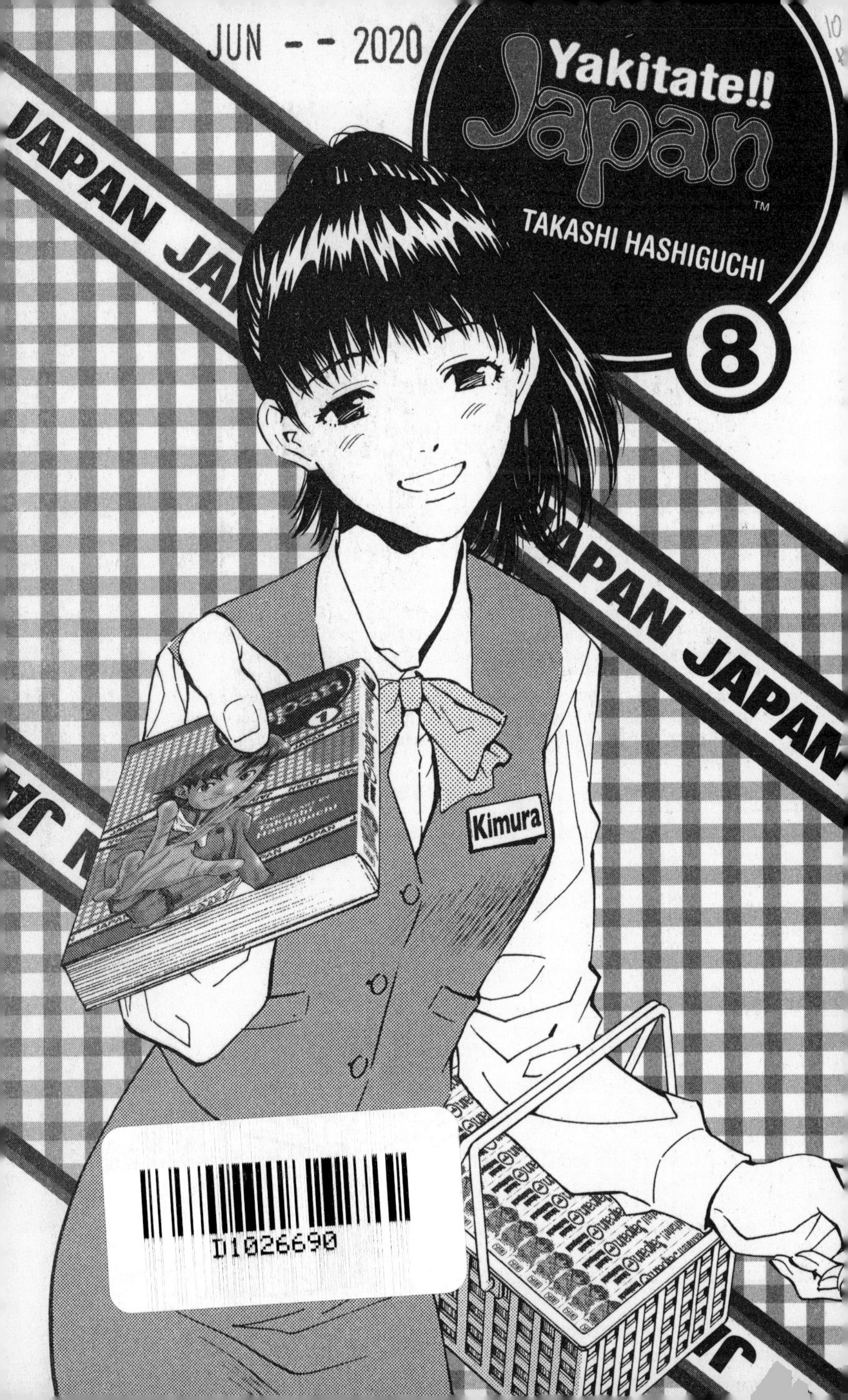
Yakitate!!
Japan™
TAKASHI HASHIGUCHI
8
JAPAN JAPAN
JAPAN JAPAN
Kimura

YAKITATE!! JAPAN
8
VIZ Media Edition

★The Story Thus Far★

Genius bread craftsman Kazuma Azuma—scouted by Pantasia baking empire scion Tsukino Azusagawa—now works at the store's South Tokyo Branch where, under the supervision of manager Ken Matsushiro, he strives to create a national bread called "Ja-pan."

Using an innovative Ja-pan experiment, Azuma became champion at the annual Pantasia Rookie Tournament. His friend at the South Tokyo branch, Kyosuke Kawachi, finished in third place.

However, their joy evaporated when they were alerted to Tsukino's half-sister Yukino's plot to take over Pantasia. Tournament runner-up Shigeru Kanmuri—who was on Yukino's payroll until recently—has a plan to stop the coup.

Kanmuri intends to bet everyone's savings on Azuma and his team winning the international bread tournament, the Monaco Cup, in Europe—a risk that could earn him 10 billion yen and save Pantasia. Now, the action moves to the casinos of Monaco!

CONTENTS

Story 60	But We Weren't Even Tardy…	3
Story 61	Ingredient Roulette	21
Story 62	World-Class	39
Story 63	Something Left Behind	59
Story 64	Ingredient Slot Machine	81
Story 65	Suwabara's New Frontier	99
Story 66	When You Crush an Apple, Use Your Teeth!	117
Story 67	Pierrot Talk	135
Story 68	Shachihoko Is a Common Name	153
Story 69	Kinoshita and the Circus	171

Research Assistance/Bakery Consultant:
Koichi Uchimura.

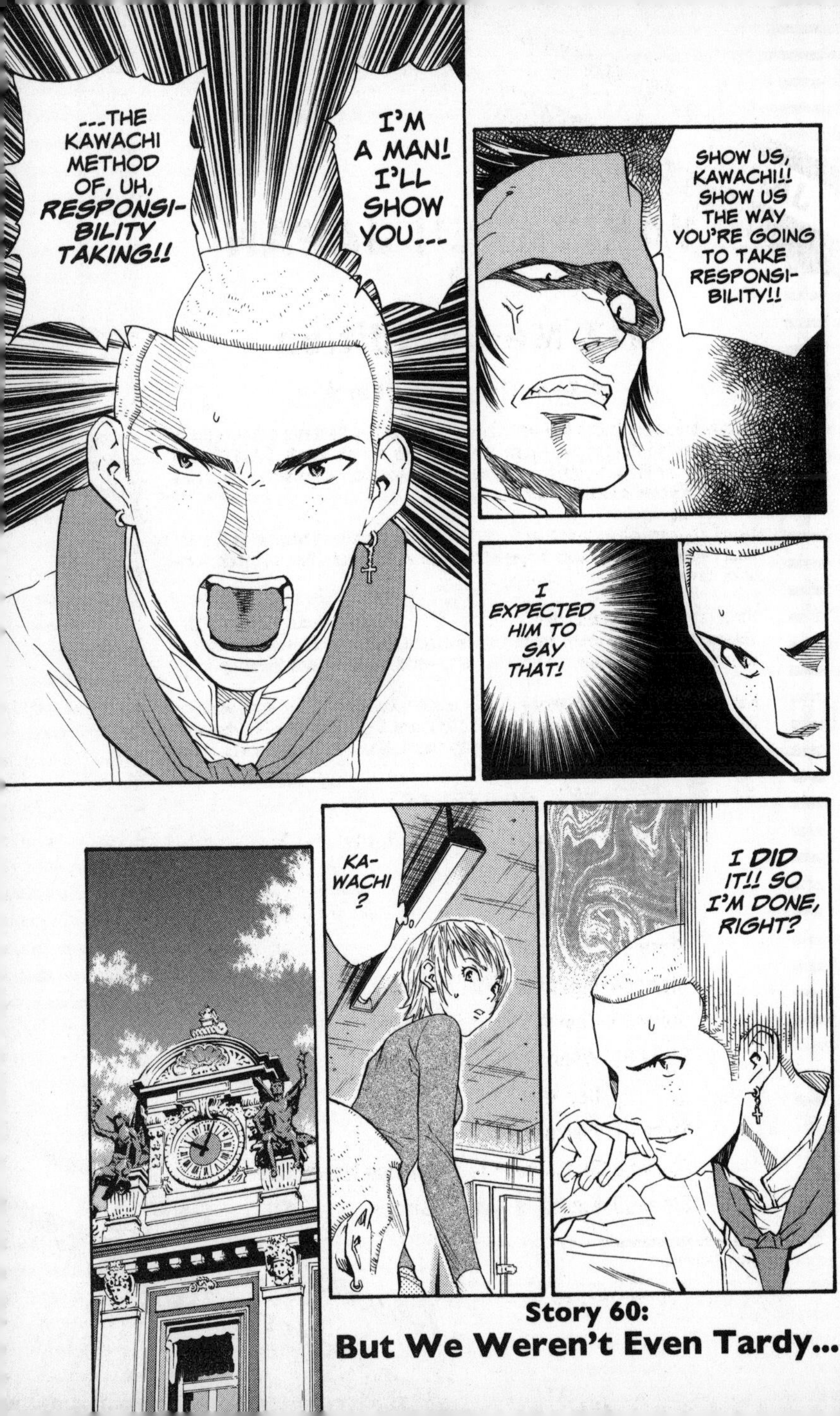
SHOW US, KAWACHI!! SHOW US THE WAY YOU'RE GOING TO TAKE RESPONSI-BILITY!!
I EXPECTED HIM TO SAY THAT!
I'M A MAN! I'LL SHOW YOU...
...THE KAWACHI METHOD OF, UH, RESPONSI-BILITY TAKING!!
I DID IT!! SO I'M DONE, RIGHT?
KA-WACHI ?

Story 60:
But We Weren't Even Tardy...

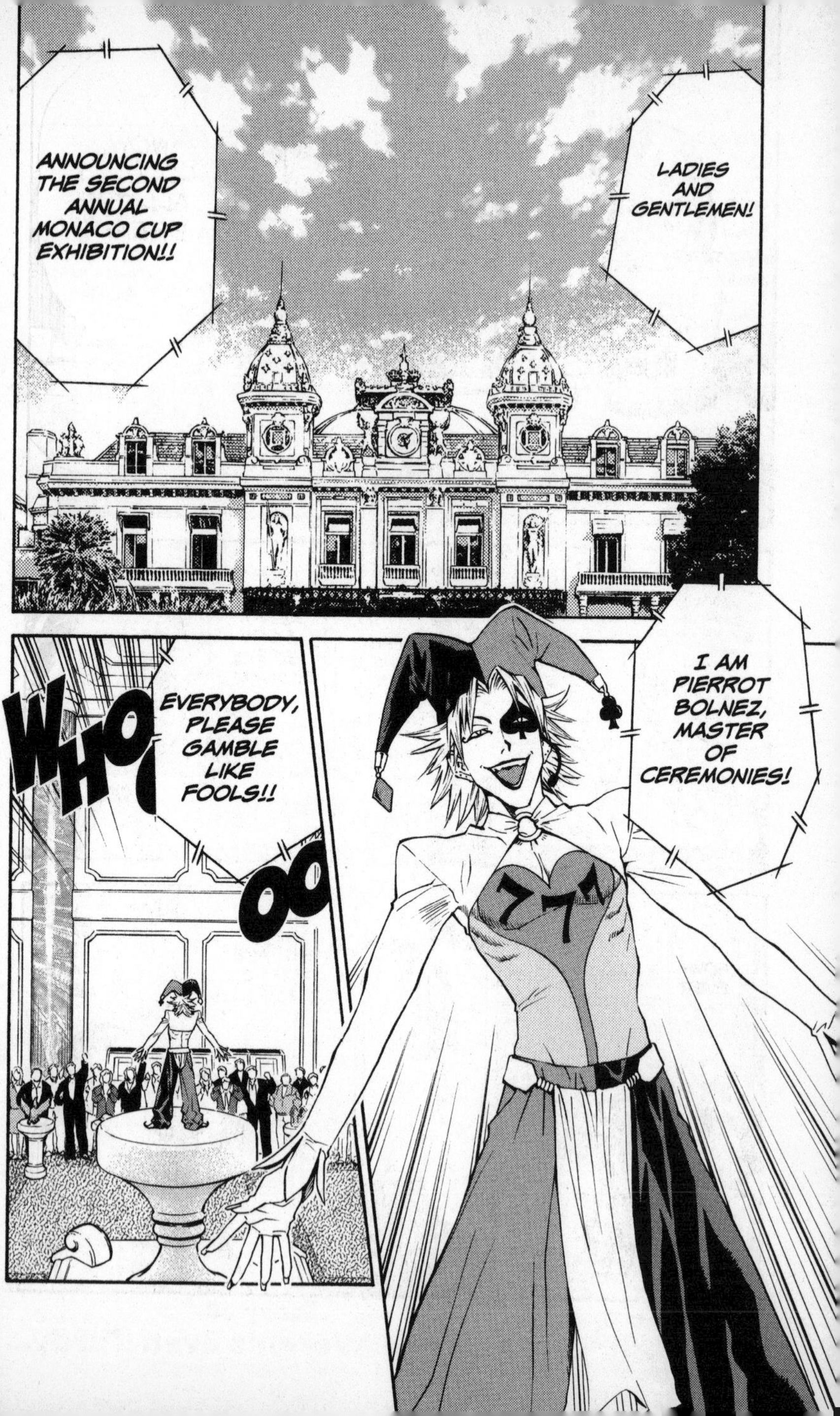
LADIES AND GENTLEMEN!
ANNOUNCING THE SECOND ANNUAL MONACO CUP EXHIBITION!!
I AM PIERROT BOLNEZ, MASTER OF CEREMONIES!
EVERYBODY, PLEASE GAMBLE LIKE FOOLS!!
WHOOO

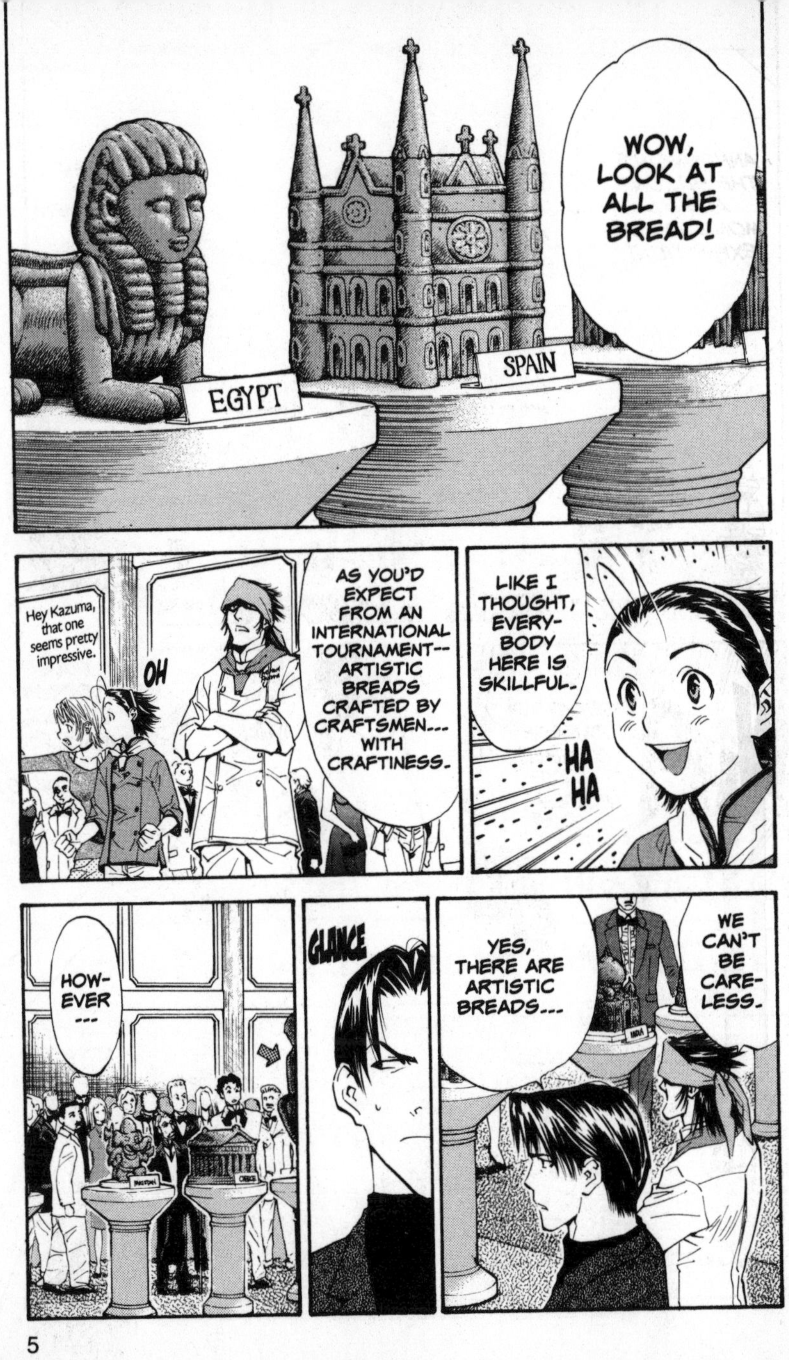
WOW, LOOK AT ALL THE BREAD!
SPAIN
EGYPT
LIKE I THOUGHT, EVERY-BODY HERE IS SKILLFUL.
HA HA
AS YOU'D EXPECT FROM AN INTERNATIONAL TOURNAMENT-- ARTISTIC BREADS CRAFTED BY CRAFTSMEN... WITH CRAFTINESS.
Hey Kazuma, that one seems pretty impressive.
OH
WE CAN'T BE CARE-LESS.
YES, THERE ARE ARTISTIC BREADS...
GLANCE
HOW-EVER ---

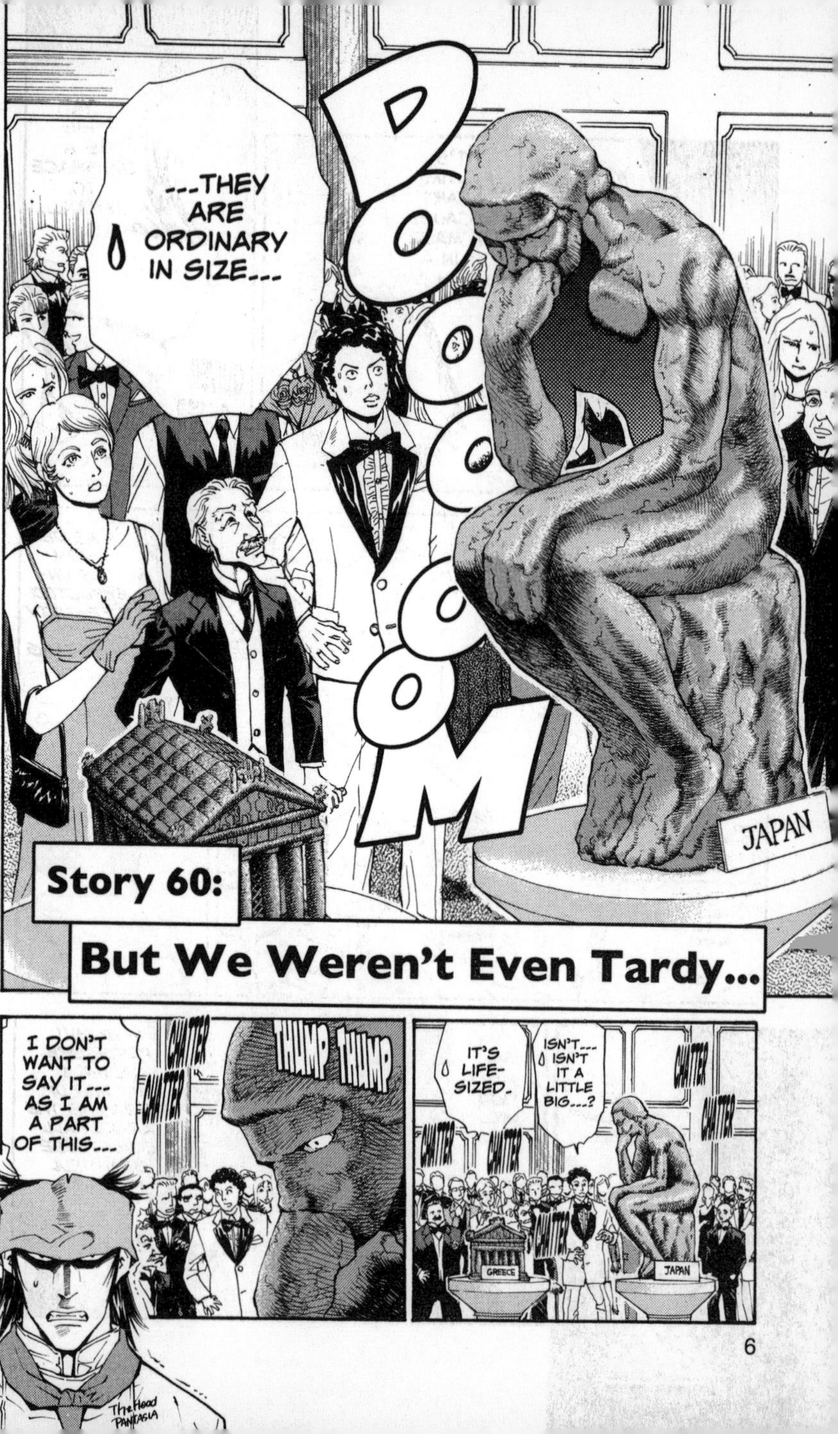
---THEY ARE ORDINARY IN SIZE---
DOOOOOM
JAPAN
Story 60:
But We Weren't Even Tardy...
CHATTER CHATTER
ISN'T--- ISN'T IT A LITTLE BIG---?
IT'S LIFE-SIZED.
CHATTER CHATTER
GREECE
JAPAN
THUMP THUMP
CHATTER CHATTER
I DON'T WANT TO SAY IT--- AS I AM A PART OF THIS---

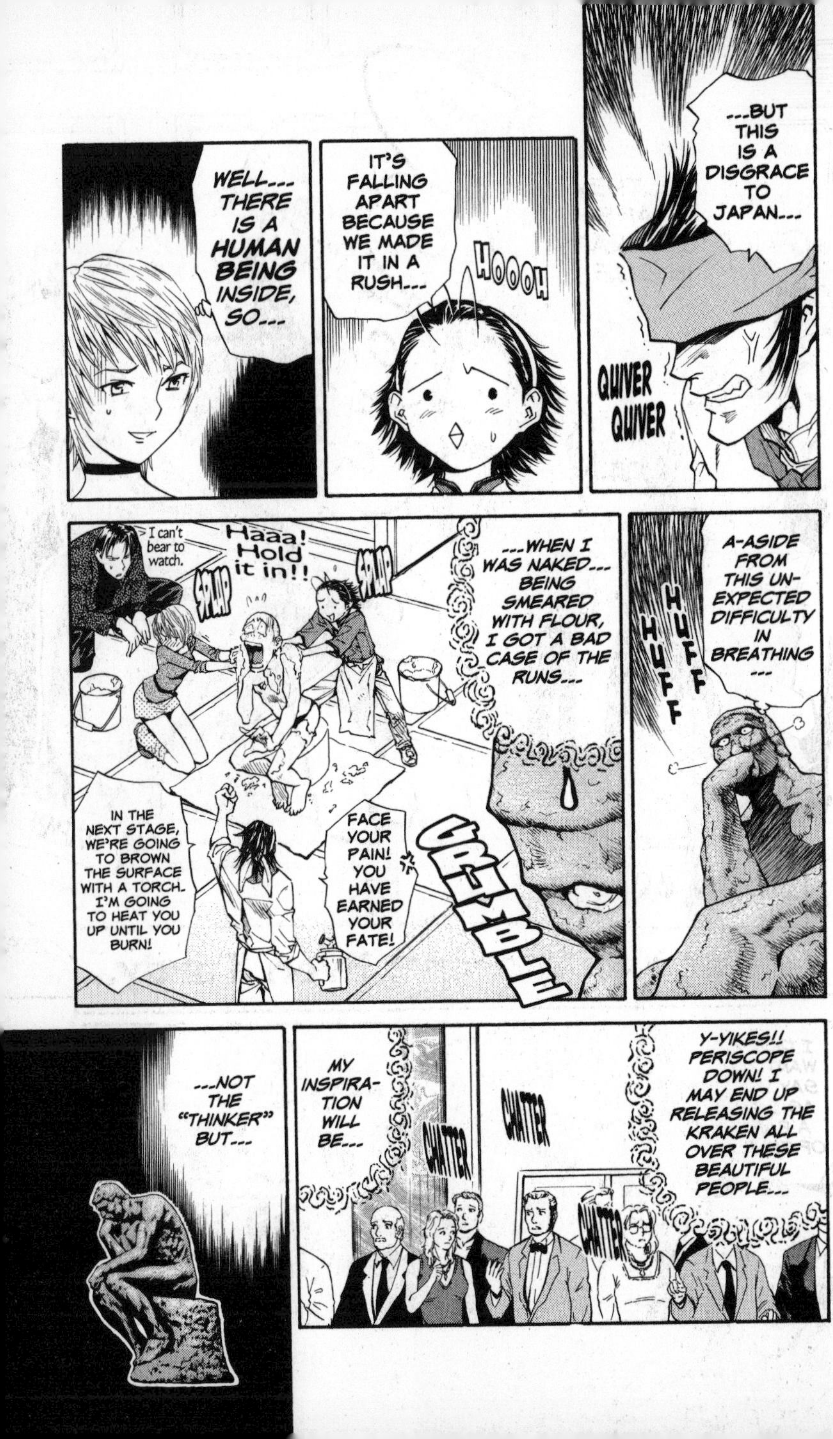
...BUT THIS IS A DISGRACE TO JAPAN...
QUIVER QUIVER
IT'S FALLING APART BECAUSE WE MADE IT IN A RUSH...
HOOOH
WELL... THERE IS A HUMAN BEING INSIDE, SO...
A-ASIDE FROM THIS UN-EXPECTED DIFFICULTY IN BREATHING...
HUFF HUFF
...WHEN I WAS NAKED... BEING SMEARED WITH FLOUR, I GOT A BAD CASE OF THE RUNS...
GRUMBLE
SPLAP
Haaa! Hold it in!!
SPLAP
I can't bear to watch.
FACE YOUR PAIN! YOU HAVE EARNED YOUR FATE!
IN THE NEXT STAGE, WE'RE GOING TO BROWN THE SURFACE WITH A TORCH. I'M GOING TO HEAT YOU UP UNTIL YOU BURN!
Y-YIKES!! PERISCOPE DOWN! I MAY END UP RELEASING THE KRAKEN ALL OVER THESE BEAUTIFUL PEOPLE...
CHATTER
CHATTER
CHATTER
MY INSPIRA-TION WILL BE...
...NOT THE "THINKER" BUT...

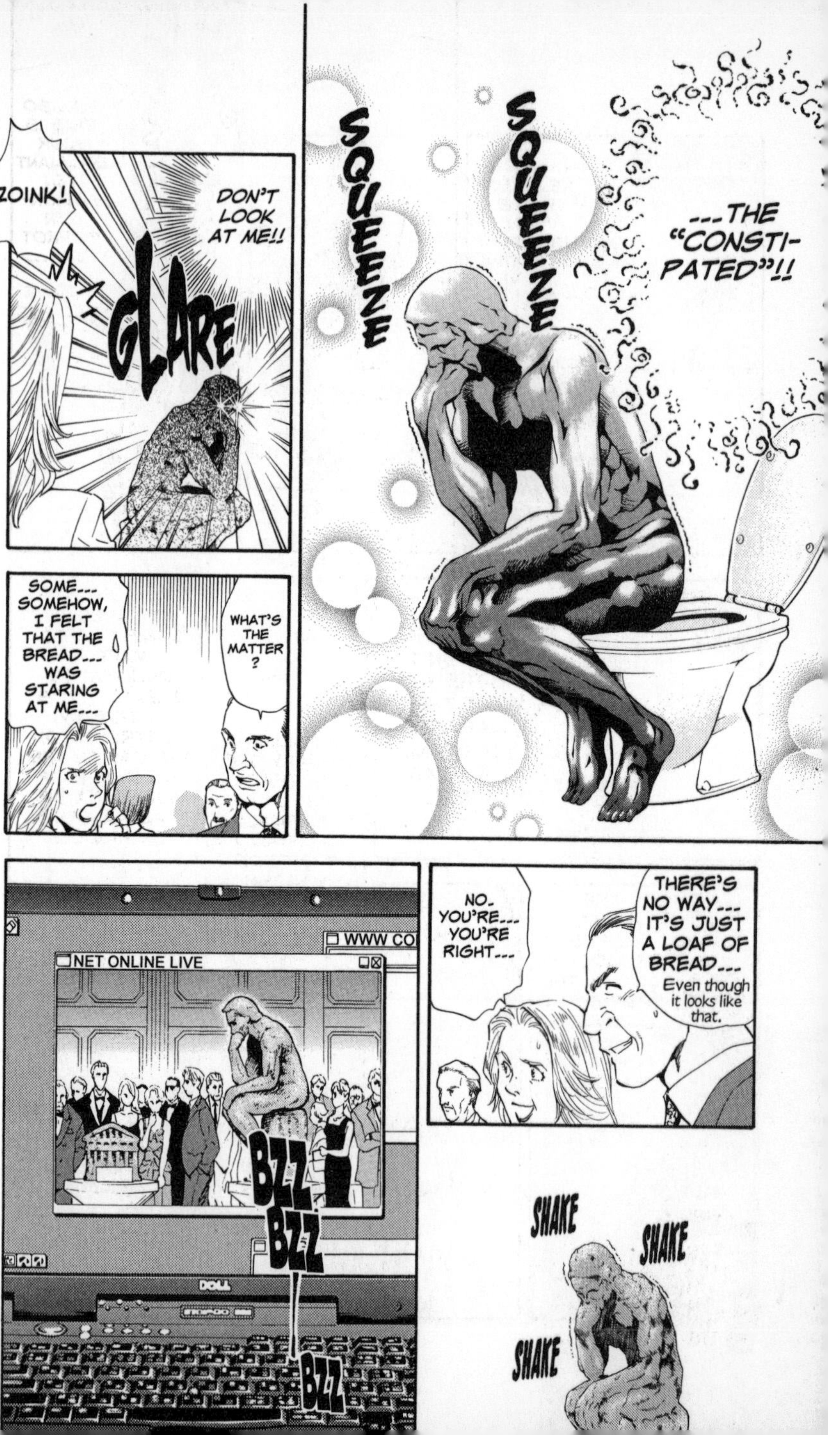
SQUEEZE
SQUEEZE
...THE "CONSTI-PATED"!!
DON'T LOOK AT ME!!
GLARE
ZOINK!
WHAT'S THE MATTER?
SOME... SOMEHOW, I FELT THAT THE BREAD... WAS STARING AT ME...
THERE'S NO WAY... IT'S JUST A LOAF OF BREAD...
Even though it looks like that.
NO. YOU'RE... YOU'RE RIGHT...
SHAKE
SHAKE
SHAKE
WWW CO
NET ONLINE LIVE
BZZ
BZZ
BZZ

SO....SO *THIS* IS YOUR BRILLIANT TEN BILLION-YEN PIERROT PLAN...

NOW WE'VE RENAMED IT--THE "TEN BILLION-YEN RODIN" PLAN.

I SEE.

HEE HEE

WELL....IF THE ODDS DON'T GO UP THE WAY WE WANT THEM TO, KAWACHI COULD STAND UP....OR START TO DANCE....

....MAKING A FREAKY ONE LIKE THAT IS THE ONLY OPTION. NATURALLY, THE ODDS WILL GO UP, TOO.

IT TAKES A LONG TIME TO MAKE A DECORATIVE BREAD. IF IT'S SUDDENLY DESTROYED ON THE DAY OF THE EVENT, EVEN IF SUWABARA OR AZUMA ARE ON HAND....

OF COURSE, THE ODDS CAN BE CHECKED LIVE, TOO....

THE MONACO CUP IS BROADCAST LIVE ON THE INTERNET SO GAMBLERS ACROSS THE WORLD CAN WATCH IT.

Ok, let me see.

....HOW CAN YOU LAUGH....?

□ NET ONLINE LIVE

IF JAPAN, WHICH WAS ELIMINATED LAST YEAR IN THE PRELIMINARIES, MAKES THAT KIND OF BREAD, NOBODY WOULD BET ON THEM.

TAP TAP TAP

I'M BETTING IT WILL KEEP ON RISING.

BUT IN ORDER TO EARN TEN BILLION YEN, DON'T YOU NEED 194-TO-1 ODDS?

AT THIS MOMENT IN TIME, THE ODDS ARE AT 138...

NET ONLINE LIVE

ODDS

PERU	56
SAUDI ARABIA	70
CONGO	75
MOROCCO	83
MONGOLIA	92
PAKISTAN	98
PALESTINE	108
ZAMBIA	121
INDONESIA	127
JAPAN	138
SWAZILAND	142
COSTA RICA	149

EGYPT

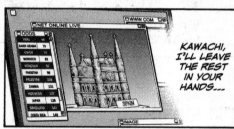

NET ONLINE LIVE

WWW COM

IMAGE

SPAIN

KAWACHI, I'LL LEAVE THE REST IN YOUR HANDS...

YOU SAID IT, SIS-TER.

THRASH THRASH

HEE HEE HEE

YOU'RE ENJOYING THIS WAY TOO MUCH.

He's working hard for us.

WHAT A HOR-RIBLE PERSON ---

BY THE WAY, MANA-GER...

10

THREE HOURS HAVE PASSED AND THE ODDS ARE AT 141... IT HASN'T INCREASED AS MUCH AS I THOUGHT...

IF THE BET IS ON ME GETTING THEM TO DO WORK, IT'S ALREADY GONE BEYOND 200-TO-1.

BY THE WAY, I WOULD LIKE EVERYBODY TO HELP OUT JUST A LITTLE BIT AROUND HERE...

PALESTINE	115
ZAMBIA	117
PAKISTAN	128
INDONESIA	133
JAPAN	141
SWAZILAND	148
COSTA RICA	152

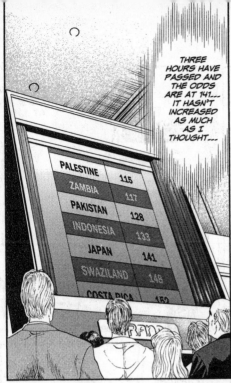

HUFF HUFF

WH-WHAT WILL HAPPEN TO ME AS A HUMAN BEING...AND WHAT OF MY FUTURE AS A BAKER...?

IF...IF I POOP LIKE THIS...THE ODDS MIGHT GO UP, BUT...

ON TOP OF THAT...MY COLON IS READY TO KICK OUT A LODGER...

GROOAAAN

GURGLE

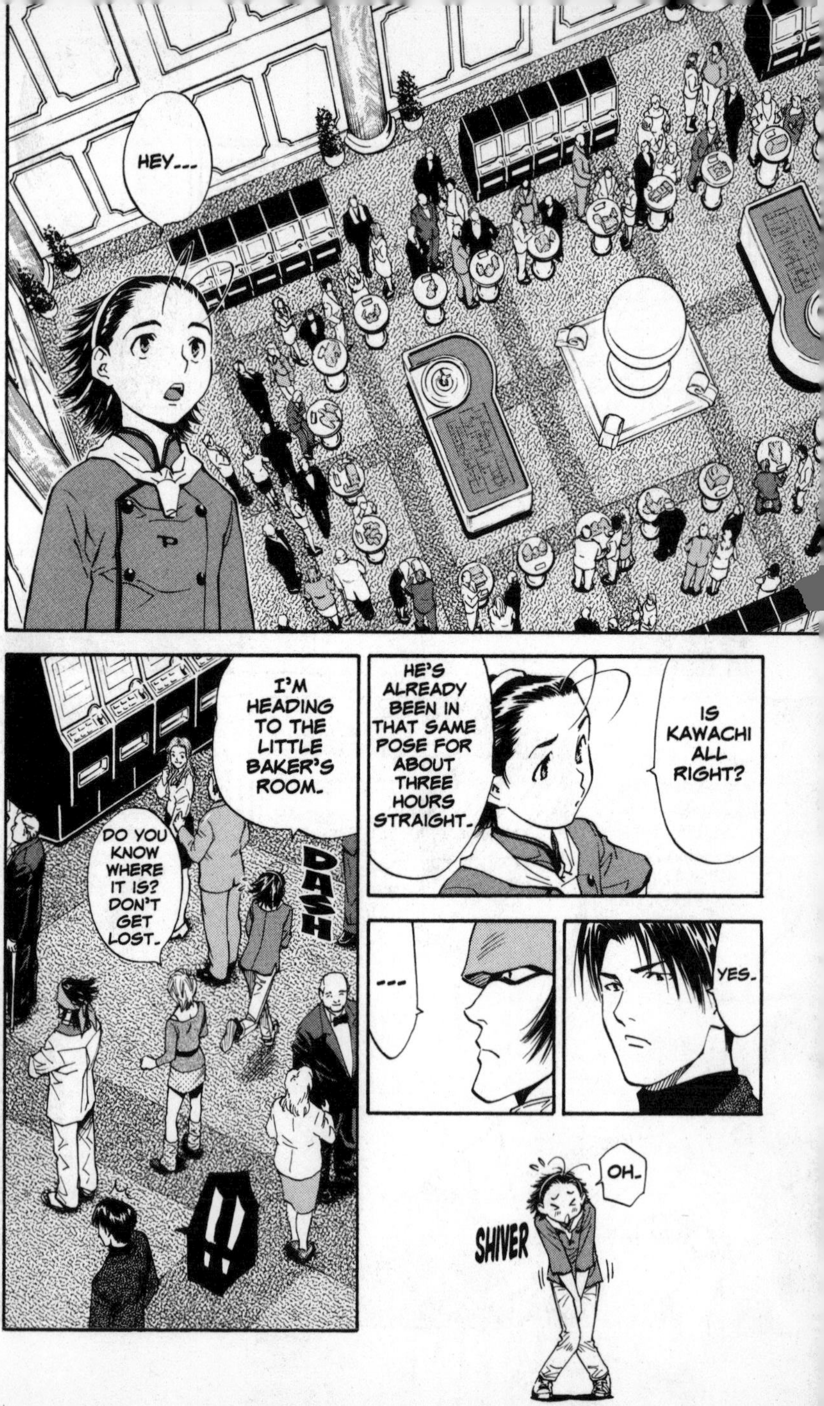
HEY...
IS KAWACHI ALL RIGHT?
HE'S ALREADY BEEN IN THAT SAME POSE FOR ABOUT THREE HOURS STRAIGHT.
YES.
...
OH.
SHIVER
I'M HEADING TO THE LITTLE BAKER'S ROOM.
DASH
DO YOU KNOW WHERE IT IS? DON'T GET LOST.
!!

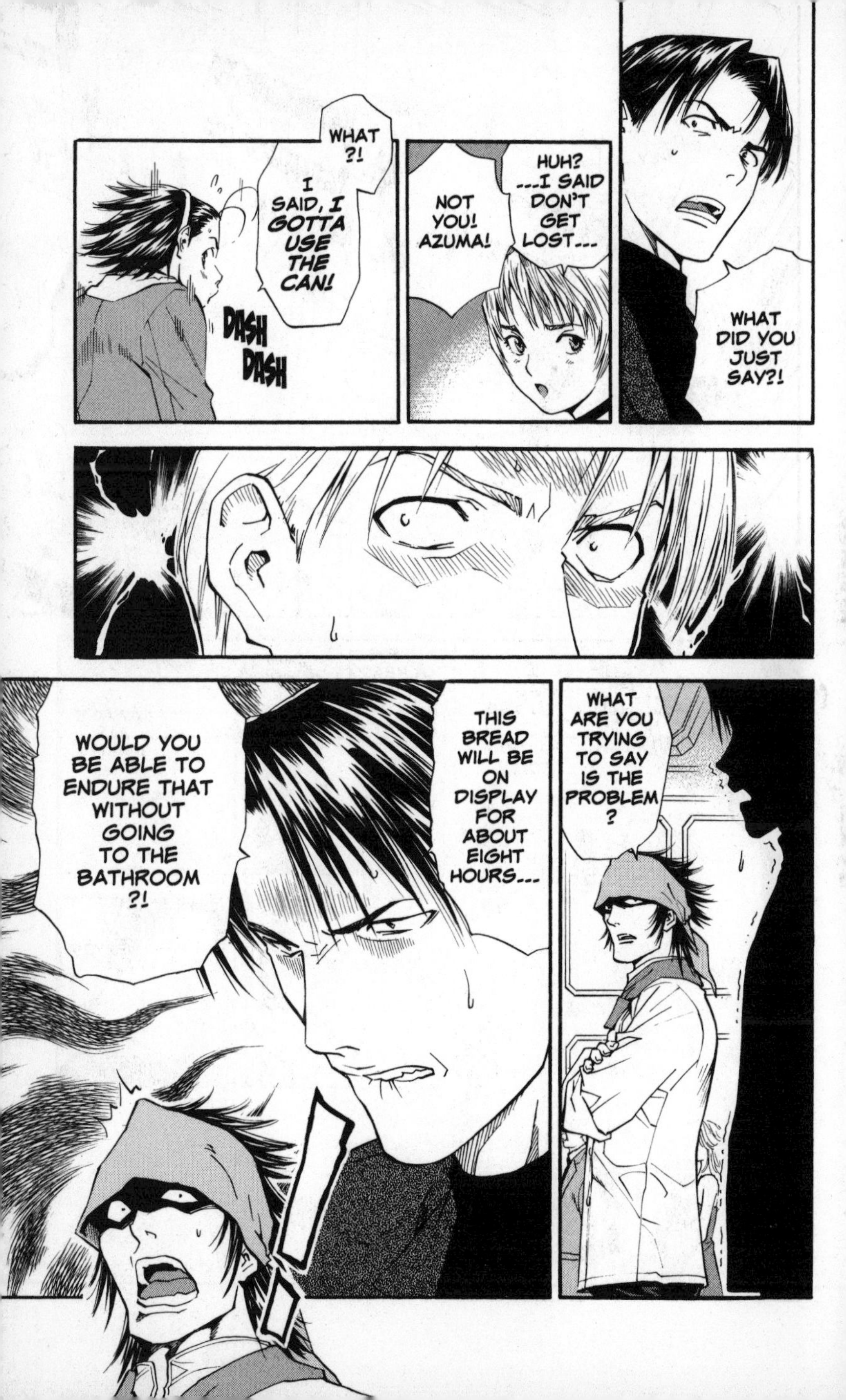
WHAT DID YOU JUST SAY?!
HUH? ---I SAID DON'T GET LOST---
NOT YOU! AZUMA!
WHAT ?!
I SAID, I GOTTA USE THE CAN!
DASH DASH
WHAT ARE YOU TRYING TO SAY IS THE PROBLEM ?
THIS BREAD WILL BE ON DISPLAY FOR ABOUT EIGHT HOURS---
WOULD YOU BE ABLE TO ENDURE THAT WITHOUT GOING TO THE BATHROOM ?!

HMMM

I'M...I'M TELLIN' YOU, THIS IS BAD...

IT...IT'S STILL 145... OH NO... THIS IS BAD...

GURRRRRGLE

...KISTAN	
...DONESIA	134
JAPAN	145
SWAZILAND	151

BLOOP BLOOP BLOOP BLOOP BLOOP

THIS IS REALLY, REALLY, REALLY BAD!!!

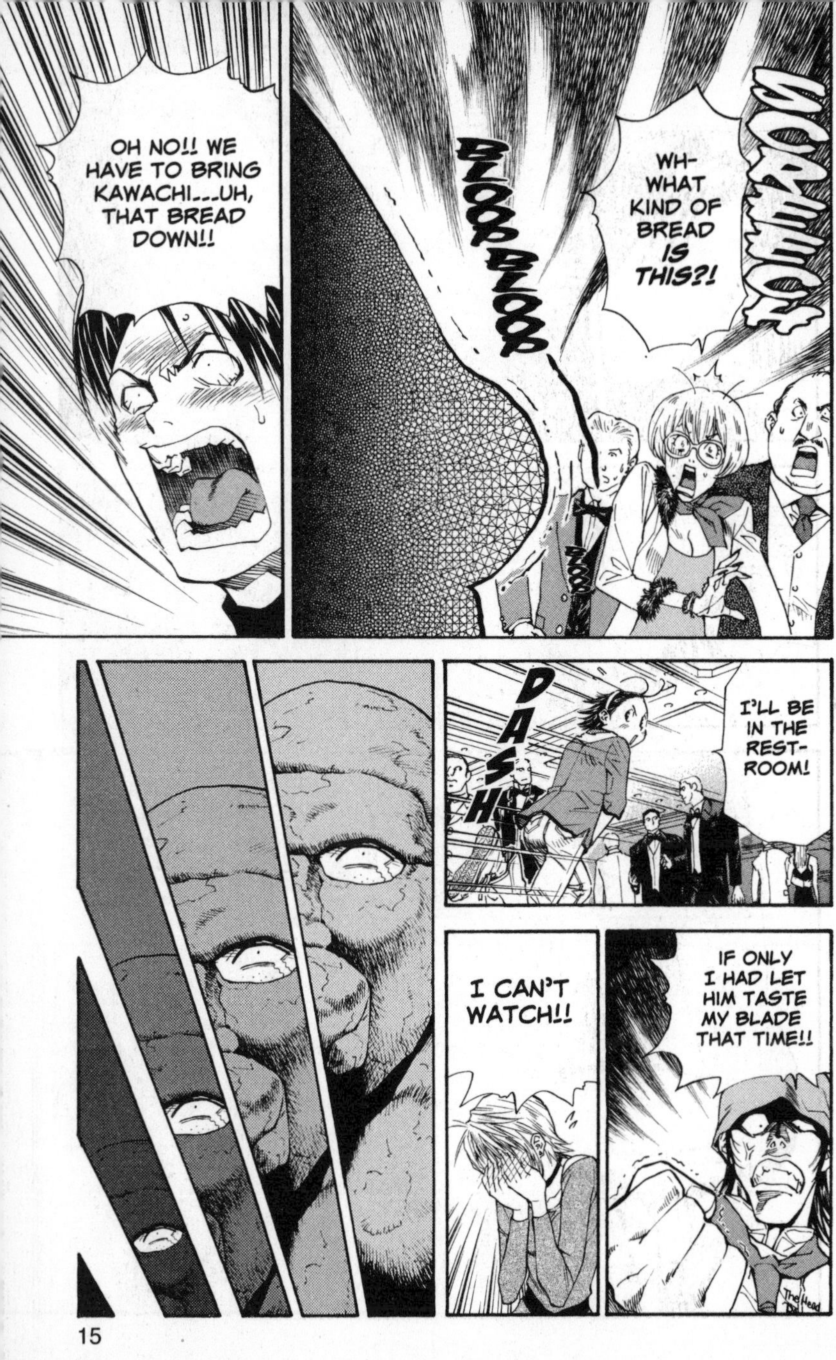
SCRUNCH
WH-WHAT KIND OF BREAD IS THIS?!
BLOOP BLOOP
OH NO!! WE HAVE TO BRING KAWACHI...UH, THAT BREAD DOWN!!
I'LL BE IN THE REST-ROOM!
DASH
IF ONLY I HAD LET HIM TASTE MY BLADE THAT TIME!!
The Head
I CAN'T WATCH!!

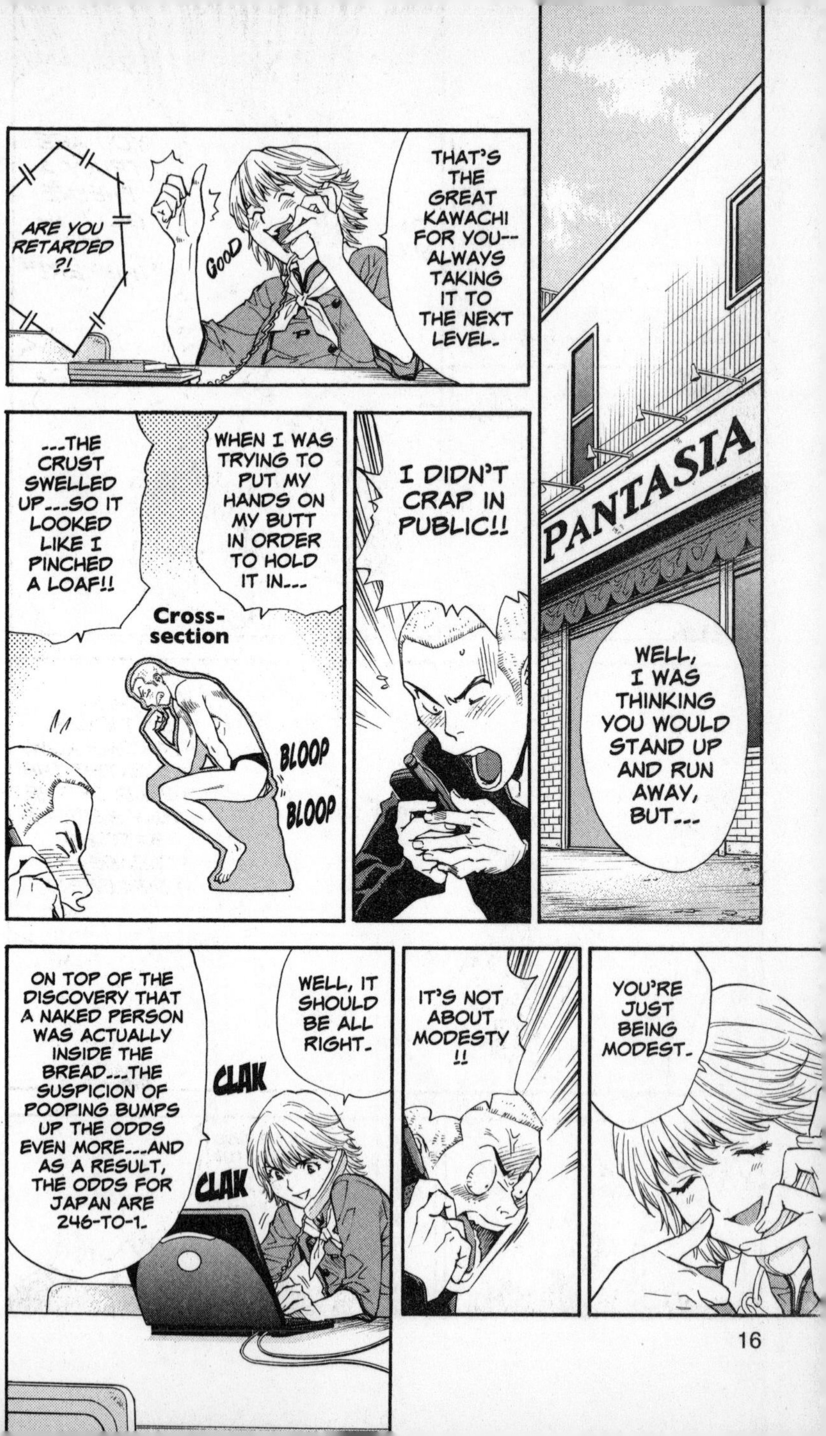
PANTASIA
WELL, I WAS THINKING YOU WOULD STAND UP AND RUN AWAY, BUT...
THAT'S THE GREAT KAWACHI FOR YOU--ALWAYS TAKING IT TO THE NEXT LEVEL.
GOOD
ARE YOU RETARDED?!
I DIDN'T CRAP IN PUBLIC!!
WHEN I WAS TRYING TO PUT MY HANDS ON MY BUTT IN ORDER TO HOLD IT IN...
...THE CRUST SWELLED UP...SO IT LOOKED LIKE I PINCHED A LOAF!!
Cross-section
BLOOP
BLOOP
YOU'RE JUST BEING MODEST.
IT'S NOT ABOUT MODESTY!!
WELL, IT SHOULD BE ALL RIGHT.
ON TOP OF THE DISCOVERY THAT A NAKED PERSON WAS ACTUALLY INSIDE THE BREAD...THE SUSPICION OF POOPING BUMPS UP THE ODDS EVEN MORE...AND AS A RESULT, THE ODDS FOR JAPAN ARE 246-TO-1.
CLAK
CLAK

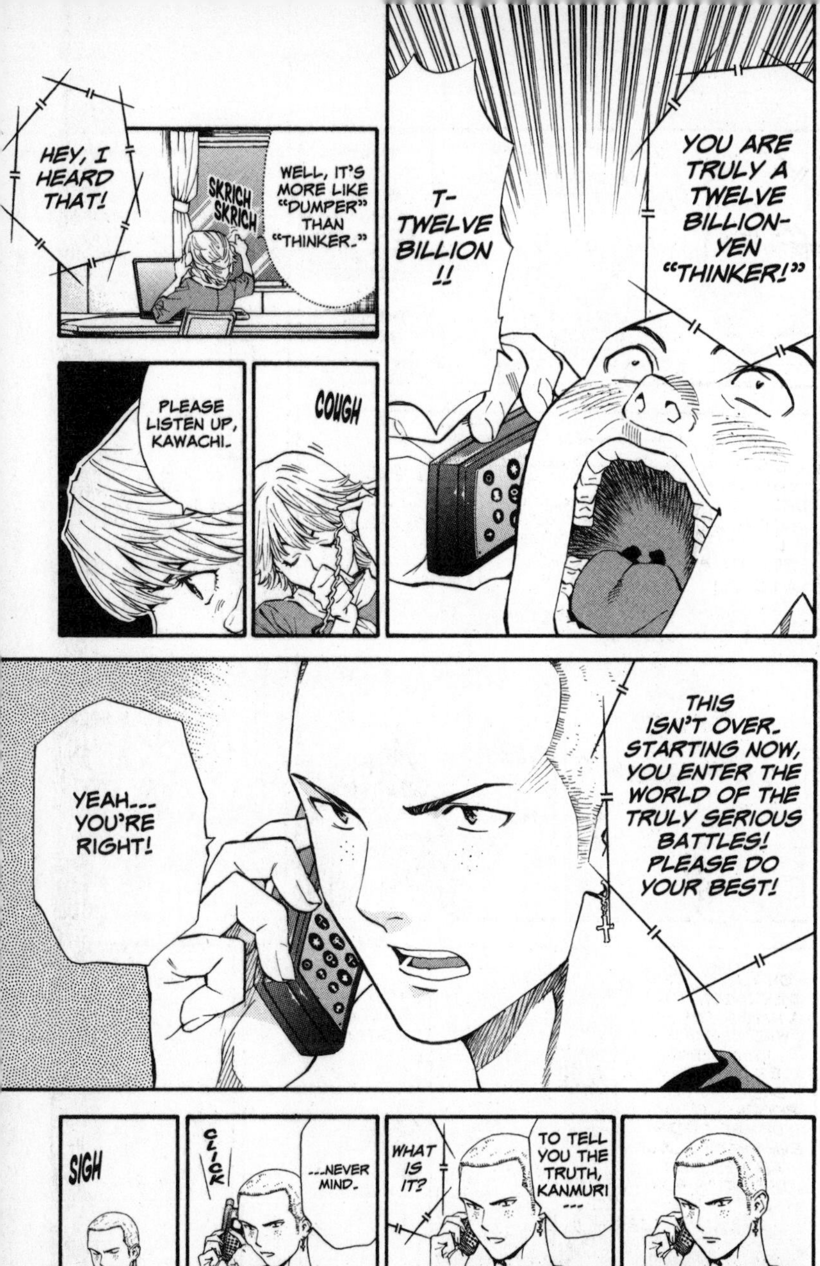
YOU ARE TRULY A TWELVE BILLION-YEN "THINKER!"
T-TWELVE BILLION !!
WELL, IT'S MORE LIKE "DUMPER" THAN "THINKER."
SKRICH SKRICH
HEY, I HEARD THAT!
COUGH
PLEASE LISTEN UP, KAWACHI.
THIS ISN'T OVER. STARTING NOW, YOU ENTER THE WORLD OF THE TRULY SERIOUS BATTLES! PLEASE DO YOUR BEST!
YEAH... YOU'RE RIGHT!
TO TELL YOU THE TRUTH, KANMURI ...
WHAT IS IT?
...NEVER MIND.
CLICK
SIGH

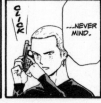

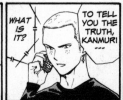

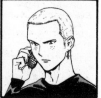

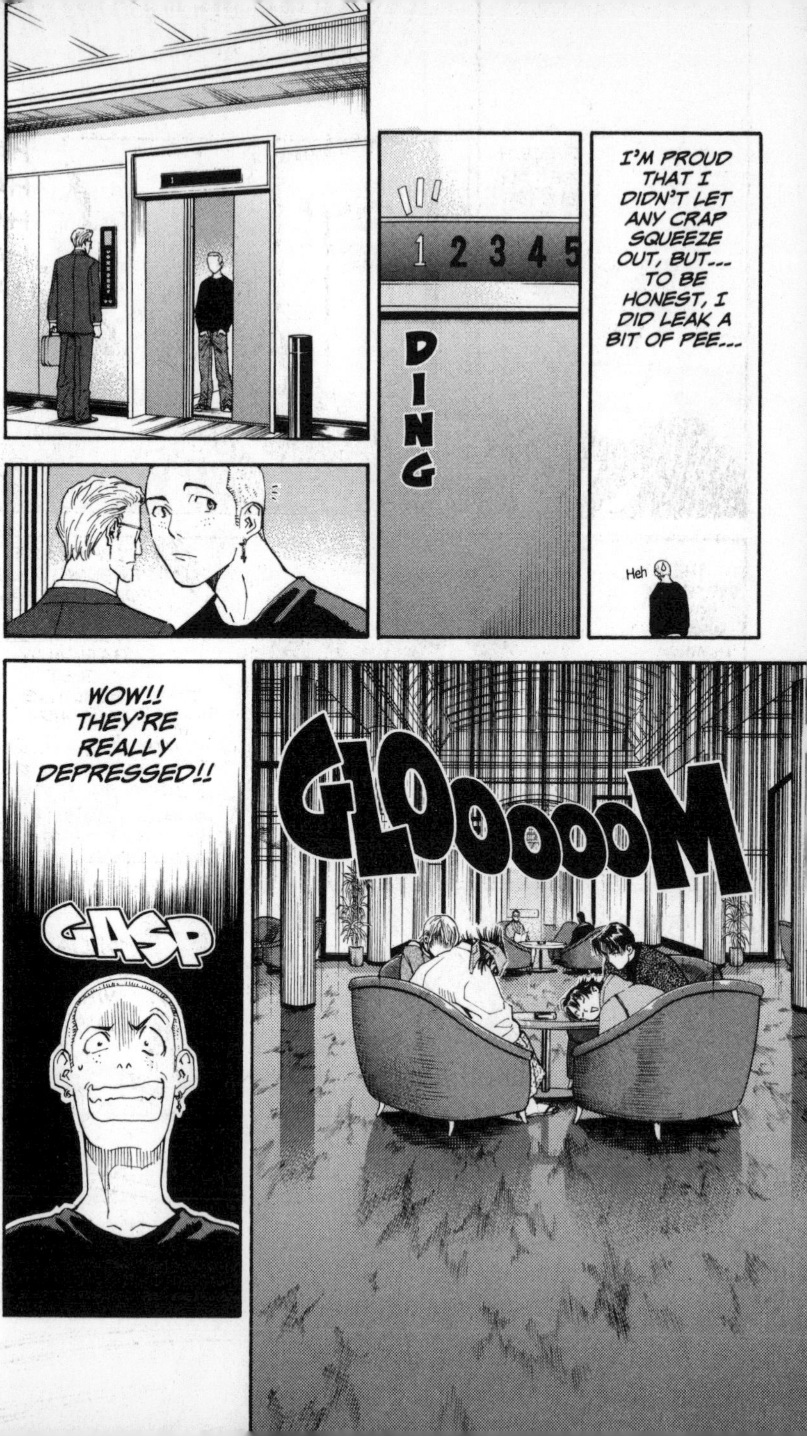
I'M PROUD THAT I DIDN'T LET ANY CRAP SQUEEZE OUT, BUT... TO BE HONEST, I DID LEAK A BIT OF PEE...
Heh
1 2 3 4 5
DING
GLOOOOOM
WOW!! THEY'RE REALLY DEPRESSED!!
GASP

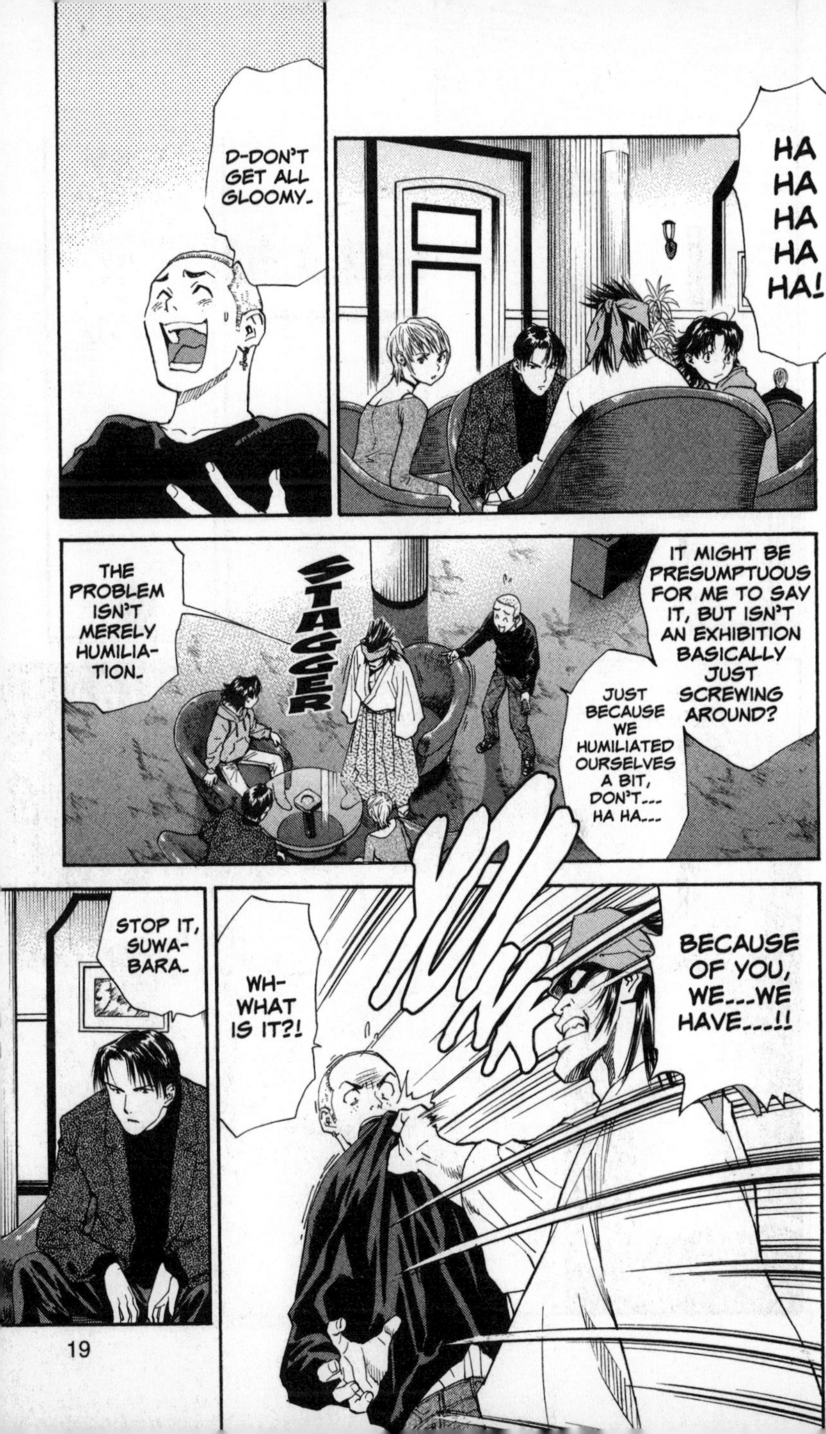
HA HA HA HA HA!
D-DON'T GET ALL GLOOMY...
IT MIGHT BE PRESUMPTUOUS FOR ME TO SAY IT, BUT ISN'T AN EXHIBITION BASICALLY JUST SCREWING AROUND?
JUST BECAUSE WE HUMILIATED OURSELVES A BIT, DON'T... HA HA...
STAGGER
THE PROBLEM ISN'T MERELY HUMILIA-TION...
BECAUSE OF YOU, WE...WE HAVE...!!
YANK
WH-WHAT IS IT?!
STOP IT, SUWA-BARA...

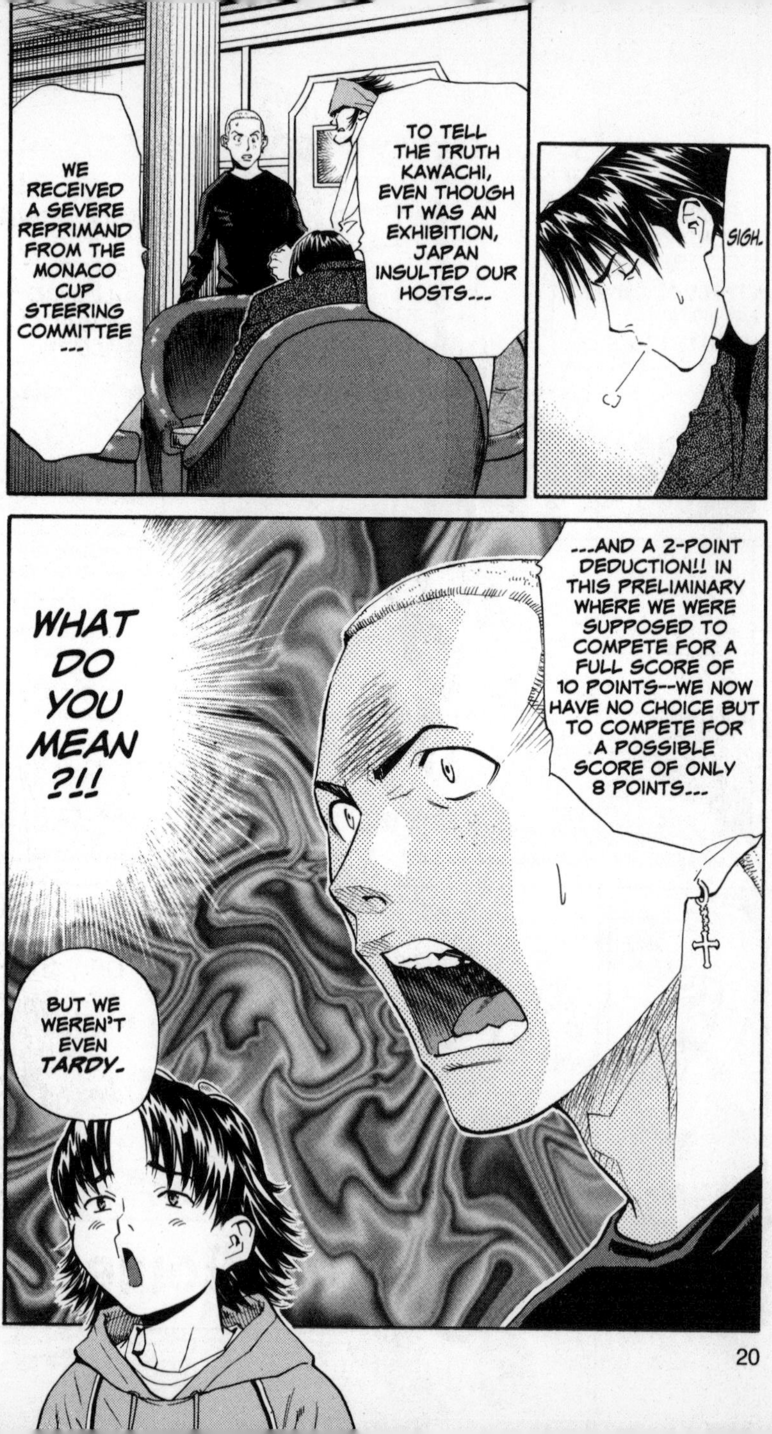
SIGH.
TO TELL THE TRUTH KAWACHI, EVEN THOUGH IT WAS AN EXHIBITION, JAPAN INSULTED OUR HOSTS...
WE RECEIVED A SEVERE REPRIMAND FROM THE MONACO CUP STEERING COMMITTEE ...
...AND A 2-POINT DEDUCTION!! IN THIS PRELIMINARY WHERE WE WERE SUPPOSED TO COMPETE FOR A FULL SCORE OF 10 POINTS--WE NOW HAVE NO CHOICE BUT TO COMPETE FOR A POSSIBLE SCORE OF ONLY 8 POINTS...
WHAT DO YOU MEAN ?!!
BUT WE WEREN'T EVEN TARDY.

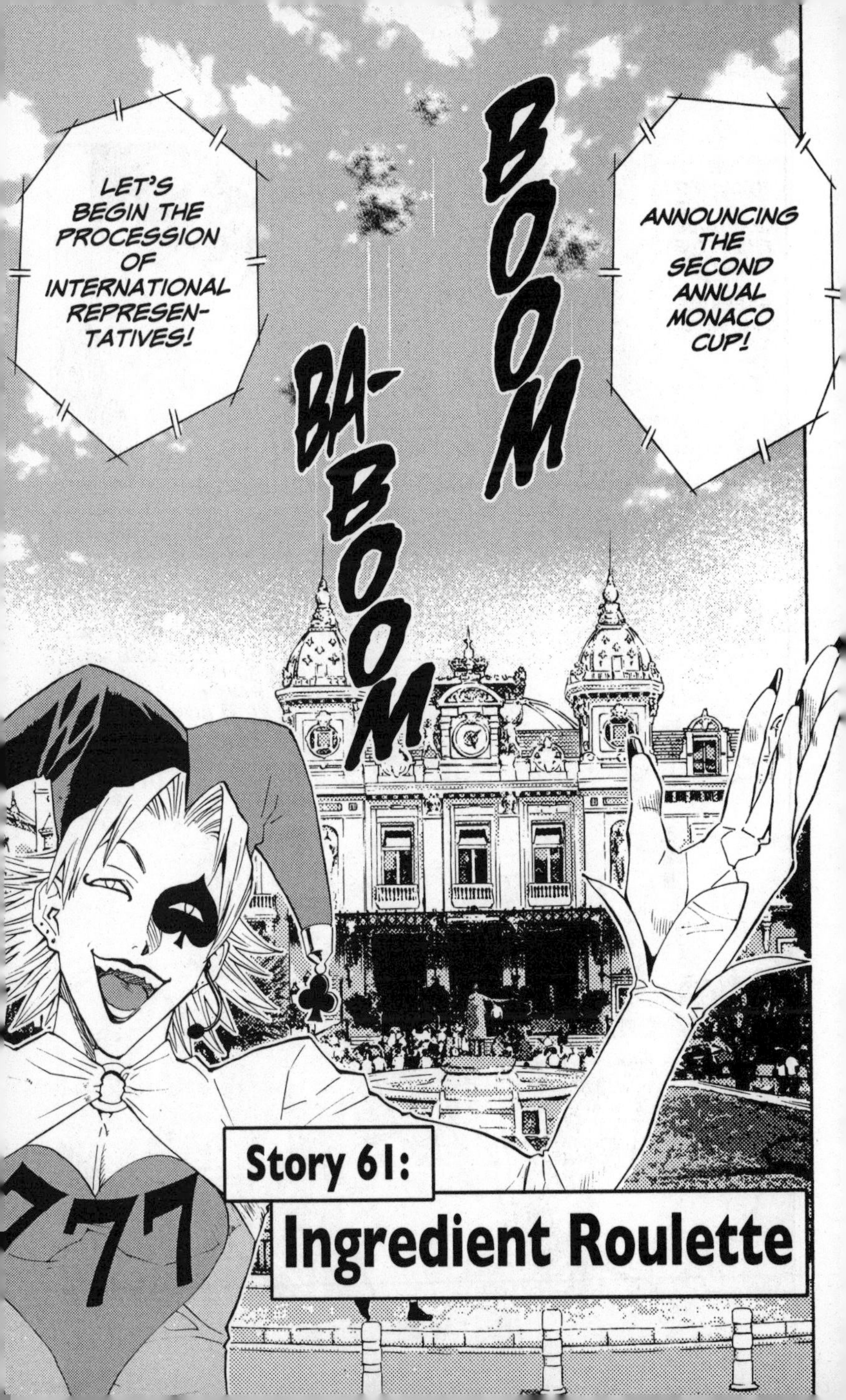
ANNOUNCING THE SECOND ANNUAL MONACO CUP!
BOOM
BA-BOOM
LET'S BEGIN THE PROCESSION OF INTERNATIONAL REPRESEN-TATIVES!
777

Story 61: Ingredient Roulette

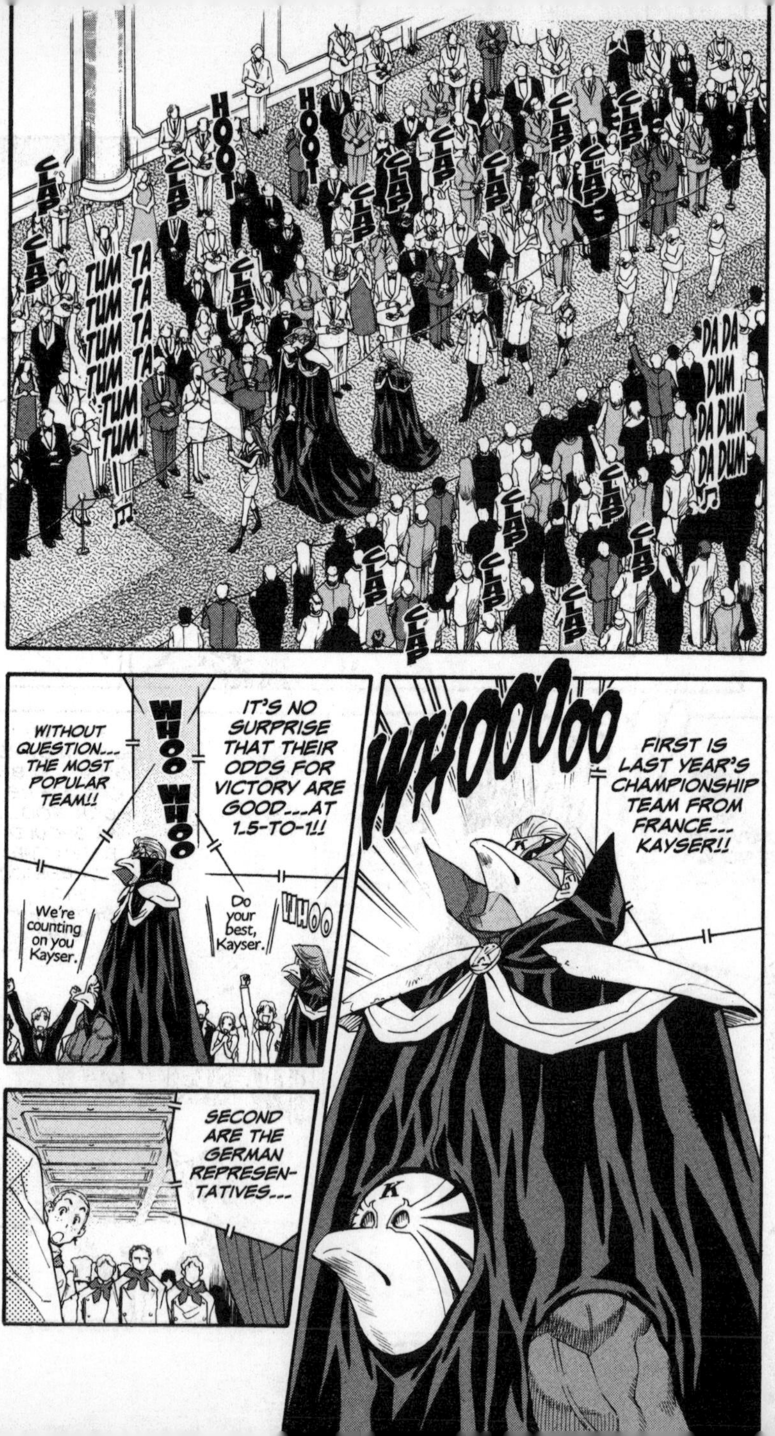
DA DA DUM DA DUM DA DUM
CLAP CLAP
CLAP CLAP
CLAP CLAP
CLAP CLAP
CLAP CLAP
CLAP CLAP
CLAP CLAP
HOOT
HOOT
CLAP CLAP
TA TA TA
TUM TUM TUM TUM TUM TUM
CLAP CLAP
WHOOOOOO
FIRST IS LAST YEAR'S CHAMPIONSHIP TEAM FROM FRANCE... KAYSER!!
IT'S NO SURPRISE THAT THEIR ODDS FOR VICTORY ARE GOOD...AT 1.5-TO-1!!
WHOO WHOO WHOO
WITHOUT QUESTION... THE MOST POPULAR TEAM!!
WHOO
Do your best, Kayser.
We're counting on you Kayser.
SECOND ARE THE GERMAN REPRESEN-TATIVES...

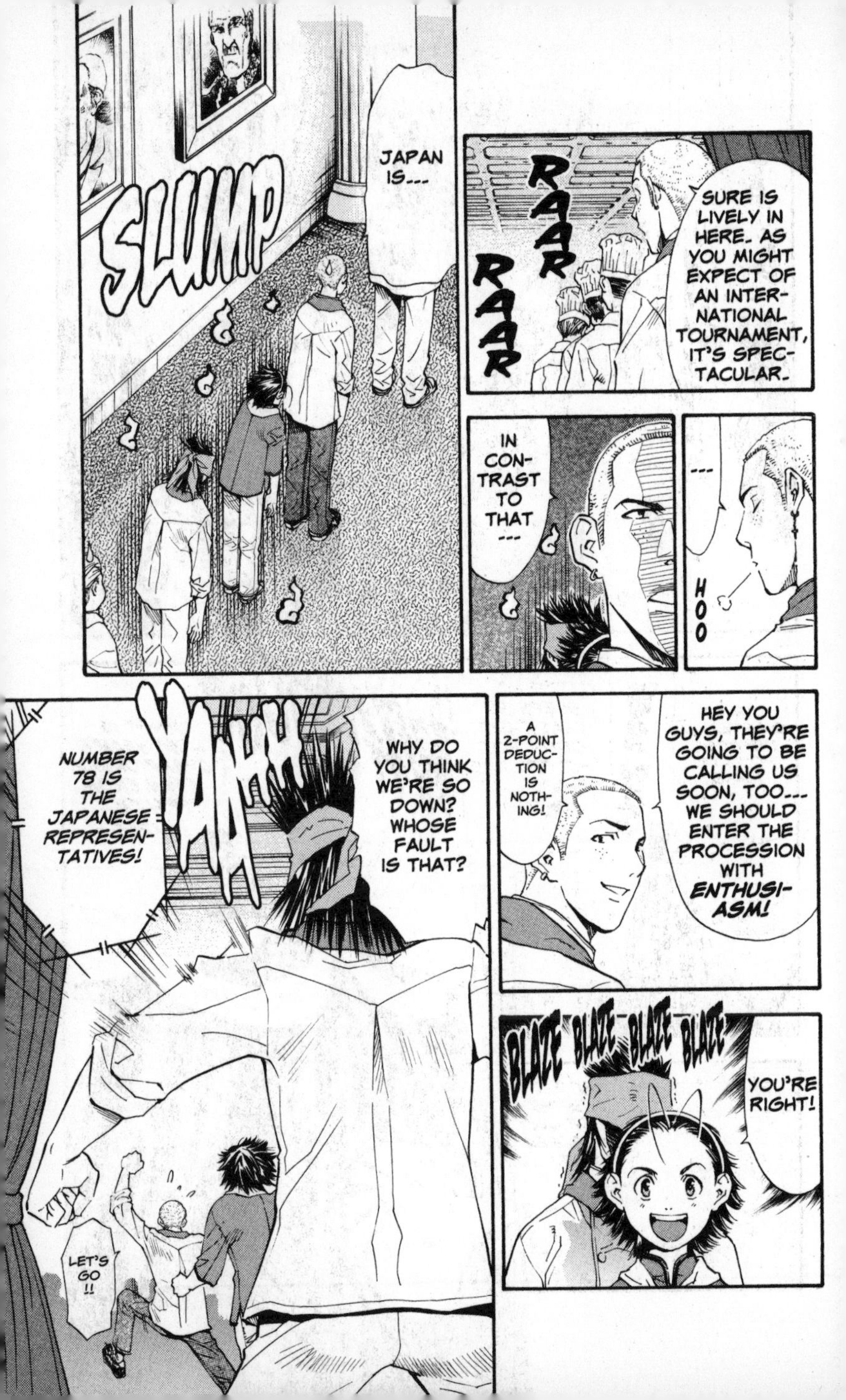
RAAR
RAAR
SURE IS LIVELY IN HERE. AS YOU MIGHT EXPECT OF AN INTERNATIONAL TOURNAMENT, IT'S SPECTACULAR.
...
HOO
IN CONTRAST TO THAT...
JAPAN IS...
SLUMP
HEY YOU GUYS, THEY'RE GOING TO BE CALLING US SOON, TOO... WE SHOULD ENTER THE PROCESSION WITH ENTHUSIASM!
A 2-POINT DEDUCTION IS NOTHING!
BLAZE BLAZE BLAZE BLAZE
YOU'RE RIGHT!
WHY DO YOU THINK WE'RE SO DOWN? WHOSE FAULT IS THAT?
YAHH
NUMBER 78 IS THE JAPANESE REPRESENTATIVES!
LET'S GO!!

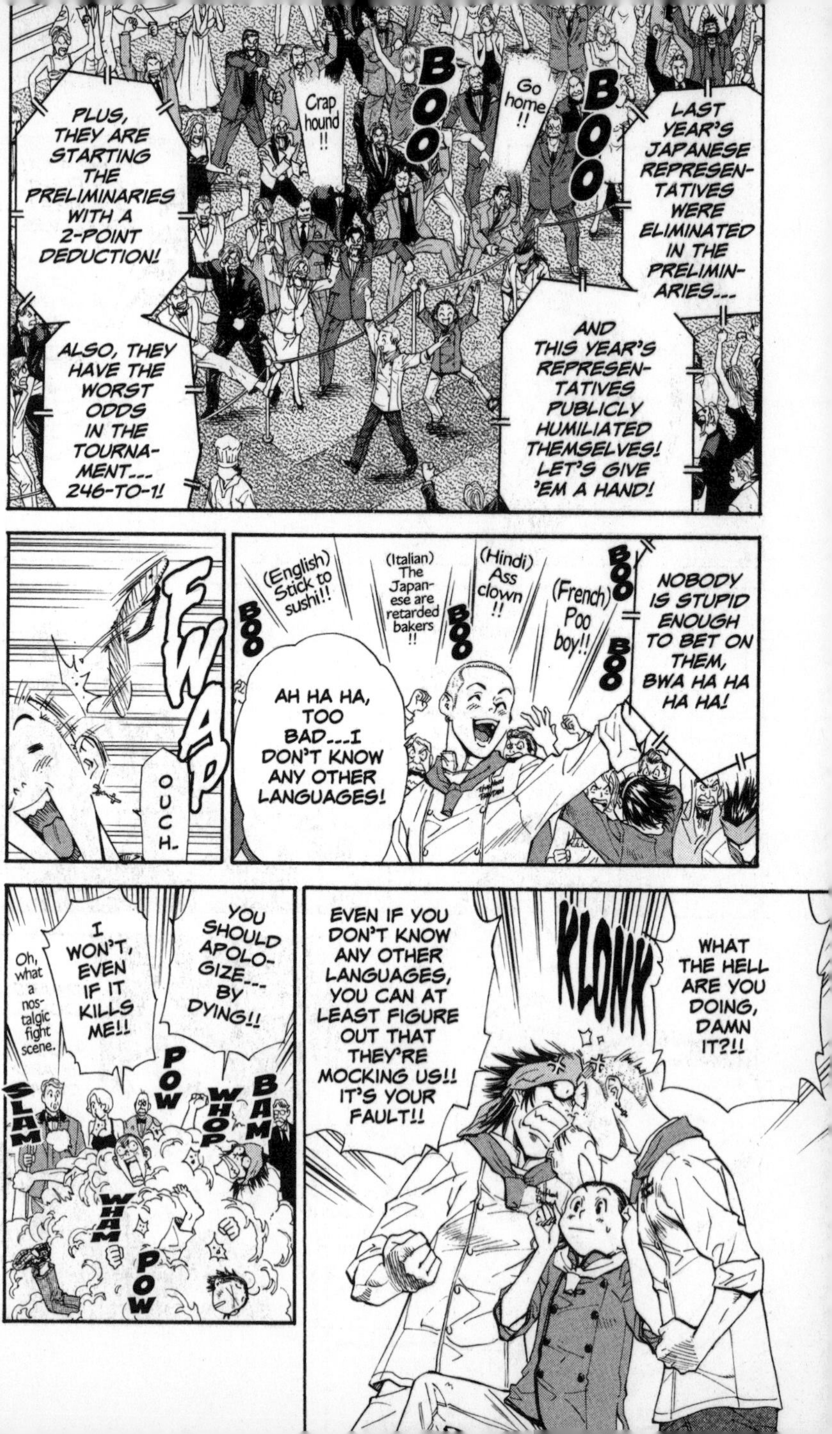
LAST YEAR'S JAPANESE REPRESEN-TATIVES WERE ELIMINATED IN THE PRELIMIN-ARIES---
AND THIS YEAR'S REPRESEN-TATIVES PUBLICLY HUMILIATED THEMSELVES! LET'S GIVE 'EM A HAND!
BOO
Go home!!
BOO
Crap hound!!
PLUS, THEY ARE STARTING THE PRELIMINARIES WITH A 2-POINT DEDUCTION!
ALSO, THEY HAVE THE WORST ODDS IN THE TOURNA-MENT--- 246-TO-1!
NOBODY IS STUPID ENOUGH TO BET ON THEM, BWA HA HA HA HA!
BOO
BOO
(French) Poo boy!!
(Hindi) Ass clown!!
BOO
(Italian) The Japan-ese are retarded bakers!!
(English) Stick to sushi!!
BOO
AH HA HA, TOO BAD---I DON'T KNOW ANY OTHER LANGUAGES!
FWAP
OUCH.
WHAT THE HELL ARE YOU DOING, DAMN IT?!!
KLONK
EVEN IF YOU DON'T KNOW ANY OTHER LANGUAGES, YOU CAN AT LEAST FIGURE OUT THAT THEY'RE MOCKING US!! IT'S YOUR FAULT!!
YOU SHOULD APOLO-GIZE--- BY DYING!!
I WON'T, EVEN IF IT KILLS ME!!
Oh, what a nos-talgic fight scene.
BAM
WHOP
POW
SLAM
WHAM
POW

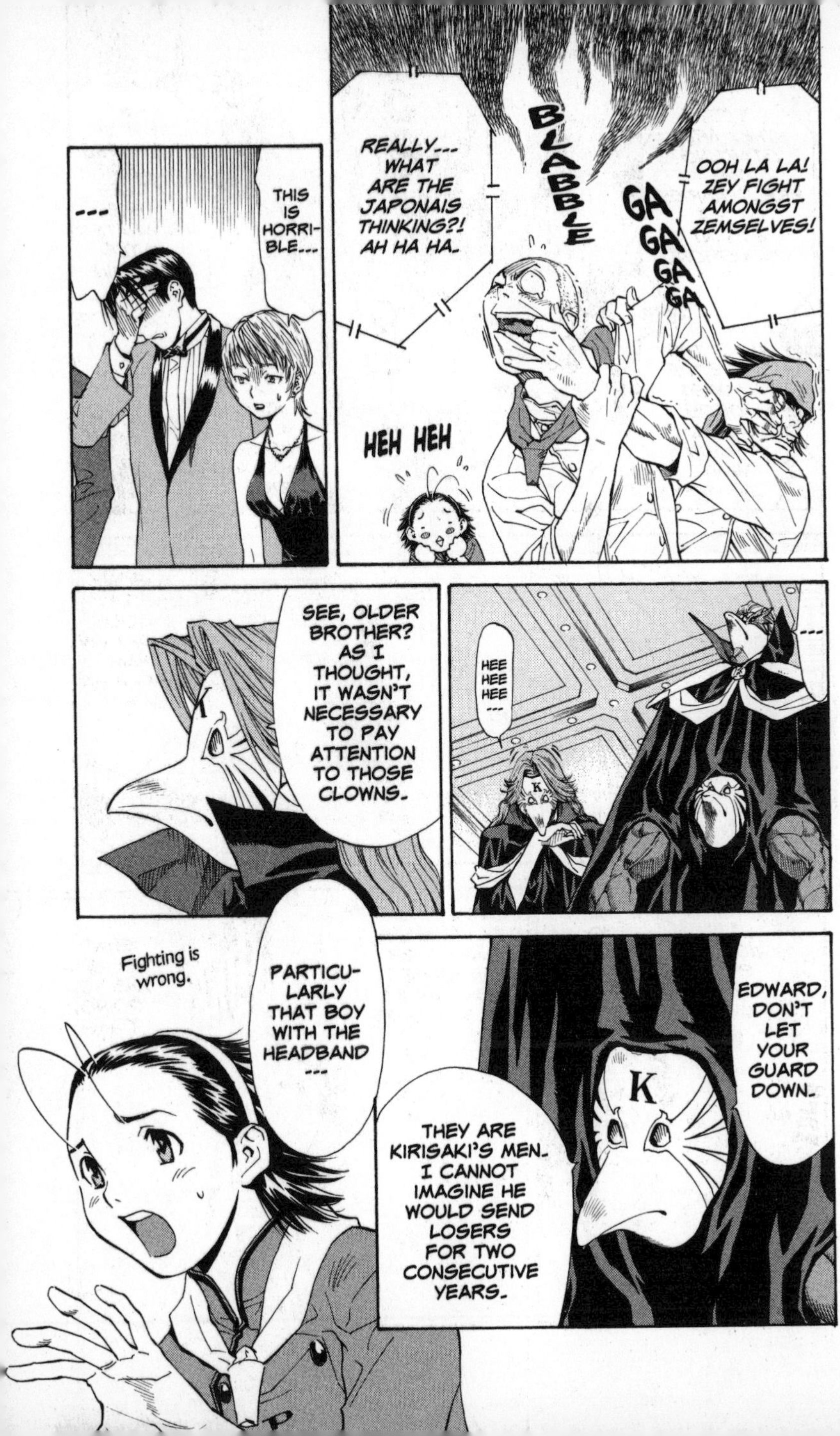
OOH LA LA! ZEY FIGHT AMONGST ZEMSELVES!
GA GA GA GA
BLABBLE
REALLY... WHAT ARE THE JAPONAIS THINKING?! AH HA HA.
HEH HEH
THIS IS HORRI-BLE...
...
...
HEE HEE HEE ...
SEE, OLDER BROTHER? AS I THOUGHT, IT WASN'T NECESSARY TO PAY ATTENTION TO THOSE CLOWNS.
EDWARD, DON'T LET YOUR GUARD DOWN.
THEY ARE KIRISAKI'S MEN. I CANNOT IMAGINE HE WOULD SEND LOSERS FOR TWO CONSECUTIVE YEARS.
PARTICU-LARLY THAT BOY WITH THE HEADBAND ...
Fighting is wrong.

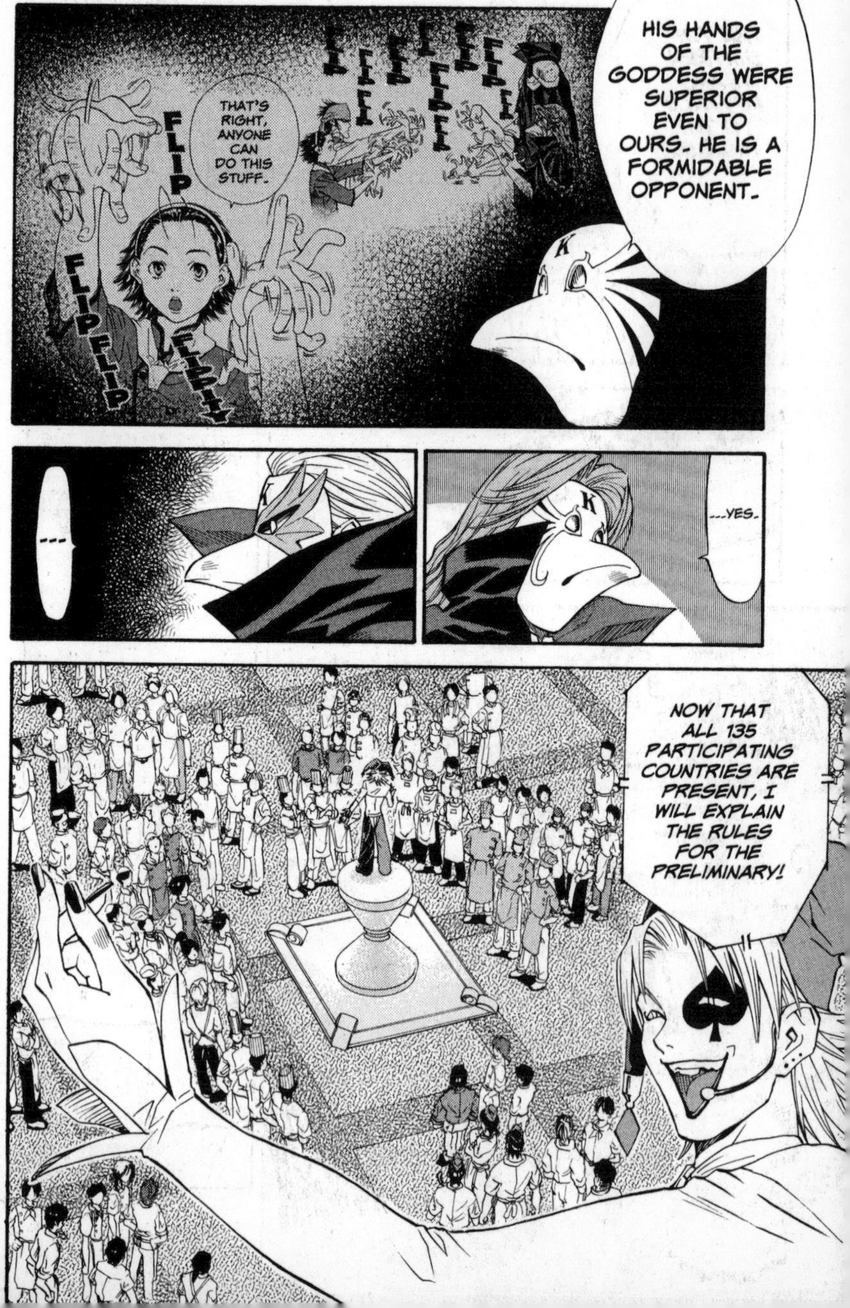
HIS HANDS OF THE GODDESS WERE SUPERIOR EVEN TO OURS. HE IS A FORMIDABLE OPPONENT.
THAT'S RIGHT, ANYONE CAN DO THIS STUFF.
FLIP
FLIP
FLIP FLIP
...YES.
...
NOW THAT ALL 135 PARTICIPATING COUNTRIES ARE PRESENT, I WILL EXPLAIN THE RULES FOR THE PRELIMINARY!

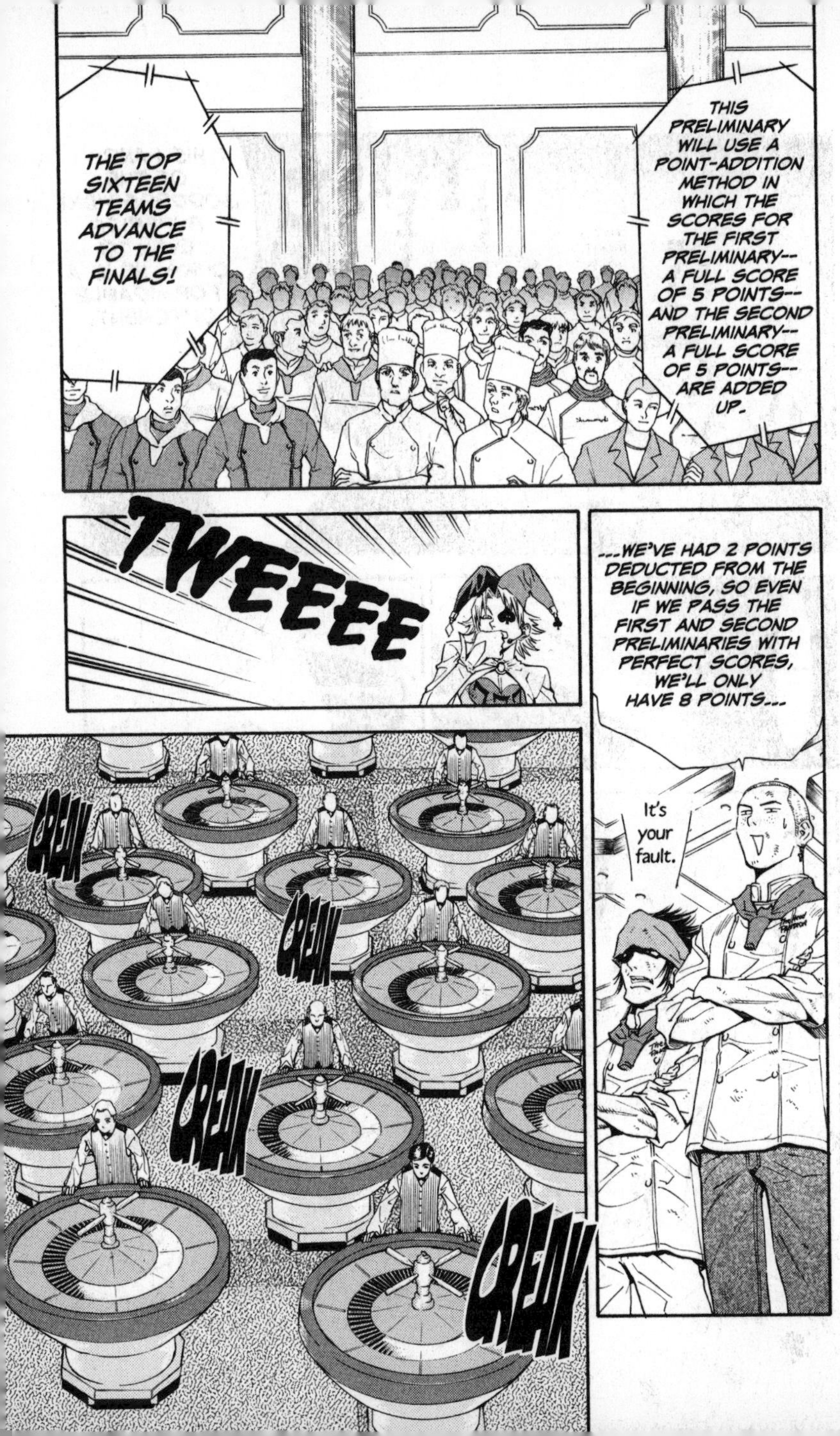
THIS PRELIMINARY WILL USE A POINT-ADDITION METHOD IN WHICH THE SCORES FOR THE FIRST PRELIMINARY-- A FULL SCORE OF 5 POINTS-- AND THE SECOND PRELIMINARY-- A FULL SCORE OF 5 POINTS-- ARE ADDED UP.
THE TOP SIXTEEN TEAMS ADVANCE TO THE FINALS!
...WE'VE HAD 2 POINTS DEDUCTED FROM THE BEGINNING, SO EVEN IF WE PASS THE FIRST AND SECOND PRELIMINARIES WITH PERFECT SCORES, WE'LL ONLY HAVE 8 POINTS...
It's your fault.
TWEEEEE
CREAK
CREAK
CREAK
CREAK

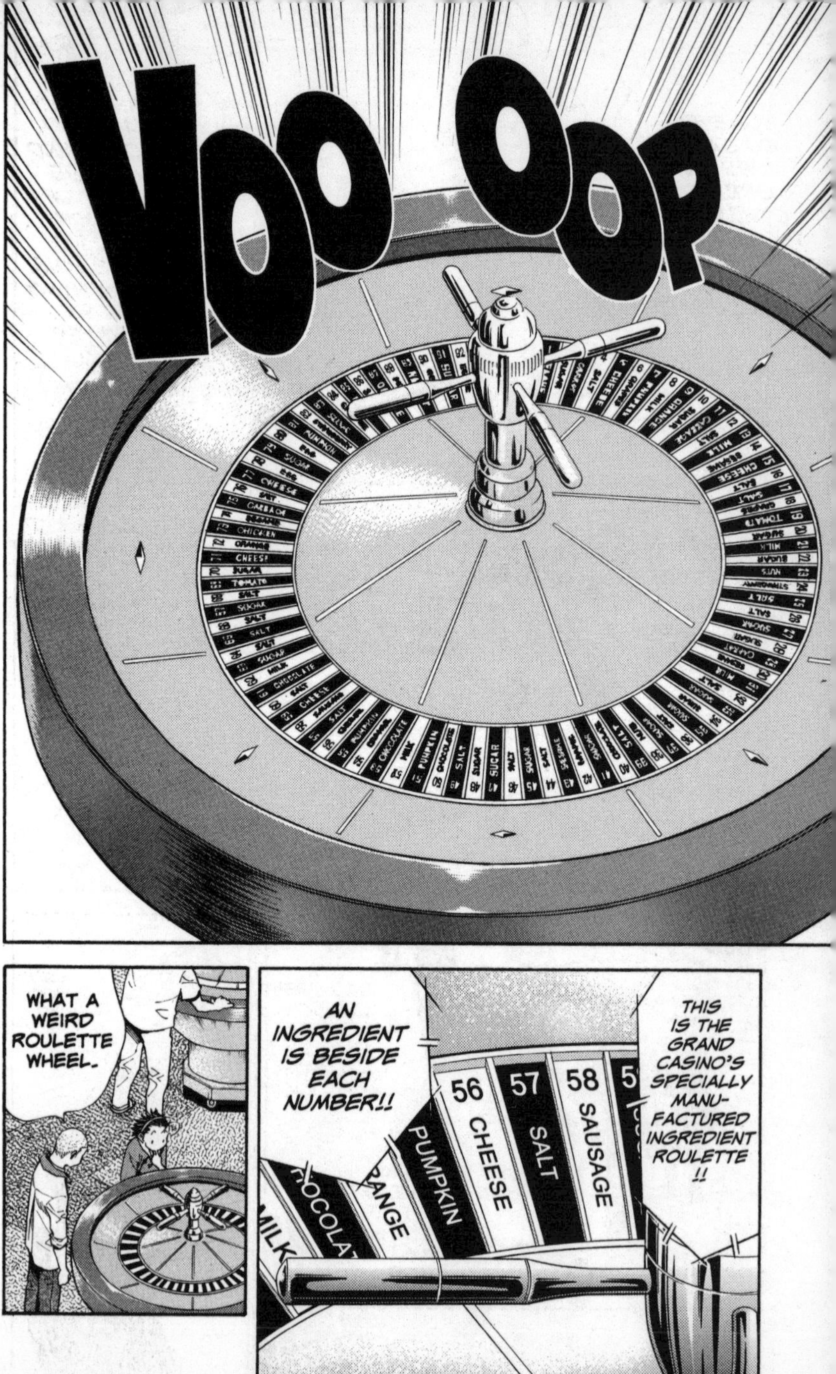
VOO OOP
THIS IS THE GRAND CASINO'S SPECIALLY MANU-FACTURED INGREDIENT ROULETTE !!
AN INGREDIENT IS BESIDE EACH NUMBER!!
56 CHEESE
57 SALT
58 SAUSAGE
PUMPKIN
MILK
WHAT A WEIRD ROULETTE WHEEL.

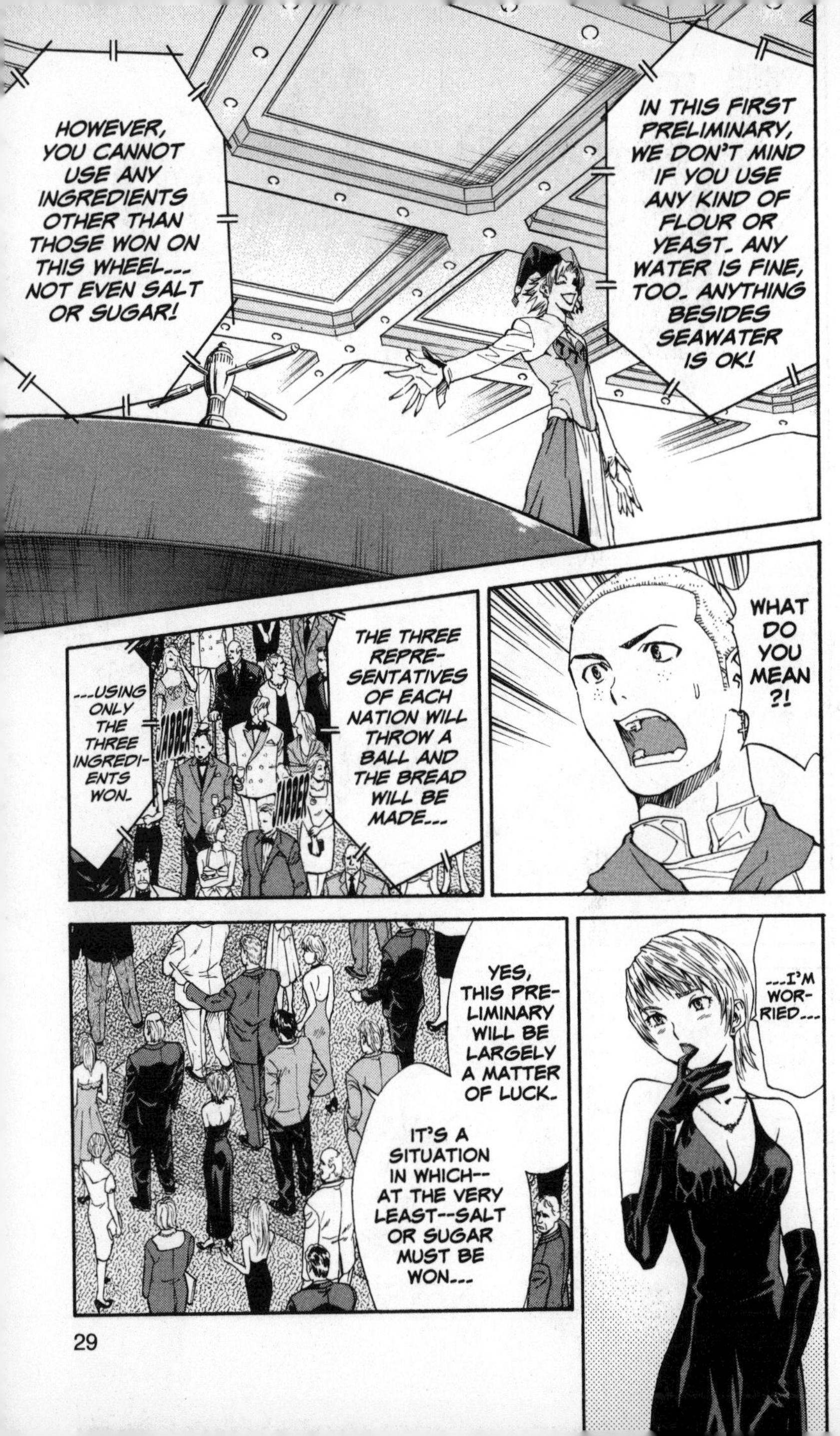
IN THIS FIRST PRELIMINARY, WE DON'T MIND IF YOU USE ANY KIND OF FLOUR OR YEAST. ANY WATER IS FINE, TOO. ANYTHING BESIDES SEAWATER IS OK!
HOWEVER, YOU CANNOT USE ANY INGREDIENTS OTHER THAN THOSE WON ON THIS WHEEL... NOT EVEN SALT OR SUGAR!
WHAT DO YOU MEAN?!
THE THREE REPRESENTATIVES OF EACH NATION WILL THROW A BALL AND THE BREAD WILL BE MADE...
...USING ONLY THE THREE INGREDIENTS WON.
JABBER
JABBER
...I'M WORRIED...
YES, THIS PRELIMINARY WILL BE LARGELY A MATTER OF LUCK.
IT'S A SITUATION IN WHICH--AT THE VERY LEAST--SALT OR SUGAR MUST BE WON...

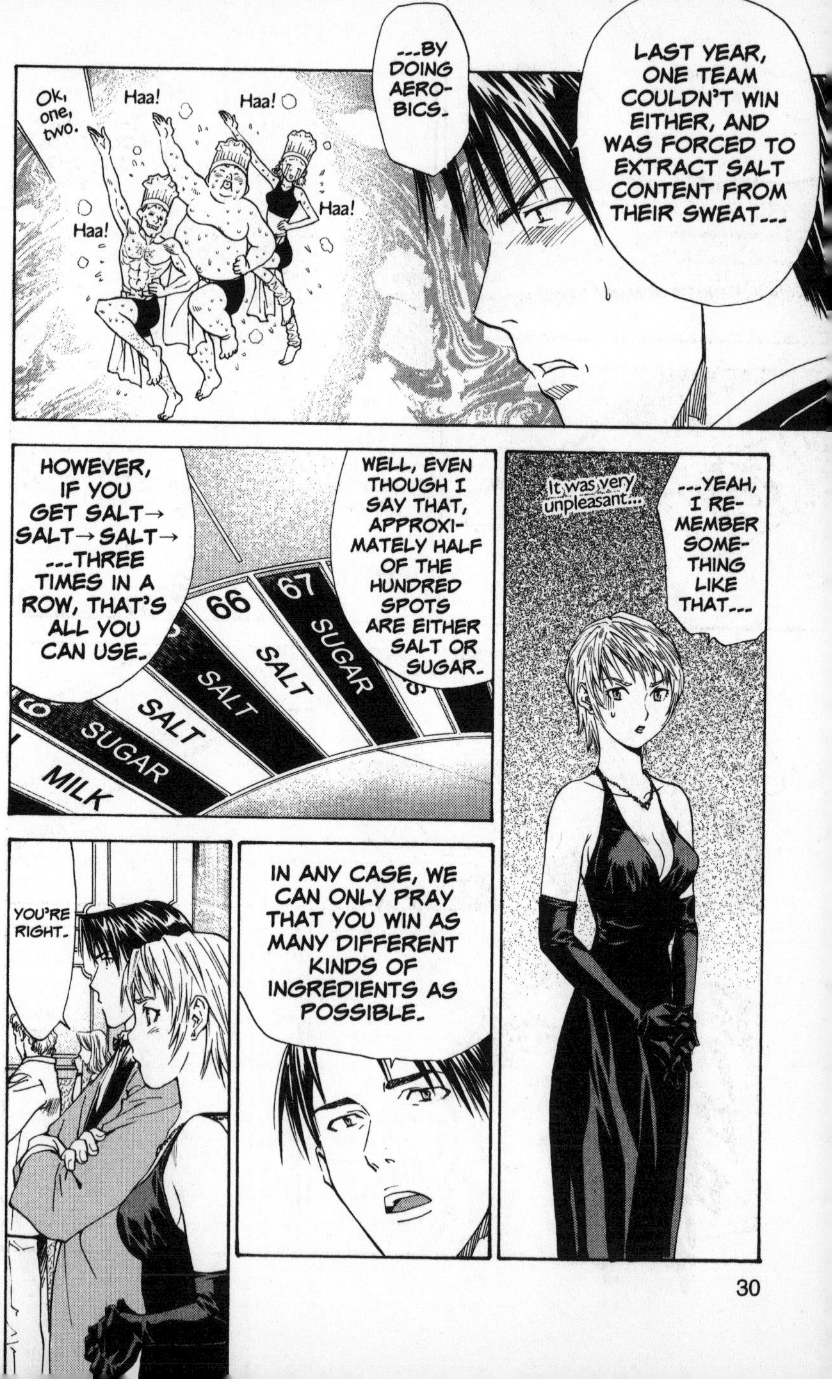
LAST YEAR, ONE TEAM COULDN'T WIN EITHER, AND WAS FORCED TO EXTRACT SALT CONTENT FROM THEIR SWEAT...
...BY DOING AERO-BICS.
Haa!
Haa!
Ok, one, two.
Haa!
Haa!
---YEAH, I RE-MEMBER SOME-THING LIKE THAT...
It was very unpleasant...
WELL, EVEN THOUGH I SAY THAT, APPROXI-MATELY HALF OF THE HUNDRED SPOTS ARE EITHER SALT OR SUGAR.
HOWEVER, IF YOU GET SALT→ SALT→ SALT→ ...THREE TIMES IN A ROW, THAT'S ALL YOU CAN USE.
67
SUGAR
66
SALT
SALT
SALT
SUGAR
MILK
IN ANY CASE, WE CAN ONLY PRAY THAT YOU WIN AS MANY DIFFERENT KINDS OF INGREDIENTS AS POSSIBLE.
YOU'RE RIGHT.

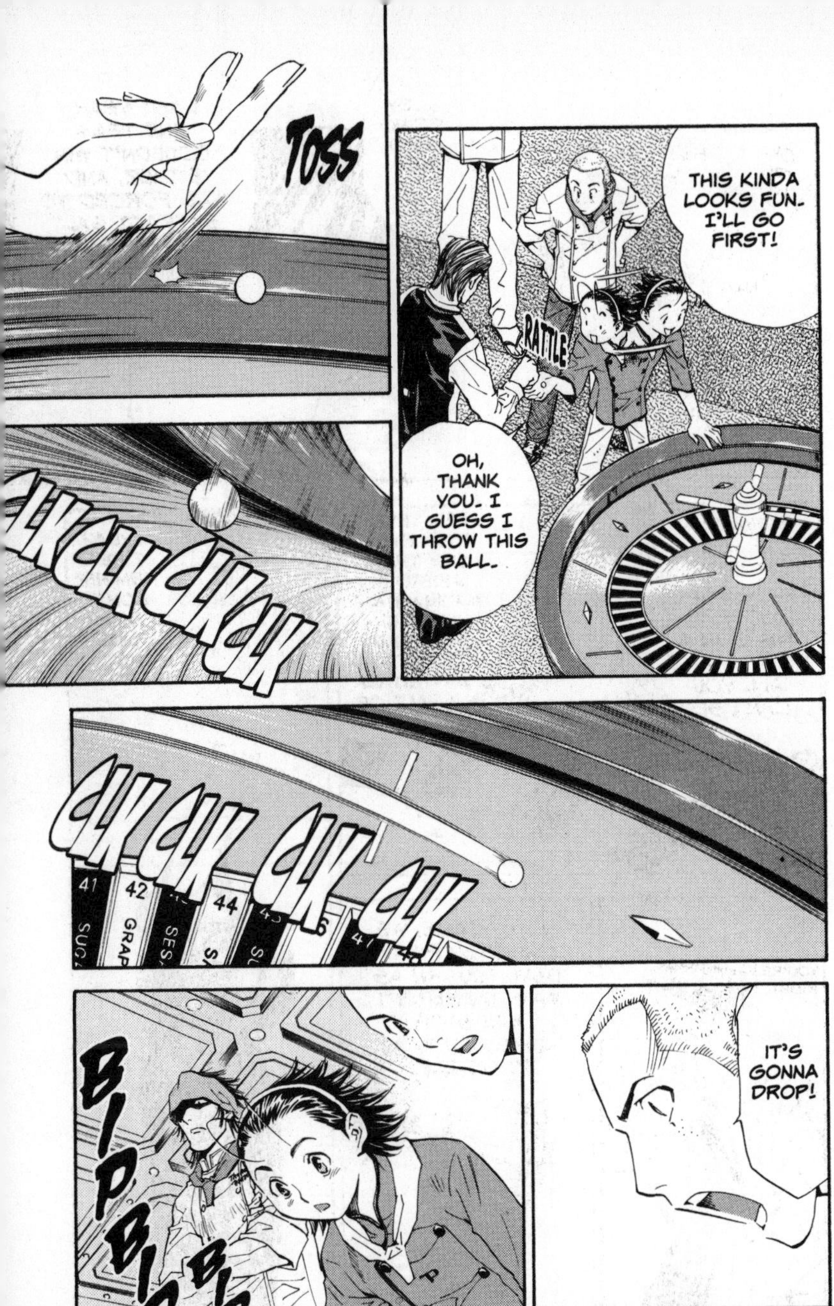
THIS KINDA LOOKS FUN. I'LL GO FIRST!
RATTLE
OH, THANK YOU. I GUESS I THROW THIS BALL.
TOSS
CLKCLK CLKCLK CLKCLK
CLK CLK CLK CLK CLK
IT'S GONNA DROP!
BIP BIP BIP BIP

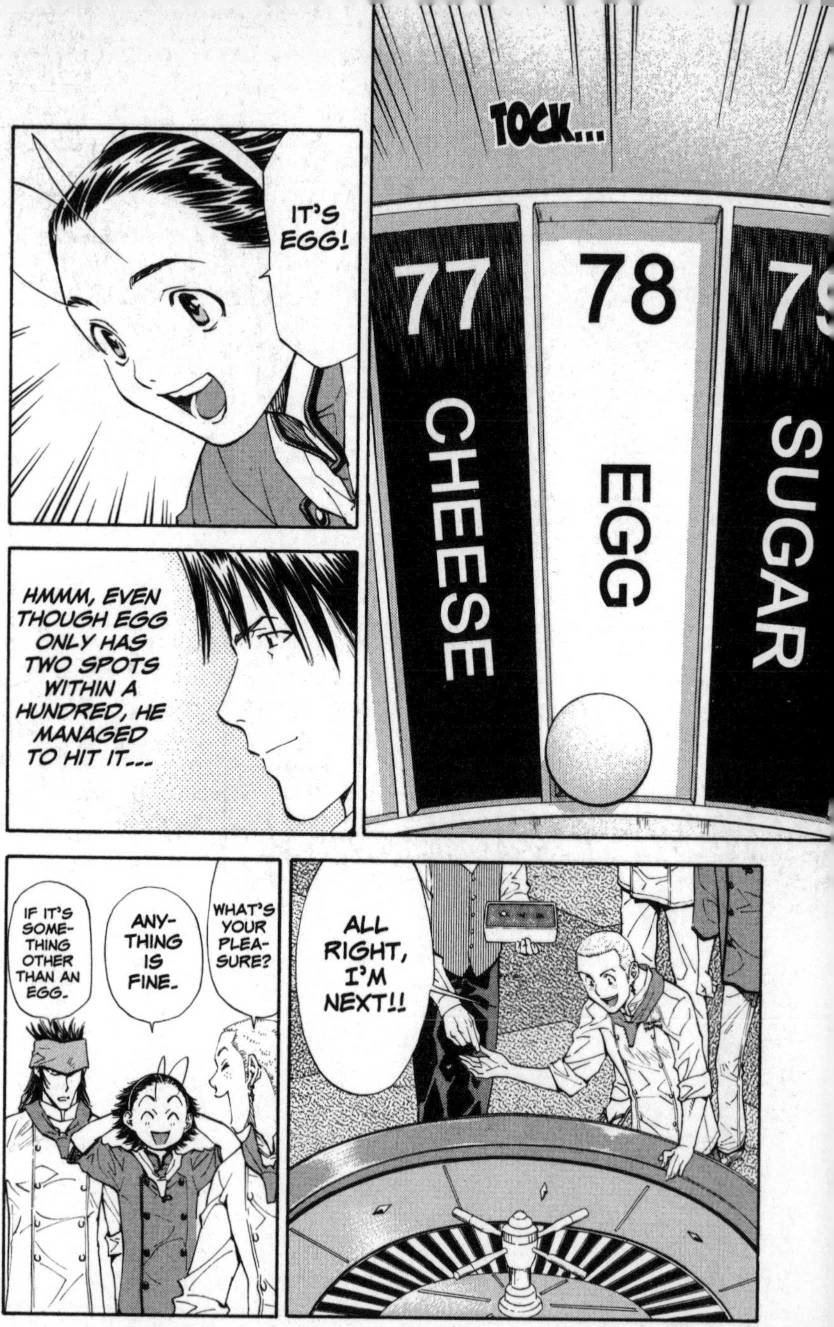
TOCK...
77
CHEESE
78
EGG
SUGAR
IT'S EGG!
HMMM, EVEN THOUGH EGG ONLY HAS TWO SPOTS WITHIN A HUNDRED, HE MANAGED TO HIT IT...
ALL RIGHT, I'M NEXT!!
WHAT'S YOUR PLEASURE?
ANYTHING IS FINE.
IF IT'S SOMETHING OTHER THAN AN EGG.

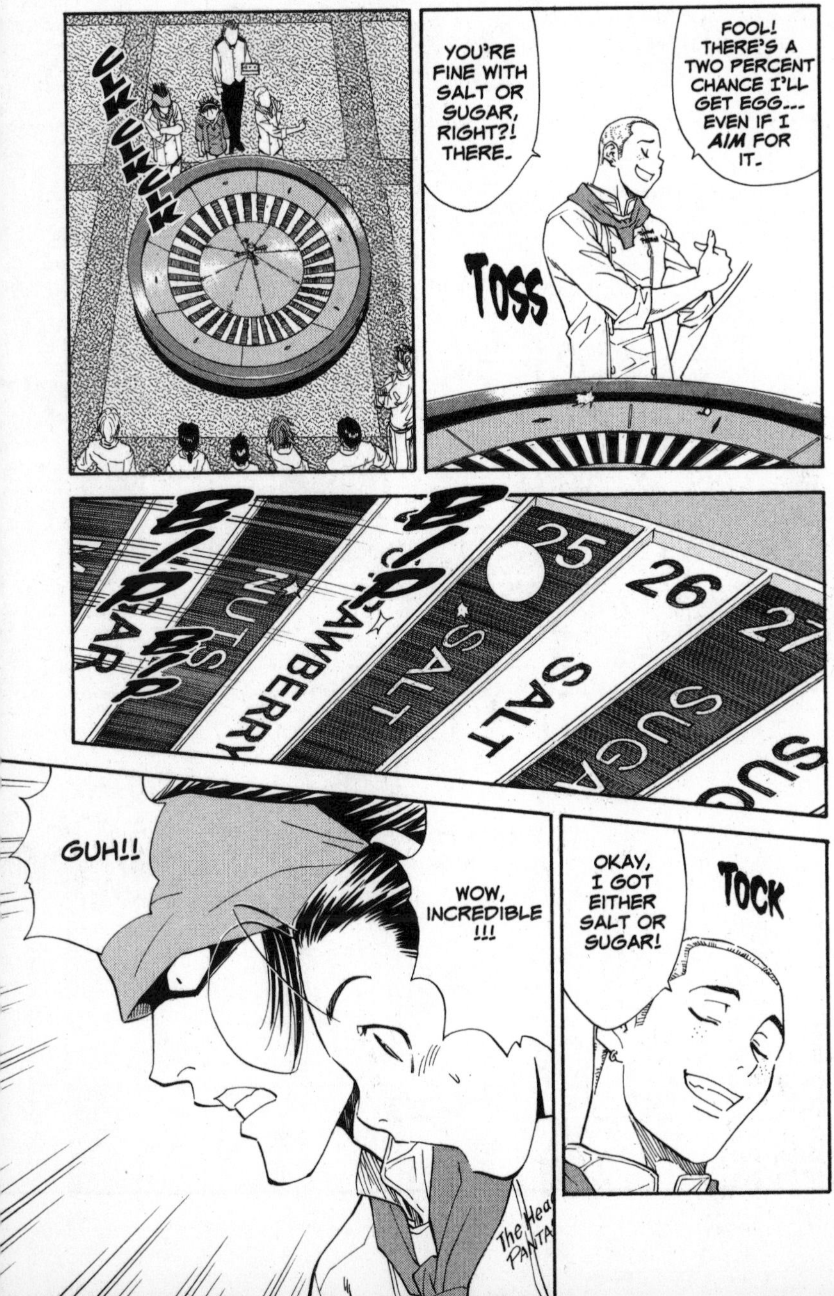
FOOL! THERE'S A TWO PERCENT CHANCE I'LL GET EGG... EVEN IF I AIM FOR IT.
YOU'RE FINE WITH SALT OR SUGAR, RIGHT?! THERE.
TOSS
25
SALT
26
SALT
27
SUGA
NUTS
OKAY, I GOT EITHER SALT OR SUGAR!
TOCK
WOW, INCREDIBLE !!!
GUH!!

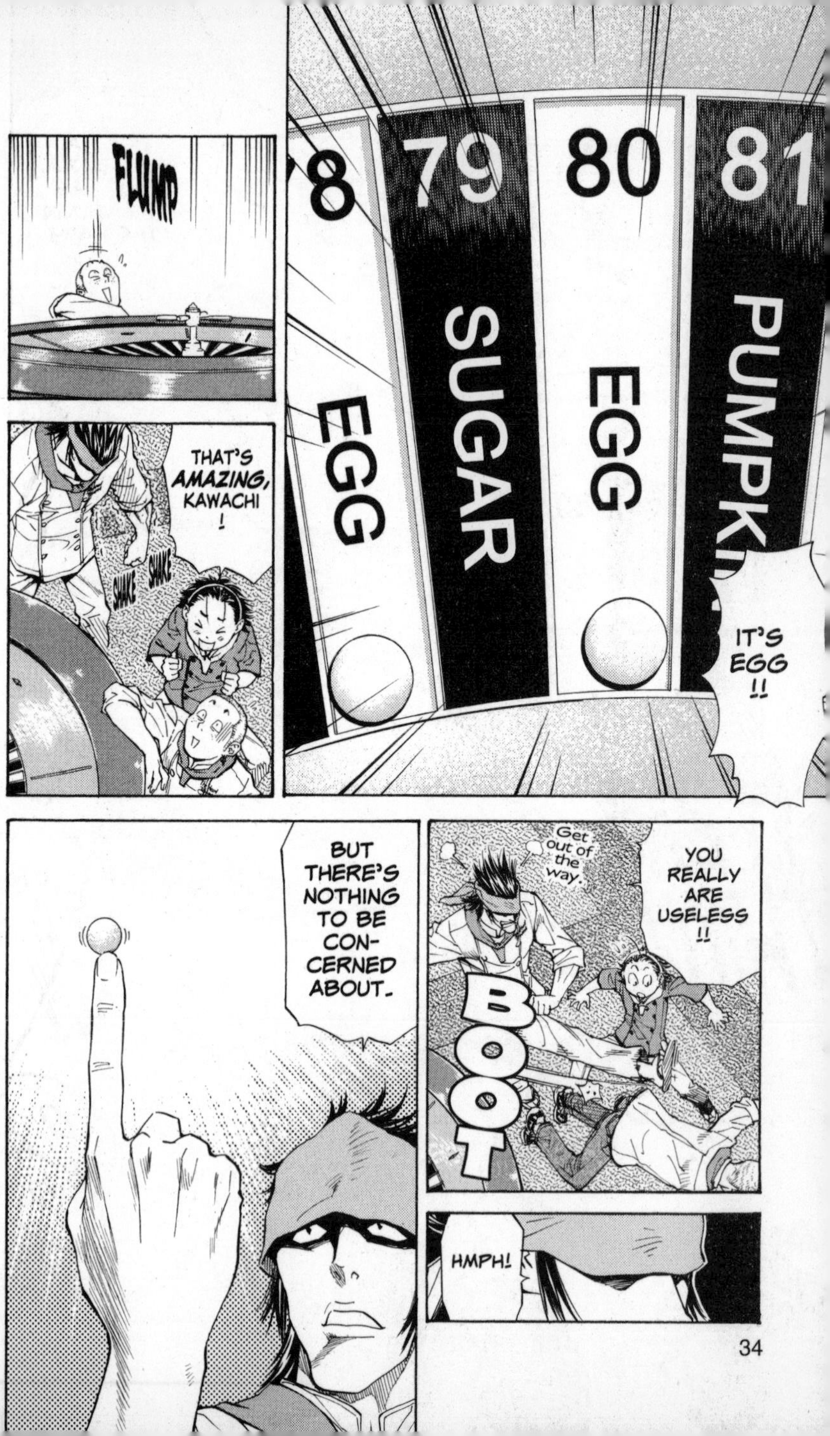
8
79
80
81
EGG
SUGAR
EGG
PUMPK
IT'S EGG!!
FLUMP
THAT'S AMAZING, KAWACHI!
SHAKE
SHAKE
YOU REALLY ARE USELESS!!
Get out of the way.
BOOT
HMPH!
BUT THERE'S NOTHING TO BE CON-CERNED ABOUT.

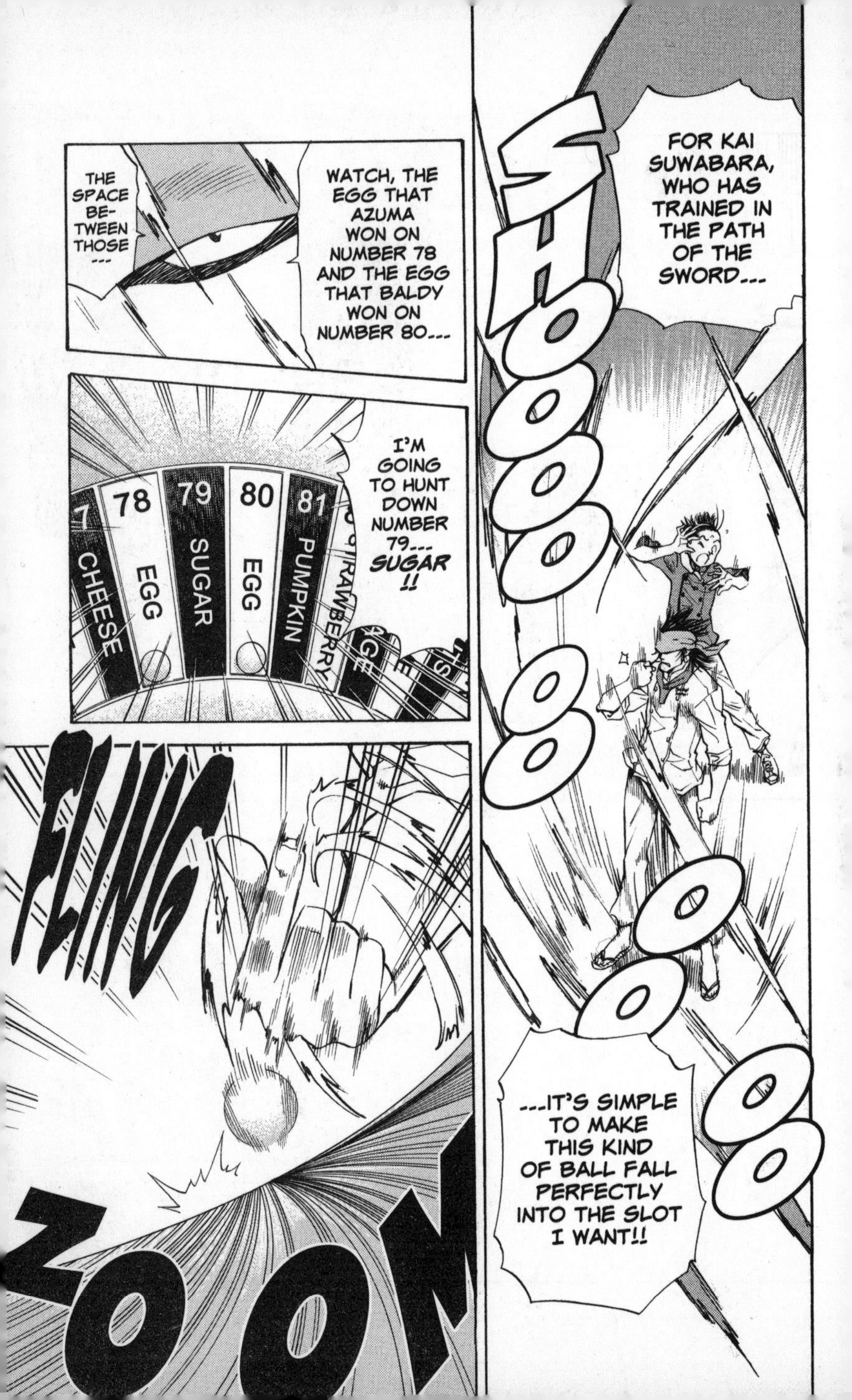
FOR KAI SUWABARA, WHO HAS TRAINED IN THE PATH OF THE SWORD...
SHOOOOOOOOOOO
...IT'S SIMPLE TO MAKE THIS KIND OF BALL FALL PERFECTLY INTO THE SLOT I WANT!!
WATCH, THE EGG THAT AZUMA WON ON NUMBER 78 AND THE EGG THAT BALDY WON ON NUMBER 80...
THE SPACE BE-TWEEN THOSE...
I'M GOING TO HUNT DOWN NUMBER 79... SUGAR!!
78
79
80
81
CHEESE
EGG
SUGAR
EGG
PUMPKIN
FLING
ZOOM

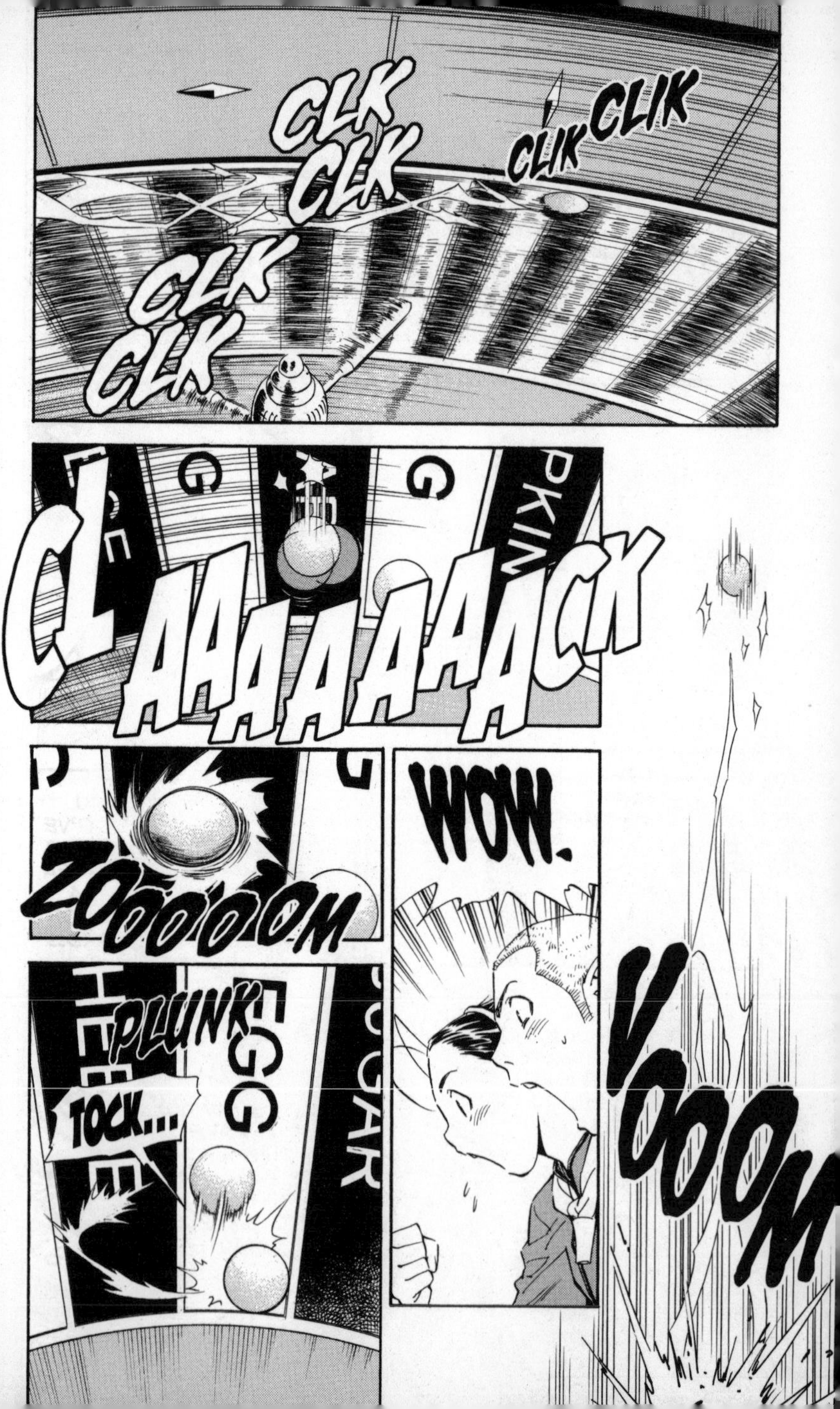
CLIK CLIK
CLK CLK
CLK CLK
CLAAAAAAACK
WOW.
VOOOM
ZOOOOOM
PLUNK
TOCK...

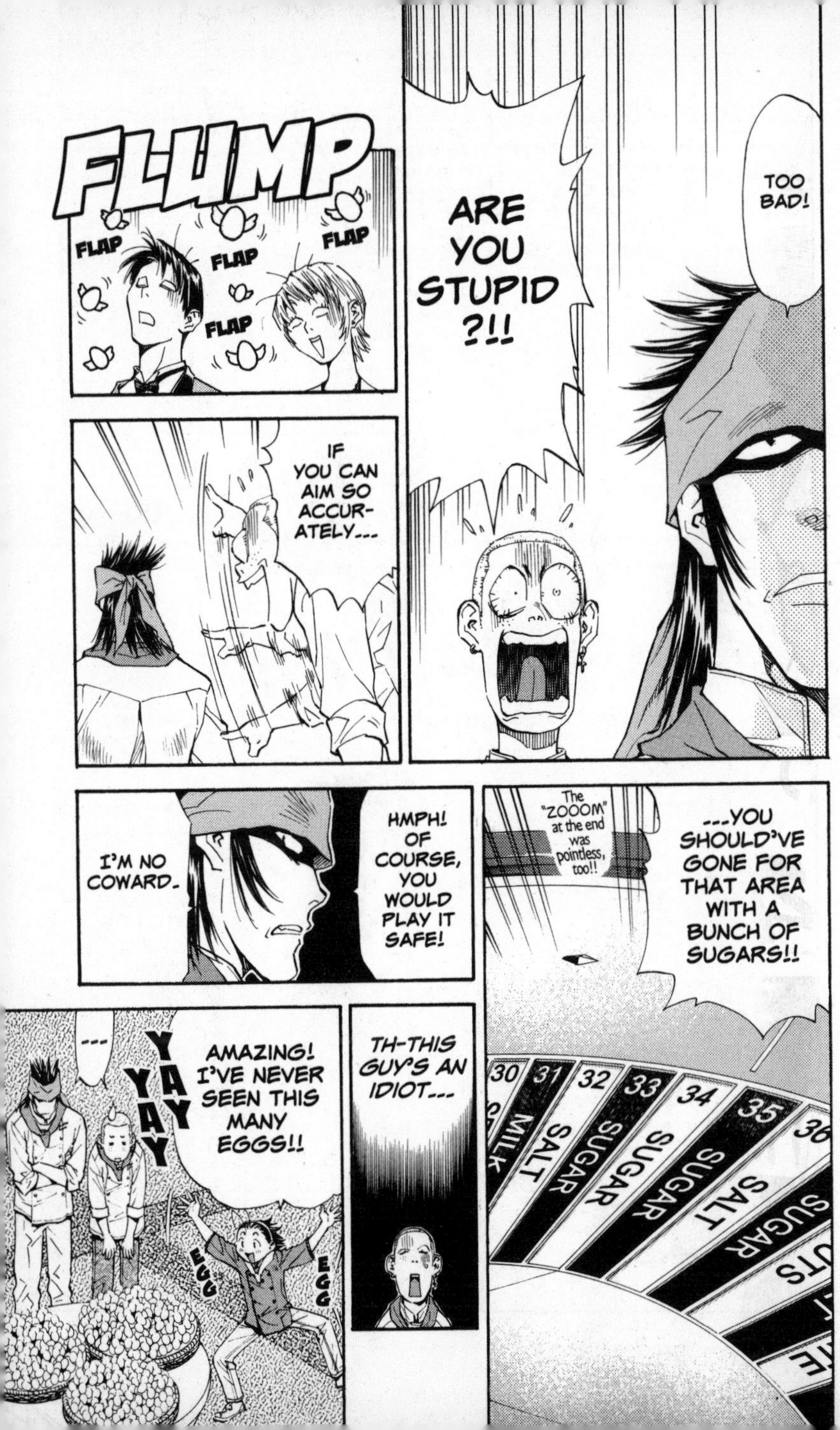
TOO BAD!
ARE YOU STUPID ?!!
FLUMP
FLAP
FLAP
FLAP
FLAP
IF YOU CAN AIM SO ACCURATELY...
...YOU SHOULD'VE GONE FOR THAT AREA WITH A BUNCH OF SUGARS!!
The "ZOOOM" at the end was pointless, too!!
30
31
32
33
34
35
36
MILK
SALT
SUGAR
SUGAR
SUGAR
SALT
SUGAR
HMPH! OF COURSE, YOU WOULD PLAY IT SAFE!
I'M NO COWARD.
TH-THIS GUY'S AN IDIOT...
AMAZING! I'VE NEVER SEEN THIS MANY EGGS!!
YAY
YAY
...
EGG
EGG

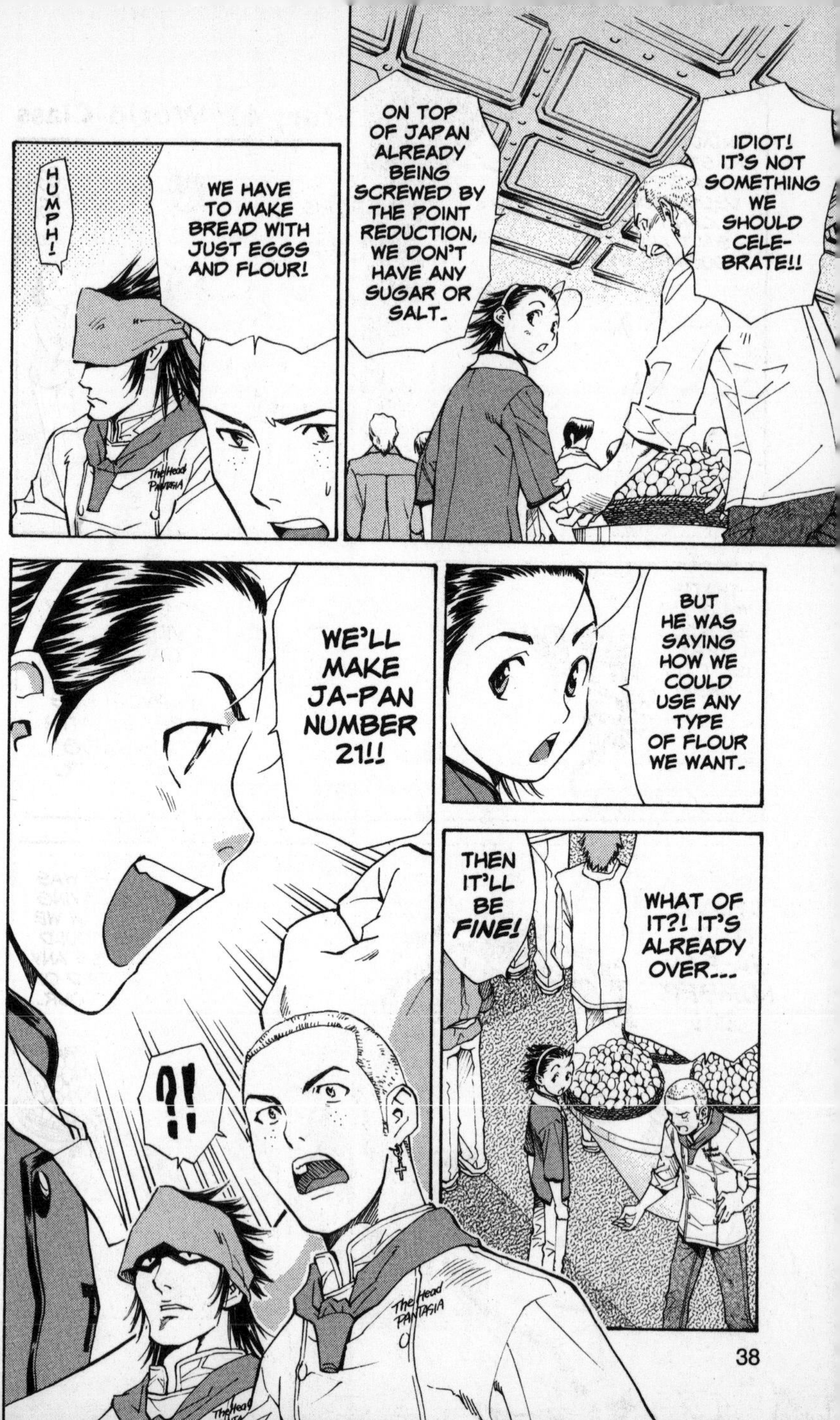
IDIOT! IT'S NOT SOMETHING WE SHOULD CELE-BRATE!!
ON TOP OF JAPAN ALREADY BEING SCREWED BY THE POINT REDUCTION, WE DON'T HAVE ANY SUGAR OR SALT.
WE HAVE TO MAKE BREAD WITH JUST EGGS AND FLOUR!
HUMPH!
BUT HE WAS SAYING HOW WE COULD USE ANY TYPE OF FLOUR WE WANT.
WHAT OF IT?! IT'S ALREADY OVER...
THEN IT'LL BE FINE!
WE'LL MAKE JA-PAN NUMBER 21!!
?!

Story 62: World-Class

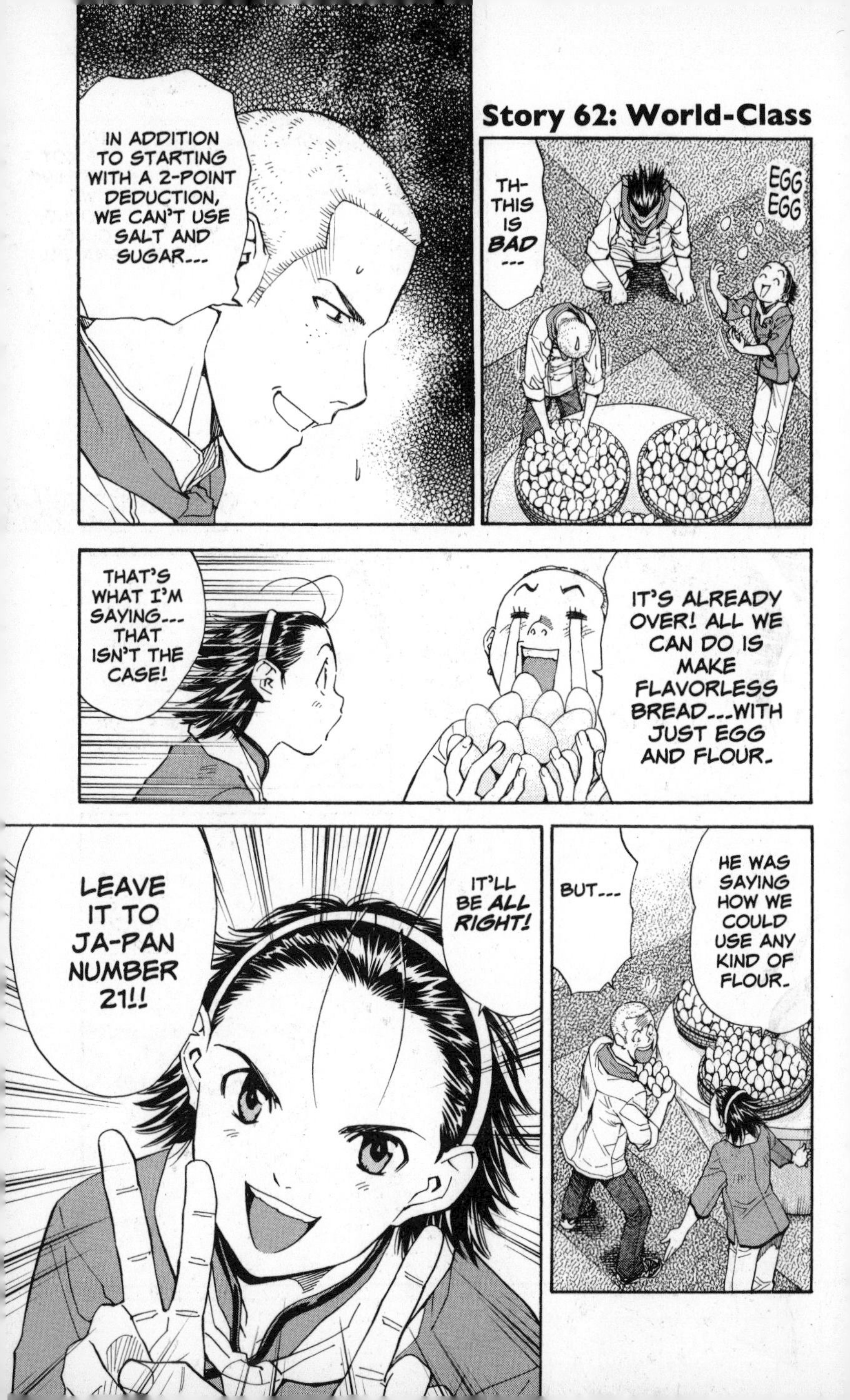
TH-THIS IS BAD...
EGG EGG
IN ADDITION TO STARTING WITH A 2-POINT DEDUCTION, WE CAN'T USE SALT AND SUGAR...
IT'S ALREADY OVER! ALL WE CAN DO IS MAKE FLAVORLESS BREAD...WITH JUST EGG AND FLOUR.
THAT'S WHAT I'M SAYING... THAT ISN'T THE CASE!
HE WAS SAYING HOW WE COULD USE ANY KIND OF FLOUR.
BUT...
IT'LL BE ALL RIGHT!
LEAVE IT TO JA-PAN NUMBER 21!!

Story 62: World-Class

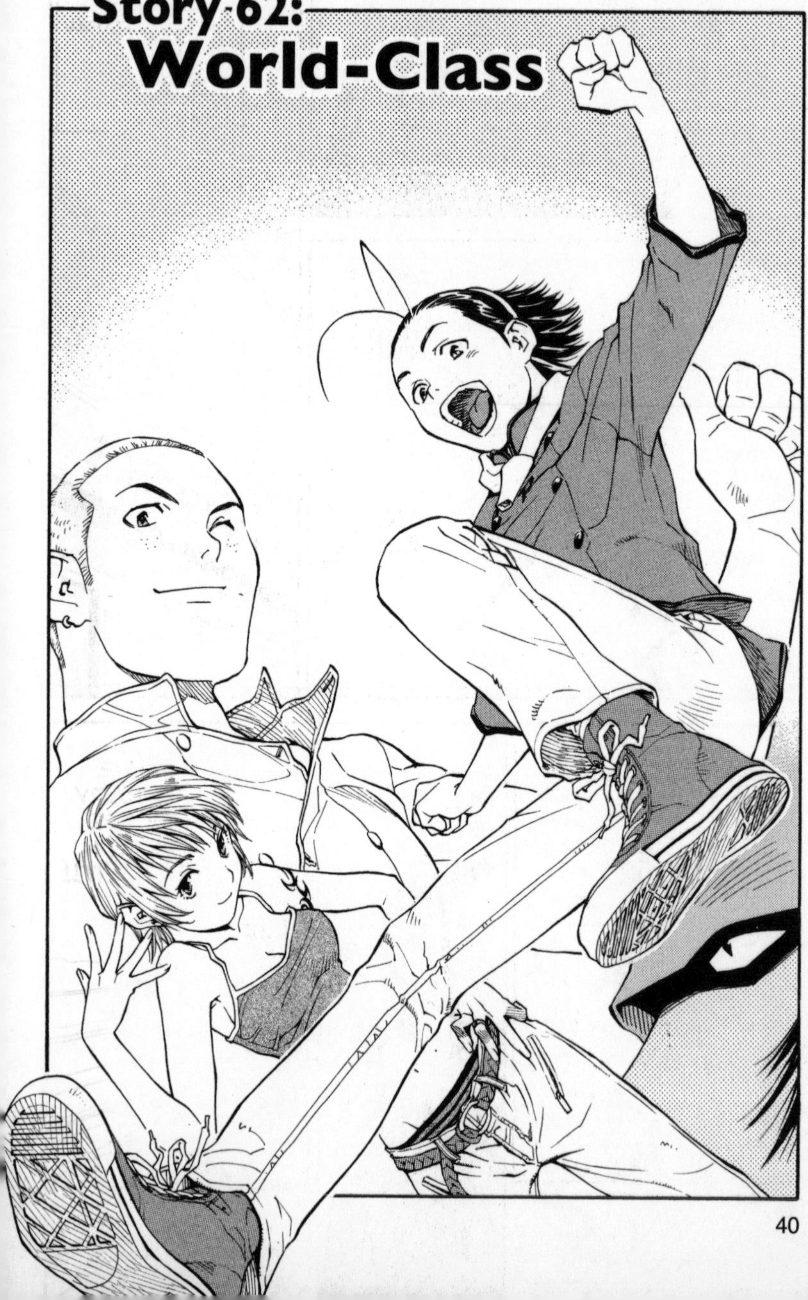

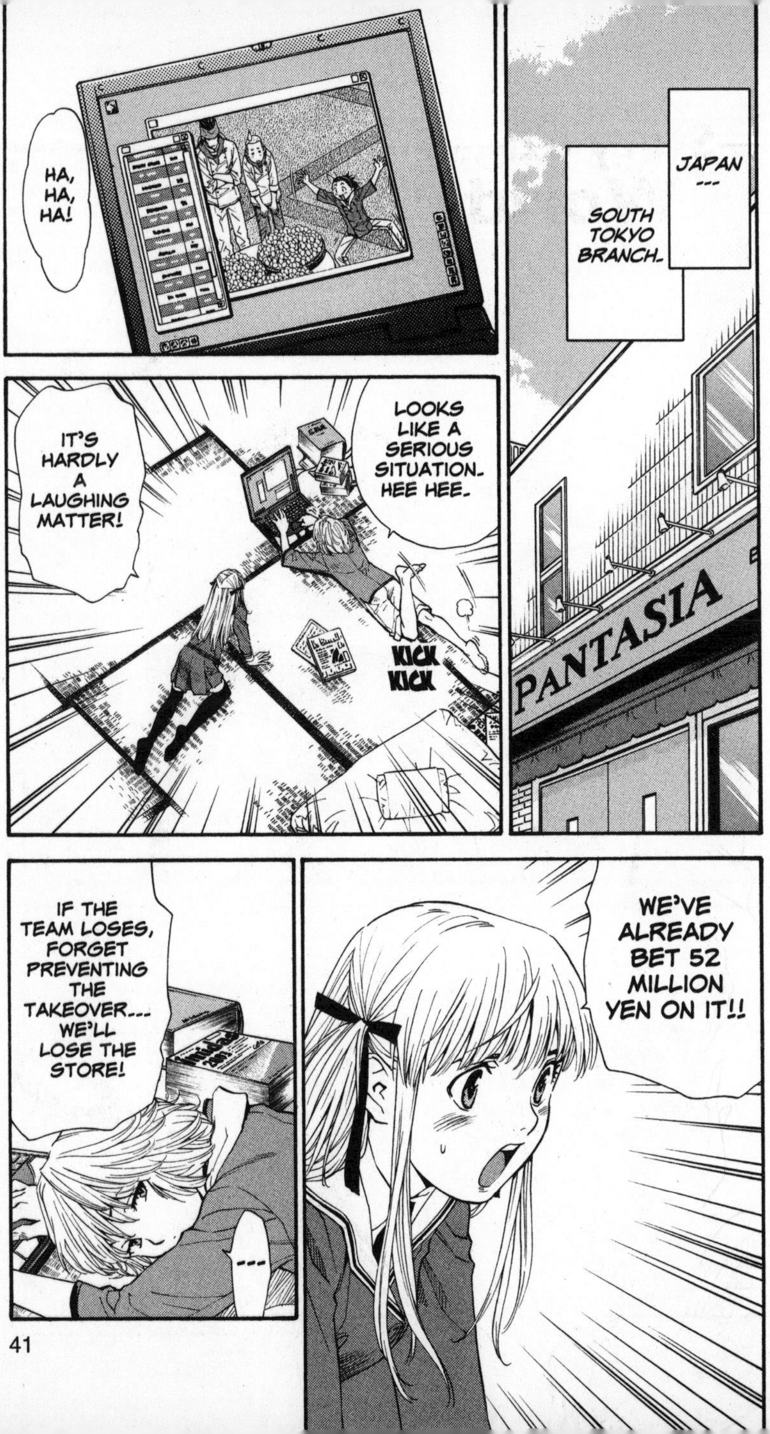
JAPAN---
SOUTH TOKYO BRANCH.
PANTASIA
HA, HA, HA!
LOOKS LIKE A SERIOUS SITUATION. HEE HEE.
IT'S HARDLY A LAUGHING MATTER!
KICK KICK
WE'VE ALREADY BET 52 MILLION YEN ON IT!!
IF THE TEAM LOSES, FORGET PREVENTING THE TAKEOVER... WE'LL LOSE THE STORE!
...

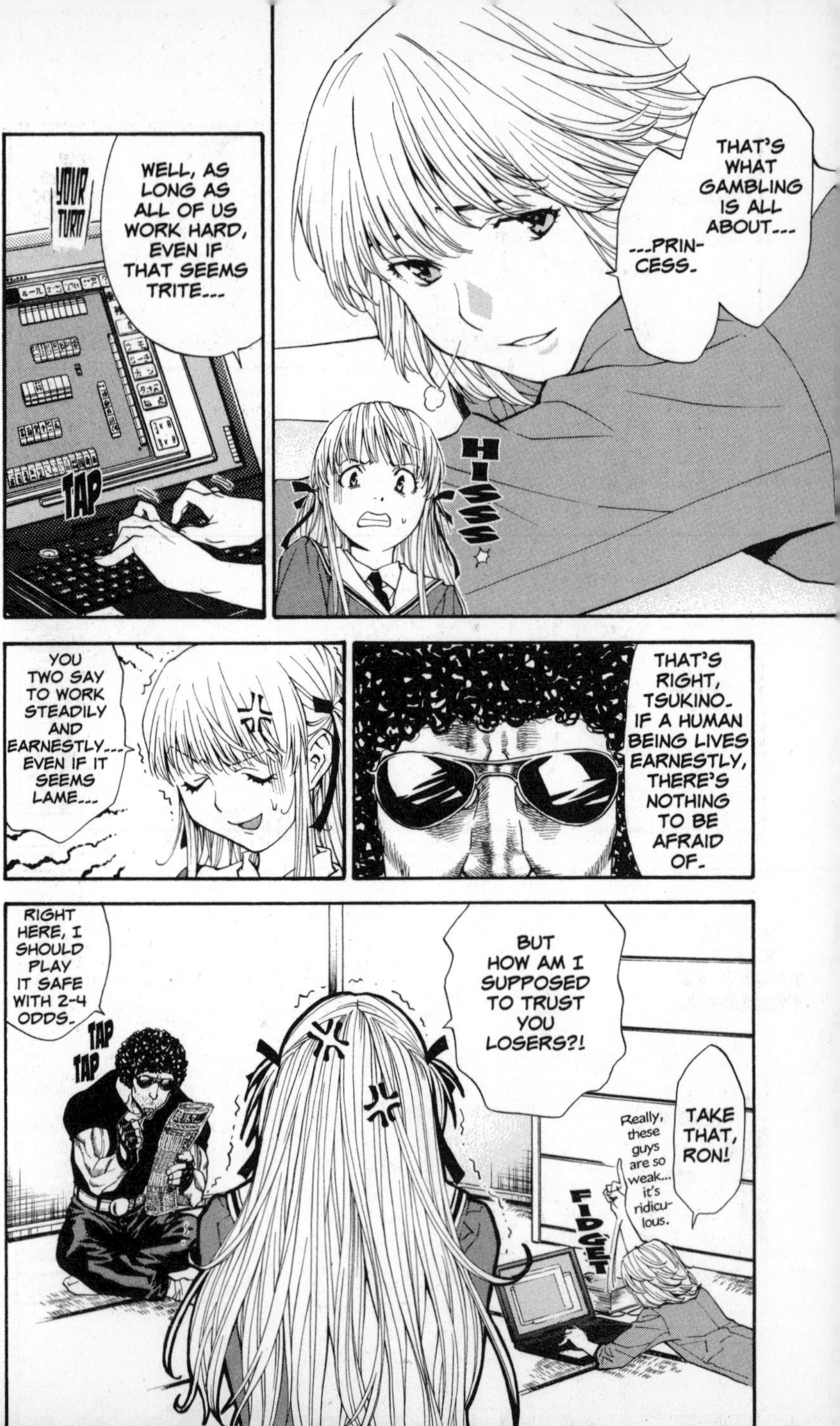
THAT'S WHAT GAMBLING IS ALL ABOUT...
...PRIN-CESS.
HISSS
YOUR TURN
WELL, AS LONG AS ALL OF US WORK HARD, EVEN IF THAT SEEMS TRITE...
TAP
THAT'S RIGHT, TSUKINO. IF A HUMAN BEING LIVES EARNESTLY, THERE'S NOTHING TO BE AFRAID OF.
YOU TWO SAY TO WORK STEADILY AND EARNESTLY... EVEN IF IT SEEMS LAME...
TAKE THAT, RON!
Really, these guys are so weak... it's ridicu-lous.
FIDGET
BUT HOW AM I SUPPOSED TO TRUST YOU LOSERS?!
RIGHT HERE, I SHOULD PLAY IT SAFE WITH 2-4 ODDS.
TAP TAP

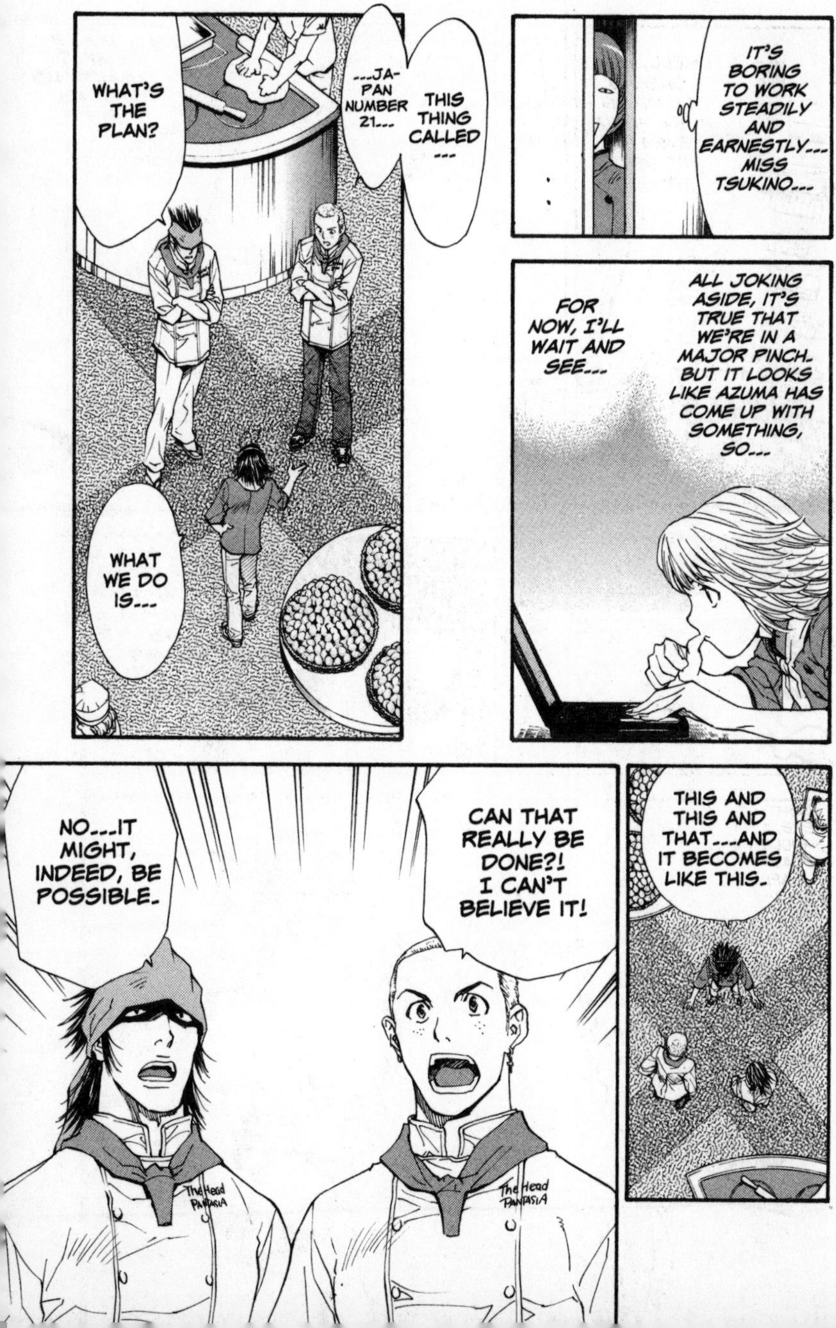
IT'S BORING TO WORK STEADILY AND EARNESTLY--- MISS TSUKINO---
ALL JOKING ASIDE, IT'S TRUE THAT WE'RE IN A MAJOR PINCH. BUT IT LOOKS LIKE AZUMA HAS COME UP WITH SOMETHING, SO---
FOR NOW, I'LL WAIT AND SEE---
THIS THING CALLED---
---JA-PAN NUMBER 21---
WHAT'S THE PLAN?
WHAT WE DO IS---
THIS AND THIS AND THAT---AND IT BECOMES LIKE THIS.
CAN THAT REALLY BE DONE?! I CAN'T BELIEVE IT!
NO---IT MIGHT, INDEED, BE POSSIBLE.
The Head PANTASIA
The Head PANTASIA

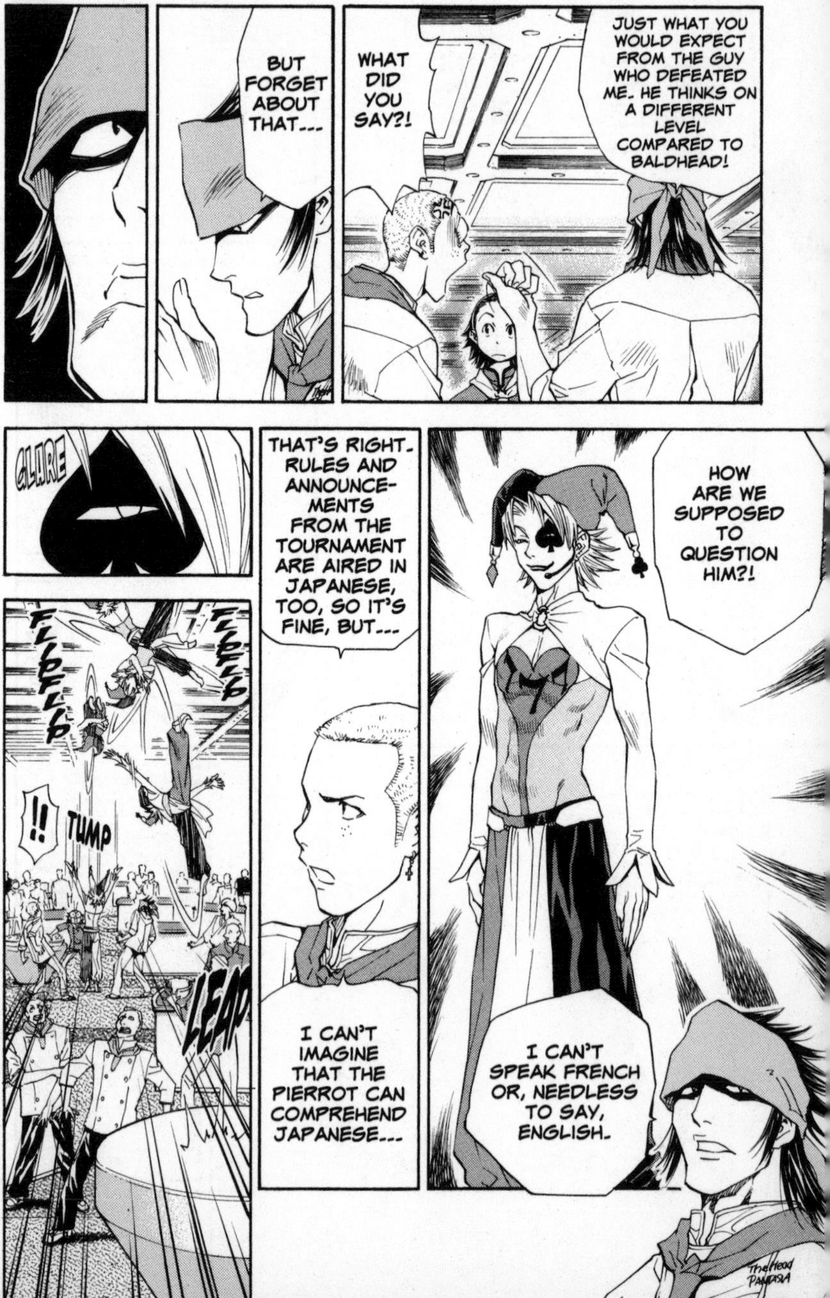
JUST WHAT YOU WOULD EXPECT FROM THE GUY WHO DEFEATED ME. HE THINKS ON A DIFFERENT LEVEL COMPARED TO BALDHEAD!
WHAT DID YOU SAY?!
BUT FORGET ABOUT THAT...
HOW ARE WE SUPPOSED TO QUESTION HIM?!
I CAN'T SPEAK FRENCH OR, NEEDLESS TO SAY, ENGLISH.
THAT'S RIGHT. RULES AND ANNOUNCEMENTS FROM THE TOURNAMENT ARE AIRED IN JAPANESE, TOO, SO IT'S FINE, BUT...
I CAN'T IMAGINE THAT THE PIERROT CAN COMPREHEND JAPANESE...
GLARE
FLIPFLIP
FLIPFLIP
!!
TUMP
LEAP

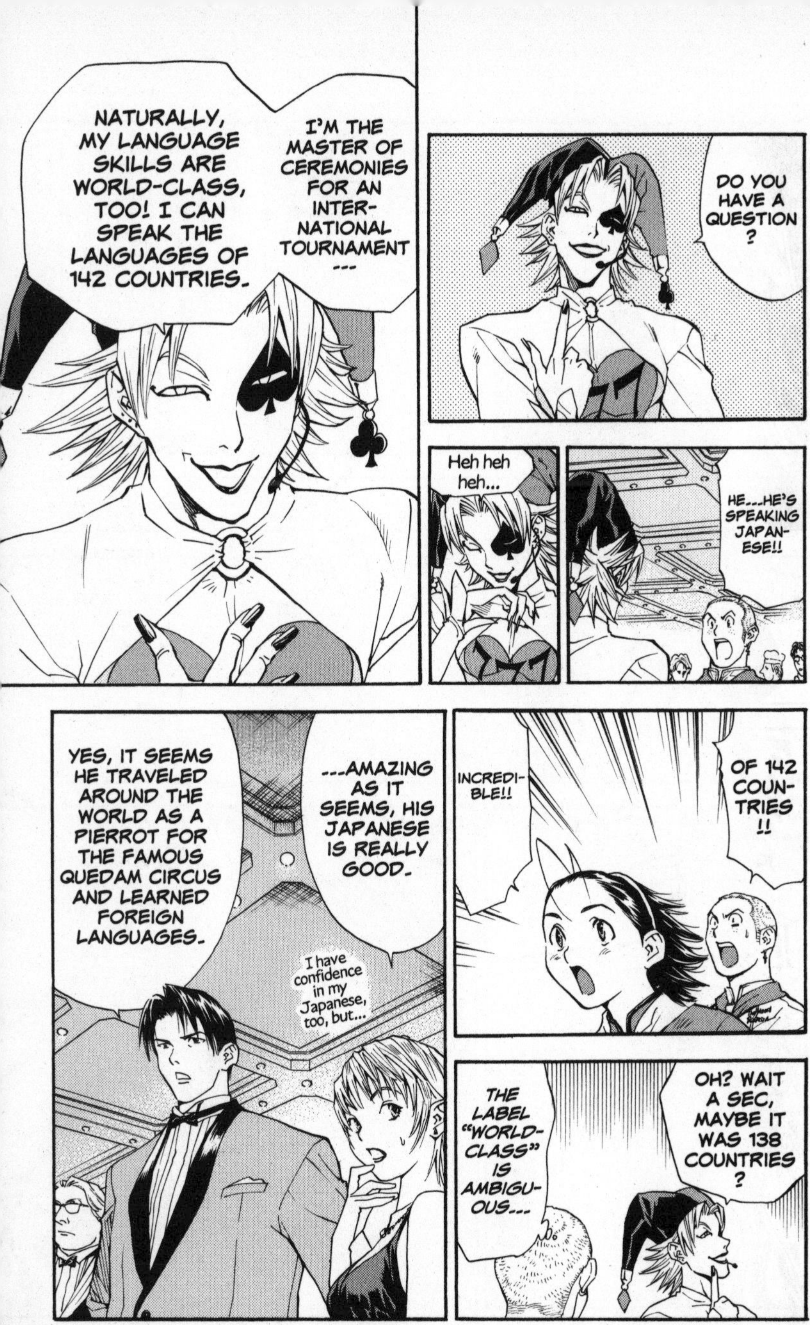
DO YOU HAVE A QUESTION?
HE...HE'S SPEAKING JAPANESE!!
Heh heh heh...
I'M THE MASTER OF CEREMONIES FOR AN INTERNATIONAL TOURNAMENT...
NATURALLY, MY LANGUAGE SKILLS ARE WORLD-CLASS, TOO! I CAN SPEAK THE LANGUAGES OF 142 COUNTRIES.
OF 142 COUNTRIES!!
INCREDIBLE!!
OH? WAIT A SEC, MAYBE IT WAS 138 COUNTRIES?
THE LABEL "WORLD-CLASS" IS AMBIGUOUS...
...AMAZING AS IT SEEMS, HIS JAPANESE IS REALLY GOOD.
YES, IT SEEMS HE TRAVELED AROUND THE WORLD AS A PIERROT FOR THE FAMOUS QUEDAM CIRCUS AND LEARNED FOREIGN LANGUAGES.
I have confidence in my Japanese, too, but...

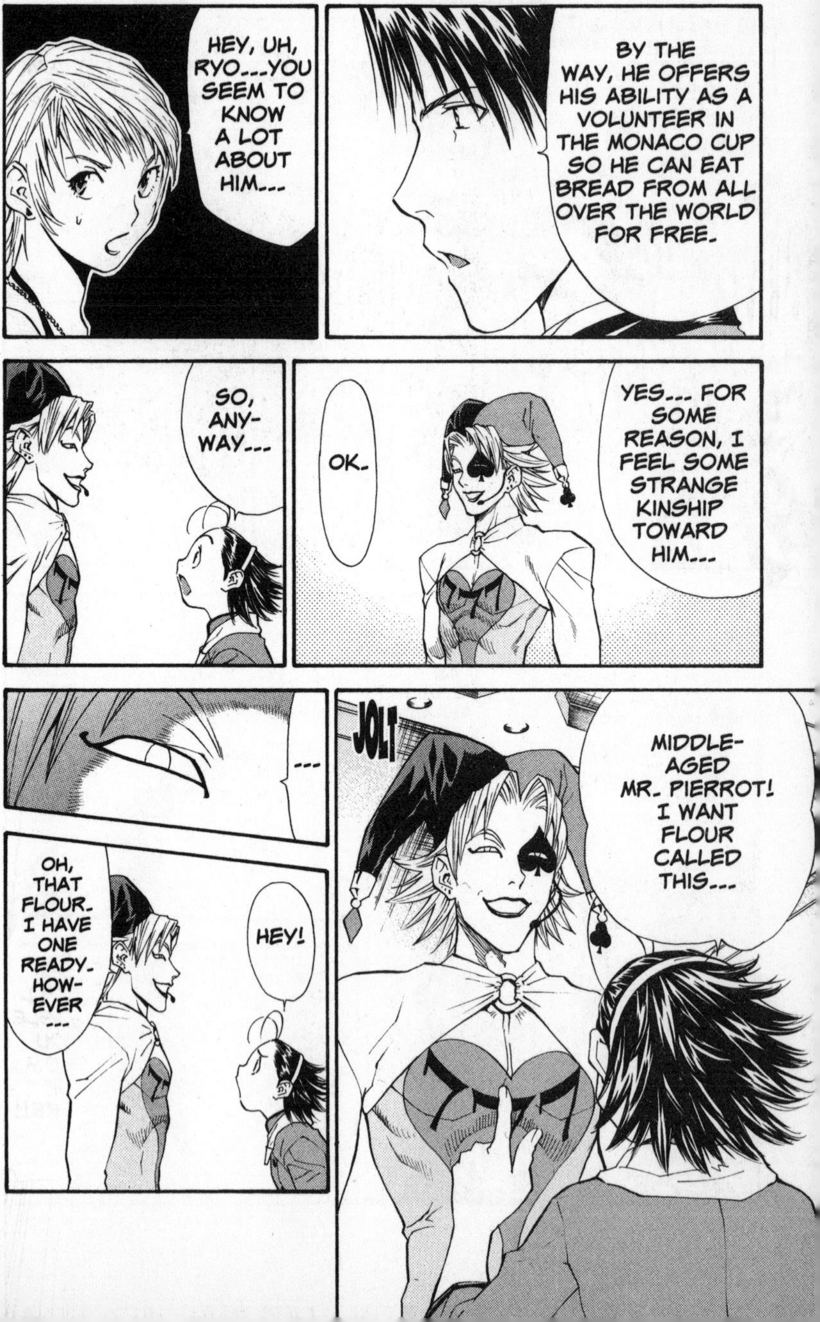
BY THE WAY, HE OFFERS HIS ABILITY AS A VOLUNTEER IN THE MONACO CUP SO HE CAN EAT BREAD FROM ALL OVER THE WORLD FOR FREE.
HEY, UH, RYO...YOU SEEM TO KNOW A LOT ABOUT HIM...
YES... FOR SOME REASON, I FEEL SOME STRANGE KINSHIP TOWARD HIM...
OK.
SO, ANY-WAY...
JOLT
MIDDLE-AGED MR. PIERROT! I WANT FLOUR CALLED THIS...
...
HEY!
OH, THAT FLOUR. I HAVE ONE READY. HOW-EVER ...

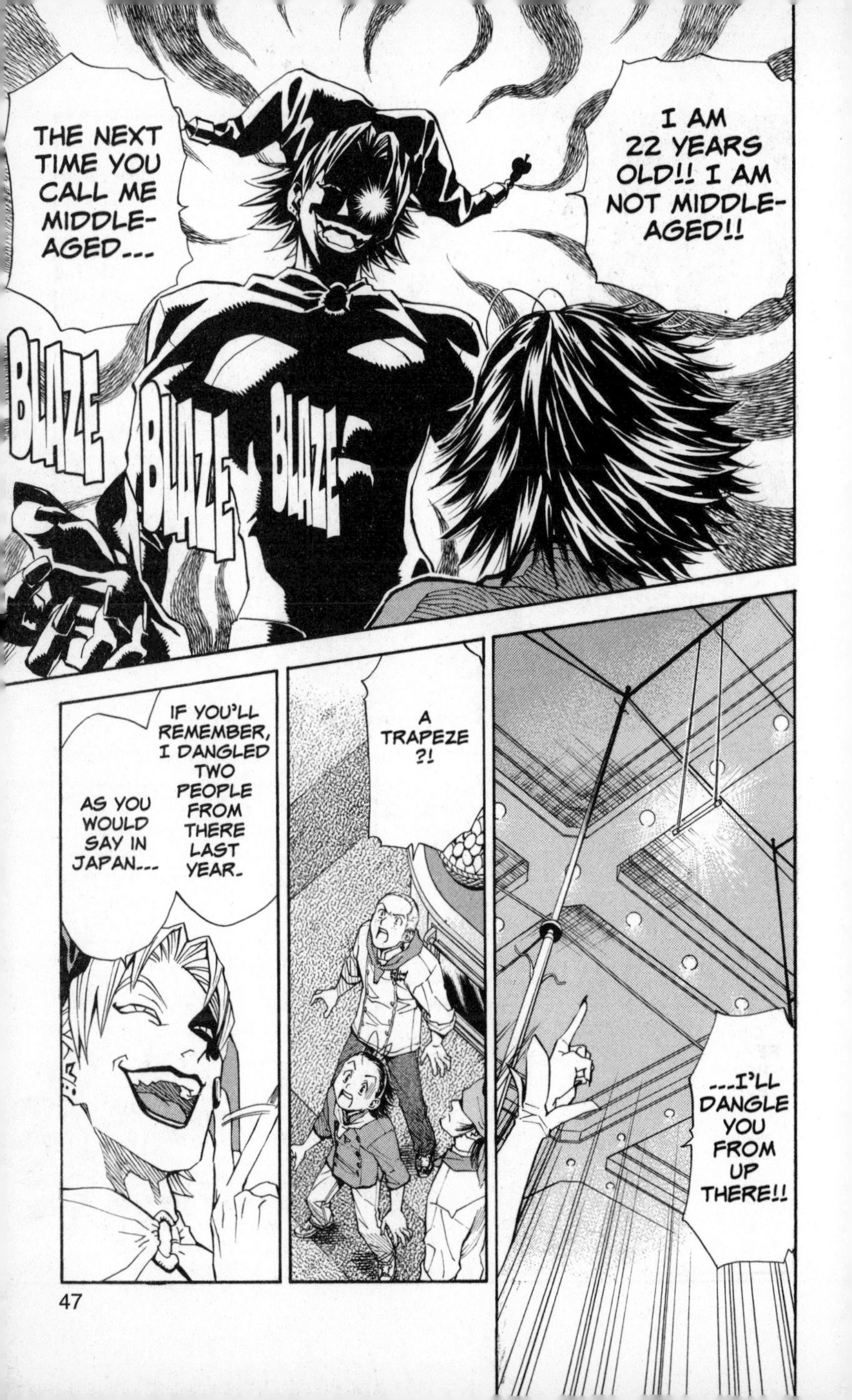

I AM 22 YEARS OLD!! I AM NOT MIDDLE-AGED!!
THE NEXT TIME YOU CALL ME MIDDLE-AGED...
BLAZE
BLAZE
BLAZE
...I'LL DANGLE YOU FROM UP THERE!!
A TRAPEZE?!
IF YOU'LL REMEMBER, I DANGLED TWO PEOPLE FROM THERE LAST YEAR.
AS YOU WOULD SAY IN JAPAN...

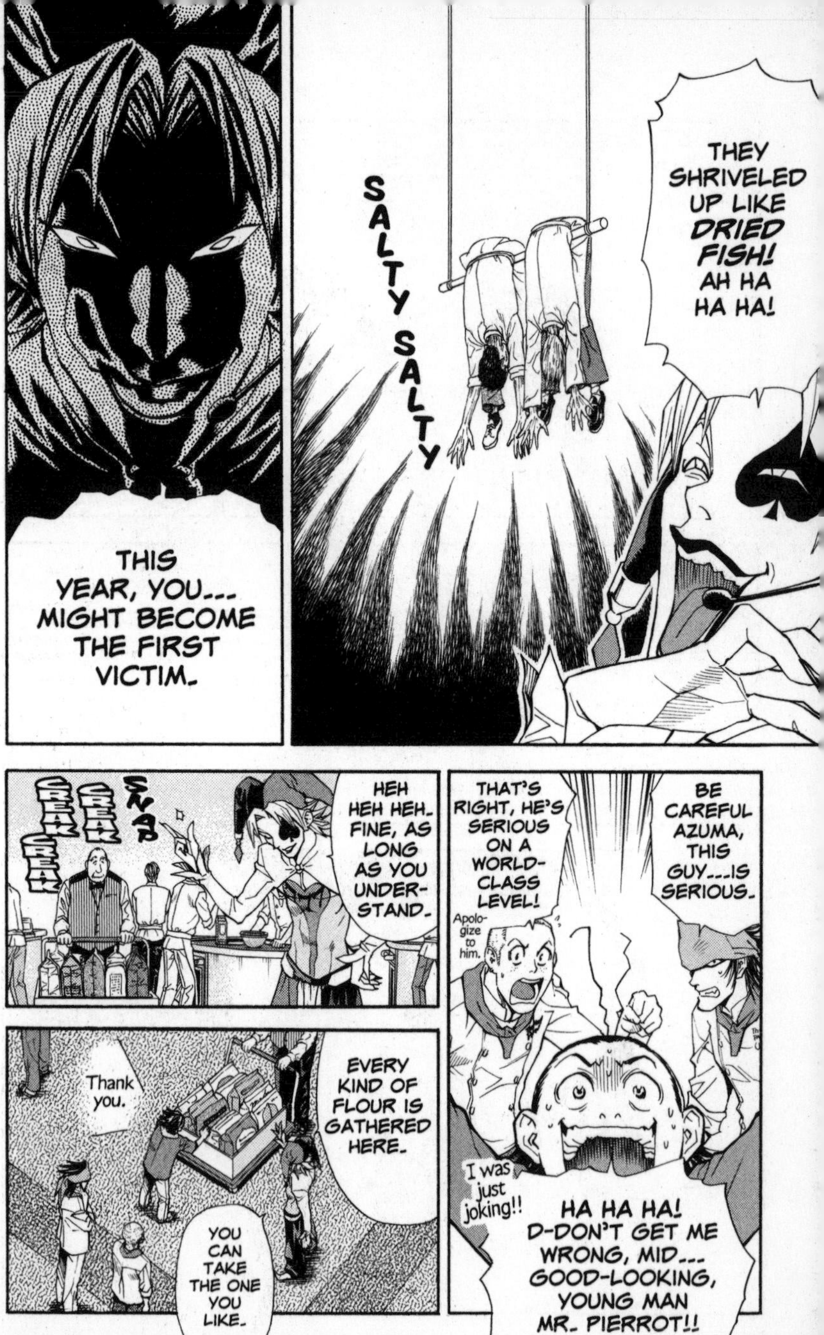

THEY SHRIVELED UP LIKE DRIED FISH! AH HA HA HA!
SALTY SALTY
THIS YEAR, YOU... MIGHT BECOME THE FIRST VICTIM.
BE CAREFUL AZUMA, THIS GUY...IS SERIOUS.
THAT'S RIGHT, HE'S SERIOUS ON A WORLD-CLASS LEVEL!
Apologize to him.
HA HA HA! D-DON'T GET ME WRONG, MID... GOOD-LOOKING, YOUNG MAN MR. PIERROT!!
I was just joking!!
HEH HEH HEH. FINE, AS LONG AS YOU UNDER-STAND.
SNAP
CREAK CREAK CREAK
EVERY KIND OF FLOUR IS GATHERED HERE.
Thank you.
YOU CAN TAKE THE ONE YOU LIKE.

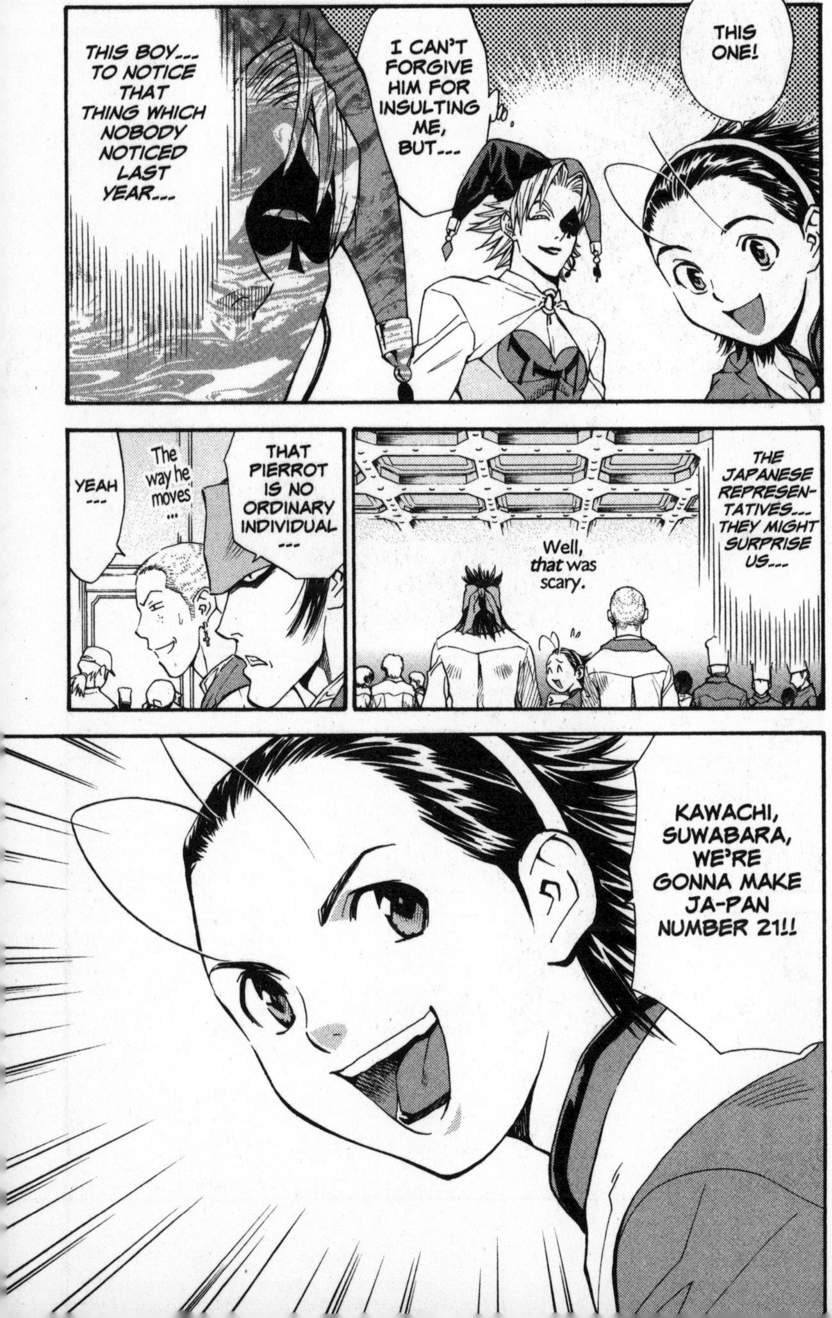
THIS ONE!
I CAN'T FORGIVE HIM FOR INSULTING ME, BUT...
THIS BOY... TO NOTICE THAT THING WHICH NOBODY NOTICED LAST YEAR...
THE JAPANESE REPRESENTATIVES... THEY MIGHT SURPRISE US...
Well, *that* was scary.
THAT PIERROT IS NO ORDINARY INDIVIDUAL...
The way he moves...
YEAH...
KAWACHI, SUWABARA, WE'RE GONNA MAKE JA-PAN NUMBER 21!!

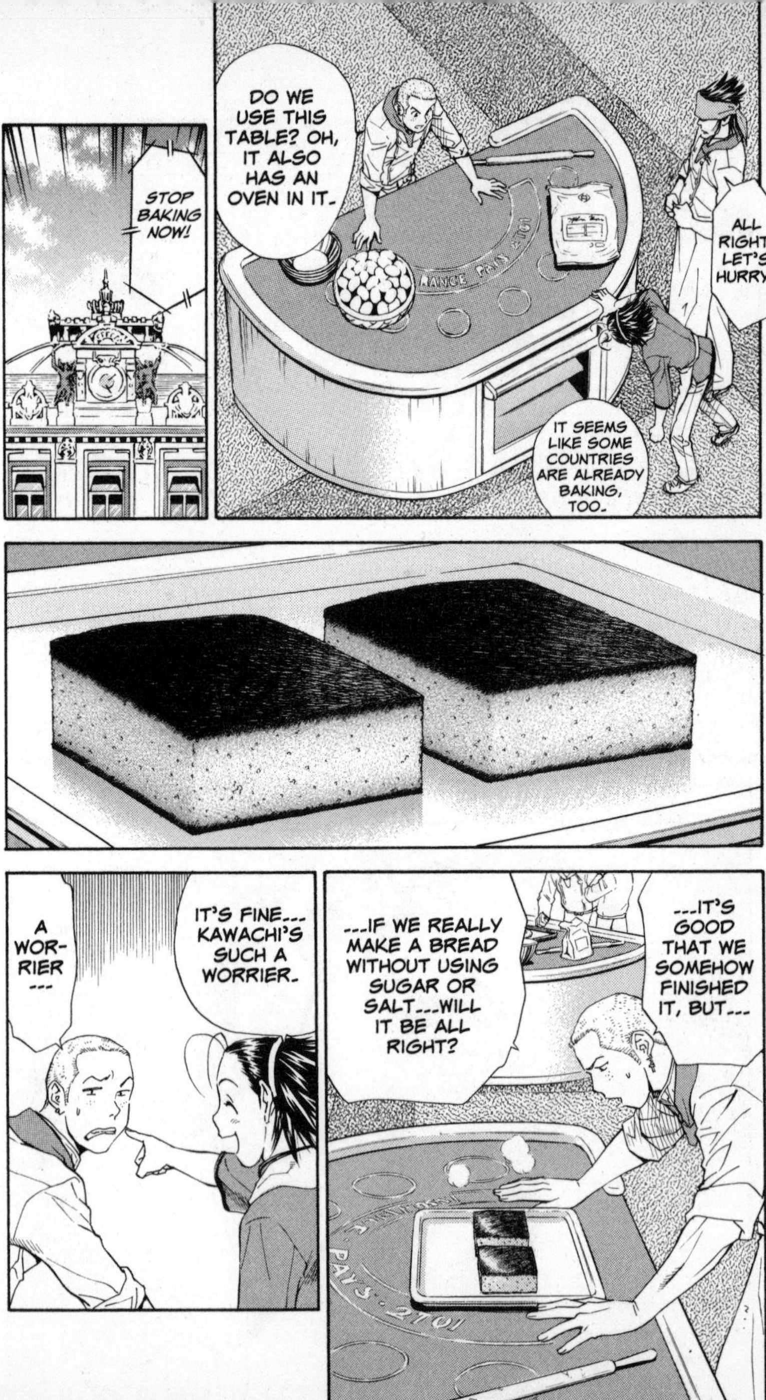
DO WE USE THIS TABLE? OH, IT ALSO HAS AN OVEN IN IT.
ALL RIGHT, LET'S HURRY.
IT SEEMS LIKE SOME COUNTRIES ARE ALREADY BAKING, TOO.
STOP BAKING NOW!
...IT'S GOOD THAT WE SOMEHOW FINISHED IT, BUT...
...IF WE REALLY MAKE A BREAD WITHOUT USING SUGAR OR SALT...WILL IT BE ALL RIGHT?
IT'S FINE... KAWACHI'S SUCH A WORRIER.
A WOR-RIER ...

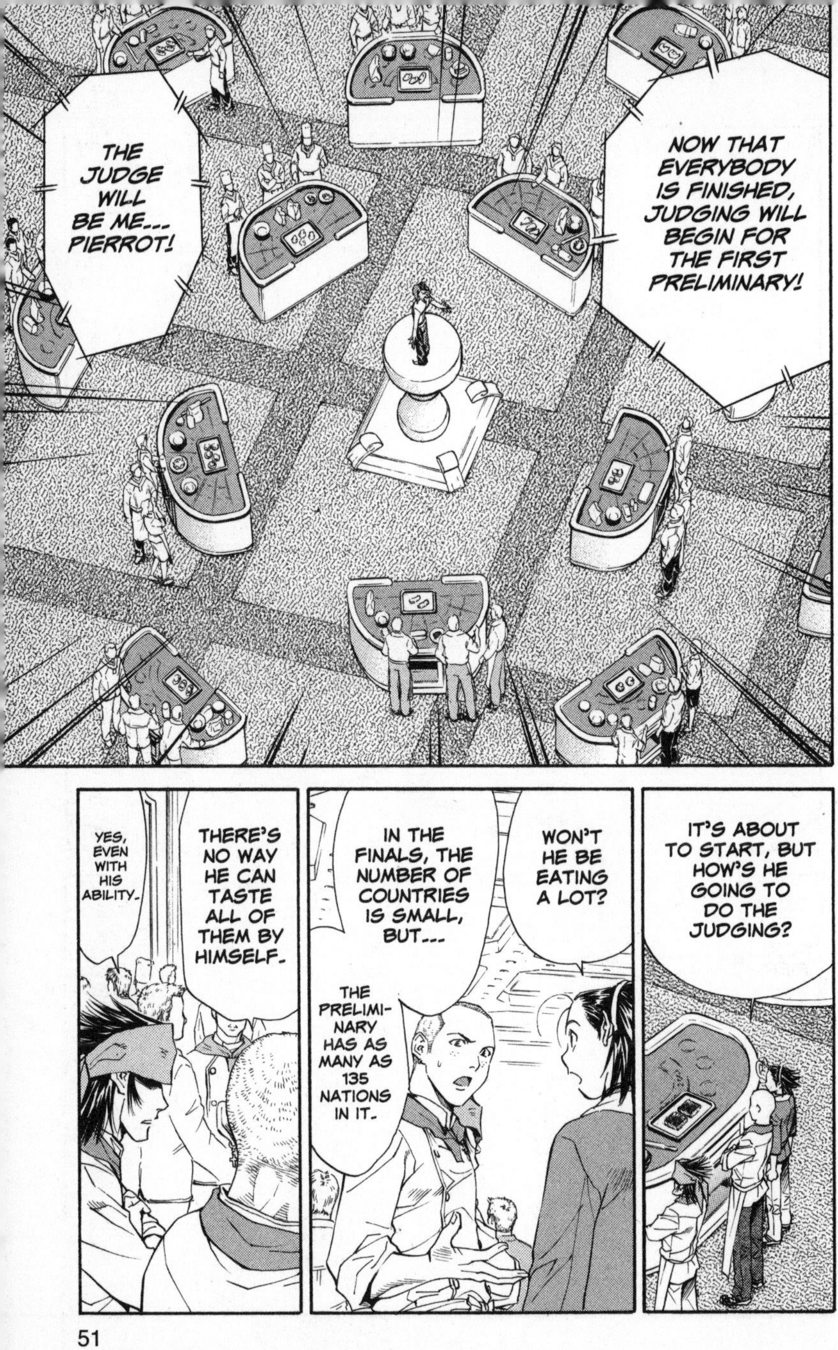
NOW THAT EVERYBODY IS FINISHED, JUDGING WILL BEGIN FOR THE FIRST PRELIMINARY!
THE JUDGE WILL BE ME... PIERROT!
IT'S ABOUT TO START, BUT HOW'S HE GOING TO DO THE JUDGING?
WON'T HE BE EATING A LOT?
IN THE FINALS, THE NUMBER OF COUNTRIES IS SMALL, BUT...
THE PRELIMINARY HAS AS MANY AS 135 NATIONS IN IT.
THERE'S NO WAY HE CAN TASTE ALL OF THEM BY HIMSELF.
YES, EVEN WITH HIS ABILITY.

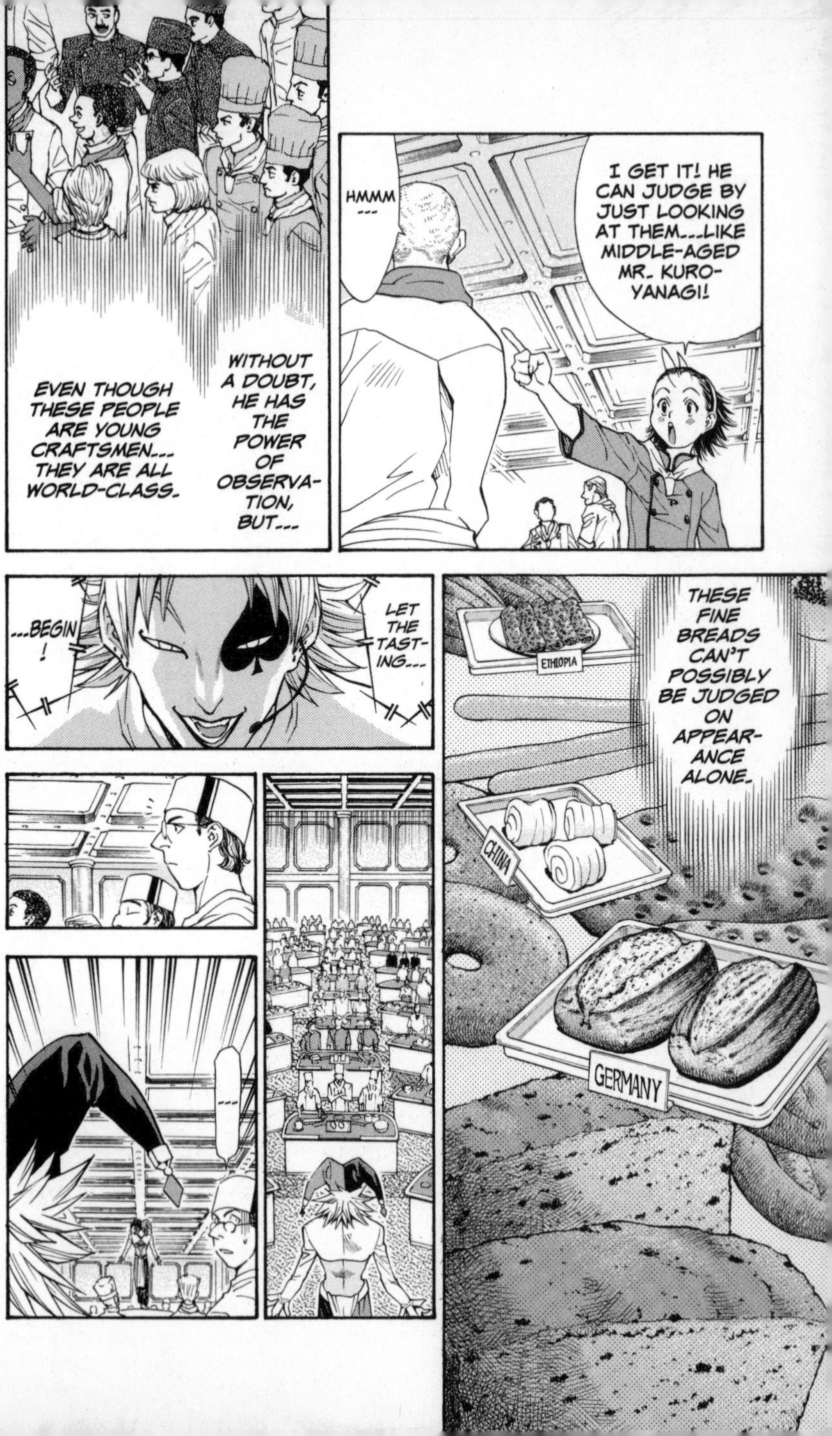
I GET IT! HE CAN JUDGE BY JUST LOOKING AT THEM...LIKE MIDDLE-AGED MR. KURO-YANAGI!
HMMM...
WITHOUT A DOUBT, HE HAS THE POWER OF OBSERVATION, BUT...
EVEN THOUGH THESE PEOPLE ARE YOUNG CRAFTSMEN... THEY ARE ALL WORLD-CLASS.
THESE FINE BREADS CAN'T POSSIBLY BE JUDGED ON APPEARANCE ALONE.
ETHIOPIA
CHINA
GERMANY
LET THE TASTING...
...BEGIN!
...

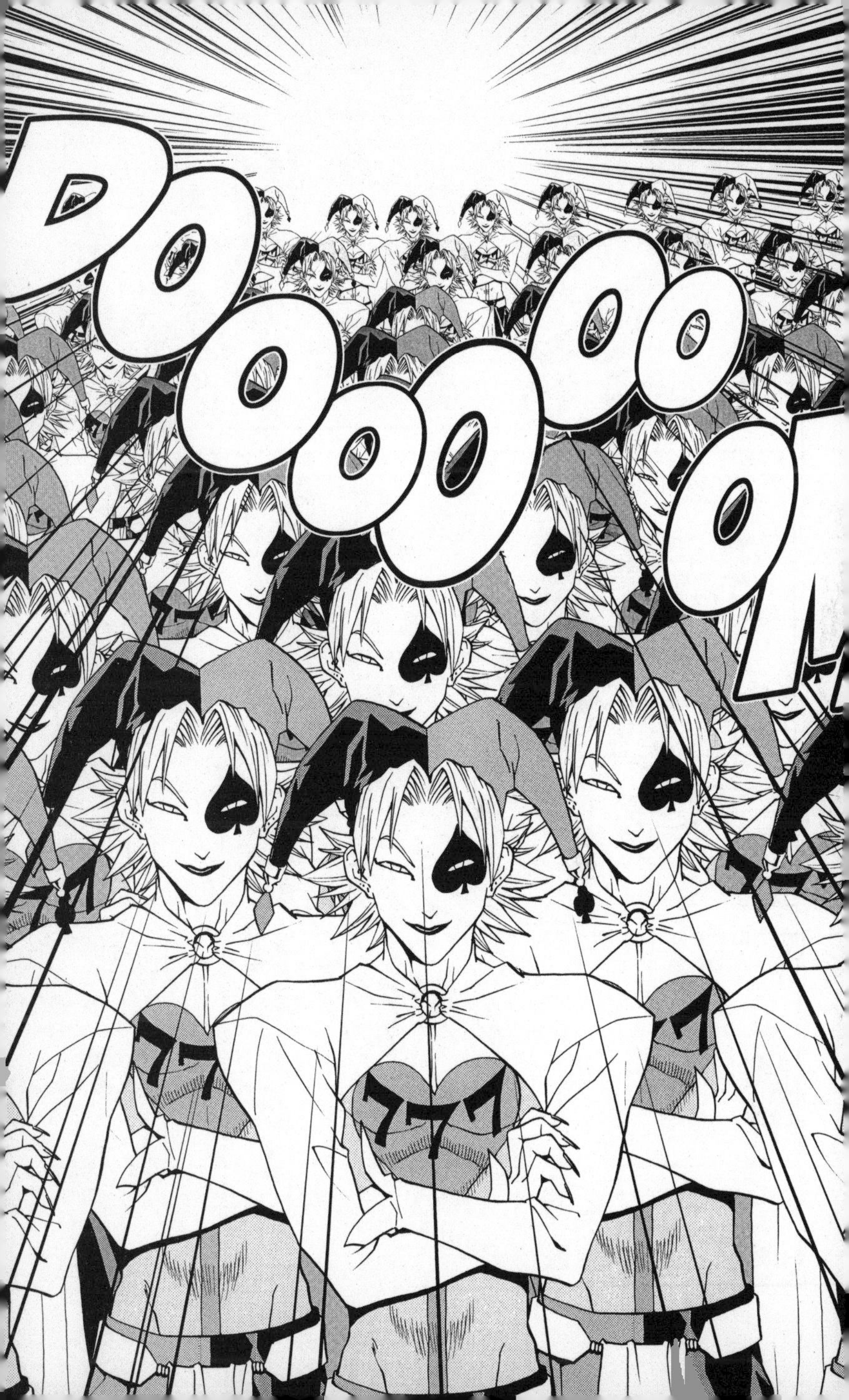
DOOOOOOOM

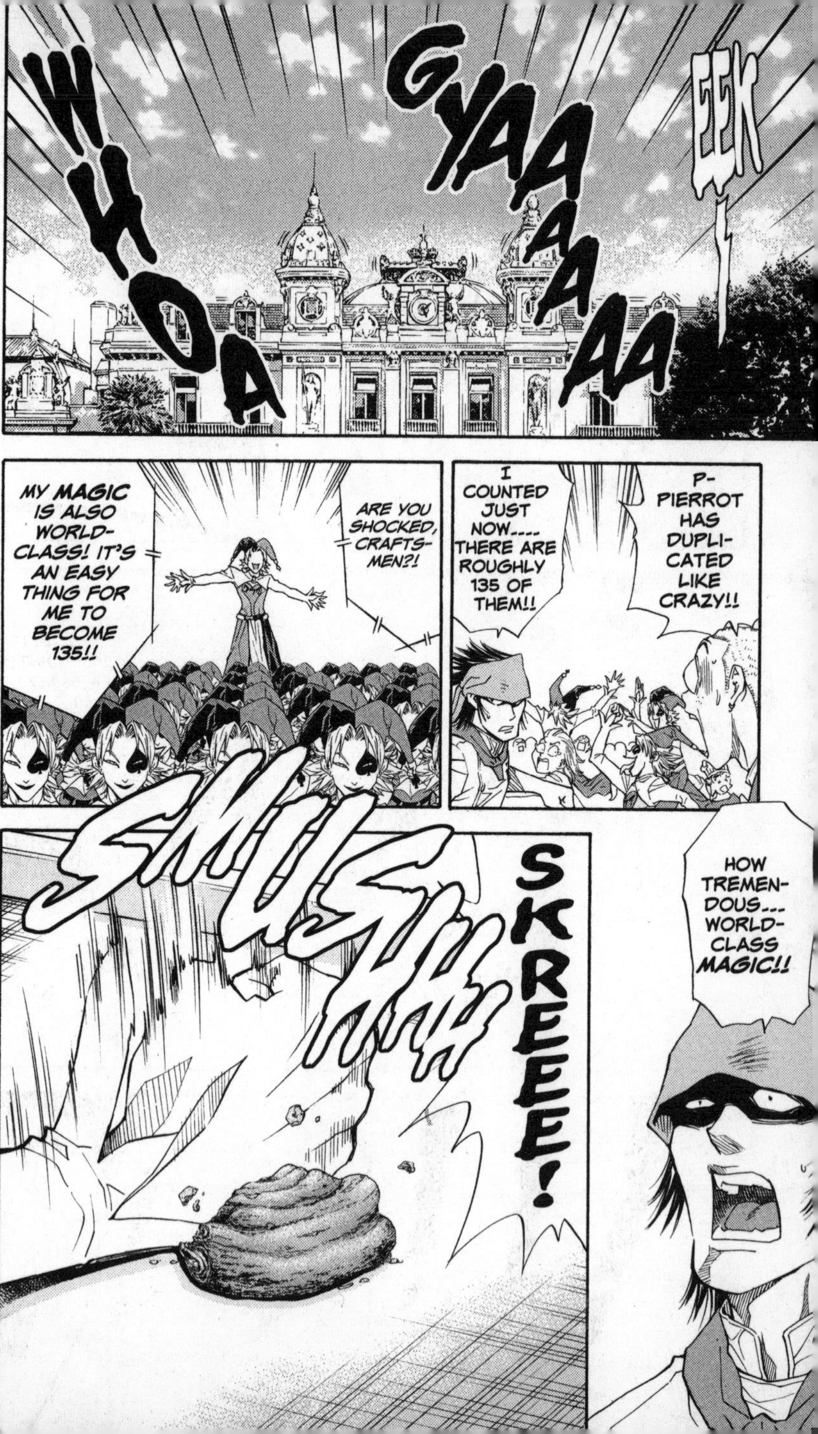
EEK!
GYAAAAAA
WHOA
P-PIERROT HAS DUPLICATED LIKE CRAZY!!
I COUNTED JUST NOW.... THERE ARE ROUGHLY 135 OF THEM!!
ARE YOU SHOCKED, CRAFTSMEN?!
MY MAGIC IS ALSO WORLD-CLASS! IT'S AN EASY THING FOR ME TO BECOME 135!!
HOW TREMENDOUS... WORLD-CLASS MAGIC!!
SKREEE!
SMUSHHH

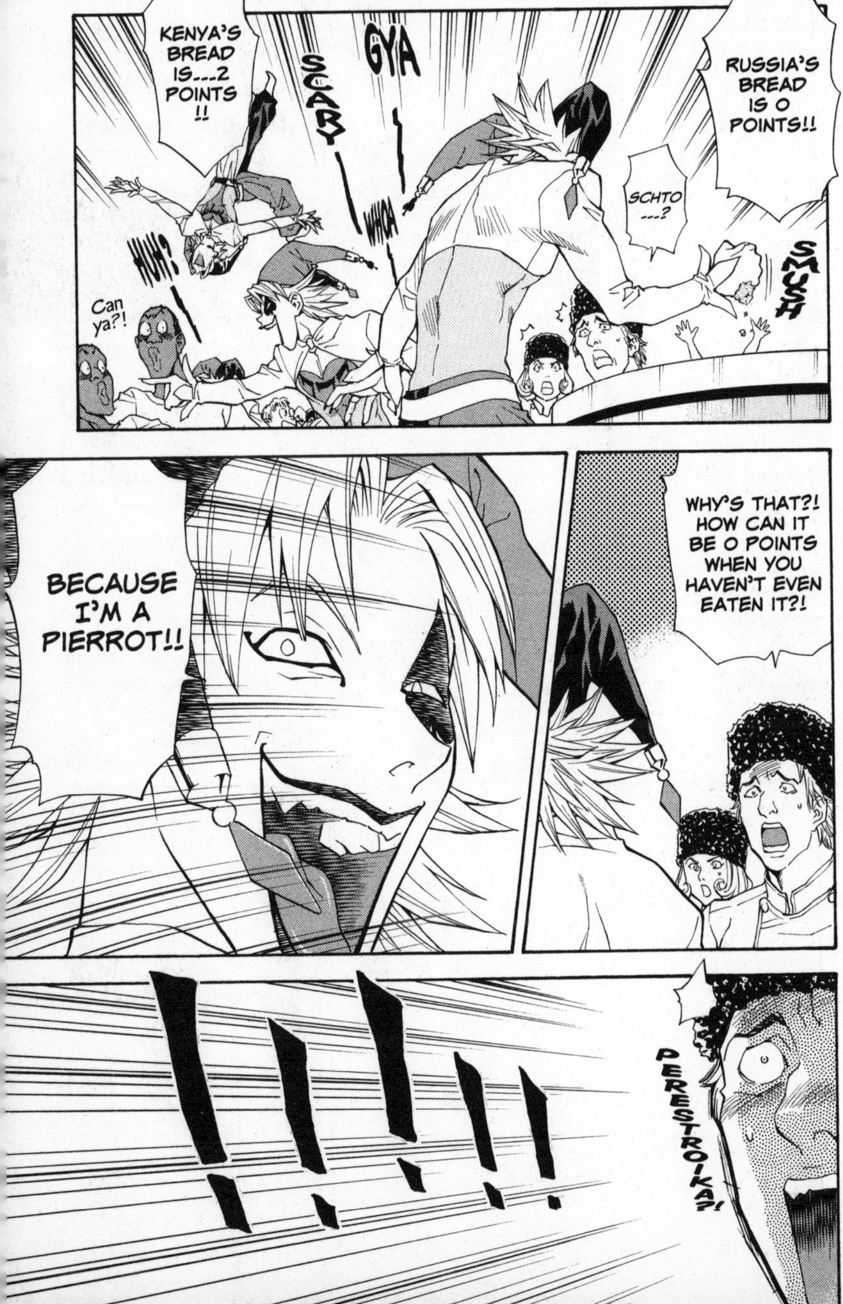
RUSSIA'S BREAD IS 0 POINTS!!
SCHTO ...?
SMUSH
GYA
KENYA'S BREAD IS...2 POINTS !!
SCARY
WHOA
HUH?
Can ya?!
WHY'S THAT?! HOW CAN IT BE 0 POINTS WHEN YOU HAVEN'T EVEN EATEN IT?!
BECAUSE I'M A PIERROT!!
PERESTROIKA?!
!!!!!

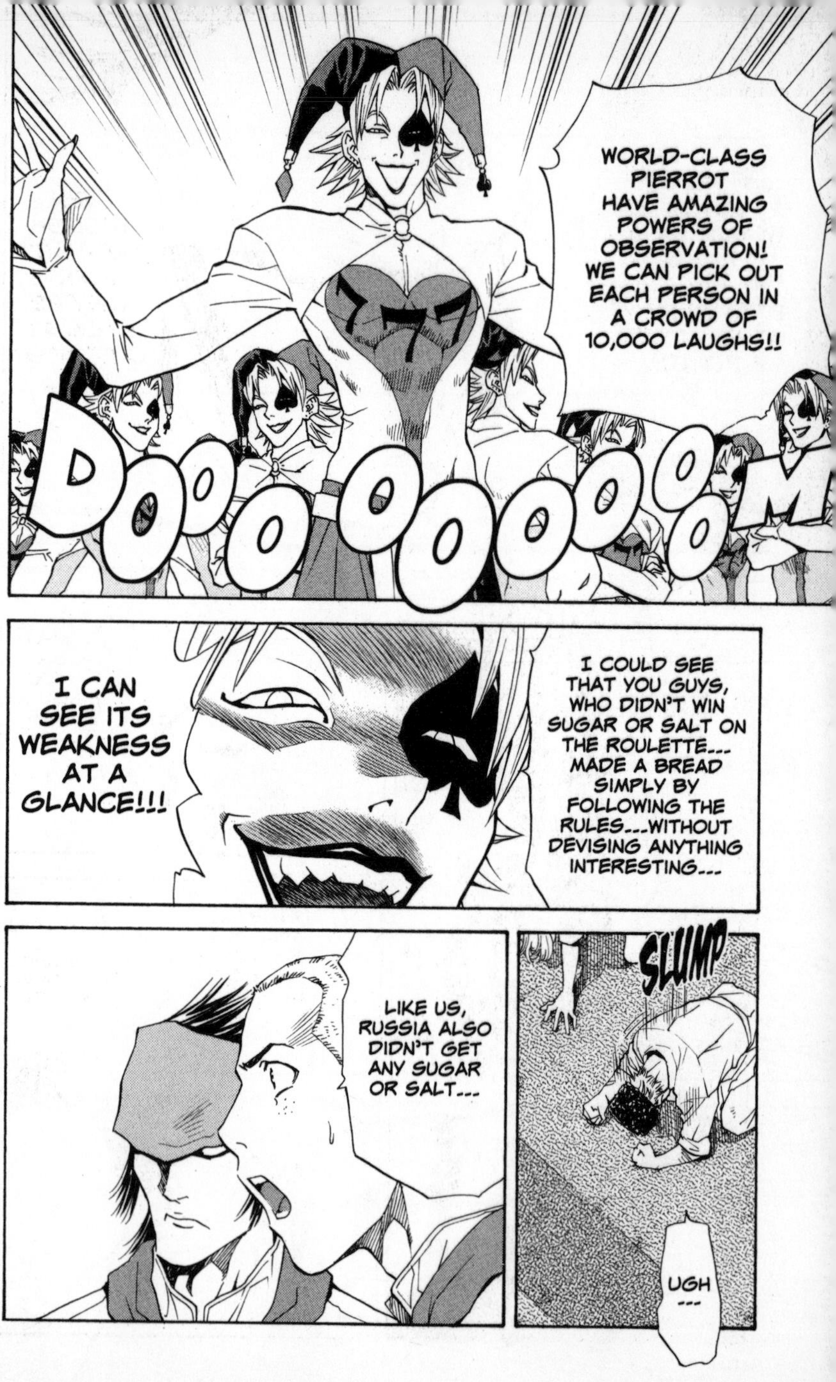
WORLD-CLASS PIERROT HAVE AMAZING POWERS OF OBSERVATION! WE CAN PICK OUT EACH PERSON IN A CROWD OF 10,000 LAUGHS!!
DOOOOOOOOOOM
I COULD SEE THAT YOU GUYS, WHO DIDN'T WIN SUGAR OR SALT ON THE ROULETTE... MADE A BREAD SIMPLY BY FOLLOWING THE RULES...WITHOUT DEVISING ANYTHING INTERESTING...
I CAN SEE ITS WEAKNESS AT A GLANCE!!!
SLUMP
UGH ...
LIKE US, RUSSIA ALSO DIDN'T GET ANY SUGAR OR SALT...

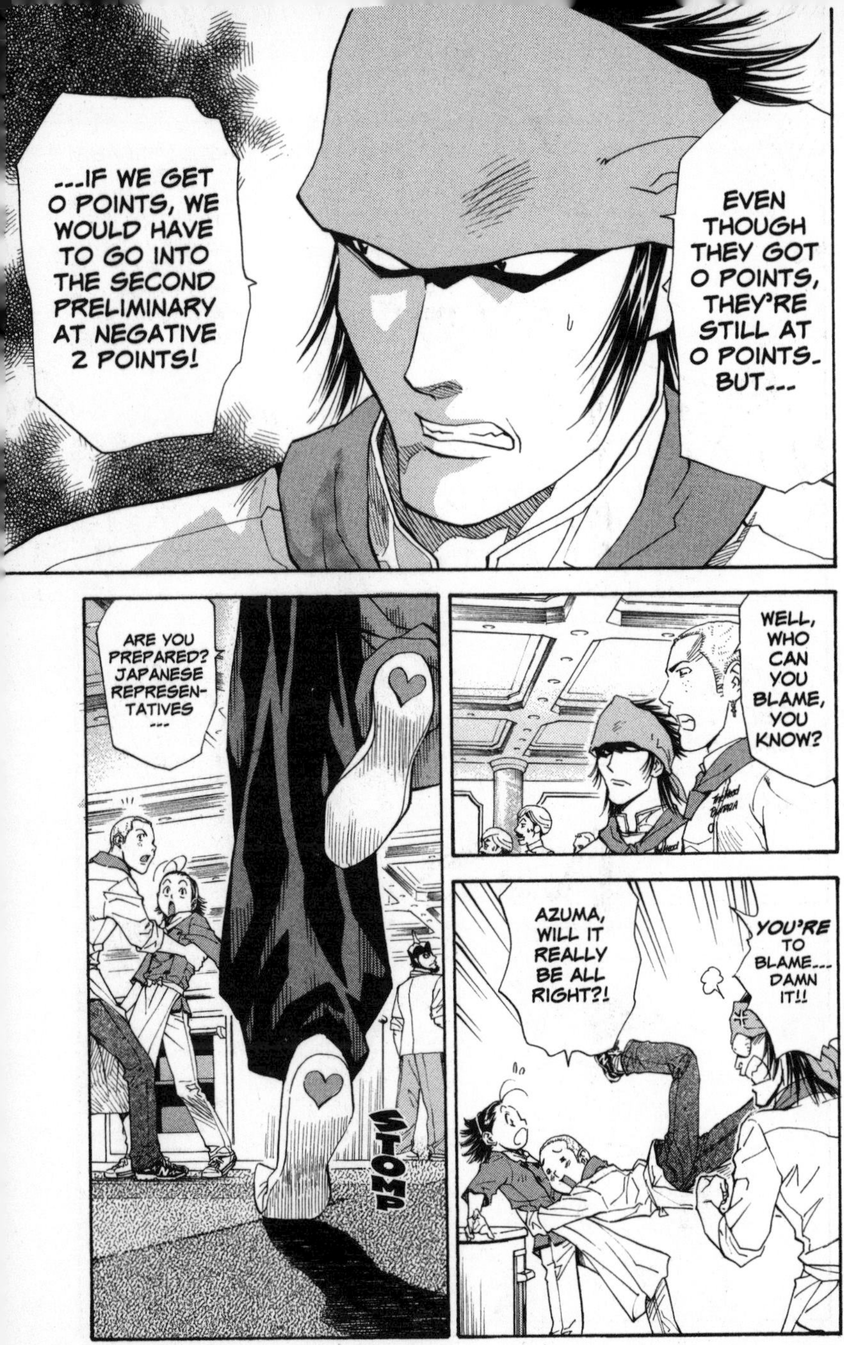
EVEN THOUGH THEY GOT 0 POINTS, THEY'RE STILL AT 0 POINTS. BUT...
...IF WE GET 0 POINTS, WE WOULD HAVE TO GO INTO THE SECOND PRELIMINARY AT NEGATIVE 2 POINTS!
WELL, WHO CAN YOU BLAME, YOU KNOW?
YOU'RE TO BLAME... DAMN IT!!
AZUMA, WILL IT REALLY BE ALL RIGHT?!
ARE YOU PREPARED? JAPANESE REPRESEN-TATIVES ...
STOMP

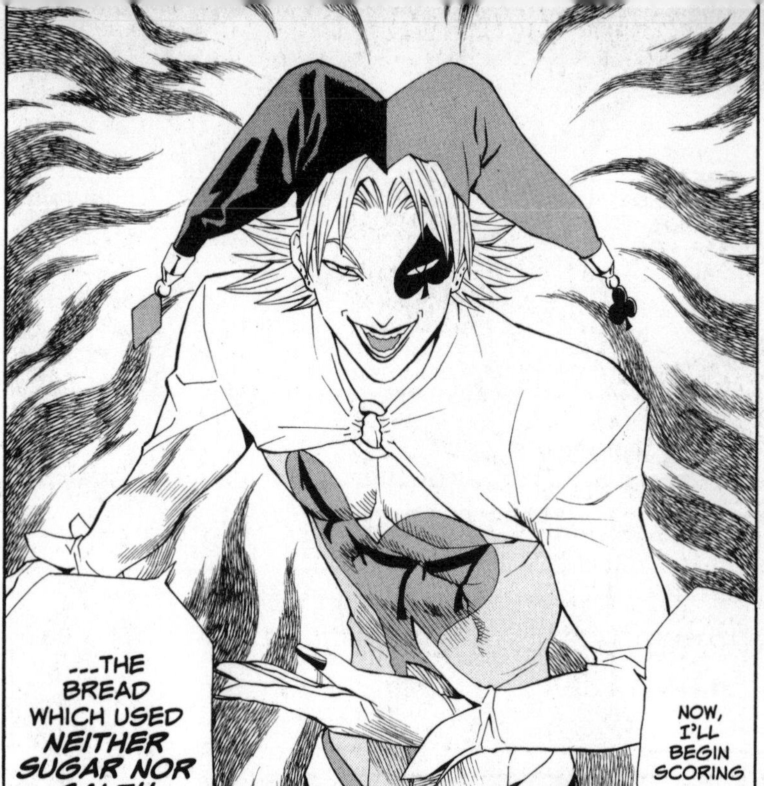
NOW, I'LL BEGIN SCORING ---
---THE BREAD WHICH USED NEITHER SUGAR NOR SALT!!

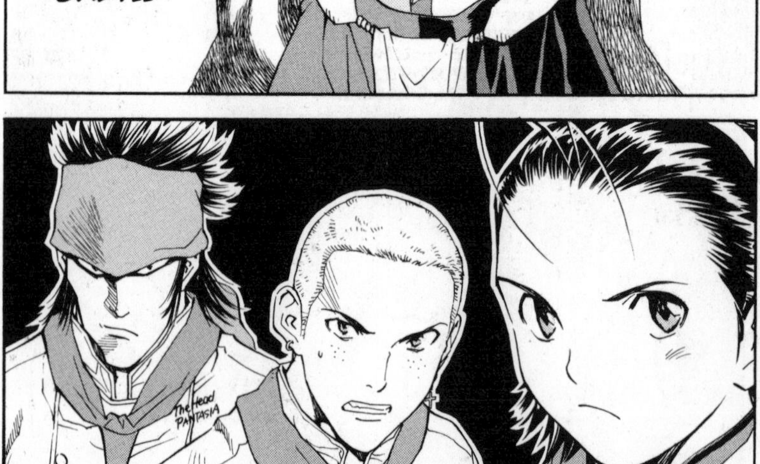
The Head PANTASIA
The Head PANTASIA

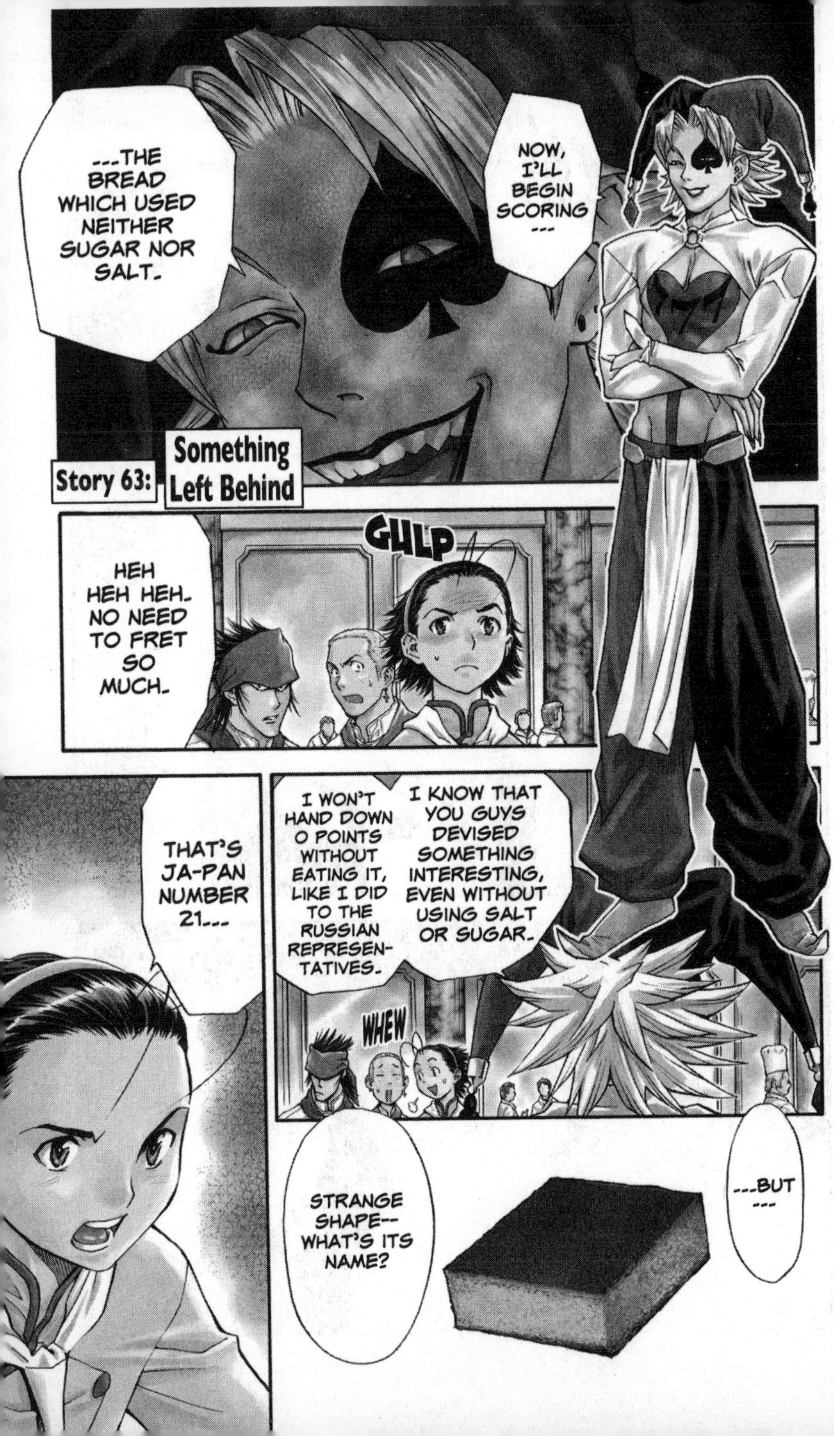
NOW, I'LL BEGIN SCORING ---
---THE BREAD WHICH USED NEITHER SUGAR NOR SALT.
Story 63: Something Left Behind
GULP
HEH HEH HEH. NO NEED TO FRET SO MUCH.
I KNOW THAT YOU GUYS DEVISED SOMETHING INTERESTING, EVEN WITHOUT USING SALT OR SUGAR.
I WON'T HAND DOWN 0 POINTS WITHOUT EATING IT, LIKE I DID TO THE RUSSIAN REPRESEN-TATIVES.
WHEW
THAT'S JA-PAN NUMBER 21...
---BUT ---
STRANGE SHAPE-- WHAT'S ITS NAME?

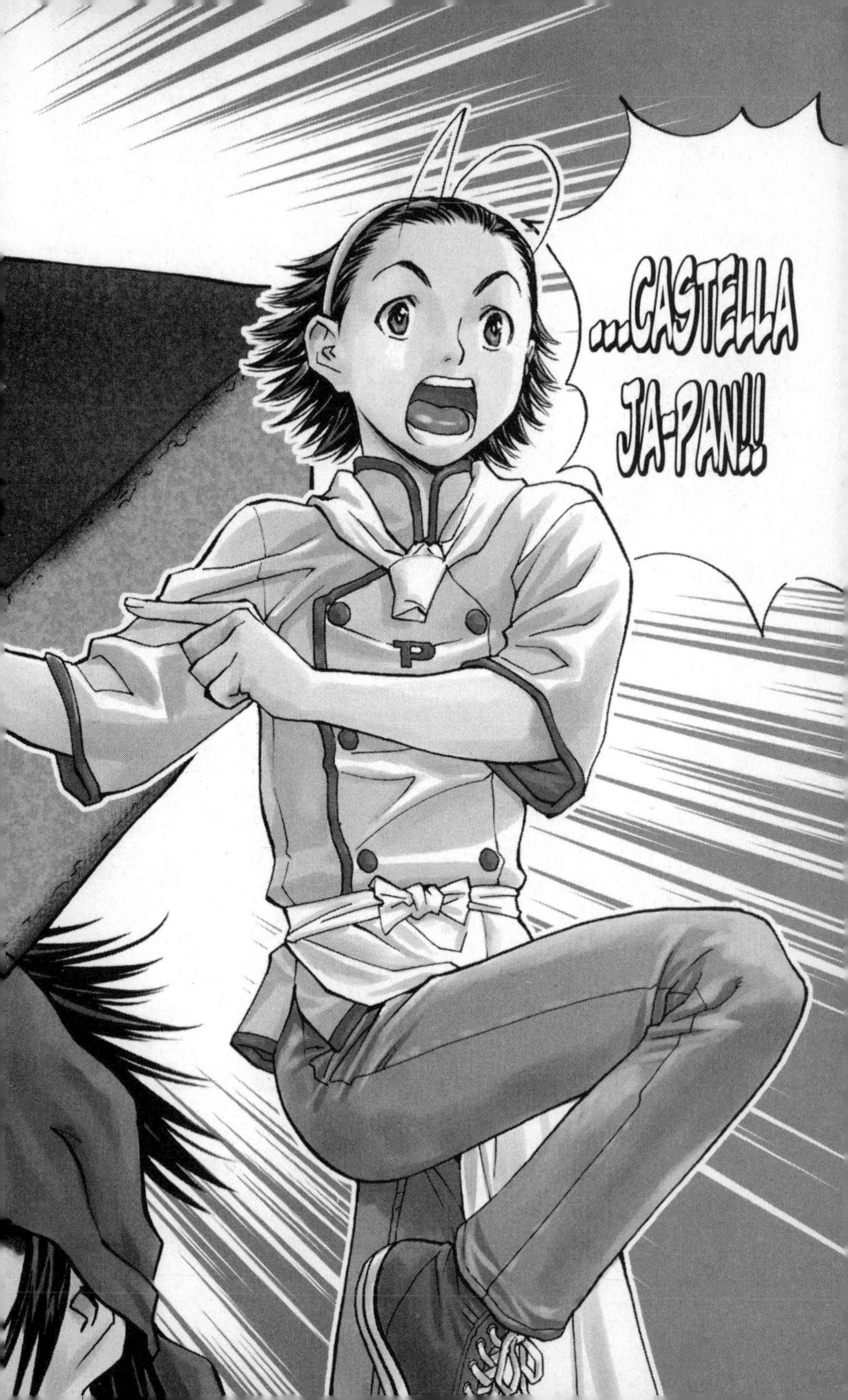
...CASTELLA JA-PAN!!

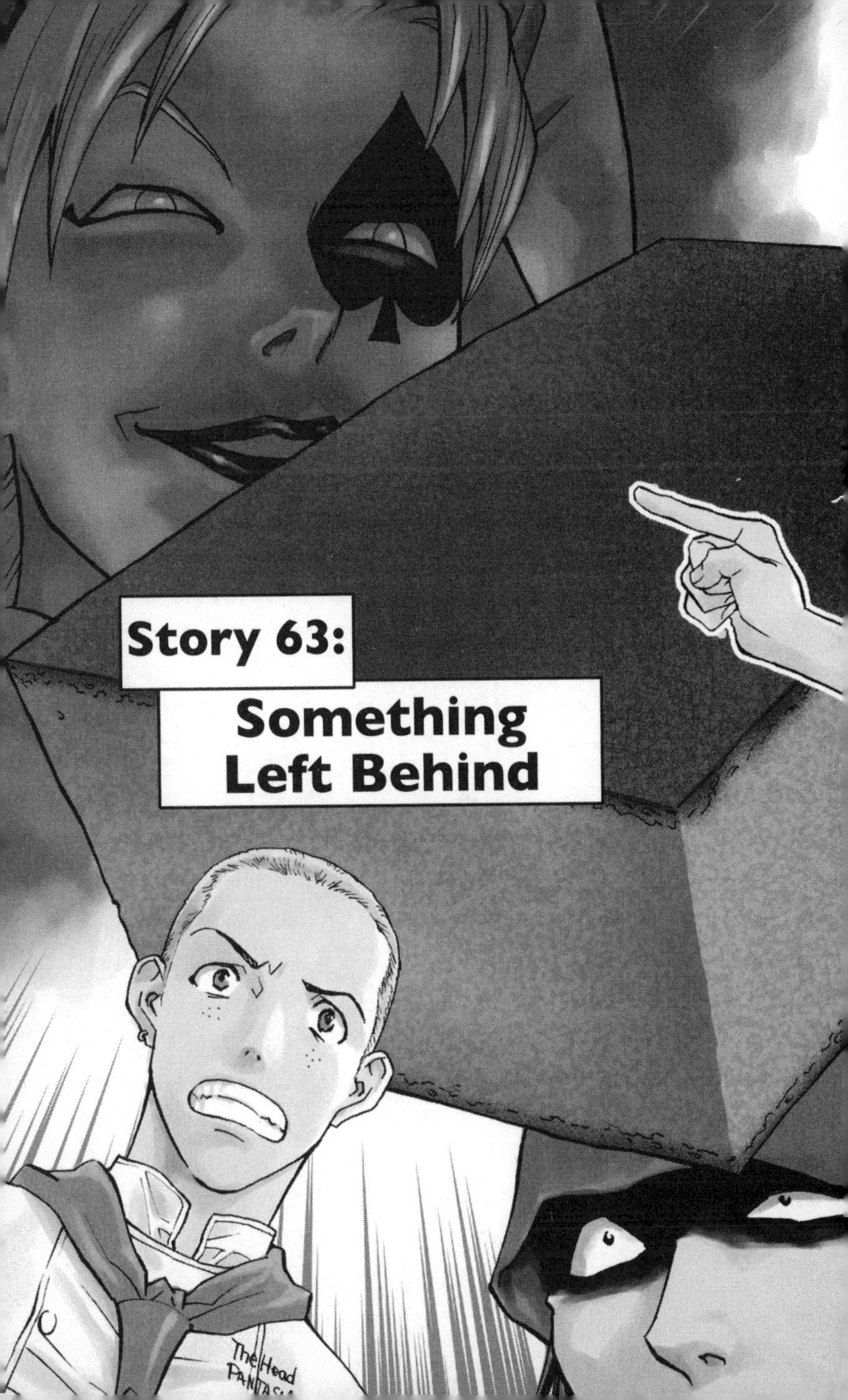
Story 63:
Something Left Behind

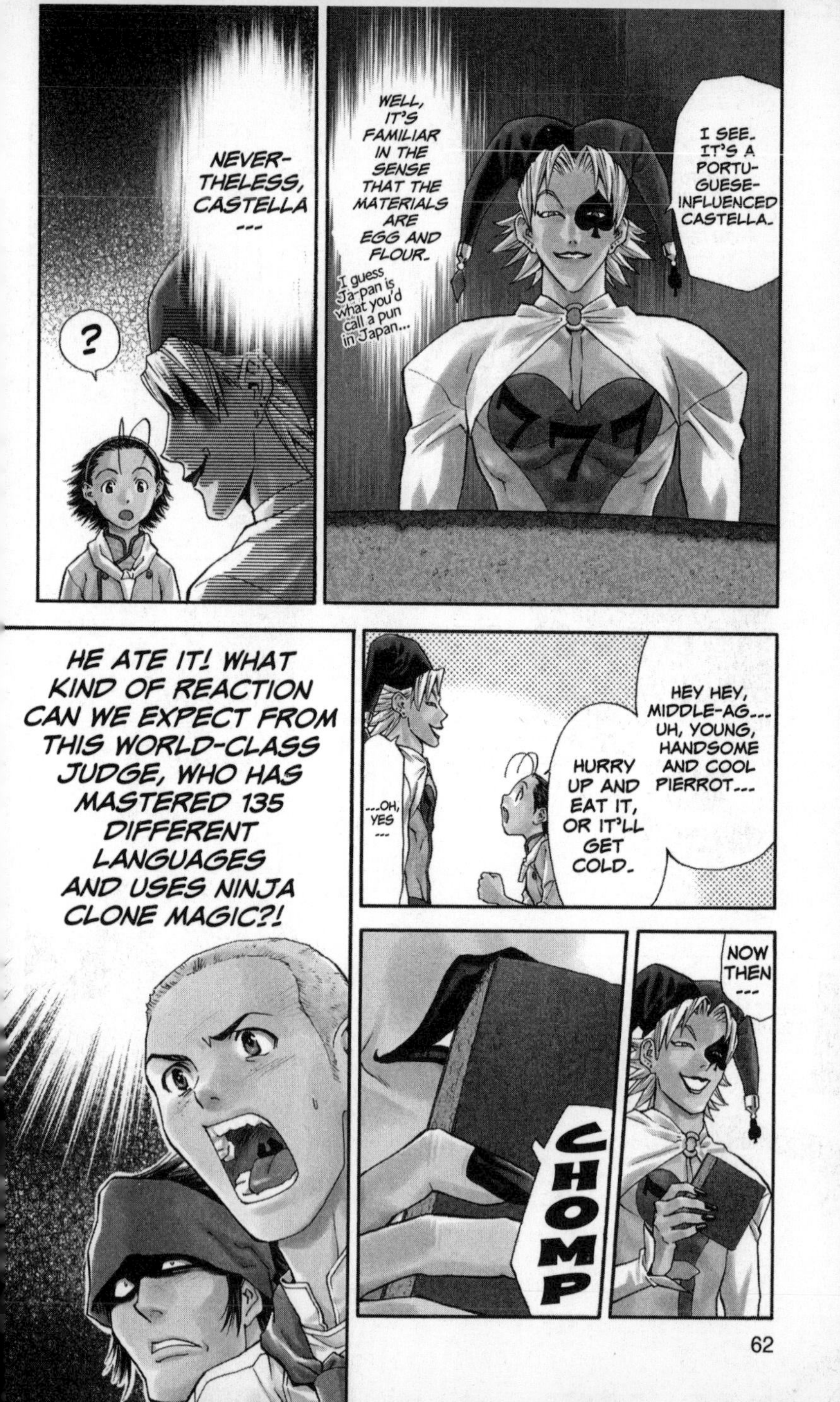
I SEE. IT'S A PORTUGUESE-INFLUENCED CASTELLA.
WELL, IT'S FAMILIAR IN THE SENSE THAT THE MATERIALS ARE EGG AND FLOUR.
I guess Ja-pan is what you'd call a pun in Japan...
NEVERTHELESS, CASTELLA ---
?
HEY HEY, MIDDLE-AG... UH, YOUNG, HANDSOME AND COOL PIERROT...
HURRY UP AND EAT IT, OR IT'LL GET COLD.
...OH, YES ---
NOW THEN ---
CHOMP
HE ATE IT! WHAT KIND OF REACTION CAN WE EXPECT FROM THIS WORLD-CLASS JUDGE, WHO HAS MASTERED 135 DIFFERENT LANGUAGES AND USES NINJA CLONE MAGIC?!

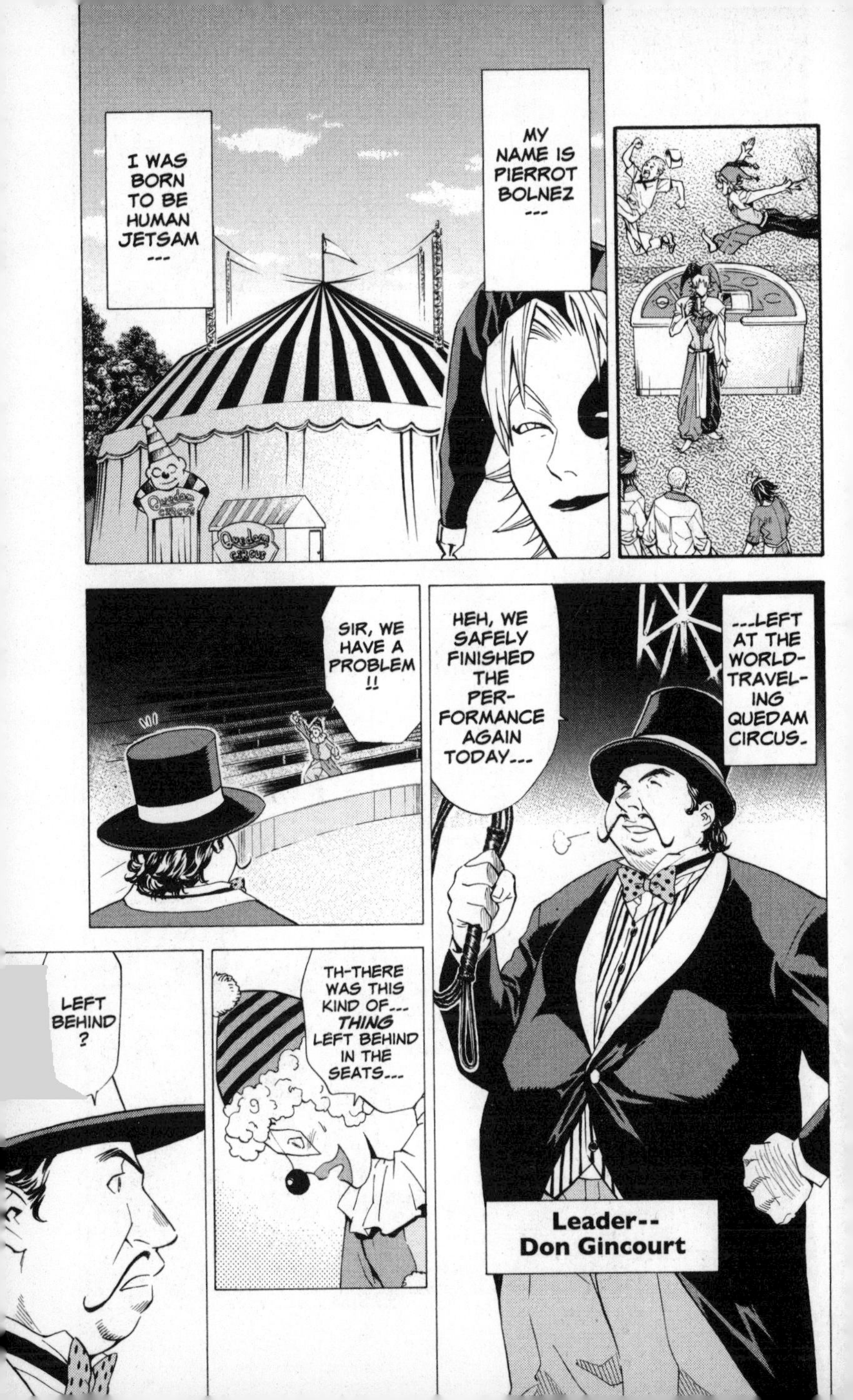
MY NAME IS PIERROT BOLNEZ ---
I WAS BORN TO BE HUMAN JETSAM ---
Quedam circus
Quedam circus
---LEFT AT THE WORLD-TRAVELING QUEDAM CIRCUS.
HEH, WE SAFELY FINISHED THE PERFORMANCE AGAIN TODAY---
Leader-- Don Gincourt
SIR, WE HAVE A PROBLEM !!
TH-THERE WAS THIS KIND OF--- *THING* LEFT BEHIND IN THE SEATS---
LEFT BEHIND ?

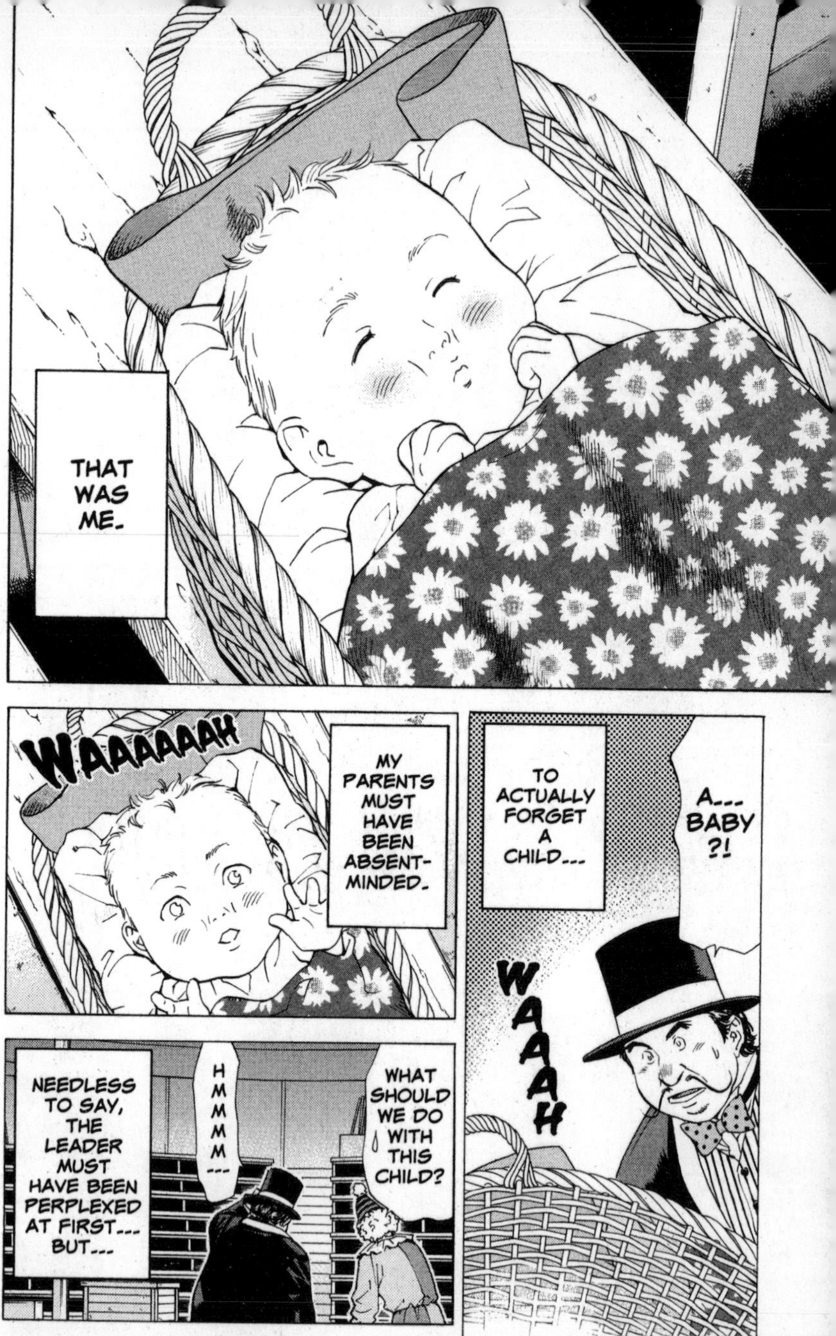
THAT WAS ME.
WAAAAAAH
MY PARENTS MUST HAVE BEEN ABSENT-MINDED.
TO ACTUALLY FORGET A CHILD...
A... BABY?!
WAAAH
NEEDLESS TO SAY, THE LEADER MUST HAVE BEEN PERPLEXED AT FIRST... BUT...
HMMMM...
WHAT SHOULD WE DO WITH THIS CHILD?

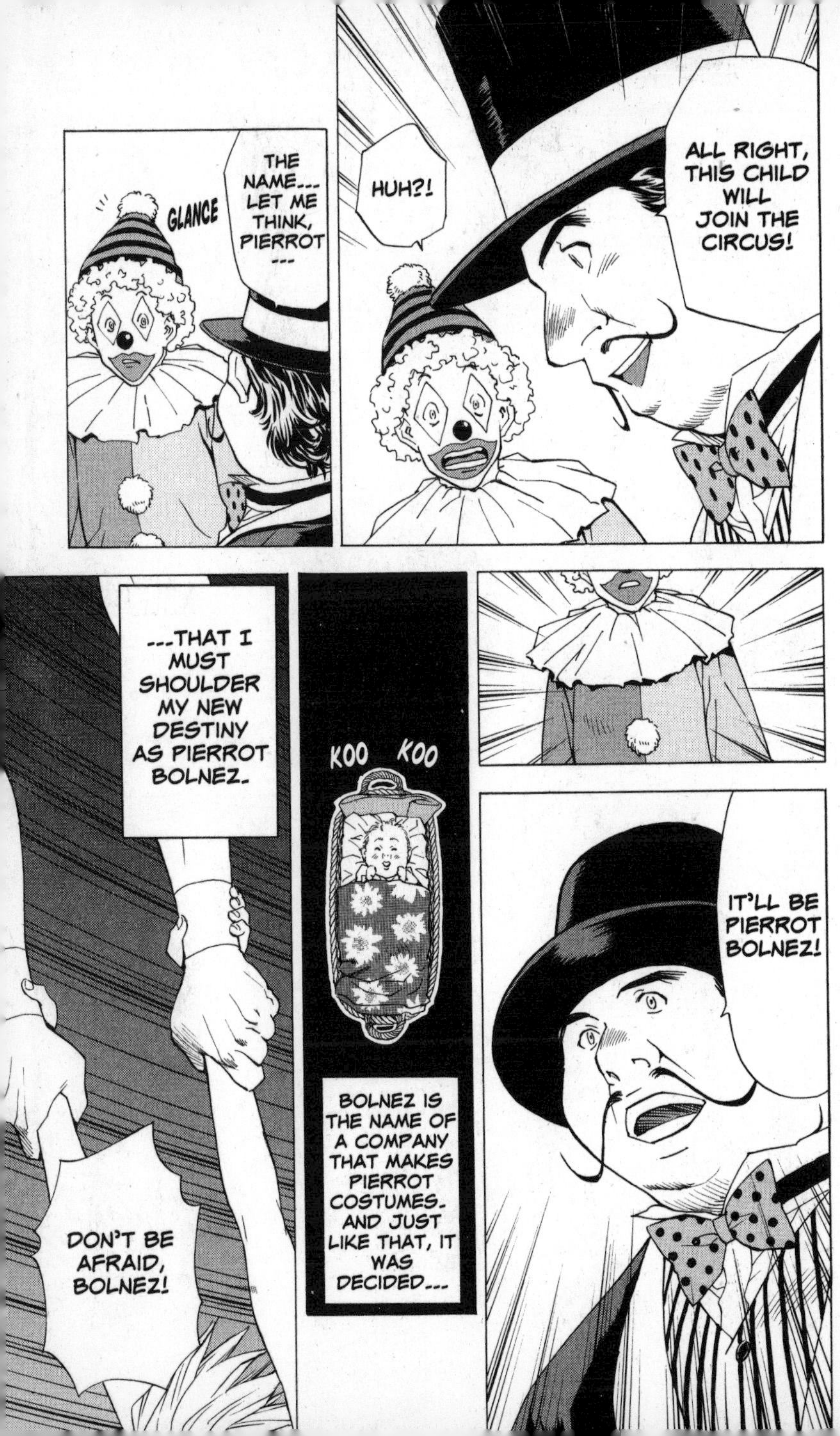
ALL RIGHT, THIS CHILD WILL JOIN THE CIRCUS!
HUH?!
THE NAME... LET ME THINK, PIERROT ...
GLANCE
IT'LL BE PIERROT BOLNEZ!
KOO KOO
BOLNEZ IS THE NAME OF A COMPANY THAT MAKES PIERROT COSTUMES. AND JUST LIKE THAT, IT WAS DECIDED...
...THAT I MUST SHOULDER MY NEW DESTINY AS PIERROT BOLNEZ.
DON'T BE AFRAID, BOLNEZ!

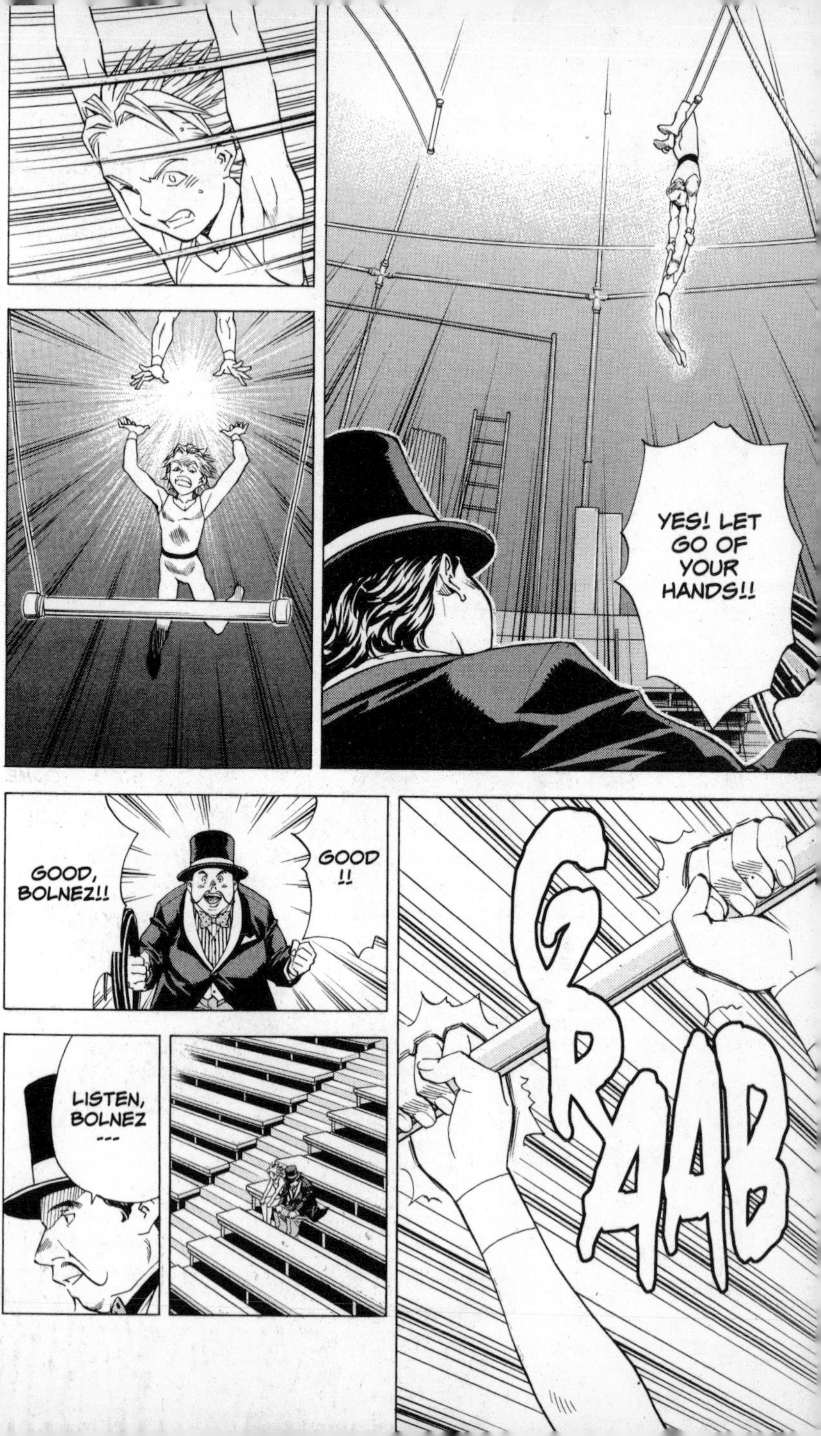
YES! LET GO OF YOUR HANDS!!
GRAAB
GOOD !!
GOOD, BOLNEZ!!
LISTEN, BOLNEZ ---

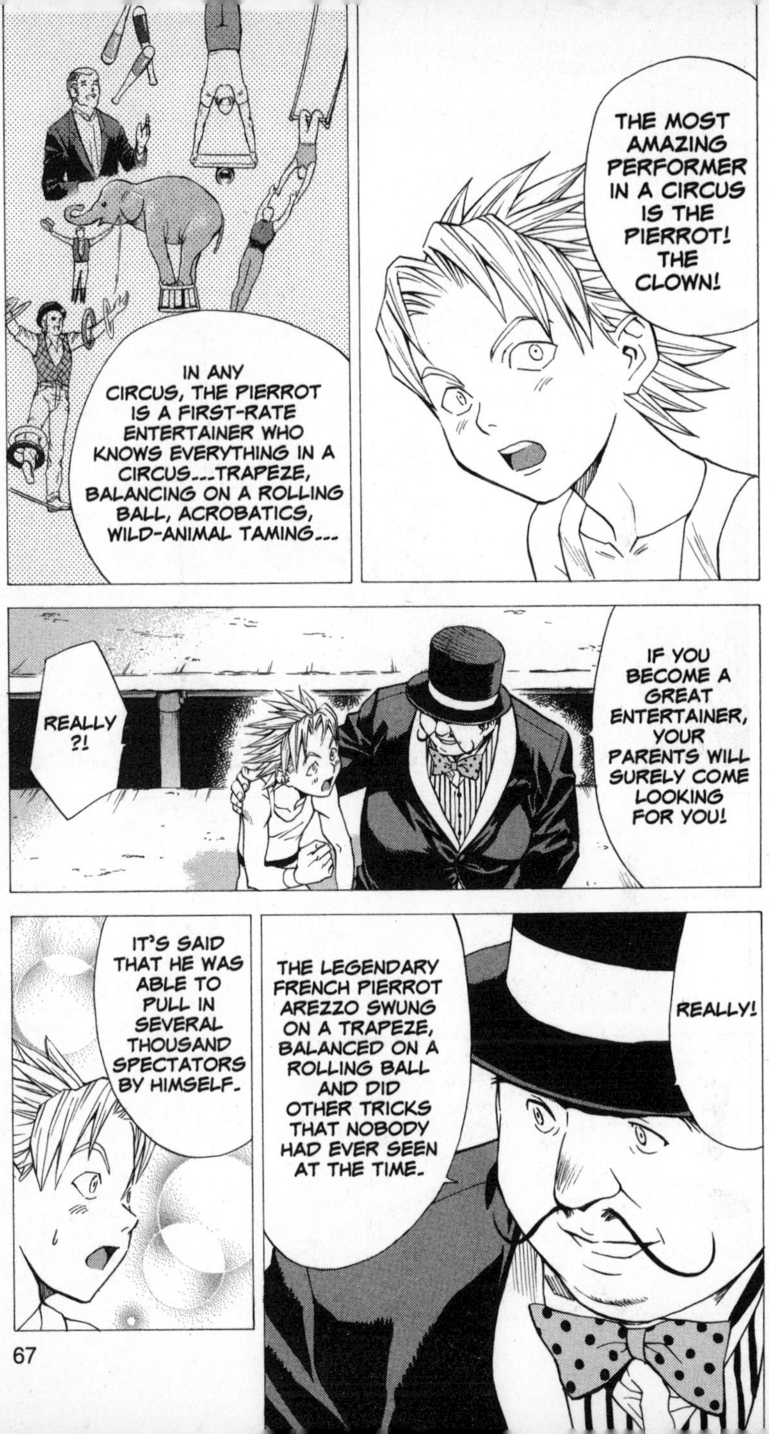
THE MOST AMAZING PERFORMER IN A CIRCUS IS THE PIERROT! THE CLOWN!
IN ANY CIRCUS, THE PIERROT IS A FIRST-RATE ENTERTAINER WHO KNOWS EVERYTHING IN A CIRCUS...TRAPEZE, BALANCING ON A ROLLING BALL, ACROBATICS, WILD-ANIMAL TAMING...
IF YOU BECOME A GREAT ENTERTAINER, YOUR PARENTS WILL SURELY COME LOOKING FOR YOU!
REALLY ?!
REALLY!
THE LEGENDARY FRENCH PIERROT AREZZO SWUNG ON A TRAPEZE, BALANCED ON A ROLLING BALL AND DID OTHER TRICKS THAT NOBODY HAD EVER SEEN AT THE TIME.
IT'S SAID THAT HE WAS ABLE TO PULL IN SEVERAL THOUSAND SPECTATORS BY HIMSELF.

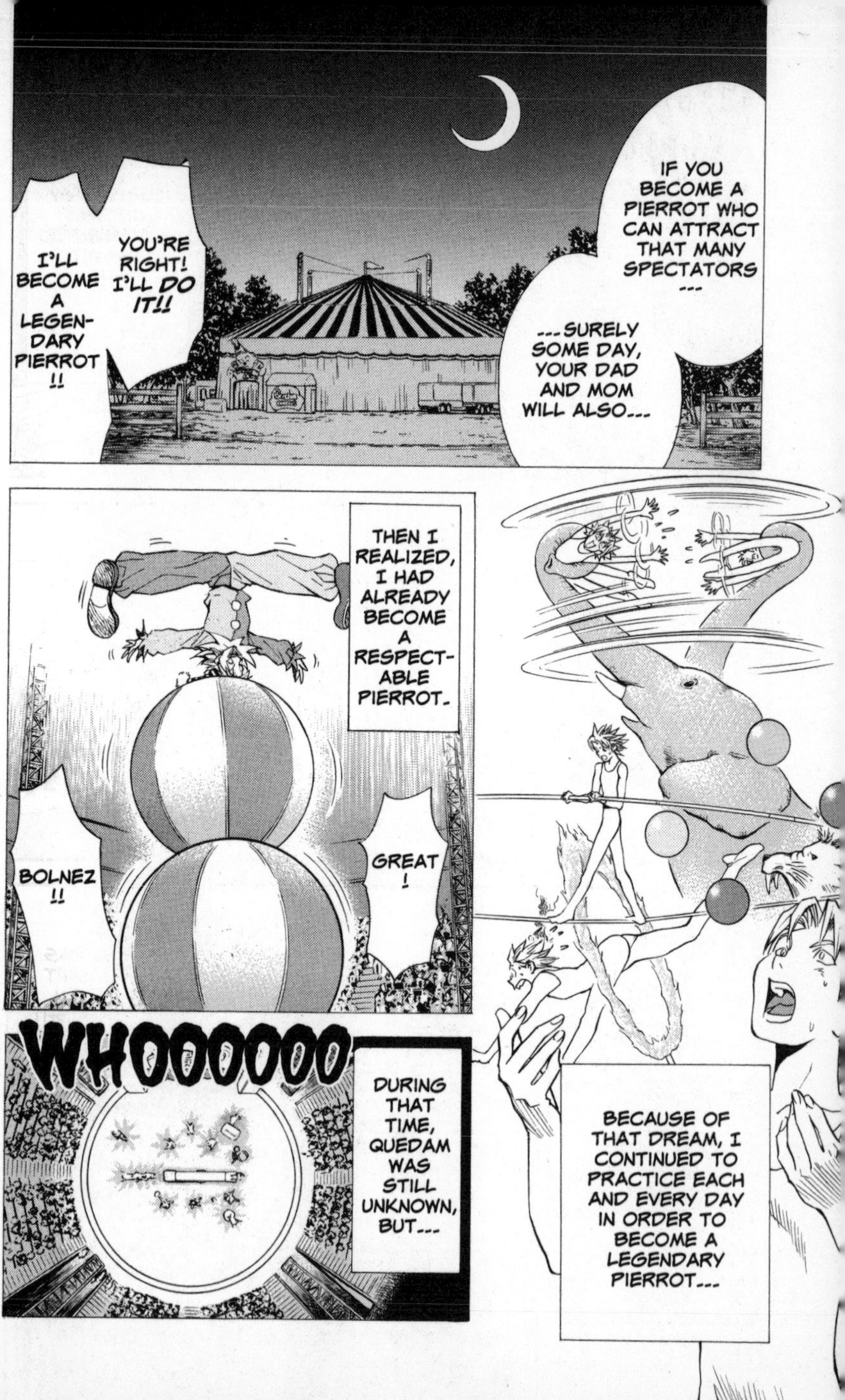
IF YOU BECOME A PIERROT WHO CAN ATTRACT THAT MANY SPECTATORS ---
---SURELY SOME DAY, YOUR DAD AND MOM WILL ALSO...
YOU'RE RIGHT! I'LL DO IT!!
I'LL BECOME A LEGENDARY PIERROT!!
BECAUSE OF THAT DREAM, I CONTINUED TO PRACTICE EACH AND EVERY DAY IN ORDER TO BECOME A LEGENDARY PIERROT...
THEN I REALIZED, I HAD ALREADY BECOME A RESPECTABLE PIERROT.
GREAT!
BOLNEZ!!
DURING THAT TIME, QUEDAM WAS STILL UNKNOWN, BUT...
WHOOOOOO

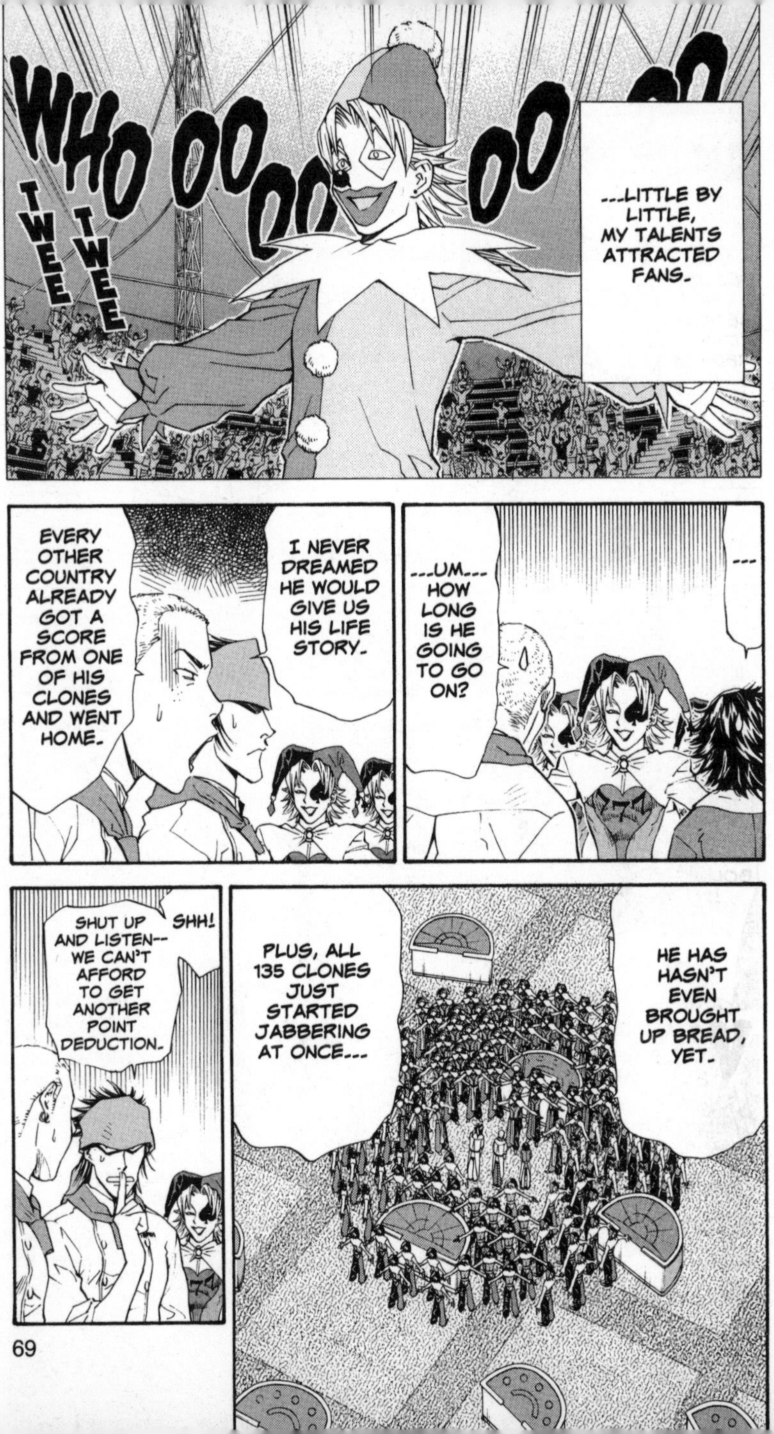
WHOOOOOOOOOO
...LITTLE BY LITTLE, MY TALENTS ATTRACTED FANS.
TWEE
TWEE
...
...UM... HOW LONG IS HE GOING TO GO ON?
I NEVER DREAMED HE WOULD GIVE US HIS LIFE STORY.
EVERY OTHER COUNTRY ALREADY GOT A SCORE FROM ONE OF HIS CLONES AND WENT HOME.
HE HAS HASN'T EVEN BROUGHT UP BREAD, YET.
PLUS, ALL 135 CLONES JUST STARTED JABBERING AT ONCE...
SHH!
SHUT UP AND LISTEN-- WE CAN'T AFFORD TO GET ANOTHER POINT DEDUCTION.

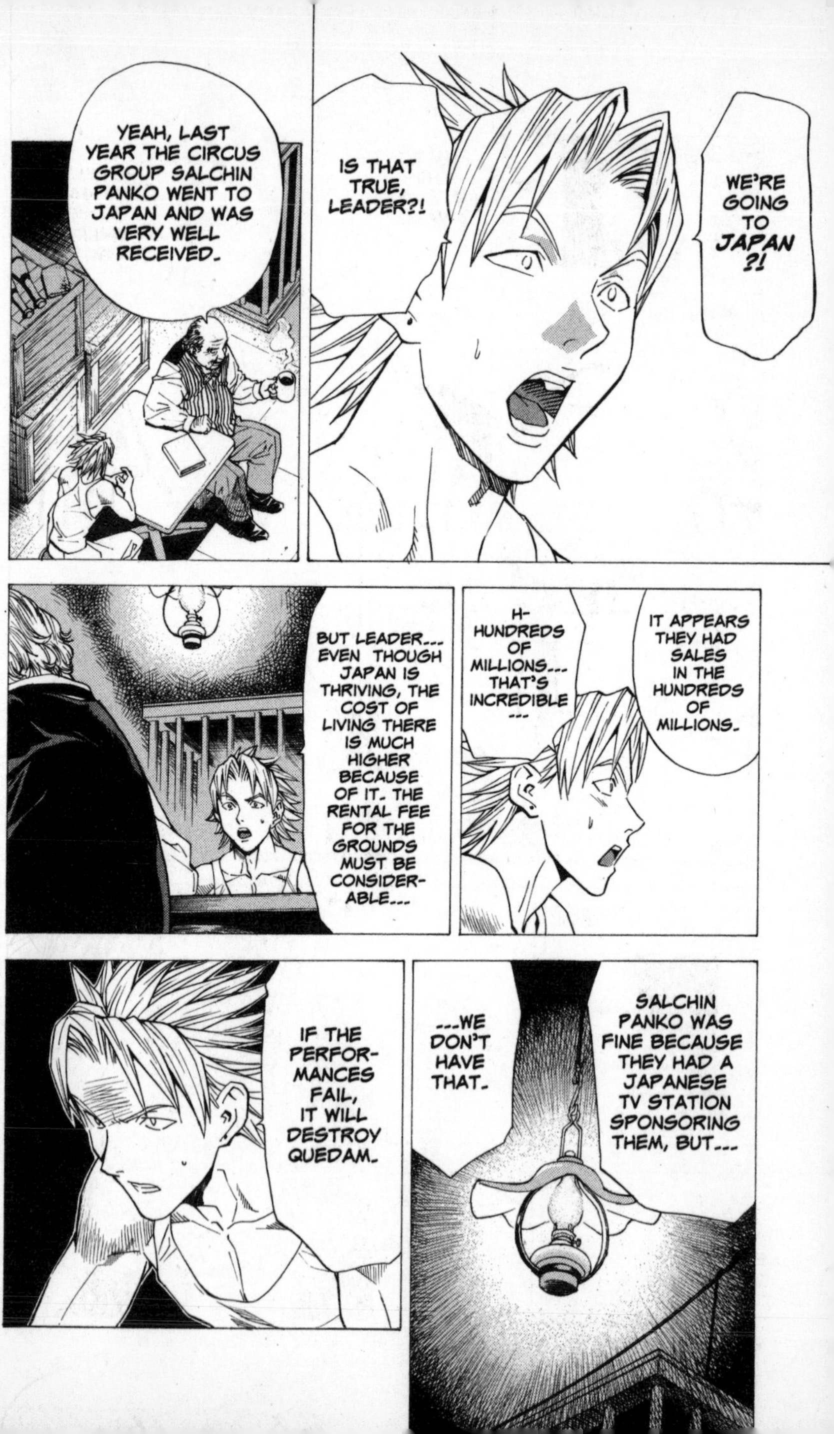
WE'RE GOING TO JAPAN?!
IS THAT TRUE, LEADER?!
YEAH, LAST YEAR THE CIRCUS GROUP SALCHIN PANKO WENT TO JAPAN AND WAS VERY WELL RECEIVED.
IT APPEARS THEY HAD SALES IN THE HUNDREDS OF MILLIONS.
H-HUNDREDS OF MILLIONS... THAT'S INCREDIBLE...
BUT LEADER... EVEN THOUGH JAPAN IS THRIVING, THE COST OF LIVING THERE IS MUCH HIGHER BECAUSE OF IT. THE RENTAL FEE FOR THE GROUNDS MUST BE CONSIDER-ABLE...
SALCHIN PANKO WAS FINE BECAUSE THEY HAD A JAPANESE TV STATION SPONSORING THEM, BUT...
...WE DON'T HAVE THAT.
IF THE PERFOR-MANCES FAIL, IT WILL DESTROY QUEDAM.

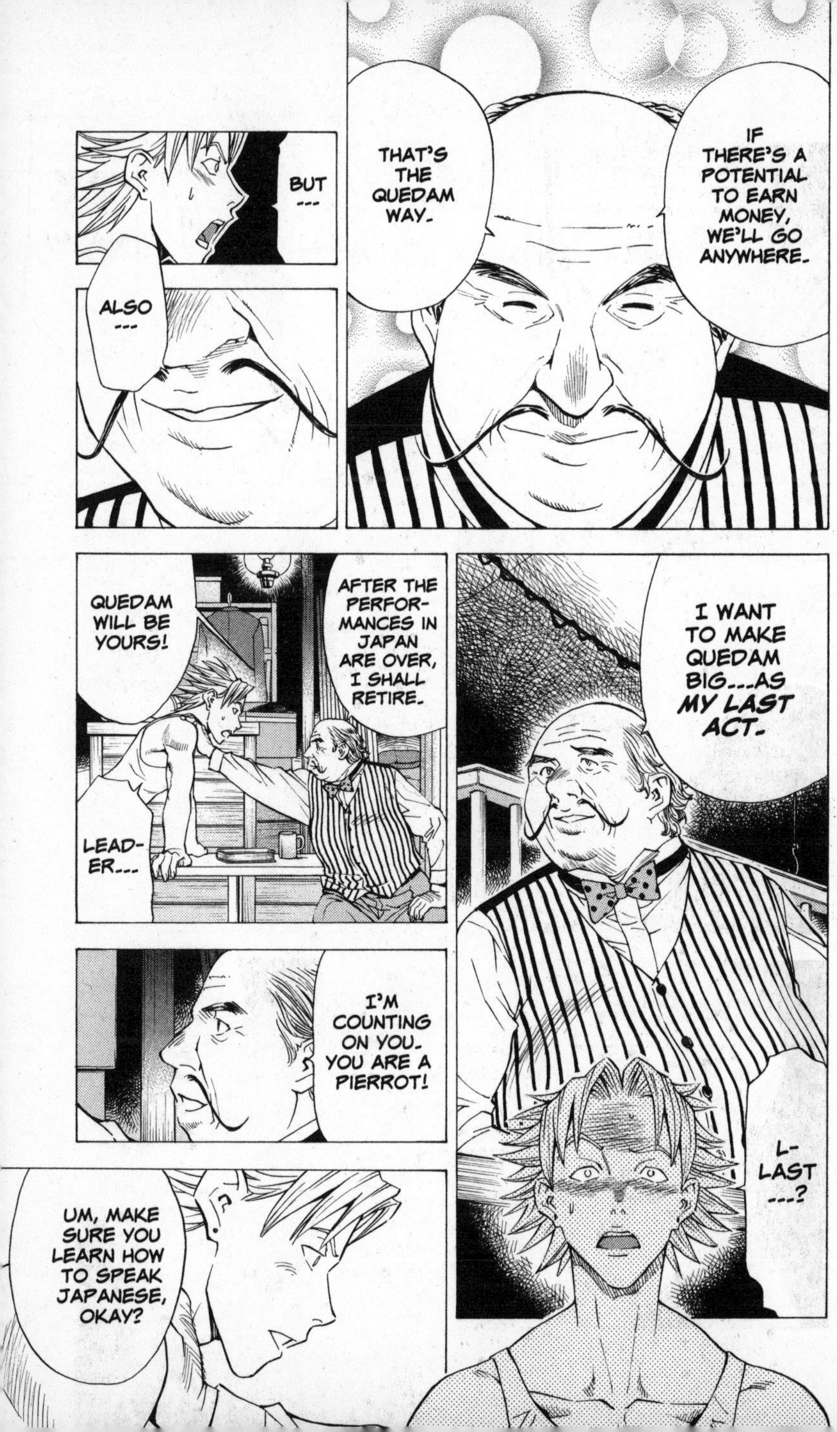
IF THERE'S A POTENTIAL TO EARN MONEY, WE'LL GO ANYWHERE.
THAT'S THE QUEDAM WAY.
BUT ---
ALSO ---
I WANT TO MAKE QUEDAM BIG...AS *MY LAST ACT.*
L- LAST ---?
AFTER THE PERFOR-MANCES IN JAPAN ARE OVER, I SHALL RETIRE.
QUEDAM WILL BE YOURS!
LEAD-ER...
I'M COUNTING ON YOU. YOU ARE A PIERROT!
UM, MAKE SURE YOU LEARN HOW TO SPEAK JAPANESE, OKAY?

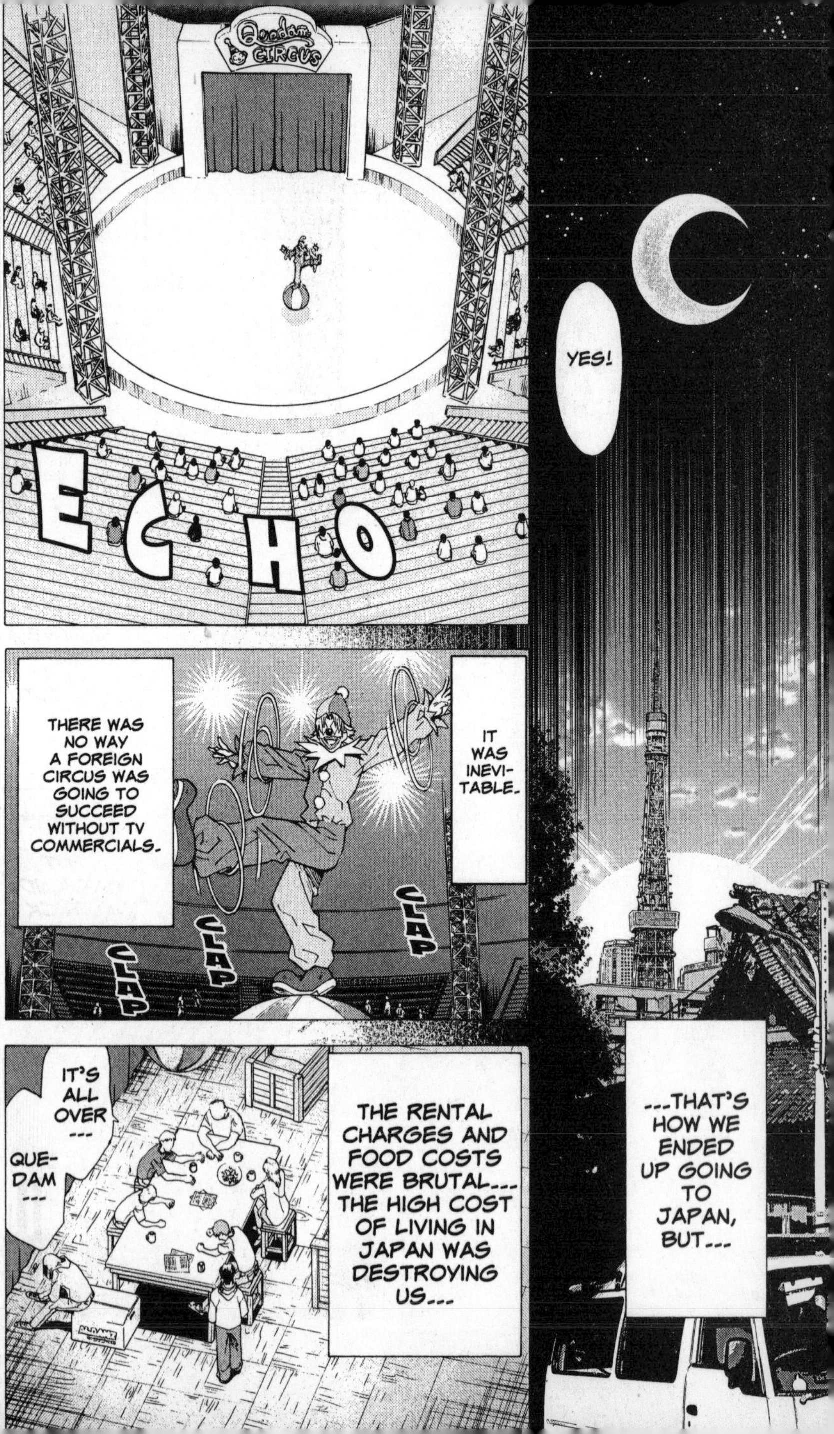
YES!
...THAT'S HOW WE ENDED UP GOING TO JAPAN, BUT...
Quedam CIRCUS
ECHO
IT WAS INEVITABLE.
THERE WAS NO WAY A FOREIGN CIRCUS WAS GOING TO SUCCEED WITHOUT TV COMMERCIALS.
CLAP
CLAP
CLAP
THE RENTAL CHARGES AND FOOD COSTS WERE BRUTAL... THE HIGH COST OF LIVING IN JAPAN WAS DESTROYING US...
IT'S ALL OVER...
QUE-DAM...

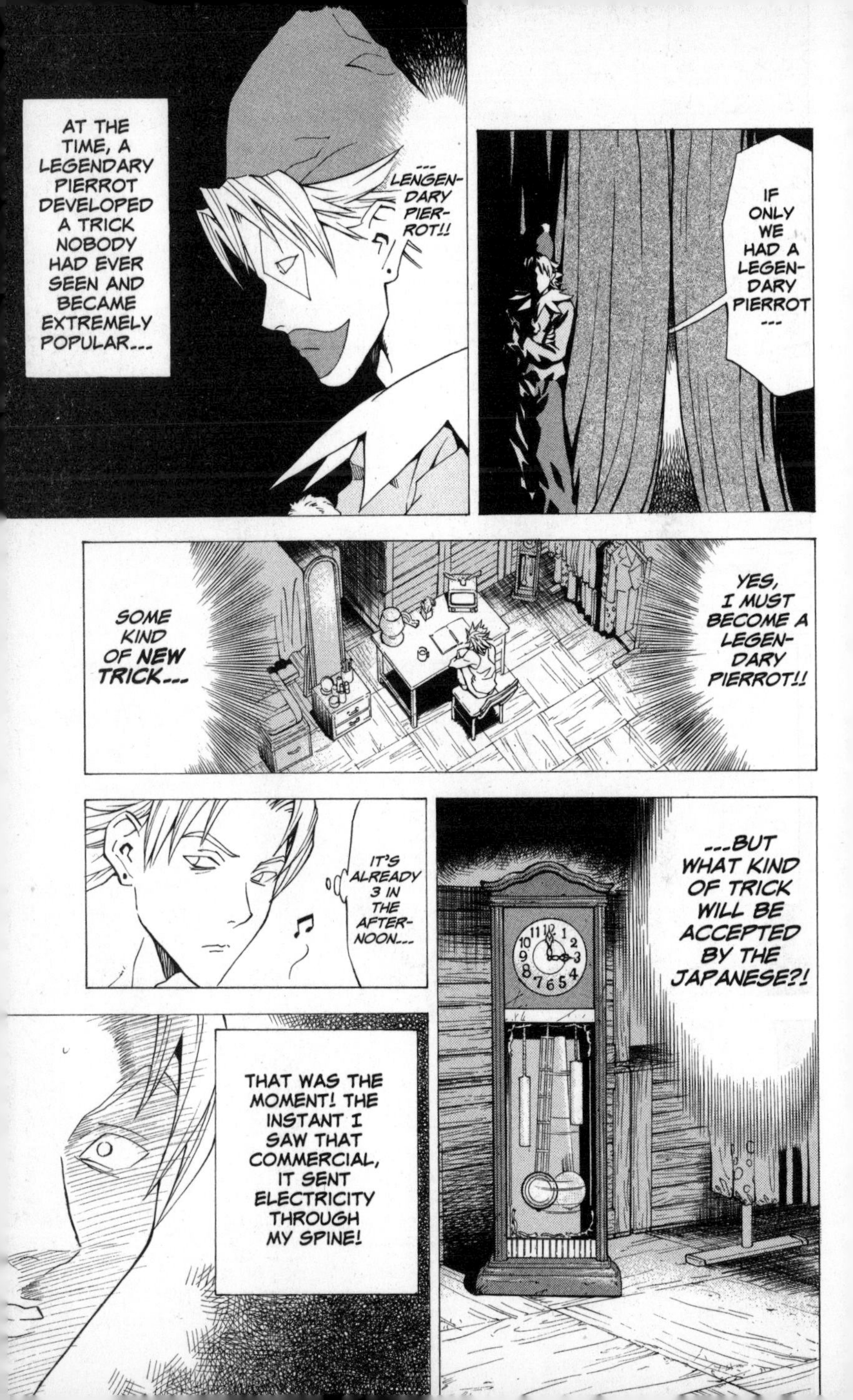
IF ONLY WE HAD A LEGENDARY PIERROT...
AT THE TIME, A LEGENDARY PIERROT DEVELOPED A TRICK NOBODY HAD EVER SEEN AND BECAME EXTREMELY POPULAR...
...LENGEN-DARY PIER-ROT!!
YES, I MUST BECOME A LEGEN-DARY PIERROT!!
SOME KIND OF NEW TRICK...
...BUT WHAT KIND OF TRICK WILL BE ACCEPTED BY THE JAPANESE?!
IT'S ALREADY 3 IN THE AFTER-NOON...
THAT WAS THE MOMENT! THE INSTANT I SAW THAT COMMERCIAL, IT SENT ELECTRICITY THROUGH MY SPINE!

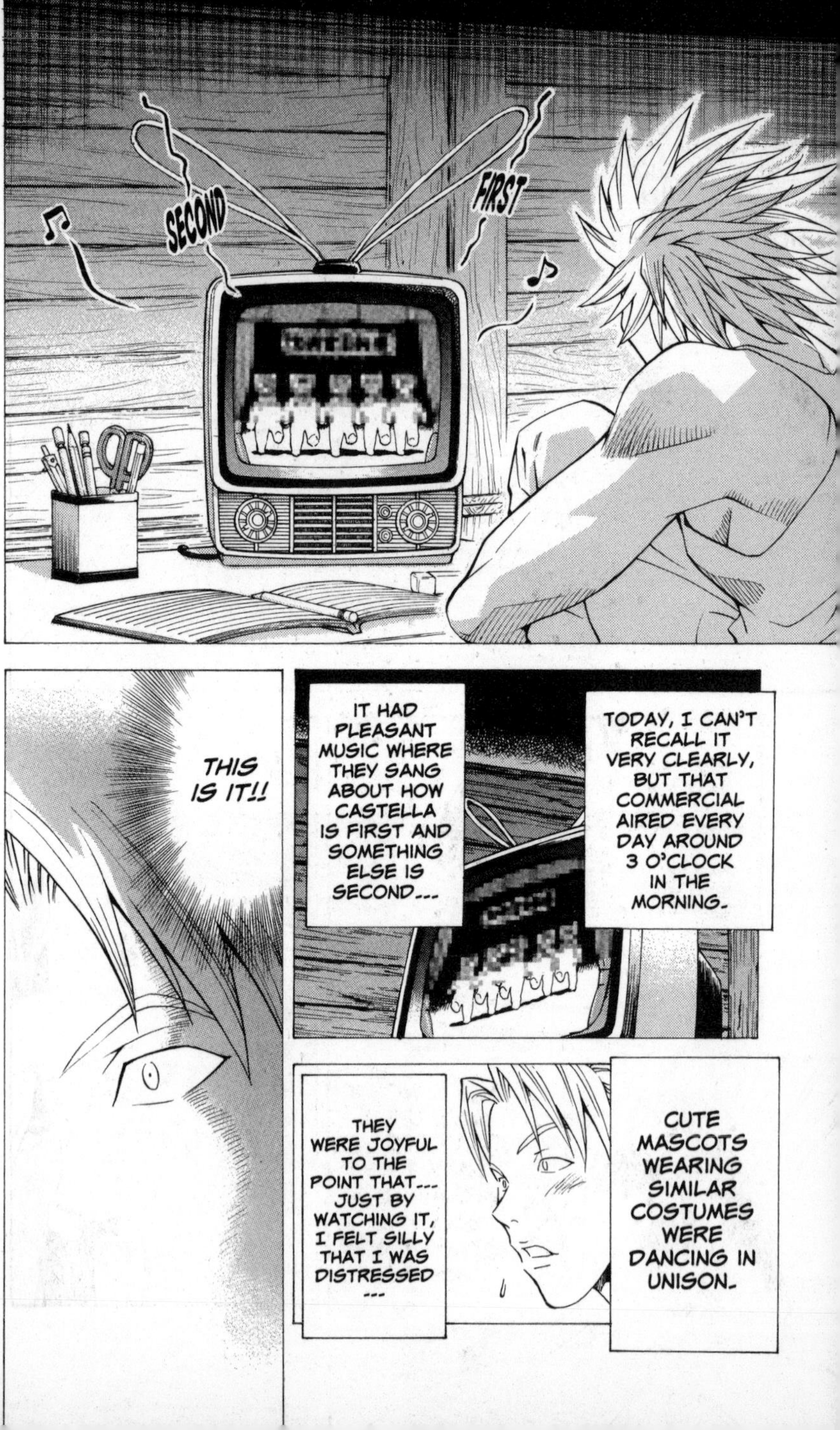
FIRST
SECOND
TODAY, I CAN'T RECALL IT VERY CLEARLY, BUT THAT COMMERCIAL AIRED EVERY DAY AROUND 3 O'CLOCK IN THE MORNING.
IT HAD PLEASANT MUSIC WHERE THEY SANG ABOUT HOW CASTELLA IS FIRST AND SOMETHING ELSE IS SECOND...
CUTE MASCOTS WEARING SIMILAR COSTUMES WERE DANCING IN UNISON.
THEY WERE JOYFUL TO THE POINT THAT... JUST BY WATCHING IT, I FELT SILLY THAT I WAS DISTRESSED ...
THIS IS IT!!

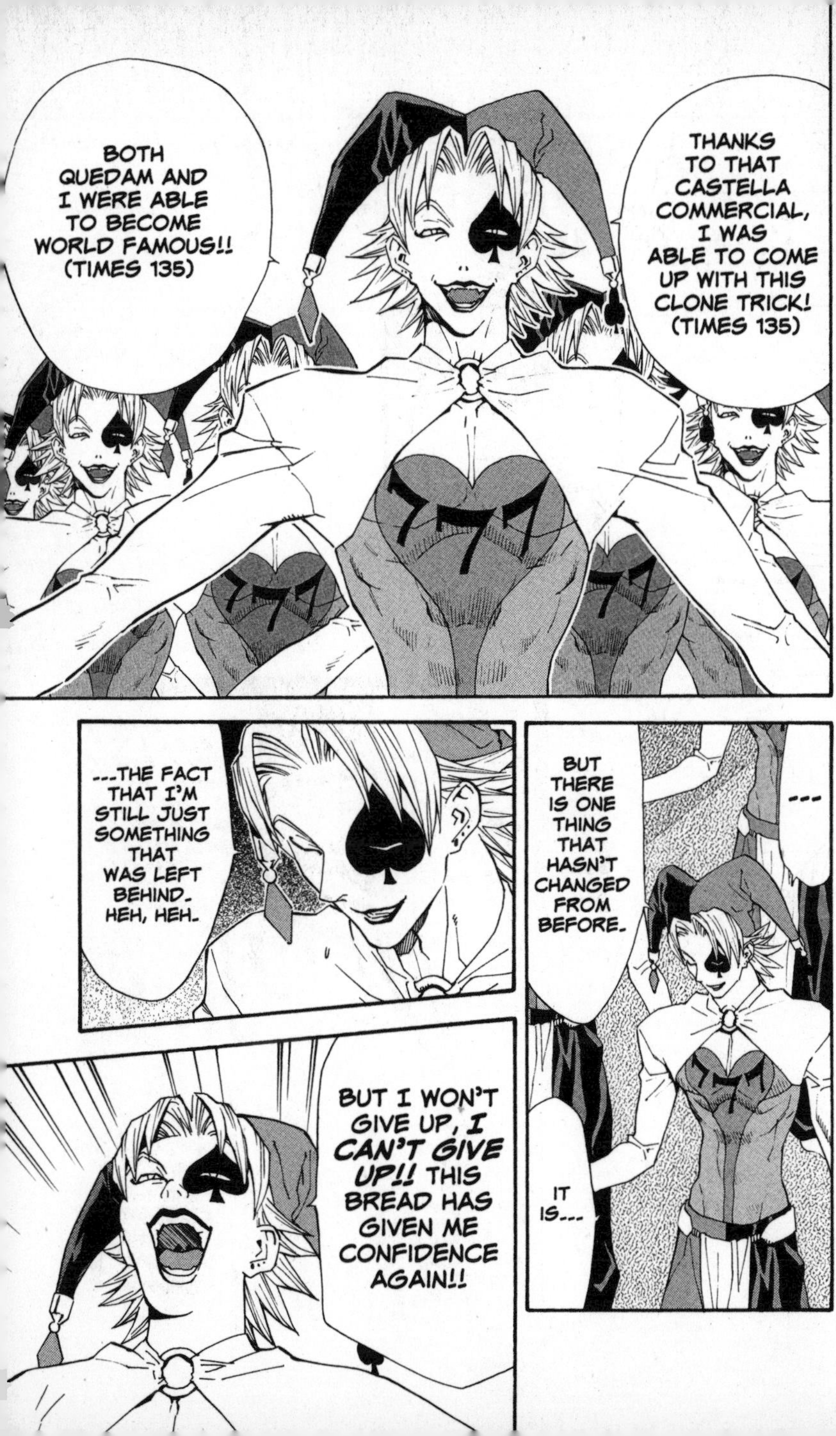
THANKS TO THAT CASTELLA COMMERCIAL, I WAS ABLE TO COME UP WITH THIS CLONE TRICK! (TIMES 135)
BOTH QUEDAM AND I WERE ABLE TO BECOME WORLD FAMOUS!! (TIMES 135)
BUT THERE IS ONE THING THAT HASN'T CHANGED FROM BEFORE.

IT IS---
---THE FACT THAT I'M STILL JUST SOMETHING THAT WAS LEFT BEHIND. HEH, HEH.
BUT I WON'T GIVE UP, *I CAN'T GIVE UP!!* THIS BREAD HAS GIVEN ME CONFIDENCE AGAIN!!

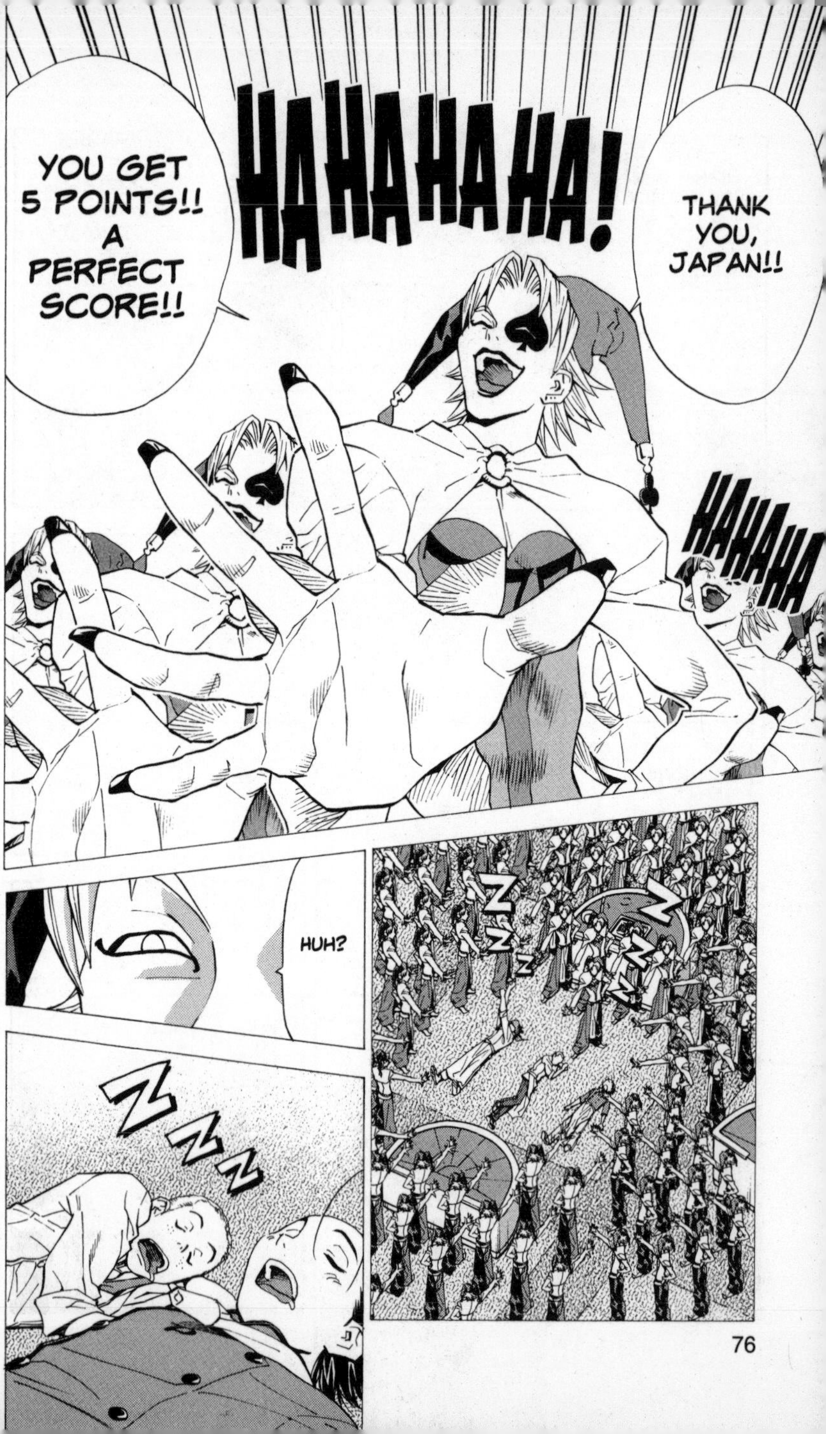

THANK YOU, JAPAN!!
HAHAHAHAHA!
YOU GET 5 POINTS!! A PERFECT SCORE!!
HAHAHA
ZZZ
HUH?
ZZZ

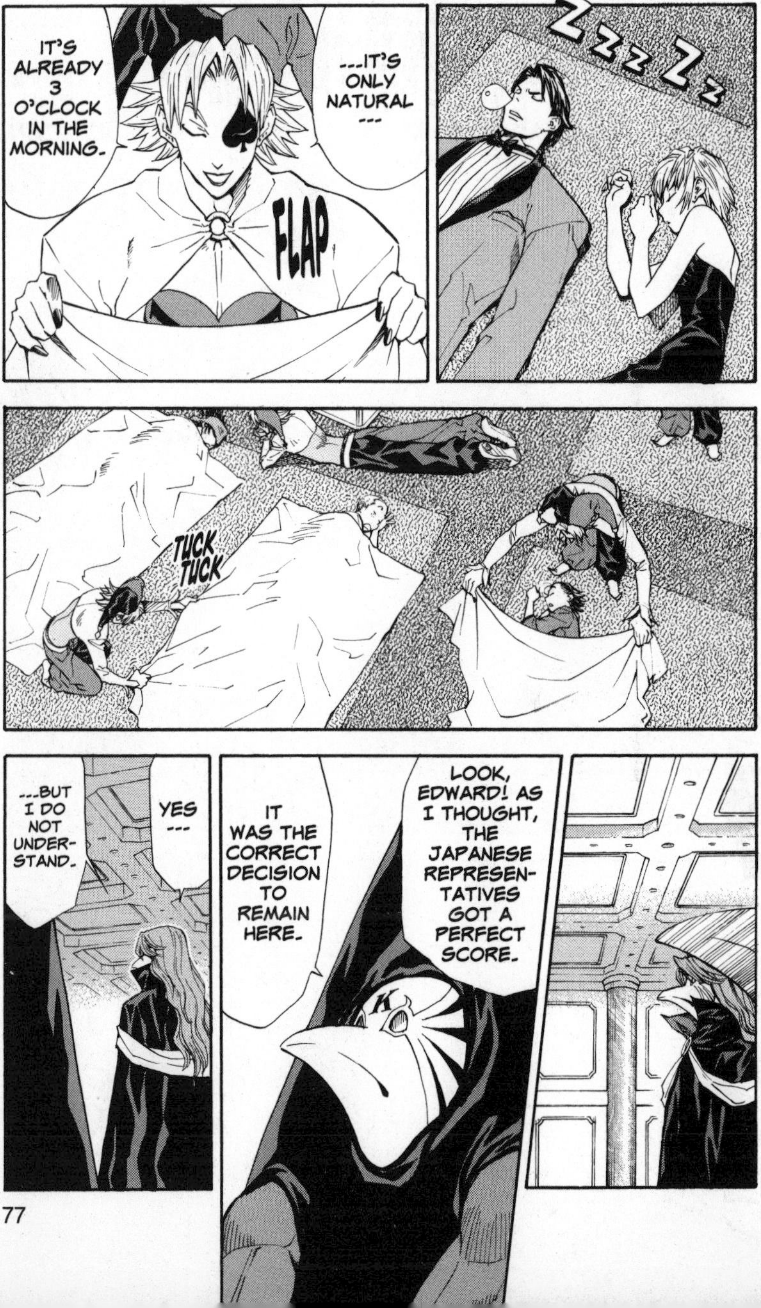
Z z z Z z
---IT'S ONLY NATURAL---
IT'S ALREADY 3 O'CLOCK IN THE MORNING.
FLAP
TUCK TUCK
LOOK, EDWARD! AS I THOUGHT, THE JAPANESE REPRESENTATIVES GOT A PERFECT SCORE.
IT WAS THE CORRECT DECISION TO REMAIN HERE.
YES---
---BUT I DO NOT UNDERSTAND.

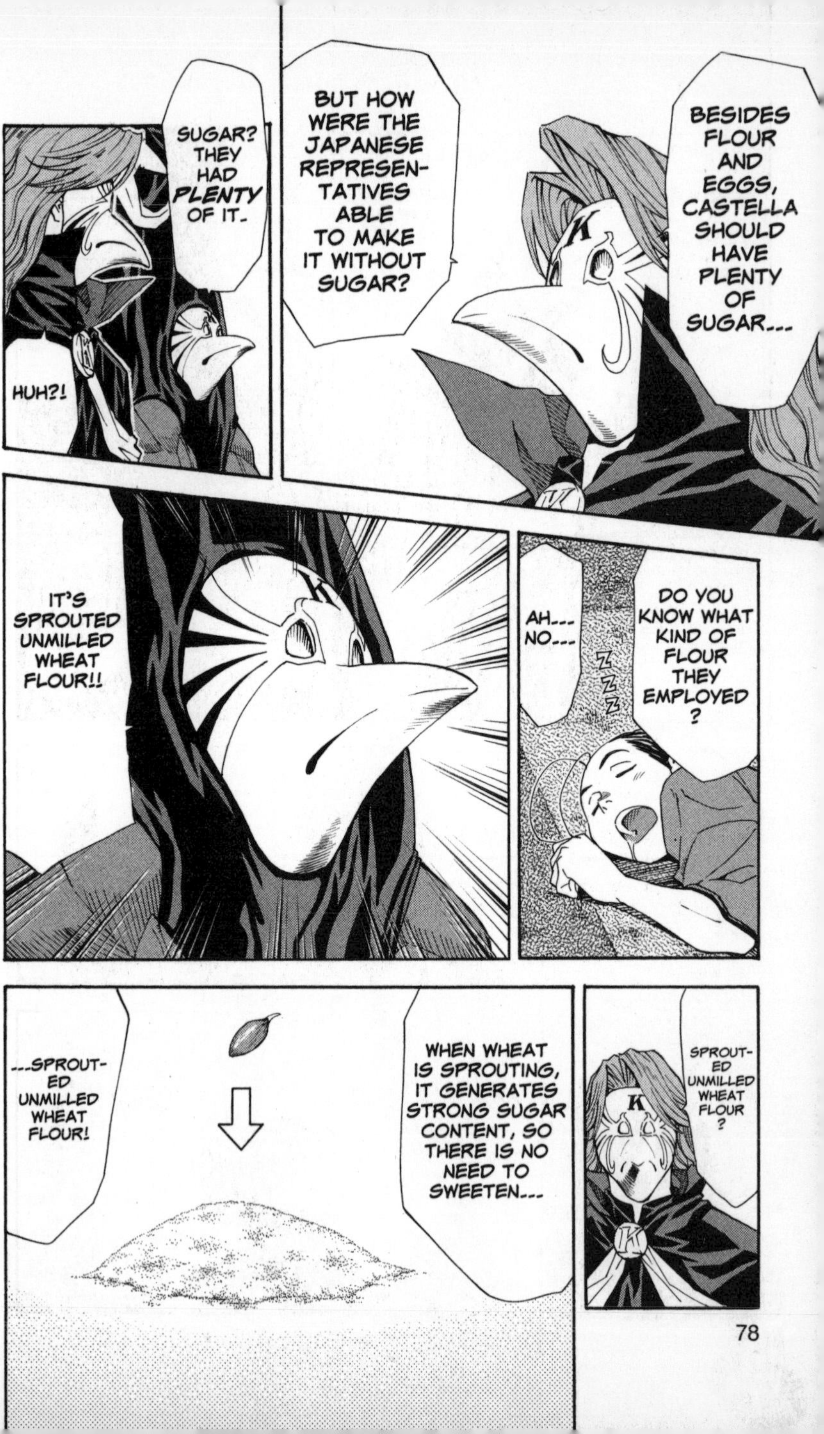

BESIDES FLOUR AND EGGS, CASTELLA SHOULD HAVE PLENTY OF SUGAR...
BUT HOW WERE THE JAPANESE REPRESEN-TATIVES ABLE TO MAKE IT WITHOUT SUGAR?
SUGAR? THEY HAD PLENTY OF IT.
HUH?!
DO YOU KNOW WHAT KIND OF FLOUR THEY EMPLOYED?
AH... NO...
Z Z Z
IT'S SPROUTED UNMILLED WHEAT FLOUR!!
SPROUT-ED UNMILLED WHEAT FLOUR?
WHEN WHEAT IS SPROUTING, IT GENERATES STRONG SUGAR CONTENT, SO THERE IS NO NEED TO SWEETEN...
...SPROUT-ED UNMILLED WHEAT FLOUR!

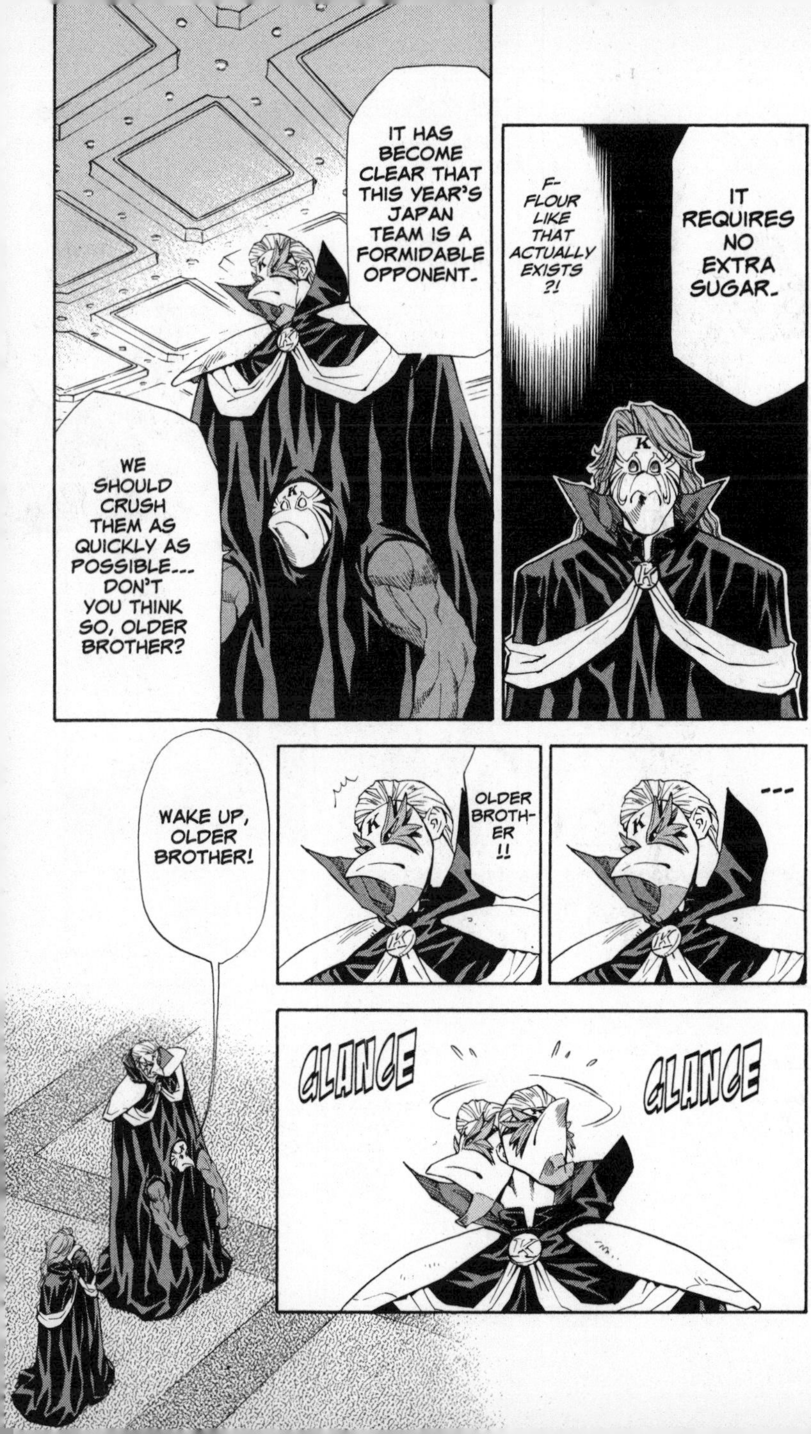
IT REQUIRES NO EXTRA SUGAR.
F-FLOUR LIKE THAT ACTUALLY EXISTS?!
IT HAS BECOME CLEAR THAT THIS YEAR'S JAPAN TEAM IS A FORMIDABLE OPPONENT.
WE SHOULD CRUSH THEM AS QUICKLY AS POSSIBLE... DON'T YOU THINK SO, OLDER BROTHER?
...
OLDER BROTHER!!
GLANCE
GLANCE
WAKE UP, OLDER BROTHER!

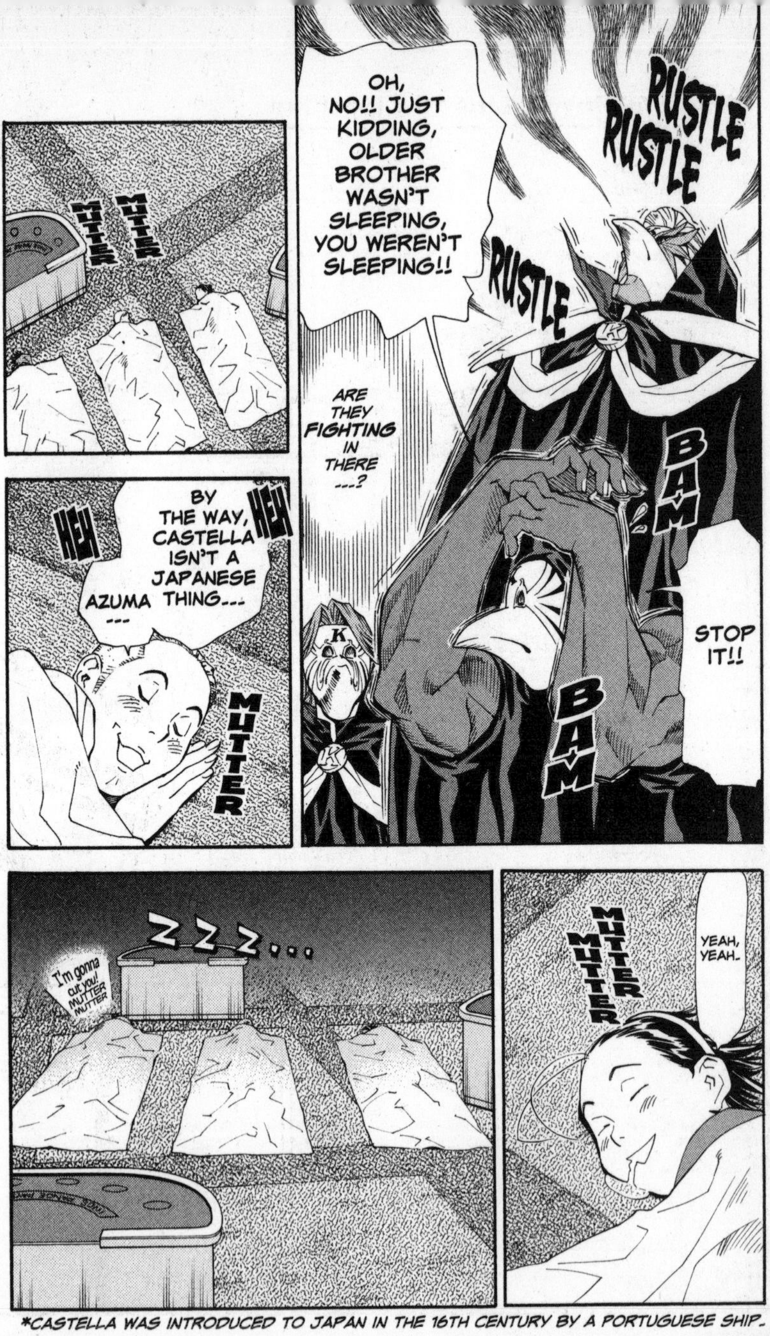
RUSTLE RUSTLE
OH, NO!! JUST KIDDING, OLDER BROTHER WASN'T SLEEPING, YOU WEREN'T SLEEPING!!
RUSTLE
ARE THEY FIGHTING IN THERE ...?
BAM
STOP IT!!
BAM
MUTTER MUTTER
HEH HEH
BY THE WAY, CASTELLA ISN'T A JAPANESE THING...
AZUMA ...
MUTTER
MUTTER MUTTER
YEAH, YEAH.
Z Z Z...
I'm gonna cut you! MUTTER MUTTER

*CASTELLA WAS INTRODUCED TO JAPAN IN THE 16TH CENTURY BY A PORTUGUESE SHIP.

Story 64: Ingredient Slot Machine

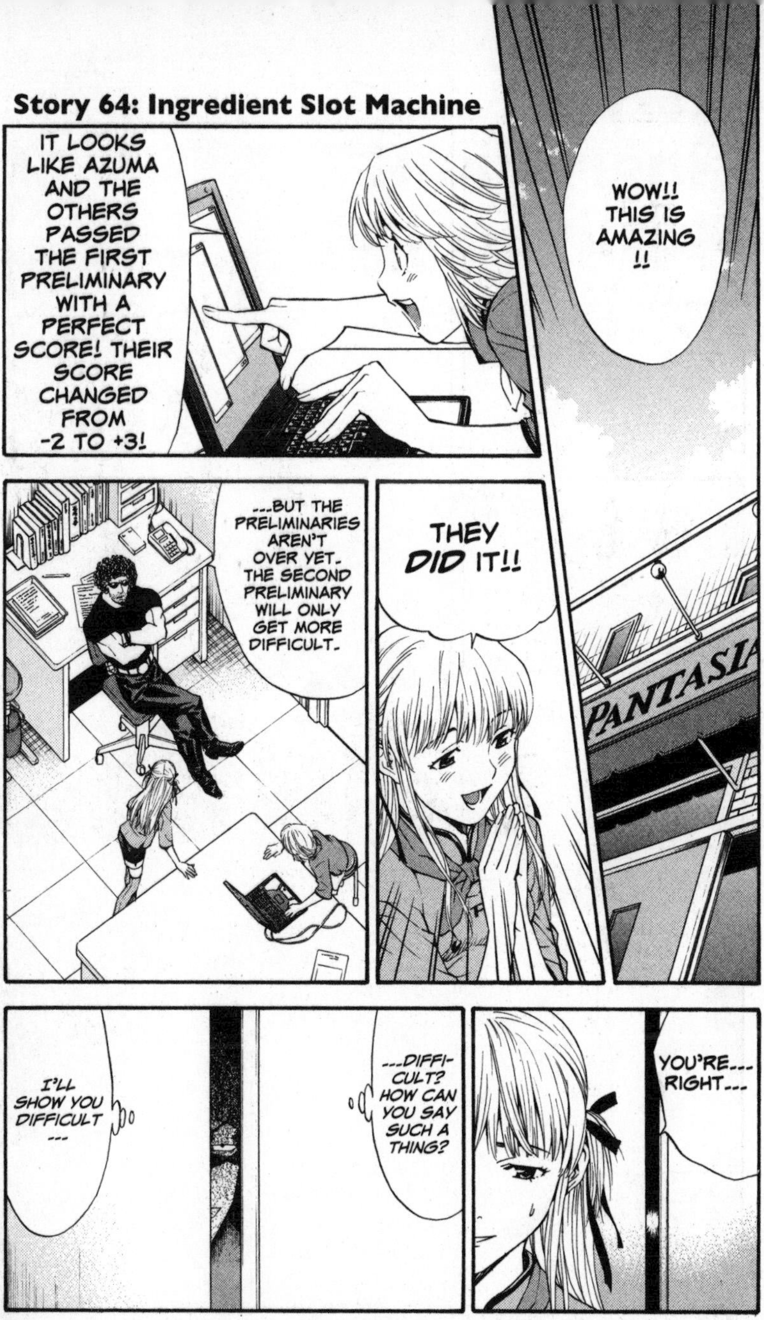
WOW!! THIS IS AMAZING!!
IT LOOKS LIKE AZUMA AND THE OTHERS PASSED THE FIRST PRELIMINARY WITH A PERFECT SCORE! THEIR SCORE CHANGED FROM -2 TO +3!
THEY DID IT!!
...BUT THE PRELIMINARIES AREN'T OVER YET. THE SECOND PRELIMINARY WILL ONLY GET MORE DIFFICULT.
PANTASIA
YOU'RE... RIGHT...
...DIFFICULT? HOW CAN YOU SAY SUCH A THING?
I'LL SHOW YOU DIFFICULT...

Story 64: Ingredient Slot Machine

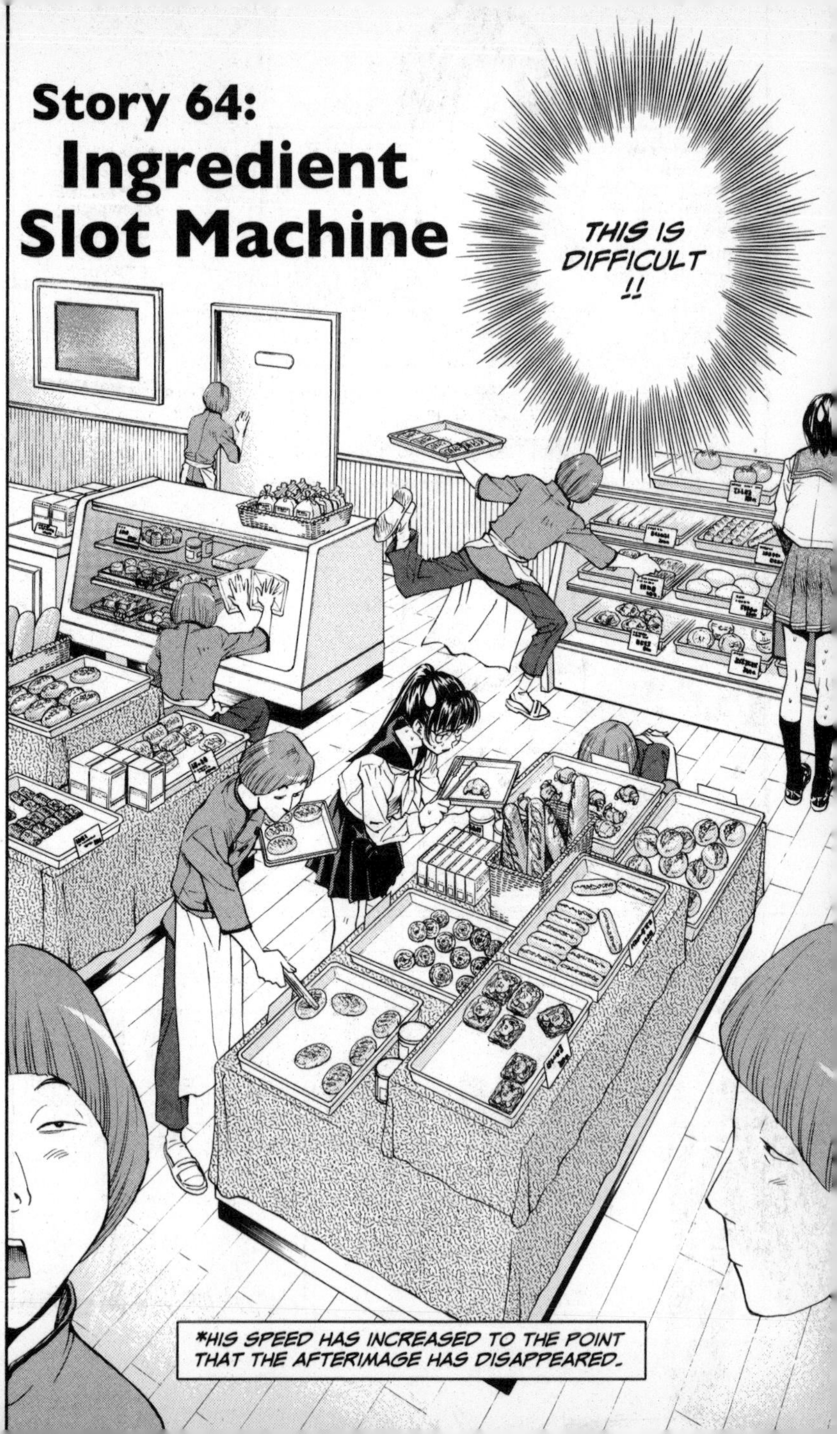
THIS IS DIFFICULT!!
*HIS SPEED HAS INCREASED TO THE POINT THAT THE AFTERIMAGE HAS DISAPPEARED.

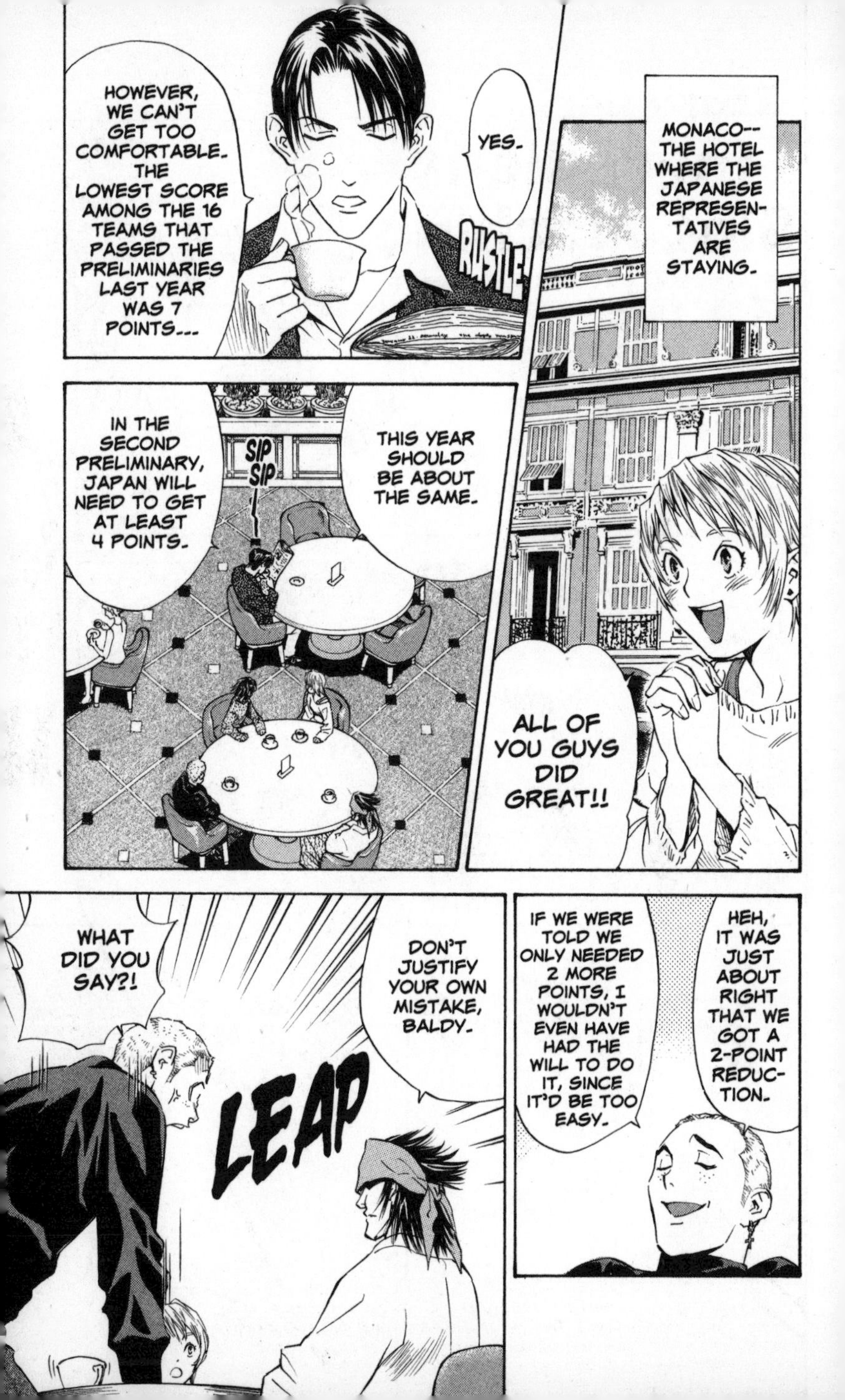
MONACO-- THE HOTEL WHERE THE JAPANESE REPRESEN-TATIVES ARE STAYING.
ALL OF YOU GUYS DID GREAT!!
YES.
RUSTLE
HOWEVER, WE CAN'T GET TOO COMFORTABLE. THE LOWEST SCORE AMONG THE 16 TEAMS THAT PASSED THE PRELIMINARIES LAST YEAR WAS 7 POINTS...
THIS YEAR SHOULD BE ABOUT THE SAME.
SIP SIP
IN THE SECOND PRELIMINARY, JAPAN WILL NEED TO GET AT LEAST 4 POINTS.
HEH, IT WAS JUST ABOUT RIGHT THAT WE GOT A 2-POINT REDUC-TION.
IF WE WERE TOLD WE ONLY NEEDED 2 MORE POINTS, I WOULDN'T EVEN HAVE HAD THE WILL TO DO IT, SINCE IT'D BE TOO EASY.
DON'T JUSTIFY YOUR OWN MISTAKE, BALDY.
WHAT DID YOU SAY?!
LEAP

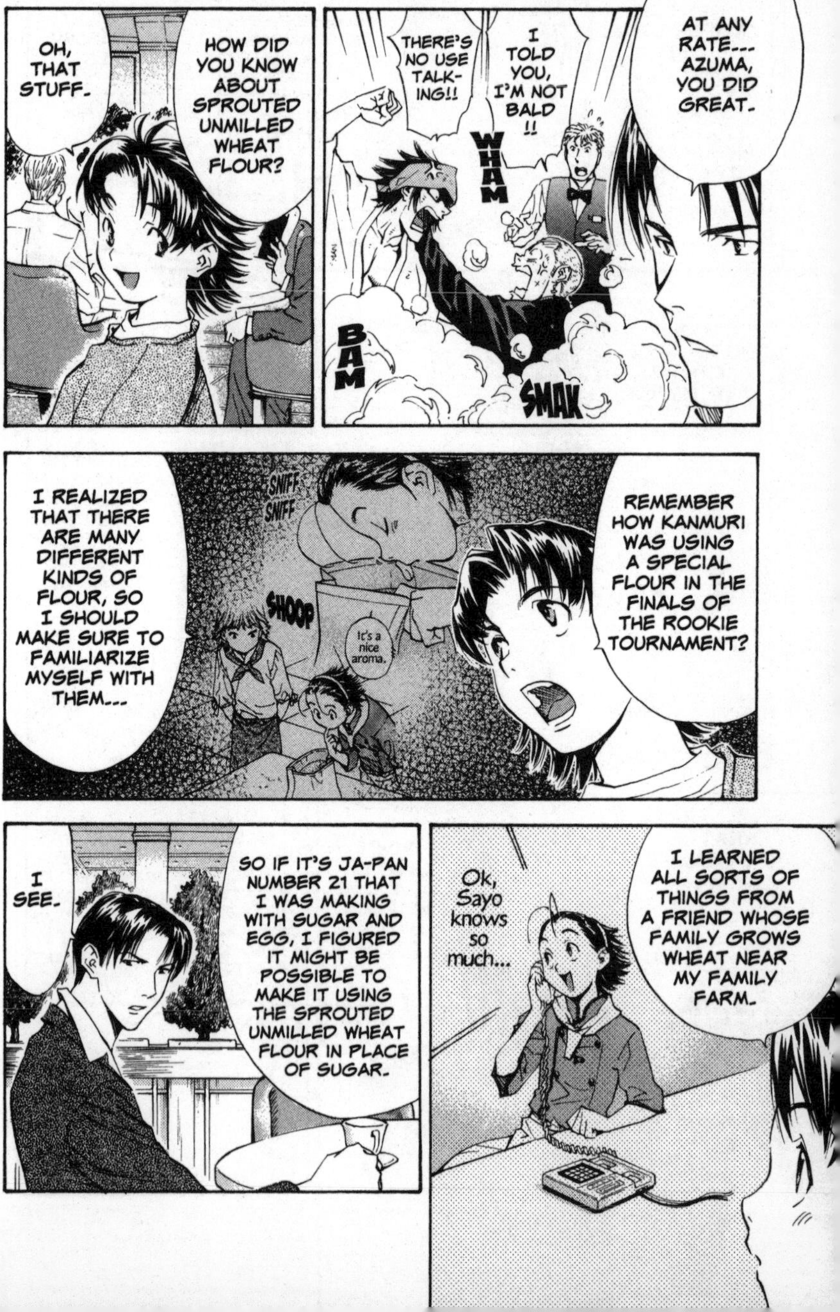
AT ANY RATE... AZUMA, YOU DID GREAT.
I TOLD YOU, I'M NOT BALD!!
THERE'S NO USE TALKING!!
WHAM
BAM
SMAK
HOW DID YOU KNOW ABOUT SPROUTED UNMILLED WHEAT FLOUR?
OH, THAT STUFF.
REMEMBER HOW KANMURI WAS USING A SPECIAL FLOUR IN THE FINALS OF THE ROOKIE TOURNAMENT?
SNIFF SNIFF
It's a nice aroma.
SHOOP
I REALIZED THAT THERE ARE MANY DIFFERENT KINDS OF FLOUR, SO I SHOULD MAKE SURE TO FAMILIARIZE MYSELF WITH THEM...
I LEARNED ALL SORTS OF THINGS FROM A FRIEND WHOSE FAMILY GROWS WHEAT NEAR MY FAMILY FARM.
Ok, Sayo knows so much...
SO IF IT'S JA-PAN NUMBER 21 THAT I WAS MAKING WITH SUGAR AND EGG, I FIGURED IT MIGHT BE POSSIBLE TO MAKE IT USING THE SPROUTED UNMILLED WHEAT FLOUR IN PLACE OF SUGAR.
I SEE.

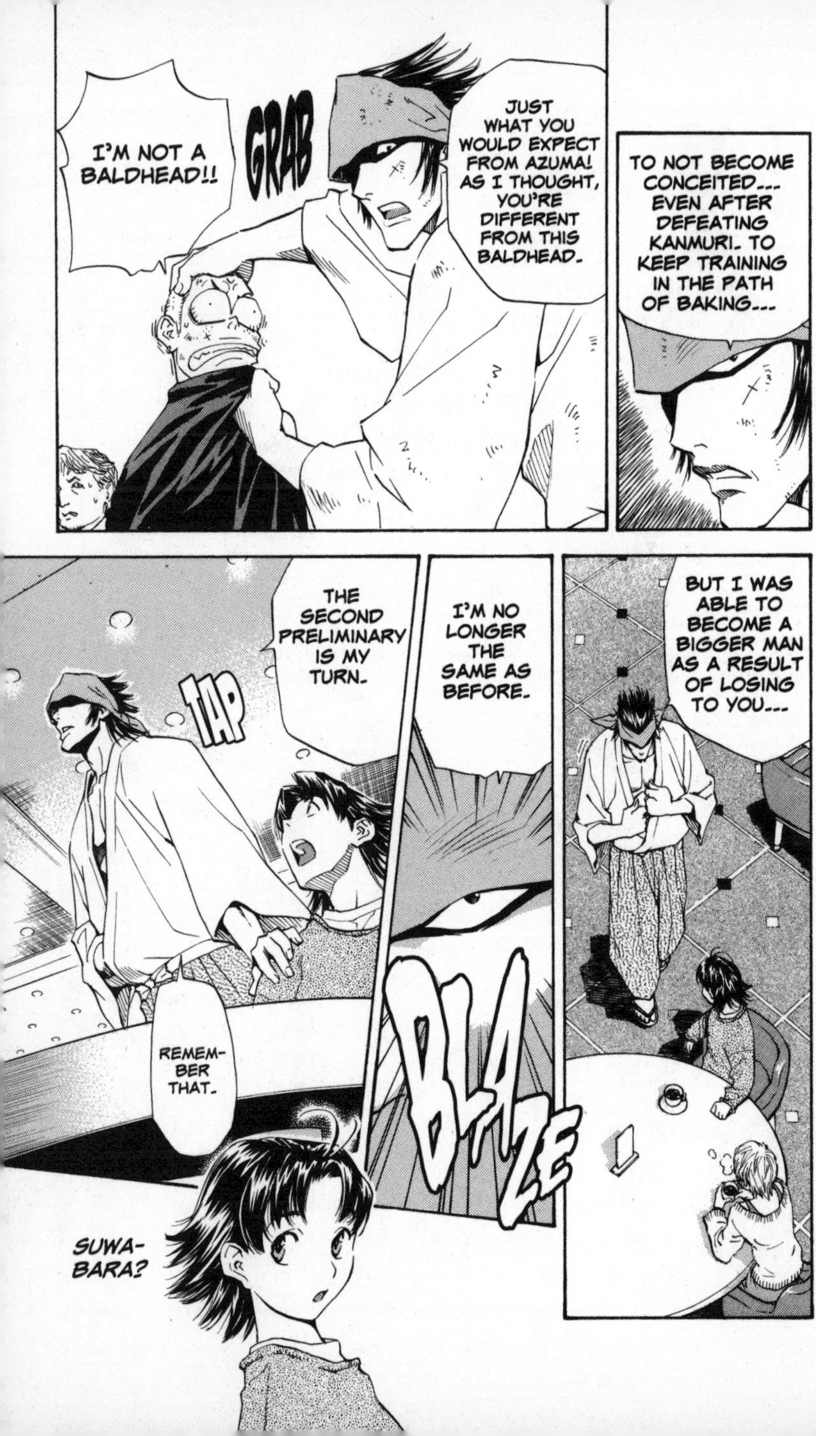
TO NOT BECOME CONCEITED... EVEN AFTER DEFEATING KANMURI, TO KEEP TRAINING IN THE PATH OF BAKING...
JUST WHAT YOU WOULD EXPECT FROM AZUMA! AS I THOUGHT, YOU'RE DIFFERENT FROM THIS BALDHEAD.
GRAB
I'M NOT A BALDHEAD!!
BUT I WAS ABLE TO BECOME A BIGGER MAN AS A RESULT OF LOSING TO YOU...
I'M NO LONGER THE SAME AS BEFORE.
BLAZE
THE SECOND PRELIMINARY IS MY TURN.
TAP
REMEMBER THAT.
SUWABARA?

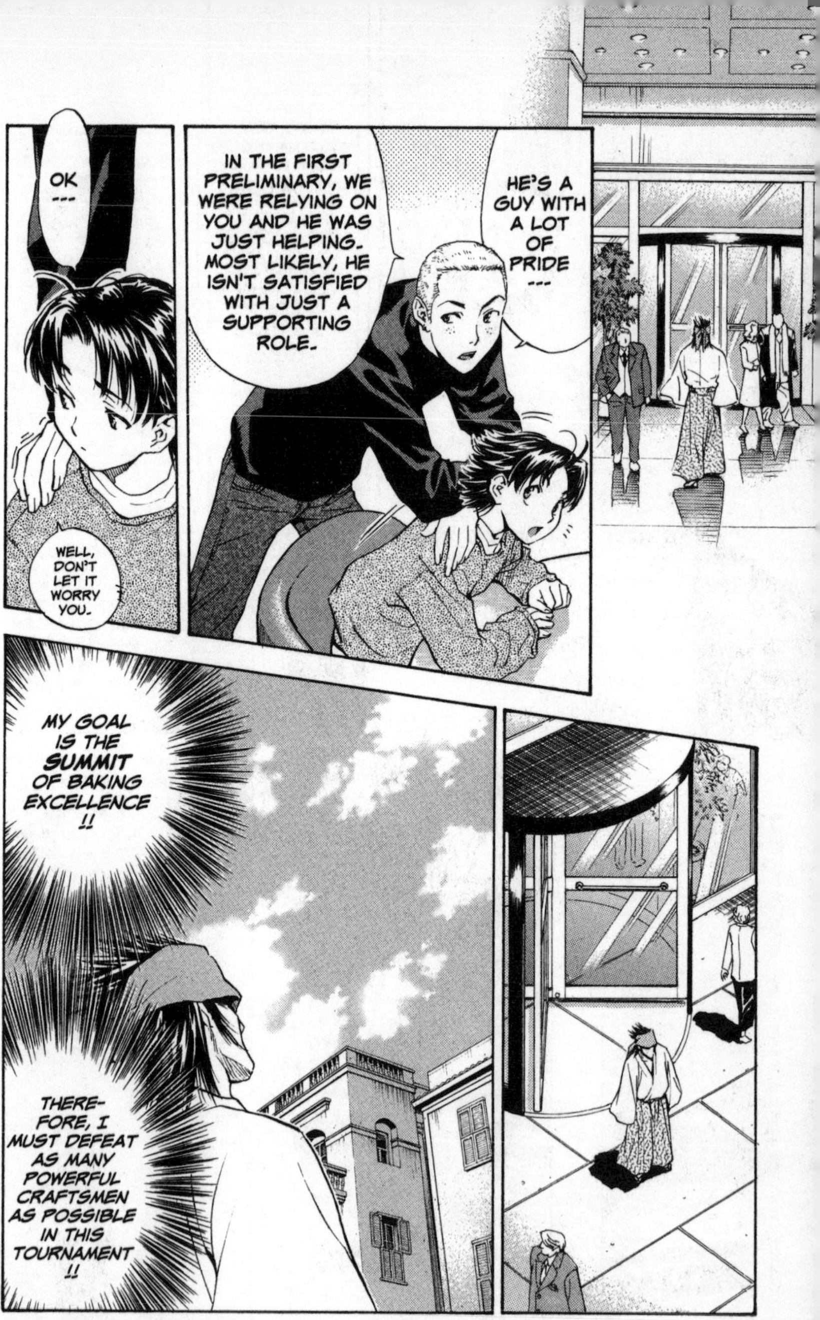
HE'S A GUY WITH A LOT OF PRIDE ---
IN THE FIRST PRELIMINARY, WE WERE RELYING ON YOU AND HE WAS JUST HELPING. MOST LIKELY, HE ISN'T SATISFIED WITH JUST A SUPPORTING ROLE.
OK ---
WELL, DON'T LET IT WORRY YOU.
MY GOAL IS THE SUMMIT OF BAKING EXCELLENCE !!
THERE-FORE, I MUST DEFEAT AS MANY POWERFUL CRAFTSMEN AS POSSIBLE IN THIS TOURNAMENT !!

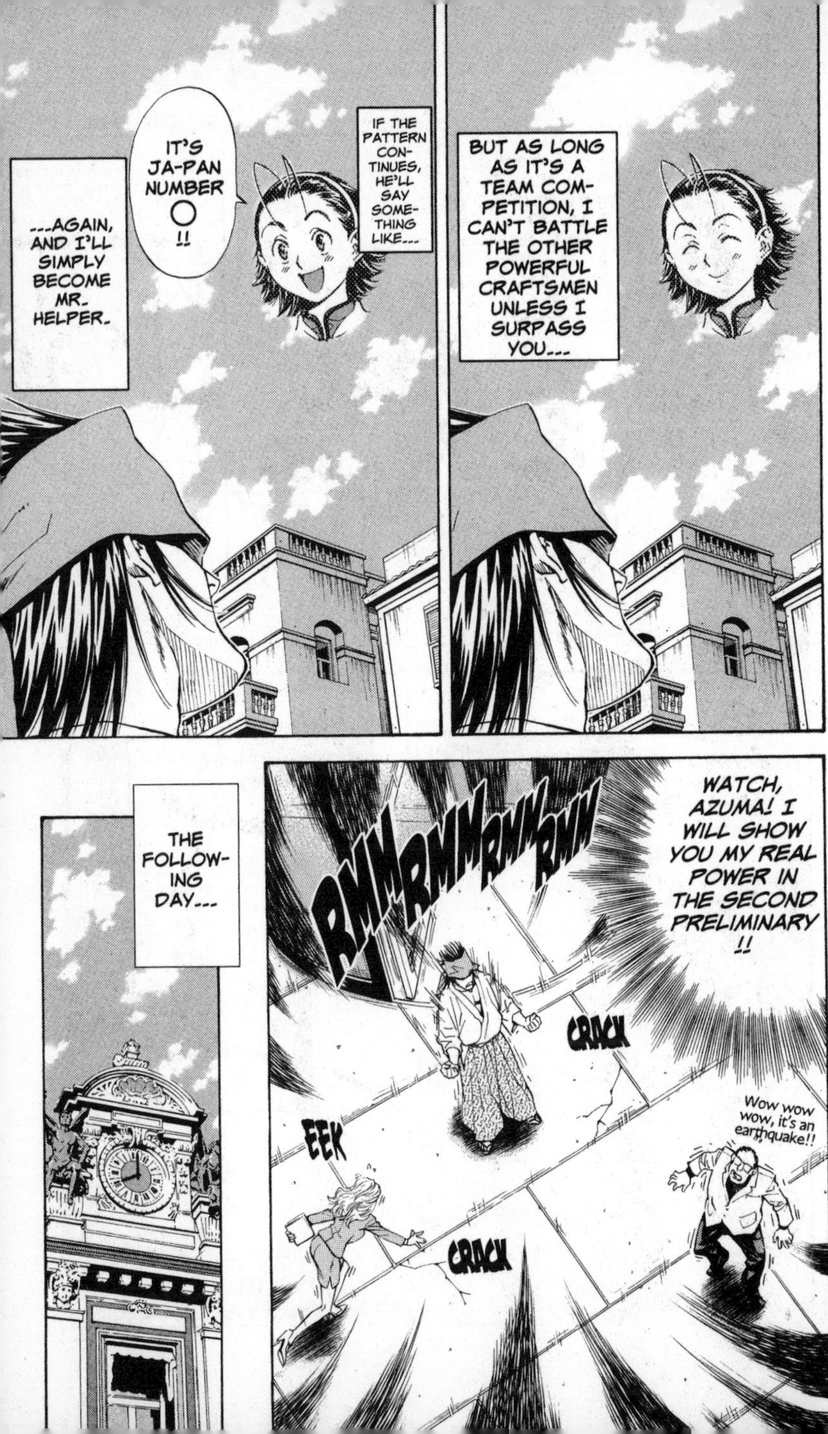
BUT AS LONG AS IT'S A TEAM COMPETITION, I CAN'T BATTLE THE OTHER POWERFUL CRAFTSMEN UNLESS I SURPASS YOU...
IF THE PATTERN CONTINUES, HE'LL SAY SOMETHING LIKE...
IT'S JA-PAN NUMBER ○ !!
...AGAIN, AND I'LL SIMPLY BECOME MR. HELPER.
WATCH, AZUMA! I WILL SHOW YOU MY REAL POWER IN THE SECOND PRELIMINARY !!
RMMMRMMMRMMRMM
CRACK
Wow wow wow, it's an earthquake!!
EEK
CRACK
THE FOLLOWING DAY...

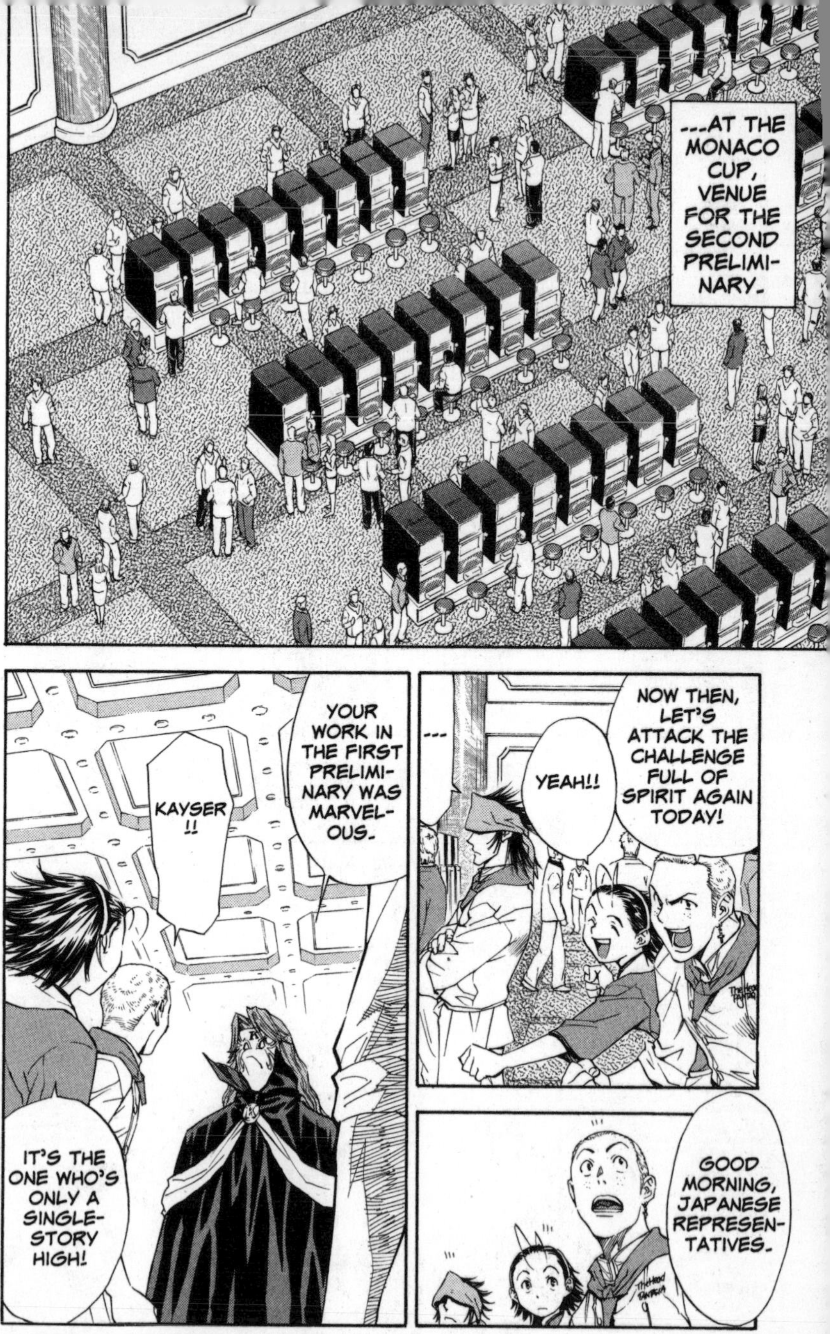
---AT THE MONACO CUP, VENUE FOR THE SECOND PRELIMINARY.
NOW THEN, LET'S ATTACK THE CHALLENGE FULL OF SPIRIT AGAIN TODAY!
YEAH!!

GOOD MORNING, JAPANESE REPRESENTATIVES.
YOUR WORK IN THE FIRST PRELIMINARY WAS MARVELOUS.
KAYSER!!
IT'S THE ONE WHO'S ONLY A SINGLE-STORY HIGH!

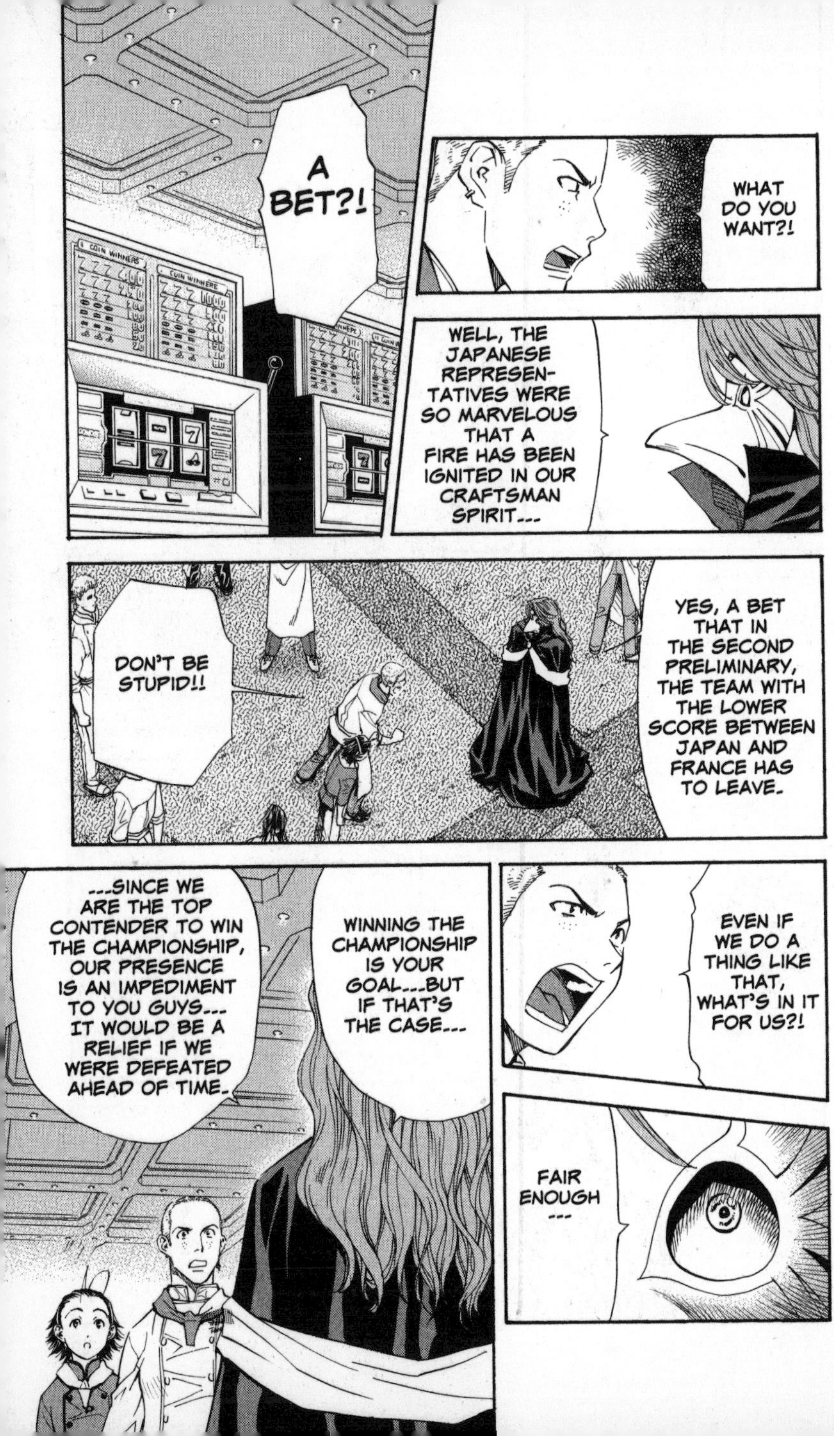
WHAT DO YOU WANT?!
WELL, THE JAPANESE REPRESEN-TATIVES WERE SO MARVELOUS THAT A FIRE HAS BEEN IGNITED IN OUR CRAFTSMAN SPIRIT...
A BET?!
YES, A BET THAT IN THE SECOND PRELIMINARY, THE TEAM WITH THE LOWER SCORE BETWEEN JAPAN AND FRANCE HAS TO LEAVE.
DON'T BE STUPID!!
EVEN IF WE DO A THING LIKE THAT, WHAT'S IN IT FOR US?!
FAIR ENOUGH...
WINNING THE CHAMPIONSHIP IS YOUR GOAL...BUT IF THAT'S THE CASE...
...SINCE WE ARE THE TOP CONTENDER TO WIN THE CHAMPIONSHIP, OUR PRESENCE IS AN IMPEDIMENT TO YOU GUYS... IT WOULD BE A RELIEF IF WE WERE DEFEATED AHEAD OF TIME.

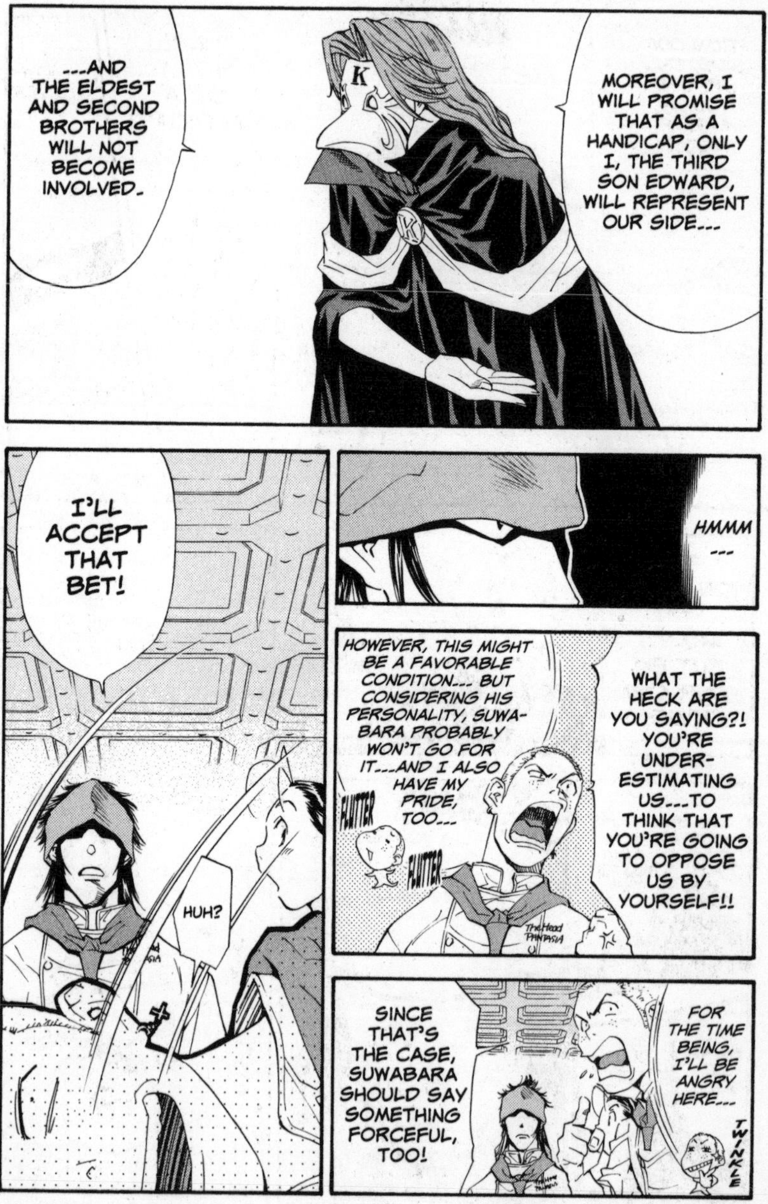
MOREOVER, I WILL PROMISE THAT AS A HANDICAP, ONLY I, THE THIRD SON EDWARD, WILL REPRESENT OUR SIDE...
...AND THE ELDEST AND SECOND BROTHERS WILL NOT BECOME INVOLVED.
HMMM ...
WHAT THE HECK ARE YOU SAYING?! YOU'RE UNDER-ESTIMATING US...TO THINK THAT YOU'RE GOING TO OPPOSE US BY YOURSELF!!
HOWEVER, THIS MIGHT BE A FAVORABLE CONDITION... BUT CONSIDERING HIS PERSONALITY, SUWA-BARA PROBABLY WON'T GO FOR IT...AND I ALSO HAVE MY PRIDE, TOO...
FLUTTER
FLUTTER
FOR THE TIME BEING, I'LL BE ANGRY HERE...
SINCE THAT'S THE CASE, SUWABARA SHOULD SAY SOMETHING FORCEFUL, TOO!
TWINKLE
I'LL ACCEPT THAT BET!
HUH?

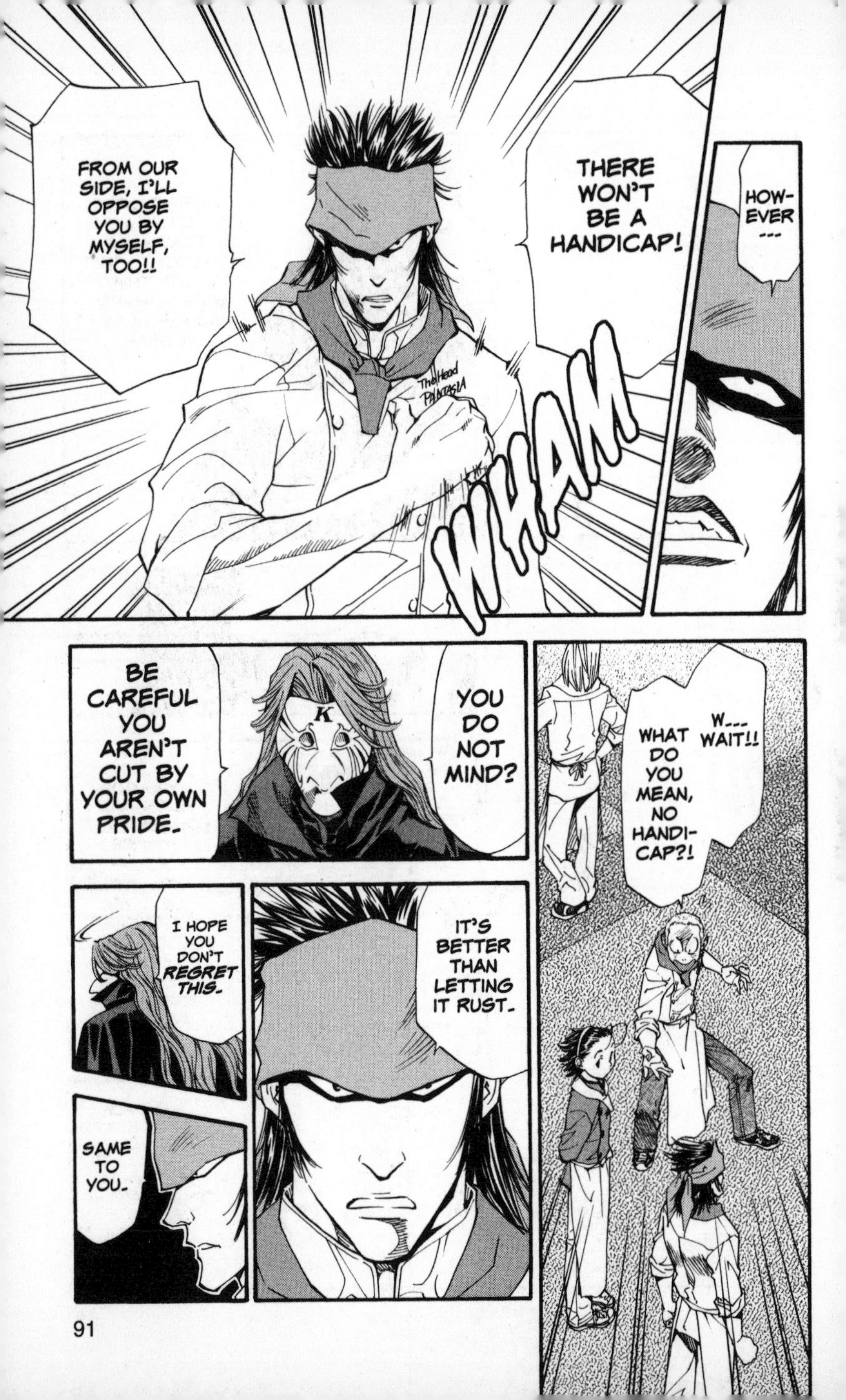
HOW-EVER---
THERE WON'T BE A HANDICAP!
WHAM
The Head PANTASIA
FROM OUR SIDE, I'LL OPPOSE YOU BY MYSELF, TOO!!
W... WAIT!!
WHAT DO YOU MEAN, NO HANDI-CAP?!
YOU DO NOT MIND?
BE CAREFUL YOU AREN'T CUT BY YOUR OWN PRIDE.
IT'S BETTER THAN LETTING IT RUST.
I HOPE YOU DON'T REGRET THIS.
SAME TO YOU.

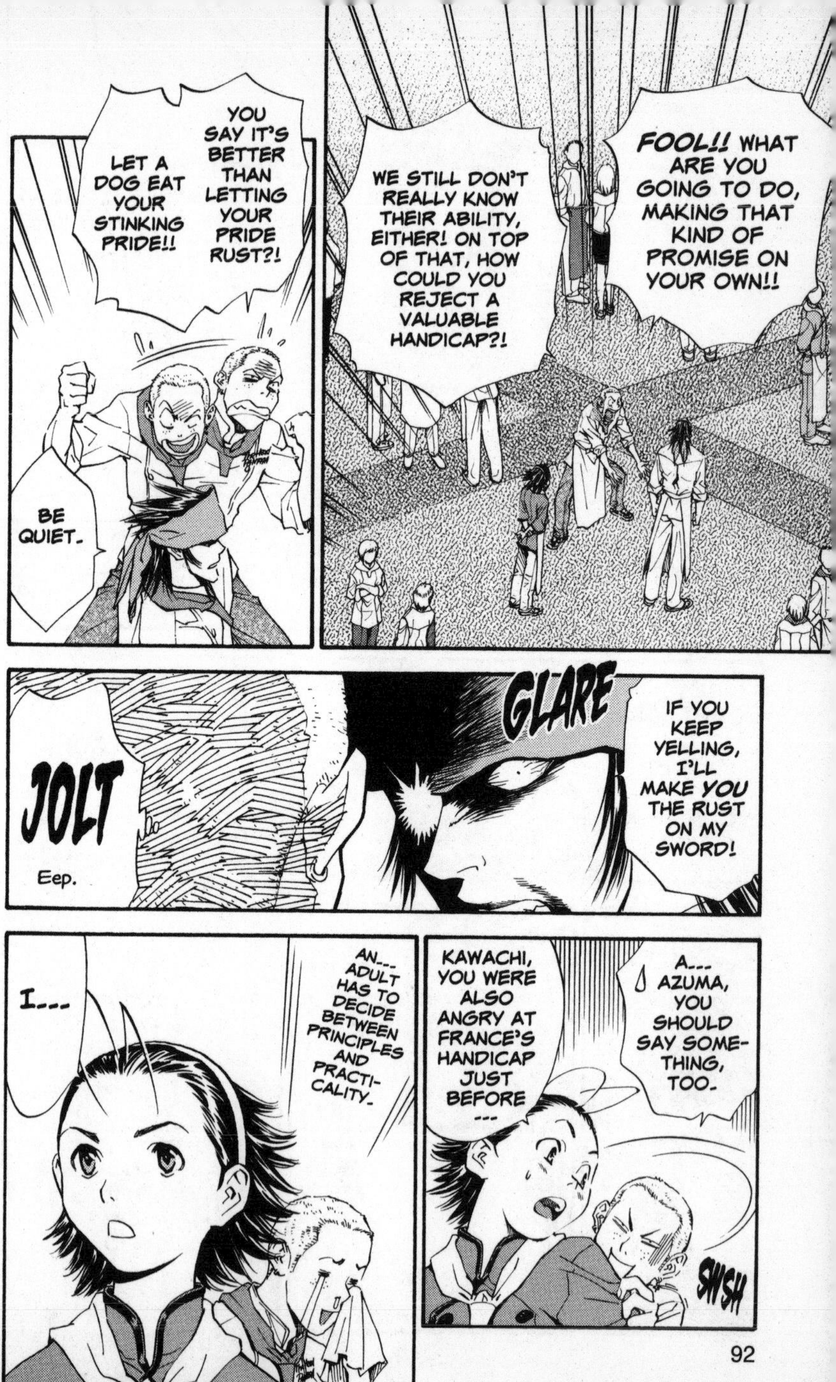
FOOL!! WHAT ARE YOU GOING TO DO, MAKING THAT KIND OF PROMISE ON YOUR OWN!!
WE STILL DON'T REALLY KNOW THEIR ABILITY, EITHER! ON TOP OF THAT, HOW COULD YOU REJECT A VALUABLE HANDICAP?!
YOU SAY IT'S BETTER THAN LETTING YOUR PRIDE RUST?!
LET A DOG EAT YOUR STINKING PRIDE!!
BE QUIET.
GLARE
IF YOU KEEP YELLING, I'LL MAKE YOU THE RUST ON MY SWORD!
JOLT
Eep.
A... AZUMA, YOU SHOULD SAY SOME-THING, TOO.
KAWACHI, YOU WERE ALSO ANGRY AT FRANCE'S HANDICAP JUST BEFORE...
SHISH
AN... ADULT HAS TO DECIDE BETWEEN PRINCIPLES AND PRACTI-CALITY.
I...

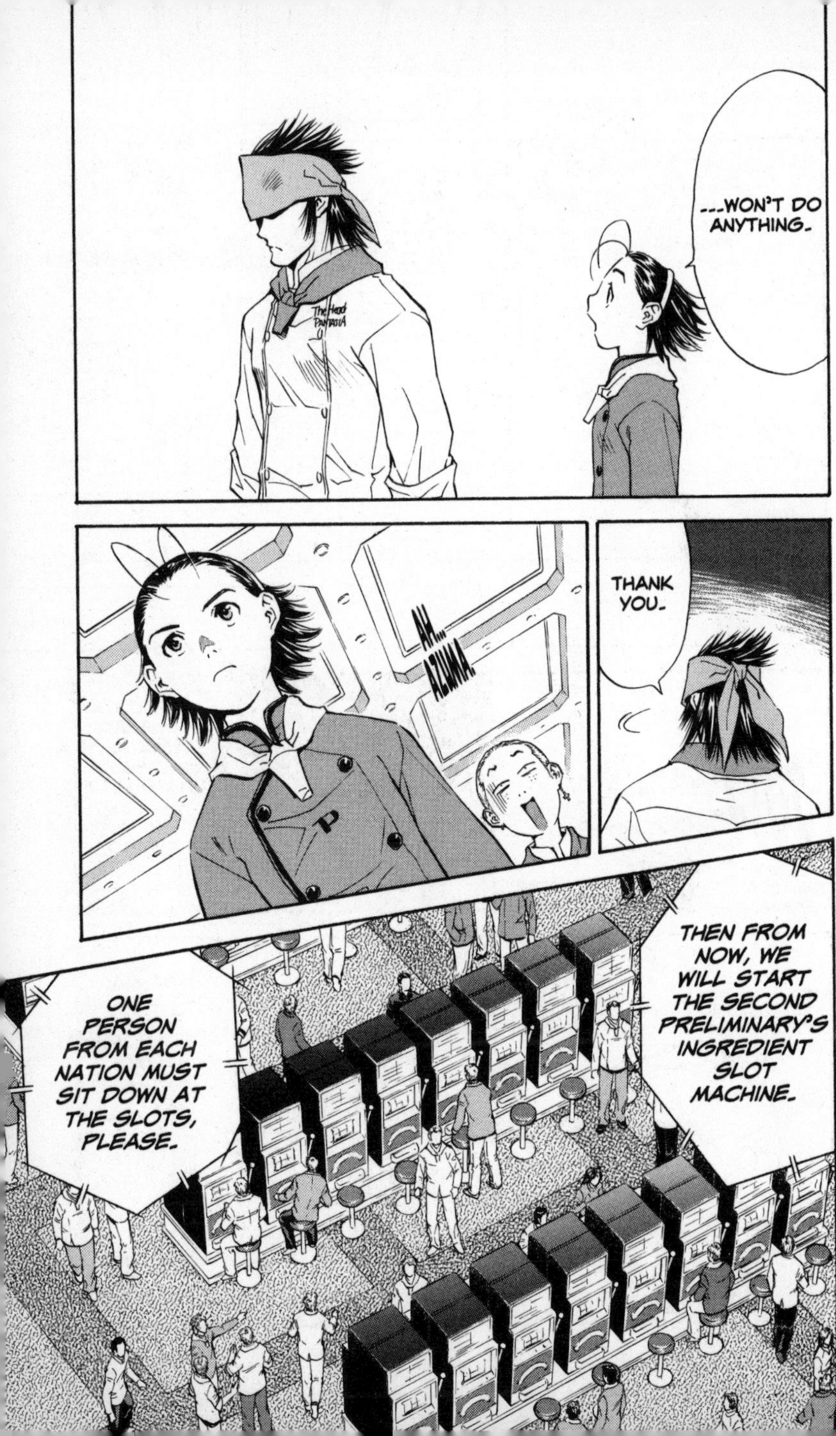
---WON'T DO ANYTHING.
The Head PANTASIA
THANK YOU.
AH... AZUMA.
THEN FROM NOW, WE WILL START THE SECOND PRELIMINARY'S INGREDIENT SLOT MACHINE.
ONE PERSON FROM EACH NATION MUST SIT DOWN AT THE SLOTS, PLEASE.

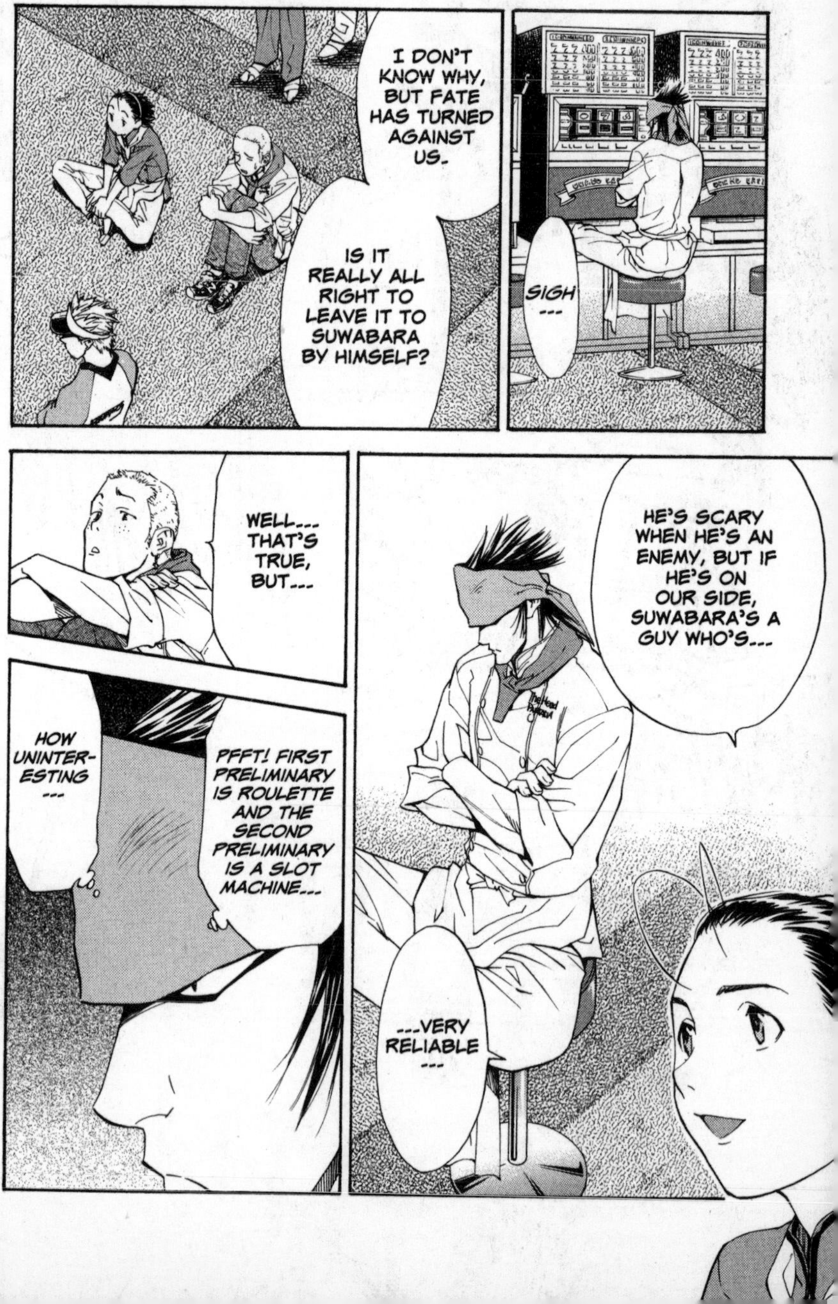
SIGH...
I DON'T KNOW WHY, BUT FATE HAS TURNED AGAINST US.
IS IT REALLY ALL RIGHT TO LEAVE IT TO SUWABARA BY HIMSELF?
HE'S SCARY WHEN HE'S AN ENEMY, BUT IF HE'S ON OUR SIDE, SUWABARA'S A GUY WHO'S...
...VERY RELIABLE...
WELL... THAT'S TRUE, BUT...
PFFT! FIRST PRELIMINARY IS ROULETTE AND THE SECOND PRELIMINARY IS A SLOT MACHINE...
HOW UNINTERESTING...

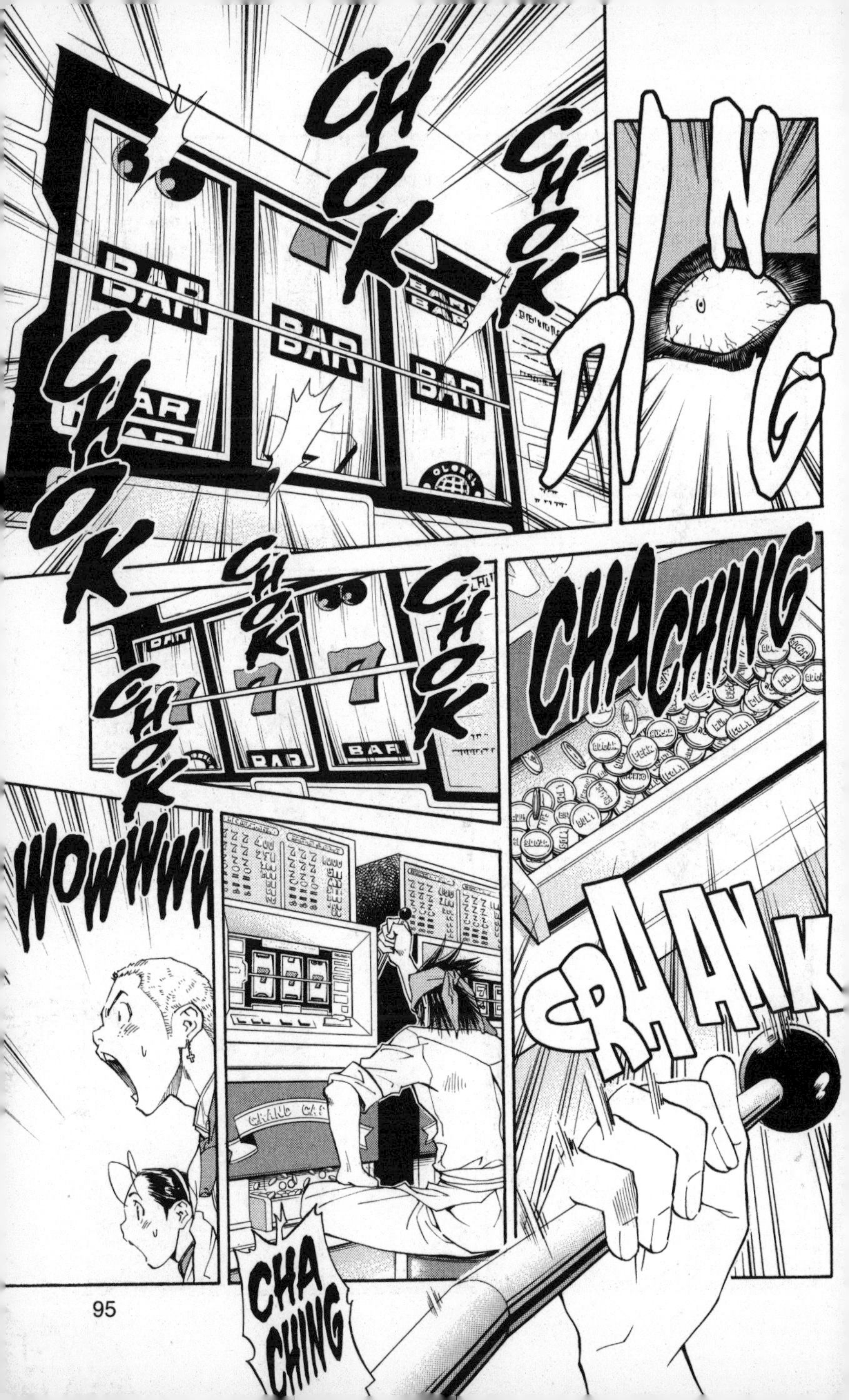
DING
CHOK
CHOK
CHOK
CHACHING
CHOK
CHOK
CHOK
CRAANK
CHA CHING
WOWWWW

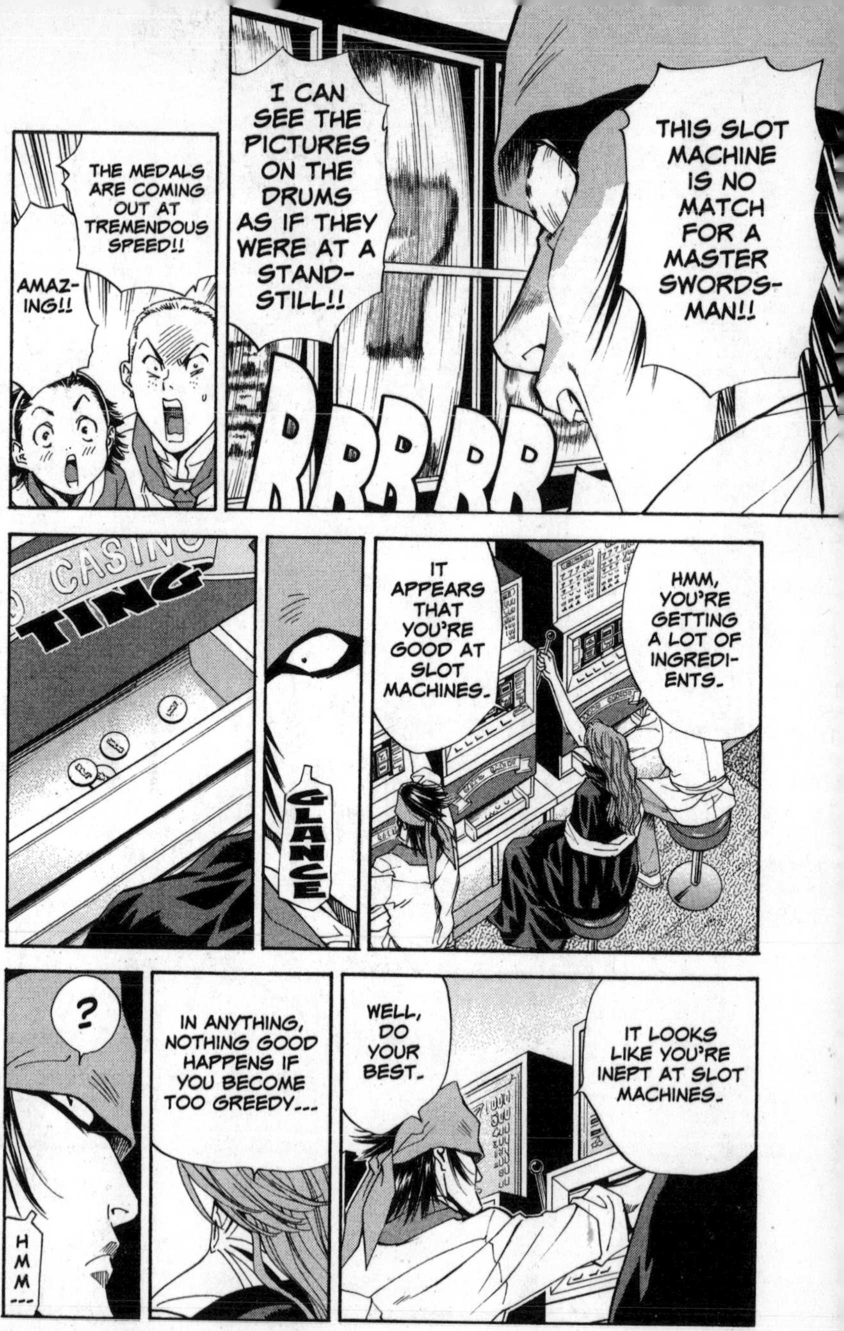

THIS SLOT MACHINE IS NO MATCH FOR A MASTER SWORDSMAN!!
I CAN SEE THE PICTURES ON THE DRUMS AS IF THEY WERE AT A STANDSTILL!!
RRRRR
THE MEDALS ARE COMING OUT AT TREMENDOUS SPEED!!
AMAZING!!
HMM, YOU'RE GETTING A LOT OF INGREDIENTS.
IT APPEARS THAT YOU'RE GOOD AT SLOT MACHINES.
GLANCE
CASINO
TING
IT LOOKS LIKE YOU'RE INEPT AT SLOT MACHINES.
WELL, DO YOUR BEST.
IN ANYTHING, NOTHING GOOD HAPPENS IF YOU BECOME TOO GREEDY...
?
HMM...

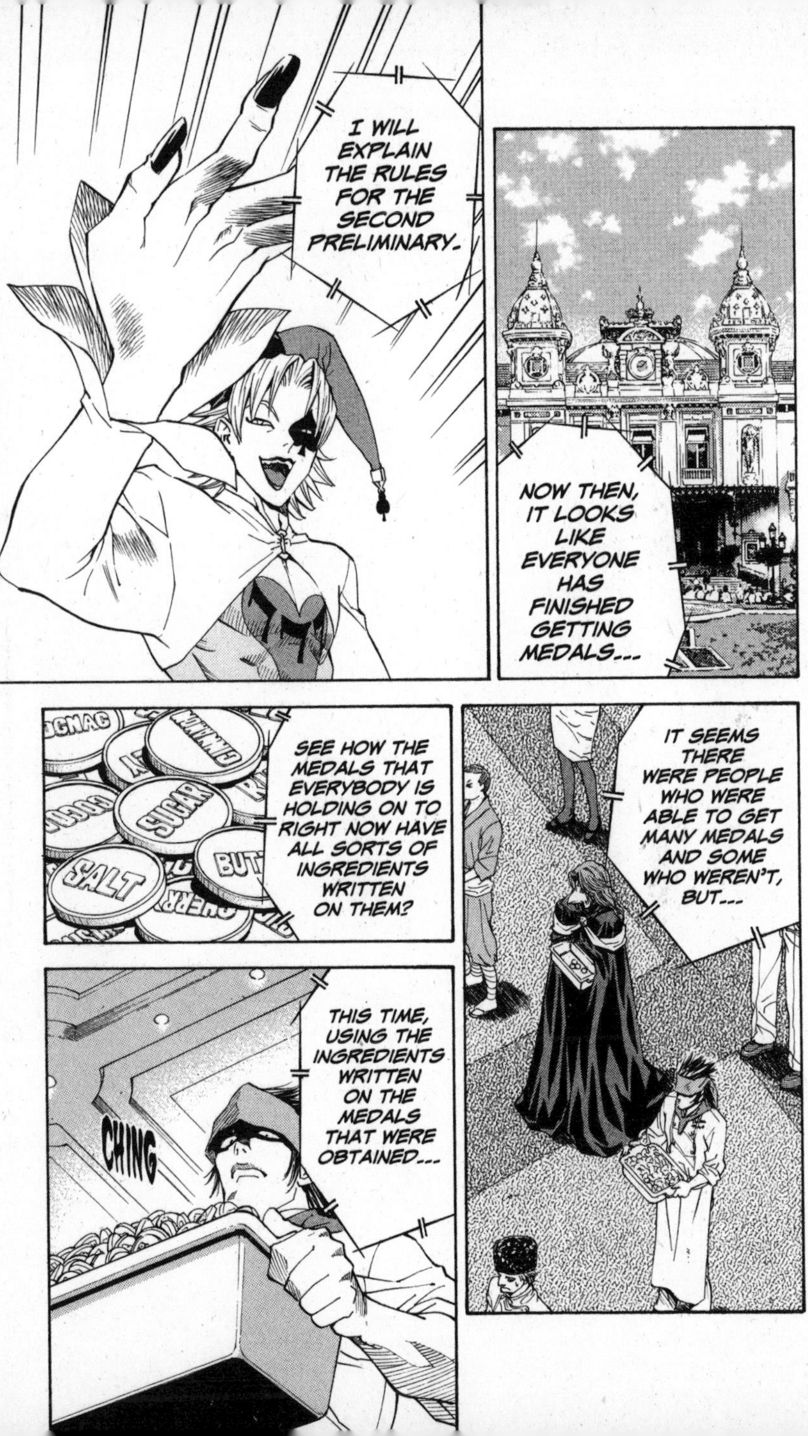
NOW THEN, IT LOOKS LIKE EVERYONE HAS FINISHED GETTING MEDALS...
I WILL EXPLAIN THE RULES FOR THE SECOND PRELIMINARY.
IT SEEMS THERE WERE PEOPLE WHO WERE ABLE TO GET MANY MEDALS AND SOME WHO WEREN'T, BUT...
SUGAR
SALT
SEE HOW THE MEDALS THAT EVERYBODY IS HOLDING ON TO RIGHT NOW HAVE ALL SORTS OF INGREDIENTS WRITTEN ON THEM?
CHING
THIS TIME, USING THE INGREDIENTS WRITTEN ON THE MEDALS THAT WERE OBTAINED...

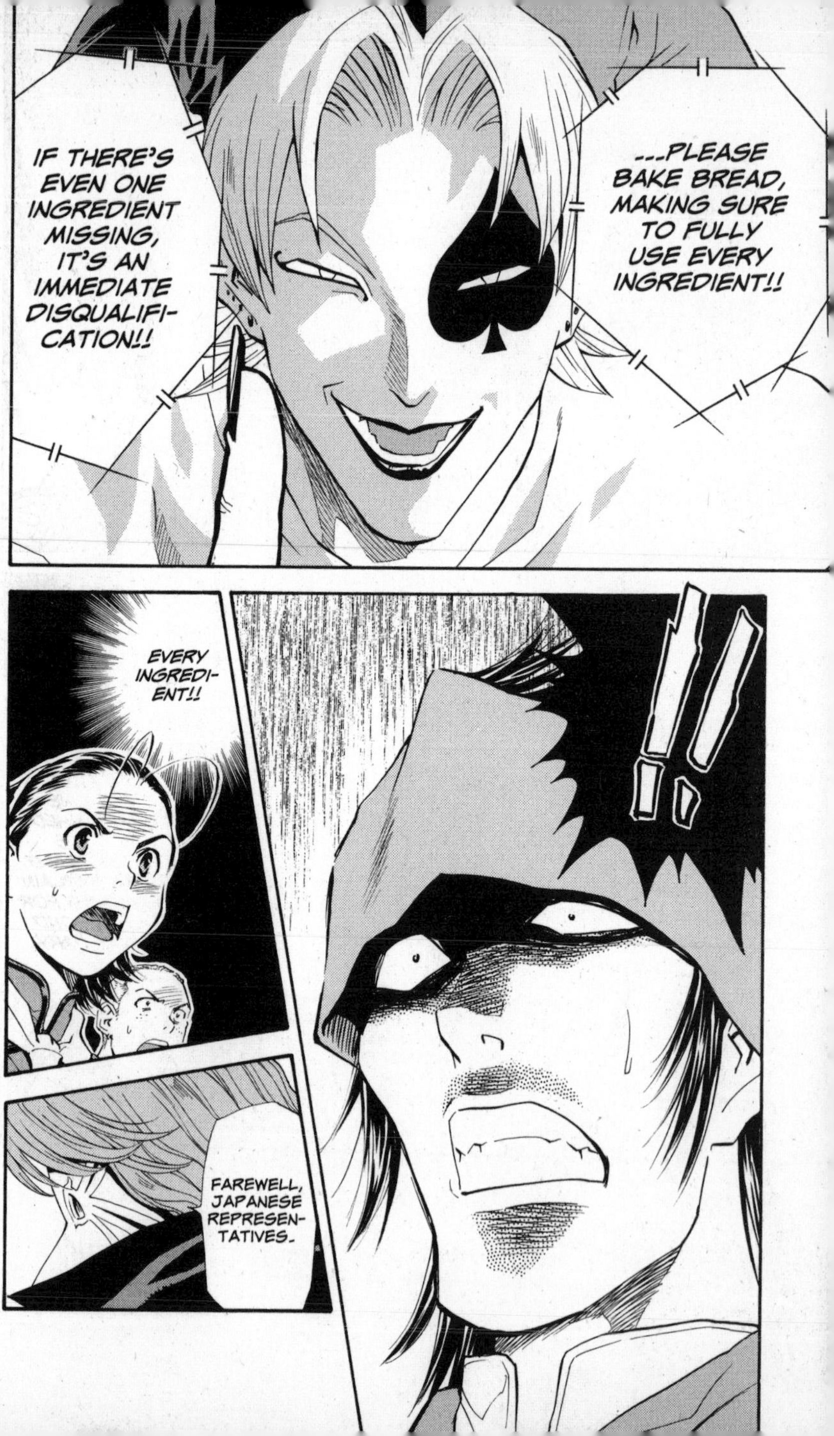
...PLEASE BAKE BREAD, MAKING SURE TO FULLY USE EVERY INGREDIENT!!
IF THERE'S EVEN ONE INGREDIENT MISSING, IT'S AN IMMEDIATE DISQUALIFI-CATION!!
!!
EVERY INGREDI-ENT!!
FAREWELL, JAPANESE REPRESEN-TATIVES.

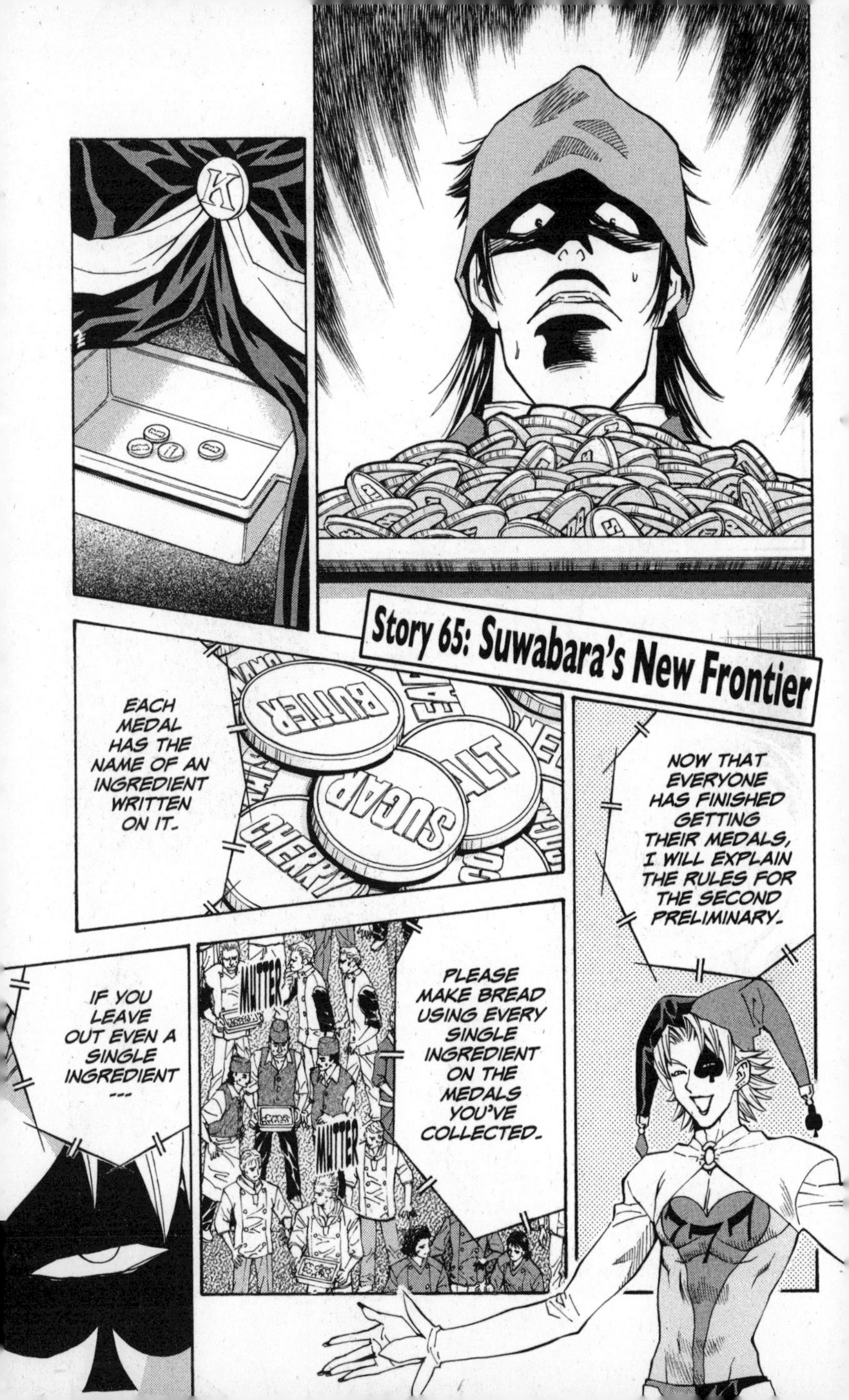
Story 65: Suwabara's New Frontier
NOW THAT EVERYONE HAS FINISHED GETTING THEIR MEDALS, I WILL EXPLAIN THE RULES FOR THE SECOND PRELIMINARY.
EACH MEDAL HAS THE NAME OF AN INGREDIENT WRITTEN ON IT.
SUGAR
CHERRY
PLEASE MAKE BREAD USING EVERY SINGLE INGREDIENT ON THE MEDALS YOU'VE COLLECTED.
IF YOU LEAVE OUT EVEN A SINGLE INGREDIENT ---

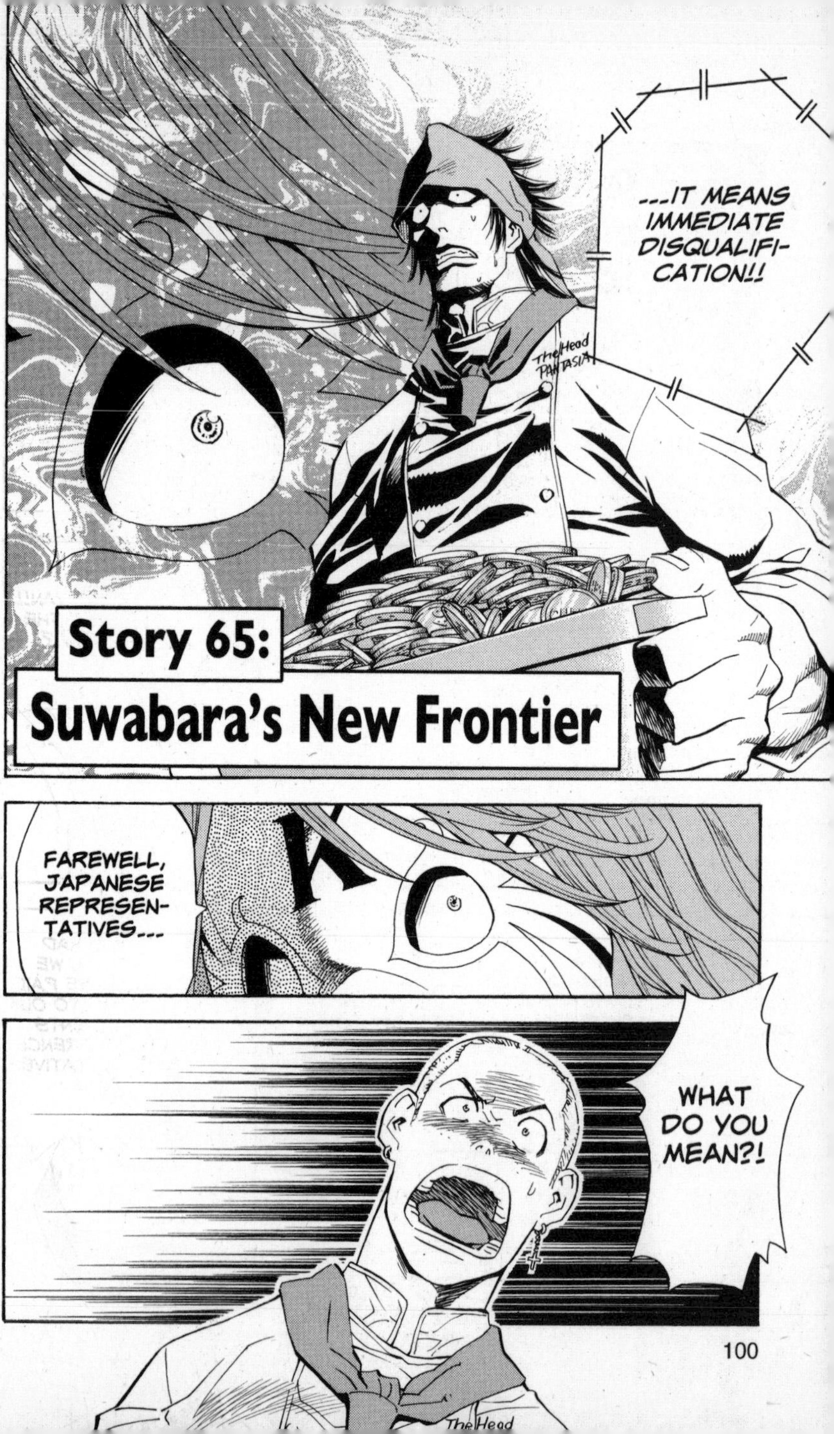

---IT MEANS IMMEDIATE DISQUALIFI- CATION!!
The Head PANTASIA
Story 65:
Suwabara's New Frontier
FAREWELL, JAPANESE REPRESEN- TATIVES---
WHAT DO YOU MEAN?!
The Head

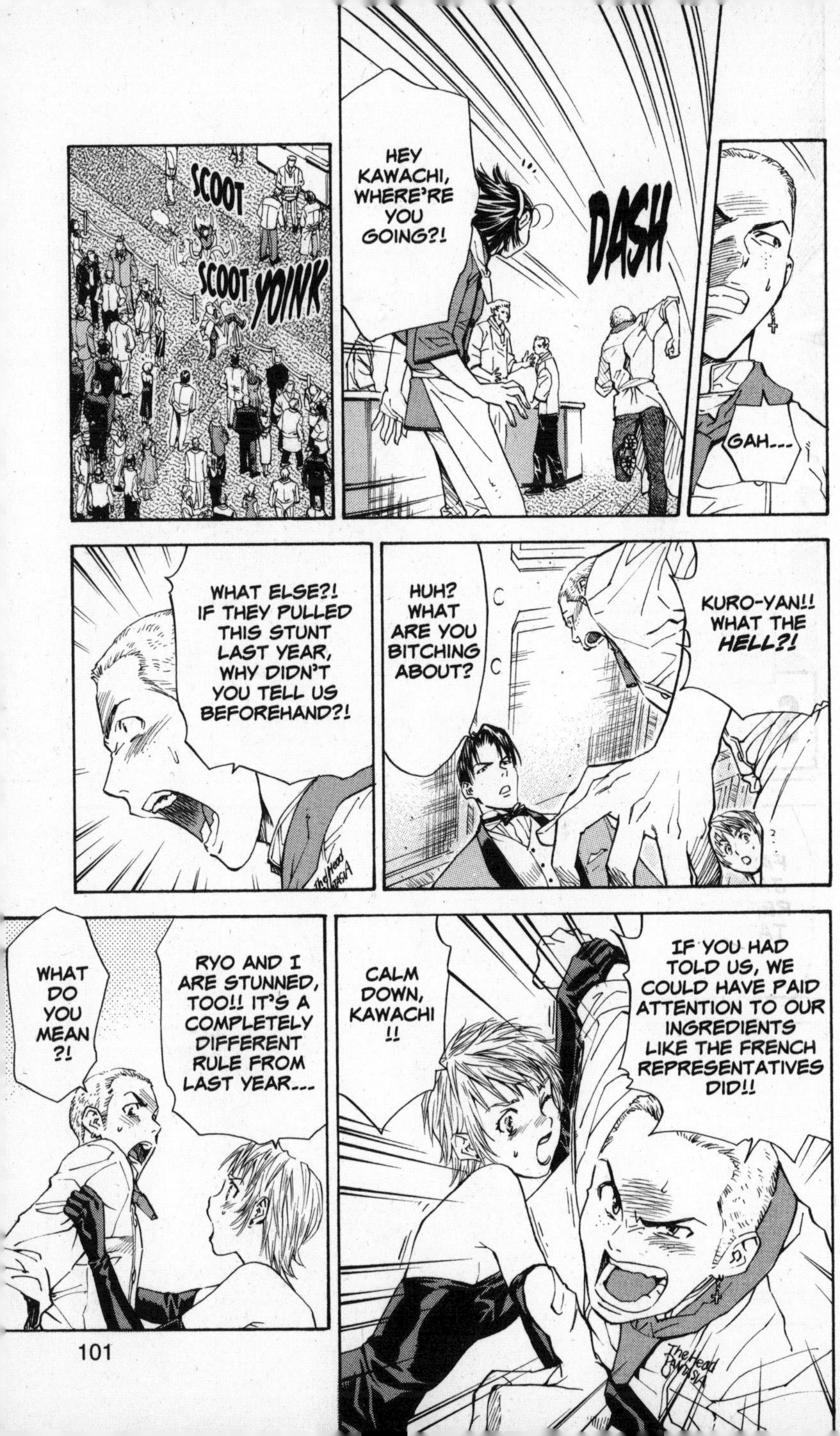
GAH...
HEY KAWACHI, WHERE'RE YOU GOING?!
DASH
SCOOT
SCOOT
YOINK
KURO-YAN!! WHAT THE HELL?!
HUH? WHAT ARE YOU BITCHING ABOUT?
WHAT ELSE?! IF THEY PULLED THIS STUNT LAST YEAR, WHY DIDN'T YOU TELL US BEFOREHAND?!
IF YOU HAD TOLD US, WE COULD HAVE PAID ATTENTION TO OUR INGREDIENTS LIKE THE FRENCH REPRESENTATIVES DID!!
CALM DOWN, KAWACHI!!
RYO AND I ARE STUNNED, TOO!! IT'S A COMPLETELY DIFFERENT RULE FROM LAST YEAR...
WHAT DO YOU MEAN?!

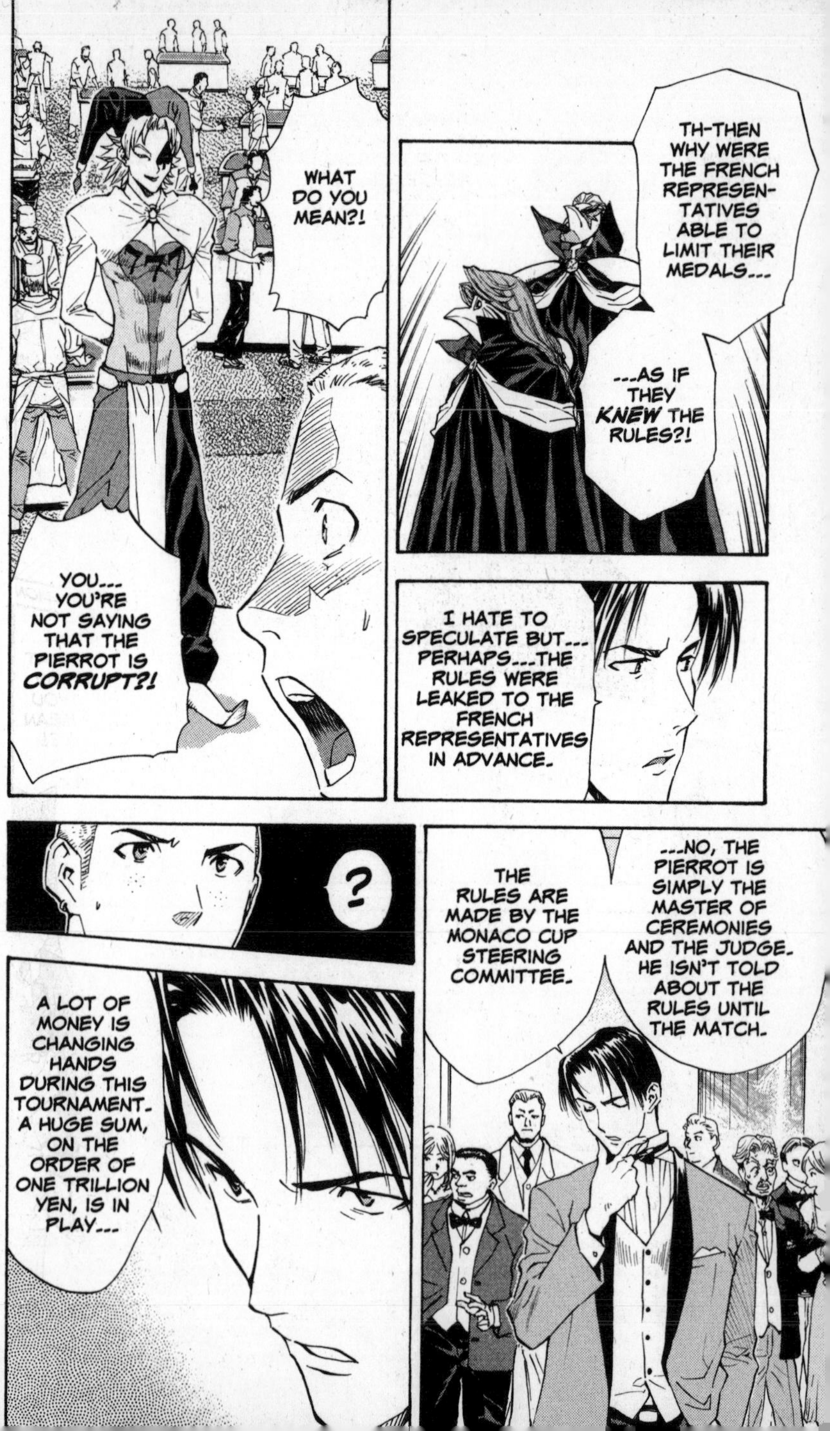
TH-THEN WHY WERE THE FRENCH REPRESEN-TATIVES ABLE TO LIMIT THEIR MEDALS...
...AS IF THEY *KNEW* THE RULES?!
I HATE TO SPECULATE BUT... PERHAPS...THE RULES WERE LEAKED TO THE FRENCH REPRESENTATIVES IN ADVANCE.
WHAT DO YOU MEAN?!
YOU... YOU'RE NOT SAYING THAT THE PIERROT IS *CORRUPT?!*
...NO, THE PIERROT IS SIMPLY THE MASTER OF CEREMONIES AND THE JUDGE. HE ISN'T TOLD ABOUT THE RULES UNTIL THE MATCH.
THE RULES ARE MADE BY THE MONACO CUP STEERING COMMITTEE.
?
A LOT OF MONEY IS CHANGING HANDS DURING THIS TOURNAMENT. A HUGE SUM, ON THE ORDER OF ONE TRILLION YEN, IS IN PLAY...

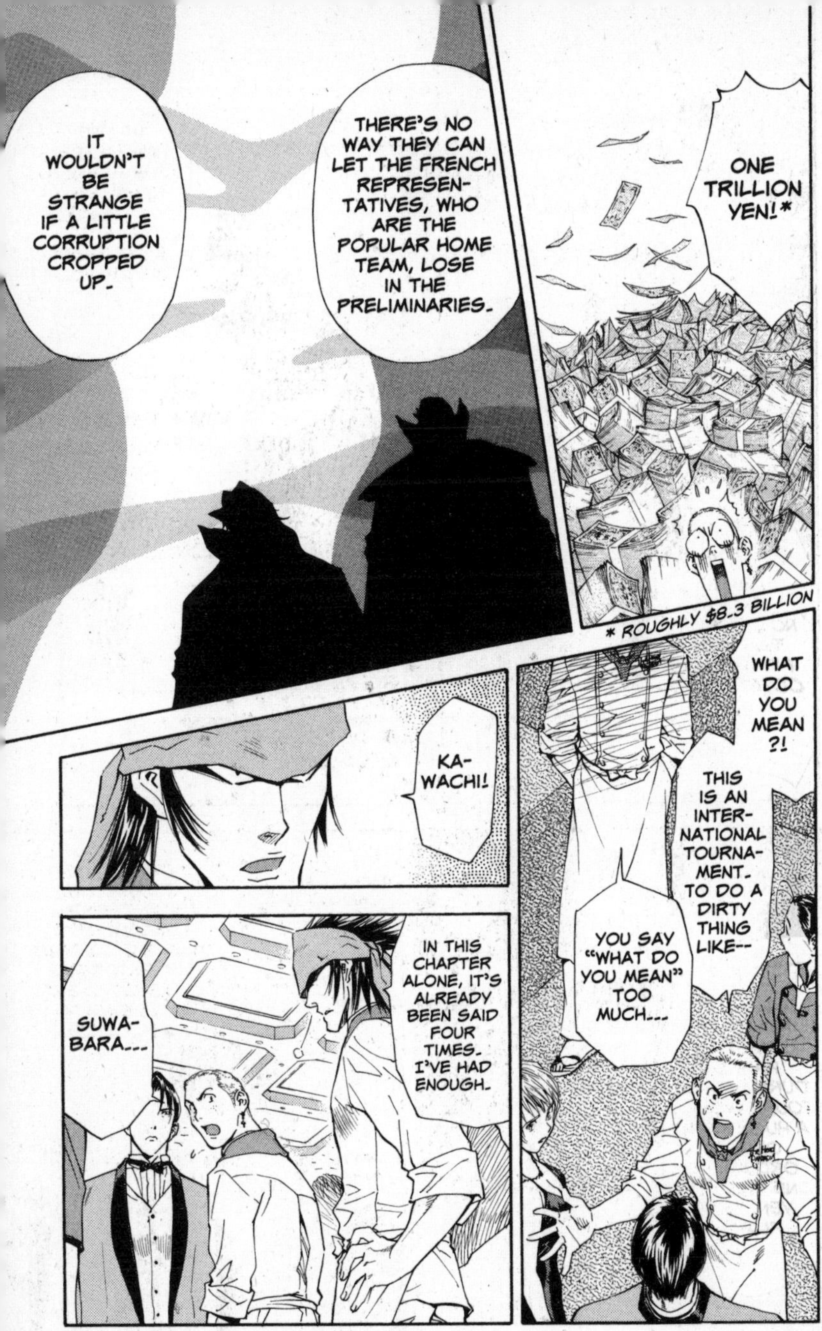
ONE TRILLION YEN!*
* ROUGHLY $8.3 BILLION
THERE'S NO WAY THEY CAN LET THE FRENCH REPRESEN-TATIVES, WHO ARE THE POPULAR HOME TEAM, LOSE IN THE PRELIMINARIES.
IT WOULDN'T BE STRANGE IF A LITTLE CORRUPTION CROPPED UP.
WHAT DO YOU MEAN?!
THIS IS AN INTER-NATIONAL TOURNA-MENT. TO DO A DIRTY THING LIKE--
YOU SAY "WHAT DO YOU MEAN" TOO MUCH...
KA-WACHI!
IN THIS CHAPTER ALONE, IT'S ALREADY BEEN SAID FOUR TIMES. I'VE HAD ENOUGH.
SUWA-BARA...

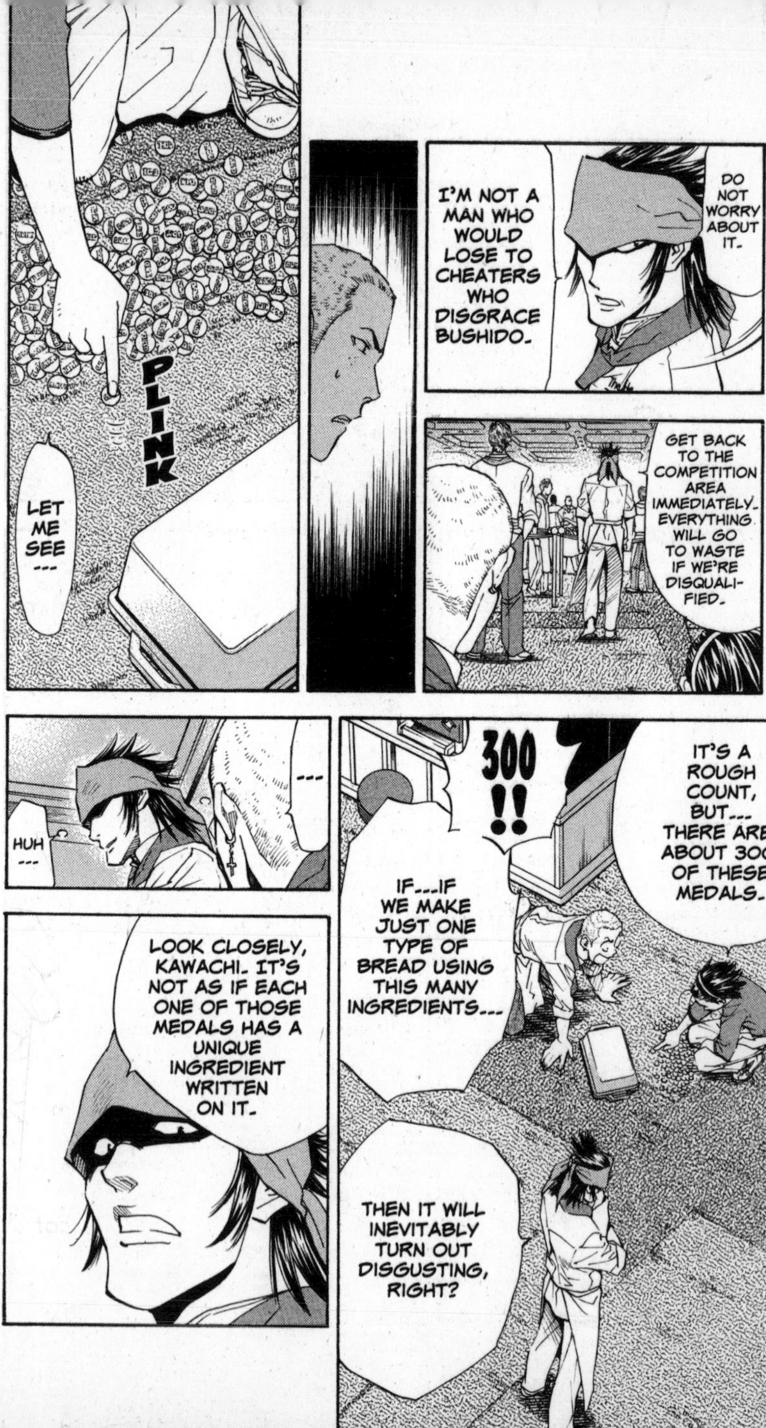
DO NOT WORRY ABOUT IT.
I'M NOT A MAN WHO WOULD LOSE TO CHEATERS WHO DISGRACE BUSHIDO.
GET BACK TO THE COMPETITION AREA IMMEDIATELY. EVERYTHING WILL GO TO WASTE IF WE'RE DISQUALIFIED.
PLINK
LET ME SEE...
IT'S A ROUGH COUNT, BUT... THERE ARE ABOUT 300 OF THESE MEDALS.
300!!
IF...IF WE MAKE JUST ONE TYPE OF BREAD USING THIS MANY INGREDIENTS...
THEN IT WILL INEVITABLY TURN OUT DISGUSTING, RIGHT?
...
HUH...
LOOK CLOSELY, KAWACHI. IT'S NOT AS IF EACH ONE OF THOSE MEDALS HAS A UNIQUE INGREDIENT WRITTEN ON IT.

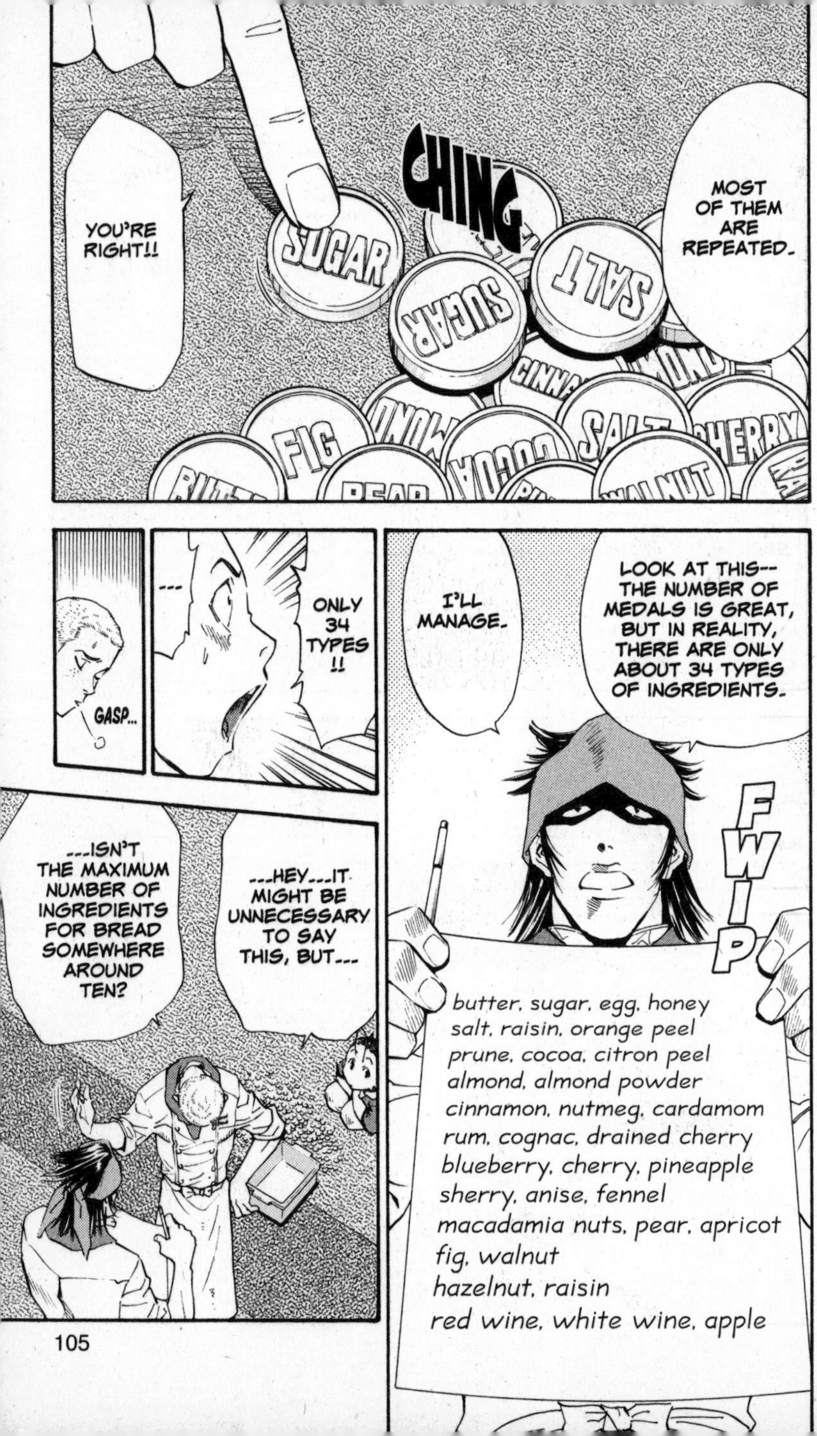
MOST OF THEM ARE REPEATED.
CHING
SUGAR
SALT
SUGAR
FIG
WALNUT
YOU'RE RIGHT!!
LOOK AT THIS-- THE NUMBER OF MEDALS IS GREAT, BUT IN REALITY, THERE ARE ONLY ABOUT 34 TYPES OF INGREDIENTS.
I'LL MANAGE.
FWIP
butter, sugar, egg, honey
salt, raisin, orange peel
prune, cocoa, citron peel
almond, almond powder
cinnamon, nutmeg, cardamom
rum, cognac, drained cherry
blueberry, cherry, pineapple
sherry, anise, fennel
macadamia nuts, pear, apricot
fig, walnut
hazelnut, raisin
red wine, white wine, apple
ONLY 34 TYPES!!
...
GASP...
...HEY...IT MIGHT BE UNNECESSARY TO SAY THIS, BUT...
...ISN'T THE MAXIMUM NUMBER OF INGREDIENTS FOR BREAD SOMEWHERE AROUND TEN?

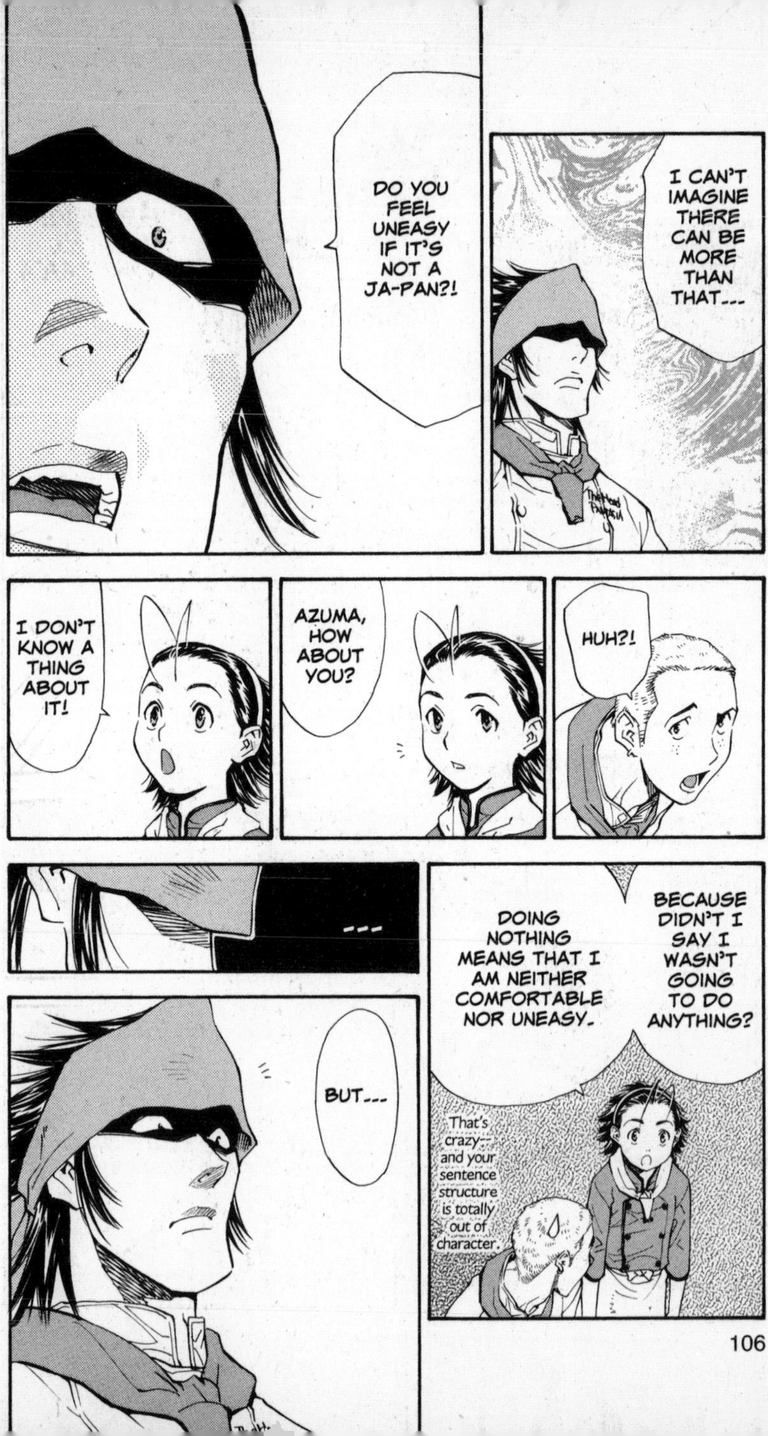
I CAN'T IMAGINE THERE CAN BE MORE THAN THAT...
DO YOU FEEL UNEASY IF IT'S NOT A JA-PAN?!
HUH?!
AZUMA, HOW ABOUT YOU?
I DON'T KNOW A THING ABOUT IT!
BECAUSE DIDN'T I SAY I WASN'T GOING TO DO ANYTHING?
DOING NOTHING MEANS THAT I AM NEITHER COMFORTABLE NOR UNEASY.
That's crazy-- and your sentence structure is totally out of character.
...
BUT...

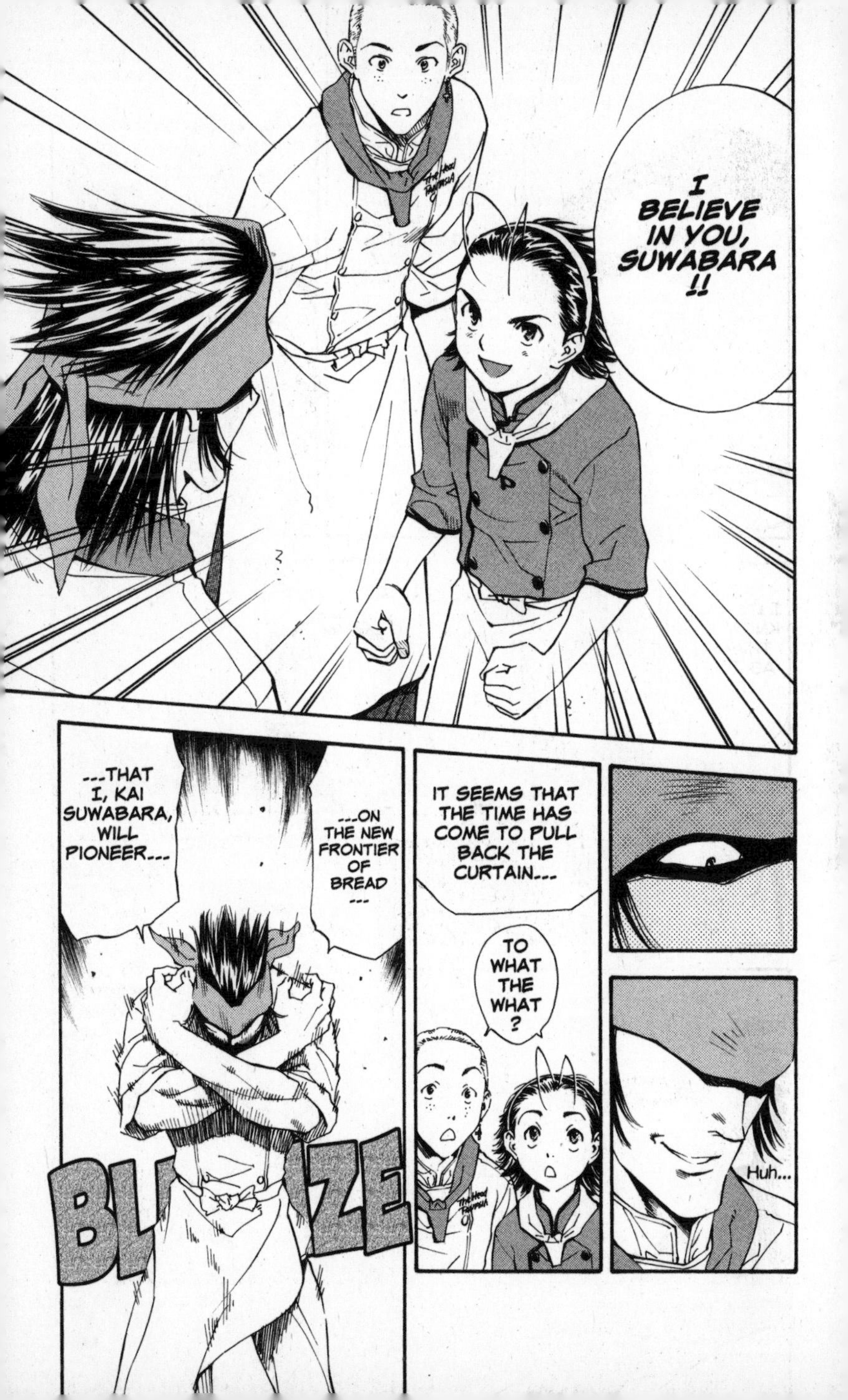
I BELIEVE IN YOU, SUWABARA !!
Huh...
IT SEEMS THAT THE TIME HAS COME TO PULL BACK THE CURTAIN...
TO WHAT THE WHAT ?
...ON THE NEW FRONTIER OF BREAD ---
...THAT I, KAI SUWABARA, WILL PIONEER...
BL ZE

LU-PAN!!

LU-PAN

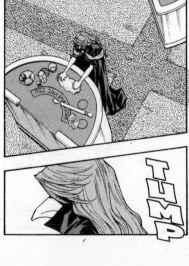

TUMP

LU...
LU-PAN
?!

What a weird name.

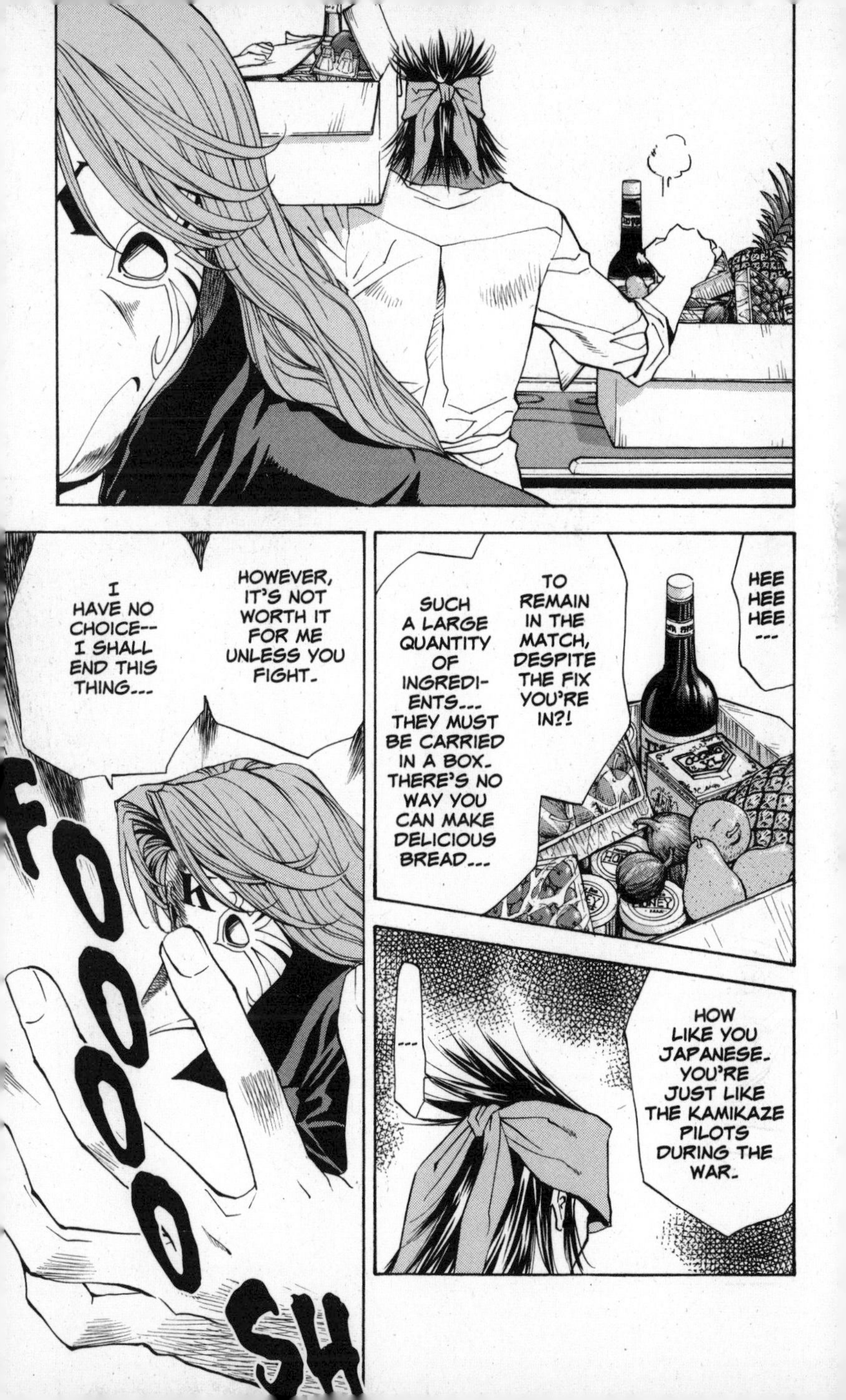
HEE HEE HEE---
TO REMAIN IN THE MATCH, DESPITE THE FIX YOU'RE IN?!
SUCH A LARGE QUANTITY OF INGREDI-ENTS--- THEY MUST BE CARRIED IN A BOX. THERE'S NO WAY YOU CAN MAKE DELICIOUS BREAD---
HOW LIKE YOU JAPANESE. YOU'RE JUST LIKE THE KAMIKAZE PILOTS DURING THE WAR.

HOWEVER, IT'S NOT WORTH IT FOR ME UNLESS YOU FIGHT.
I HAVE NO CHOICE-- I SHALL END THIS THING---
FOOOOOSH

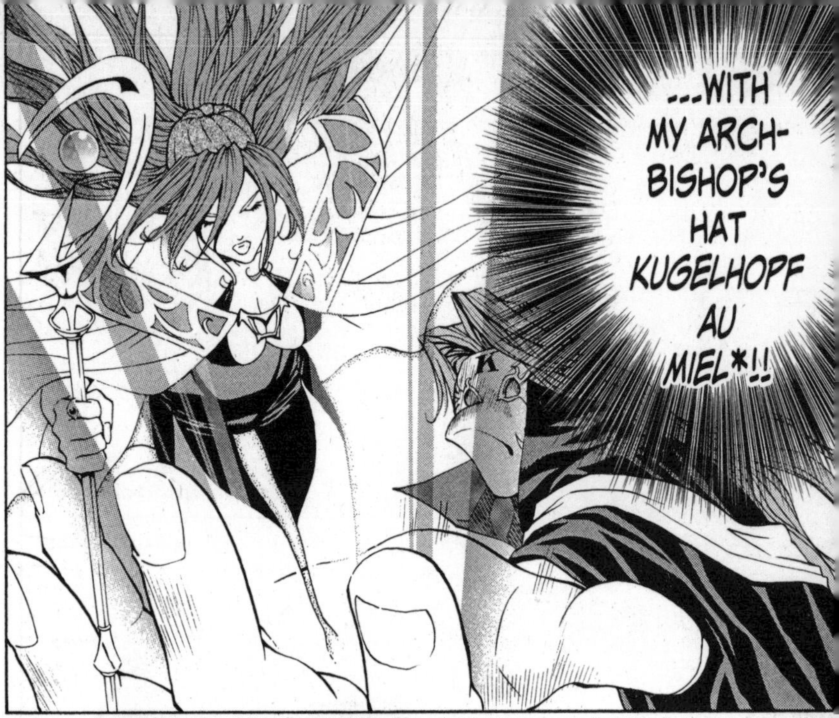
---WITH MY ARCH-BISHOP'S HAT KUGELHOPF AU MIEL*!!

* KUGELHOPF MEANS "ARCHBISHOP'S HAT." MIEL MEANS "HONEY."

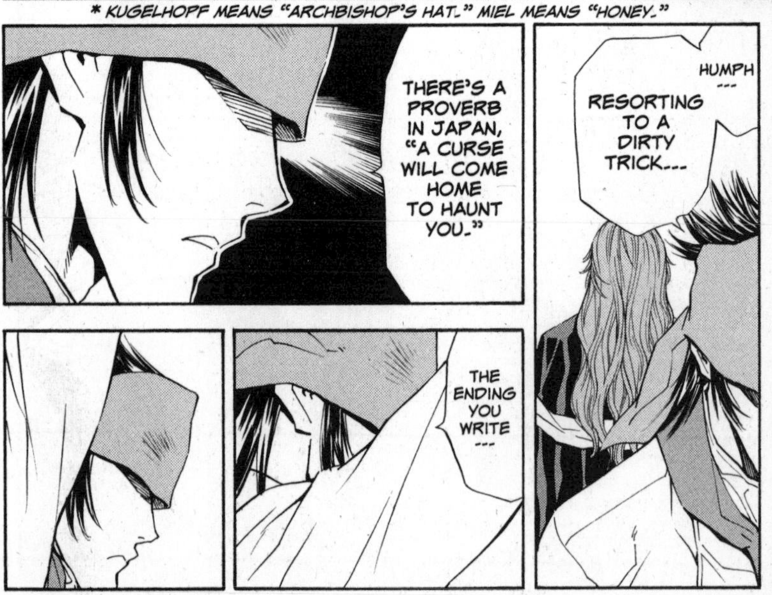
HUMPH ---
RESORTING TO A DIRTY TRICK---
THERE'S A PROVERB IN JAPAN, "A CURSE WILL COME HOME TO HAUNT YOU."
THE ENDING YOU WRITE ---

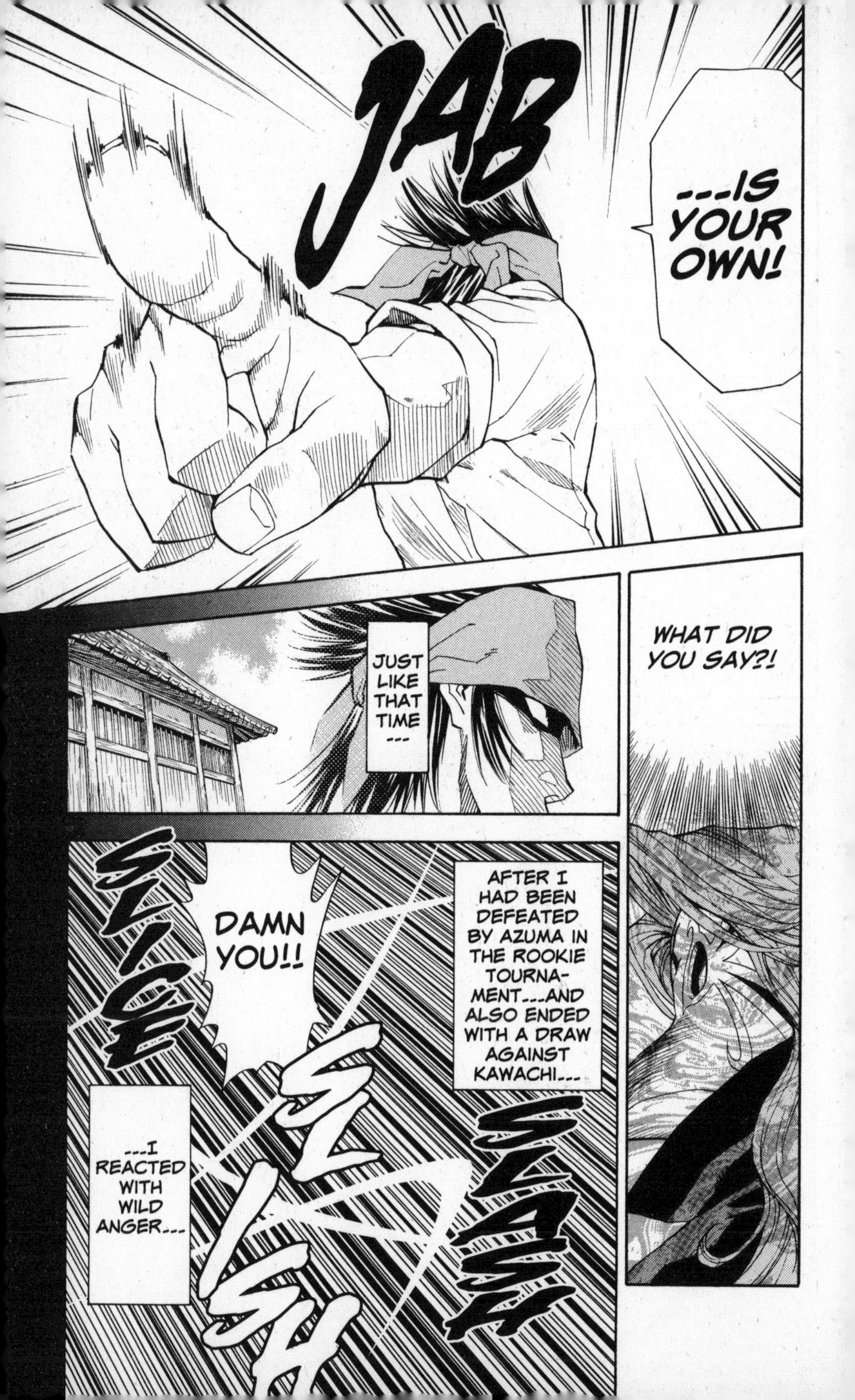
---IS YOUR OWN!
JAB
WHAT DID YOU SAY?!
JUST LIKE THAT TIME ---
AFTER I HAD BEEN DEFEATED BY AZUMA IN THE ROOKIE TOURNA-MENT---AND ALSO ENDED WITH A DRAW AGAINST KAWACHI---
DAMN YOU!!
SLASH
SLICE
---I REACTED WITH WILD ANGER---

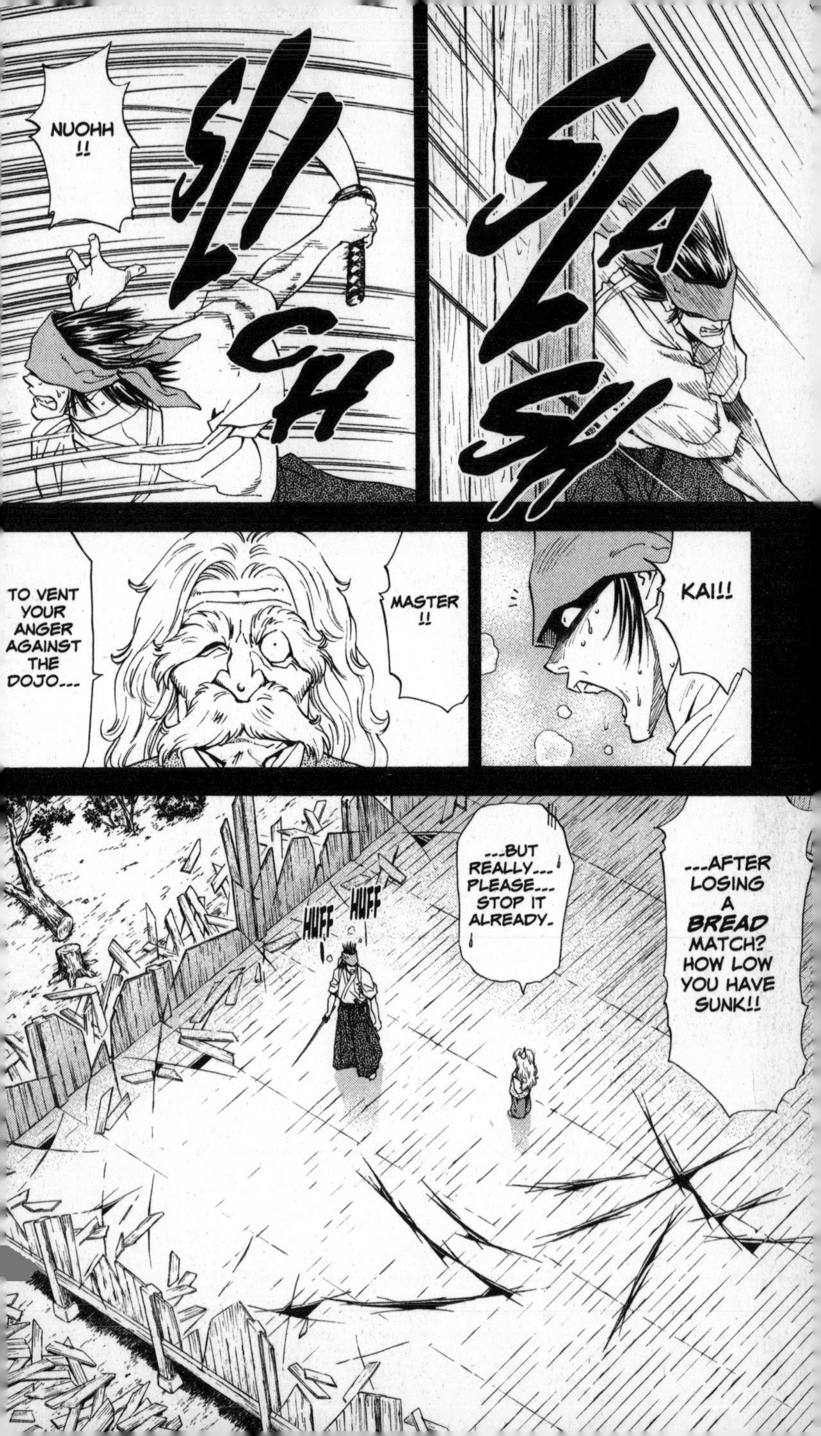
SLASH
SLICH
NUOHH!!
KAI!!
MASTER!!
TO VENT YOUR ANGER AGAINST THE DOJO...
...AFTER LOSING A BREAD MATCH? HOW LOW YOU HAVE SUNK!!
...BUT REALLY... PLEASE... STOP IT ALREADY.
HUFF
HUFF

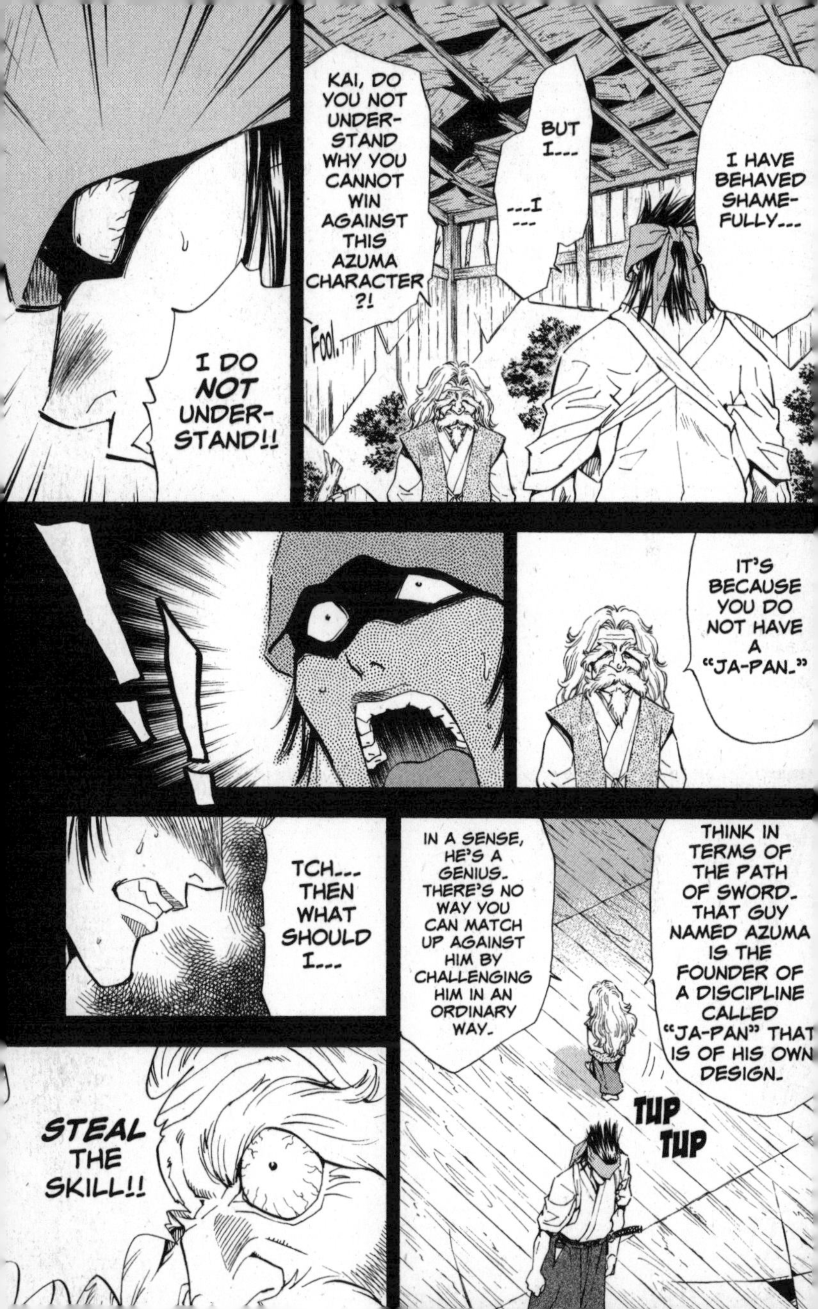
I HAVE BEHAVED SHAMEFULLY...
BUT I...
...I ...
KAI, DO YOU NOT UNDERSTAND WHY YOU CANNOT WIN AGAINST THIS AZUMA CHARACTER?!
Fool.
I DO NOT UNDERSTAND!!
IT'S BECAUSE YOU DO NOT HAVE A "JA-PAN."
!
THINK IN TERMS OF THE PATH OF SWORD. THAT GUY NAMED AZUMA IS THE FOUNDER OF A DISCIPLINE CALLED "JA-PAN" THAT IS OF HIS OWN DESIGN.
IN A SENSE, HE'S A GENIUS. THERE'S NO WAY YOU CAN MATCH UP AGAINST HIM BY CHALLENGING HIM IN AN ORDINARY WAY.
TUP TUP
TCH... THEN WHAT SHOULD I...
STEAL THE SKILL!!

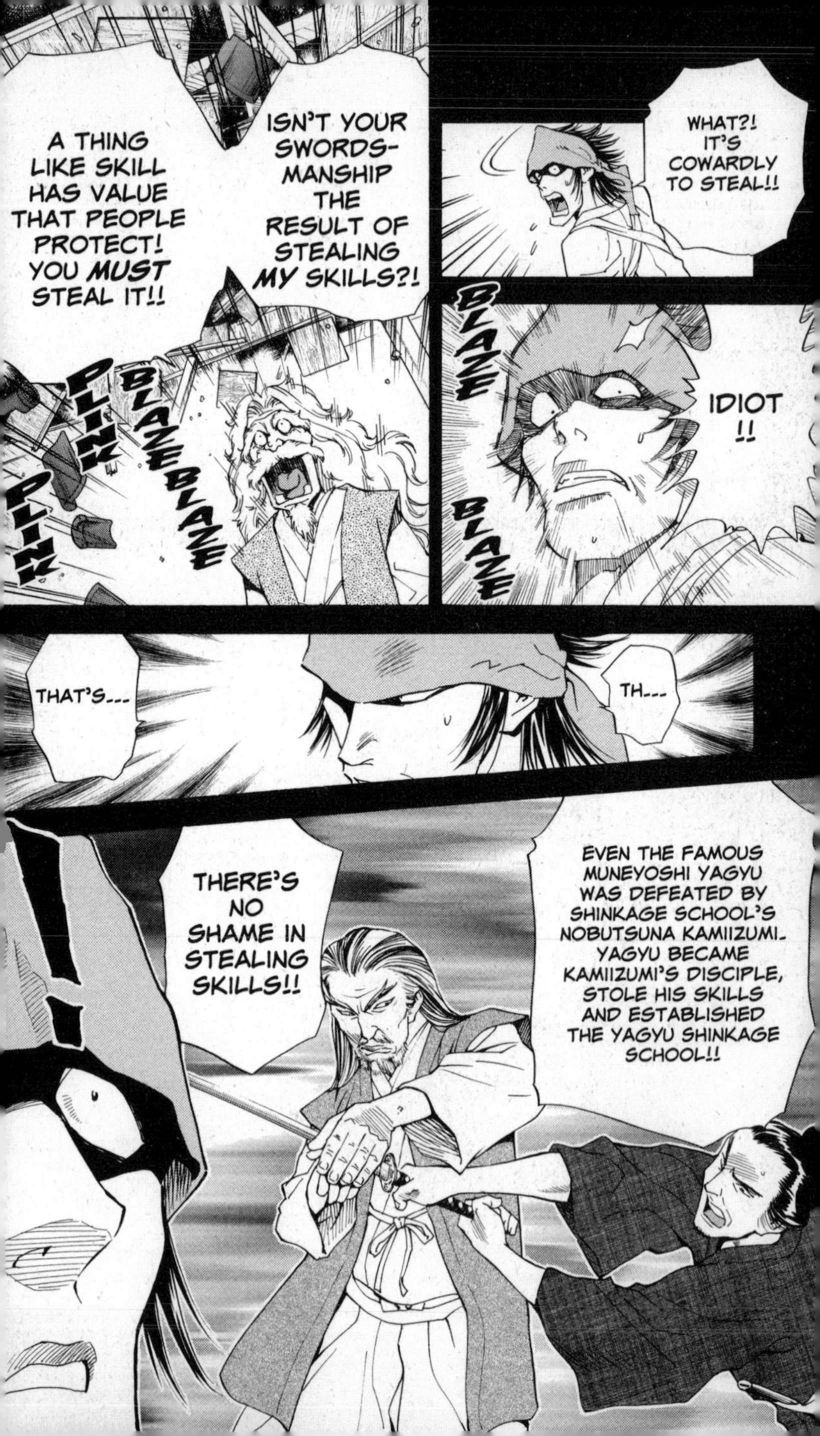
WHAT?! IT'S COWARDLY TO STEAL!!
BLAZE
IDIOT !!
BLAZE
ISN'T YOUR SWORDS-MANSHIP THE RESULT OF STEALING MY SKILLS?!
A THING LIKE SKILL HAS VALUE THAT PEOPLE PROTECT! YOU MUST STEAL IT!!
BLAZE BLAZE
PLINK
PLINK
TH---
THAT'S---
EVEN THE FAMOUS MUNEYOSHI YAGYU WAS DEFEATED BY SHINKAGE SCHOOL'S NOBUTSUNA KAMIIZUMI. YAGYU BECAME KAMIIZUMI'S DISCIPLE, STOLE HIS SKILLS AND ESTABLISHED THE YAGYU SHINKAGE SCHOOL!!
THERE'S NO SHAME IN STEALING SKILLS!!
!!

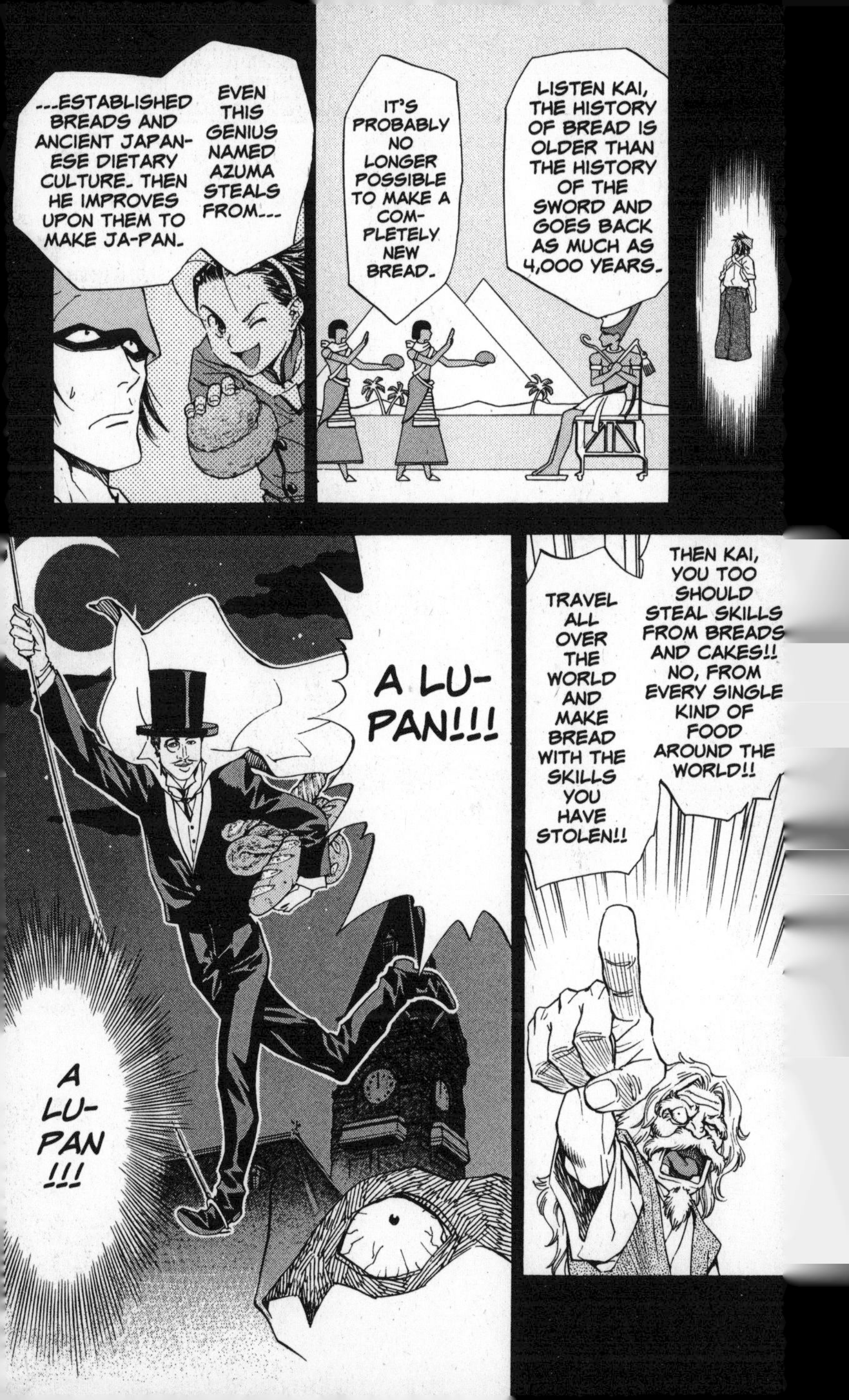
LISTEN KAI, THE HISTORY OF BREAD IS OLDER THAN THE HISTORY OF THE SWORD AND GOES BACK AS MUCH AS 4,000 YEARS.
IT'S PROBABLY NO LONGER POSSIBLE TO MAKE A COM-PLETELY NEW BREAD.
EVEN THIS GENIUS NAMED AZUMA STEALS FROM...
...ESTABLISHED BREADS AND ANCIENT JAPAN-ESE DIETARY CULTURE. THEN HE IMPROVES UPON THEM TO MAKE JA-PAN.
THEN KAI, YOU TOO SHOULD STEAL SKILLS FROM BREADS AND CAKES!! NO, FROM EVERY SINGLE KIND OF FOOD AROUND THE WORLD!!
TRAVEL ALL OVER THE WORLD AND MAKE BREAD WITH THE SKILLS YOU HAVE STOLEN!!
A LU-PAN!!!
A LU-PAN!!!

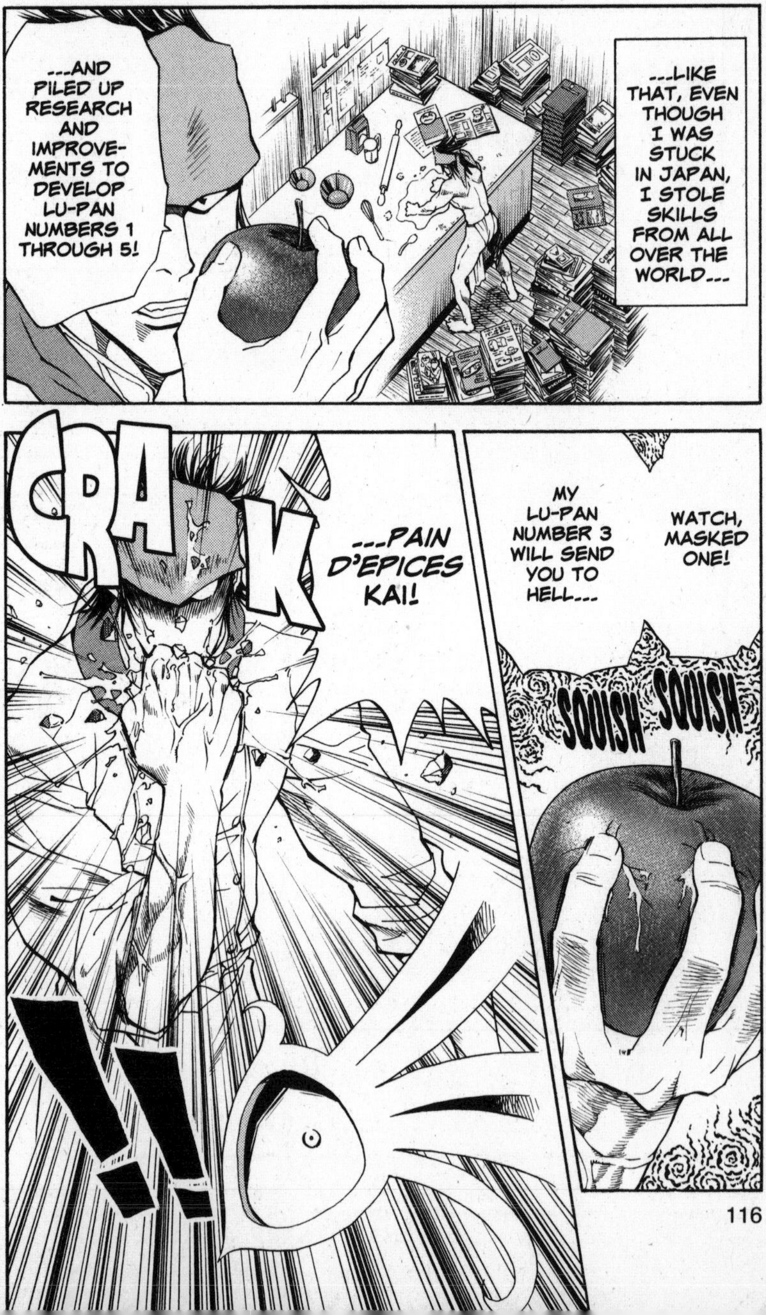
...LIKE THAT, EVEN THOUGH I WAS STUCK IN JAPAN, I STOLE SKILLS FROM ALL OVER THE WORLD...
...AND PILED UP RESEARCH AND IMPROVEMENTS TO DEVELOP LU-PAN NUMBERS 1 THROUGH 5!
WATCH, MASKED ONE!
MY LU-PAN NUMBER 3 WILL SEND YOU TO HELL...
SQUISH SQUISH
...PAIN D'EPICES KAI!
CRA K
!!!

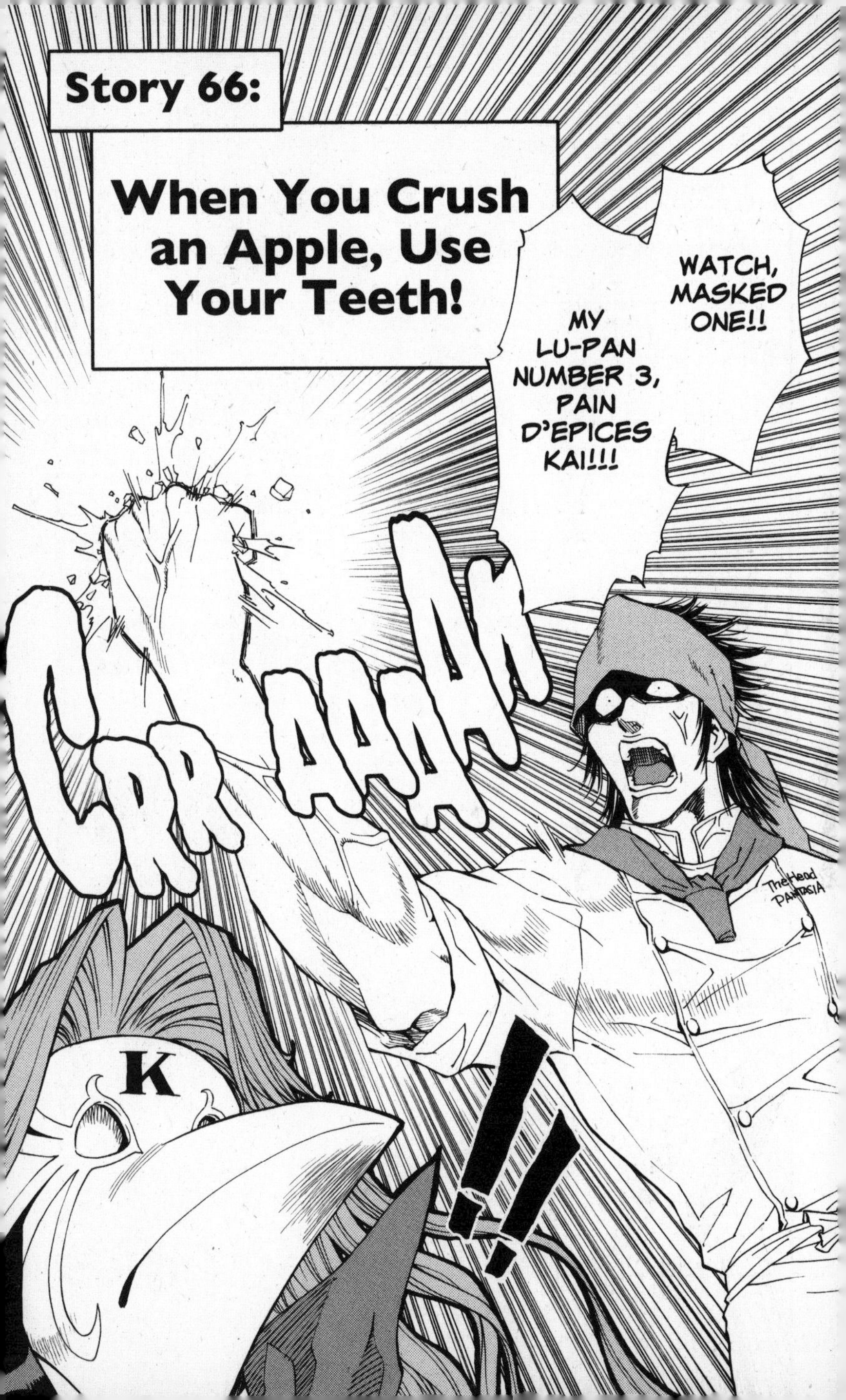
Story 66:
When You Crush an Apple, Use Your Teeth!
WATCH, MASKED ONE!!
MY LU-PAN NUMBER 3, PAIN D'EPICES KAI!!!
CRRAAAAK
The Head PANTASIA
K
!!

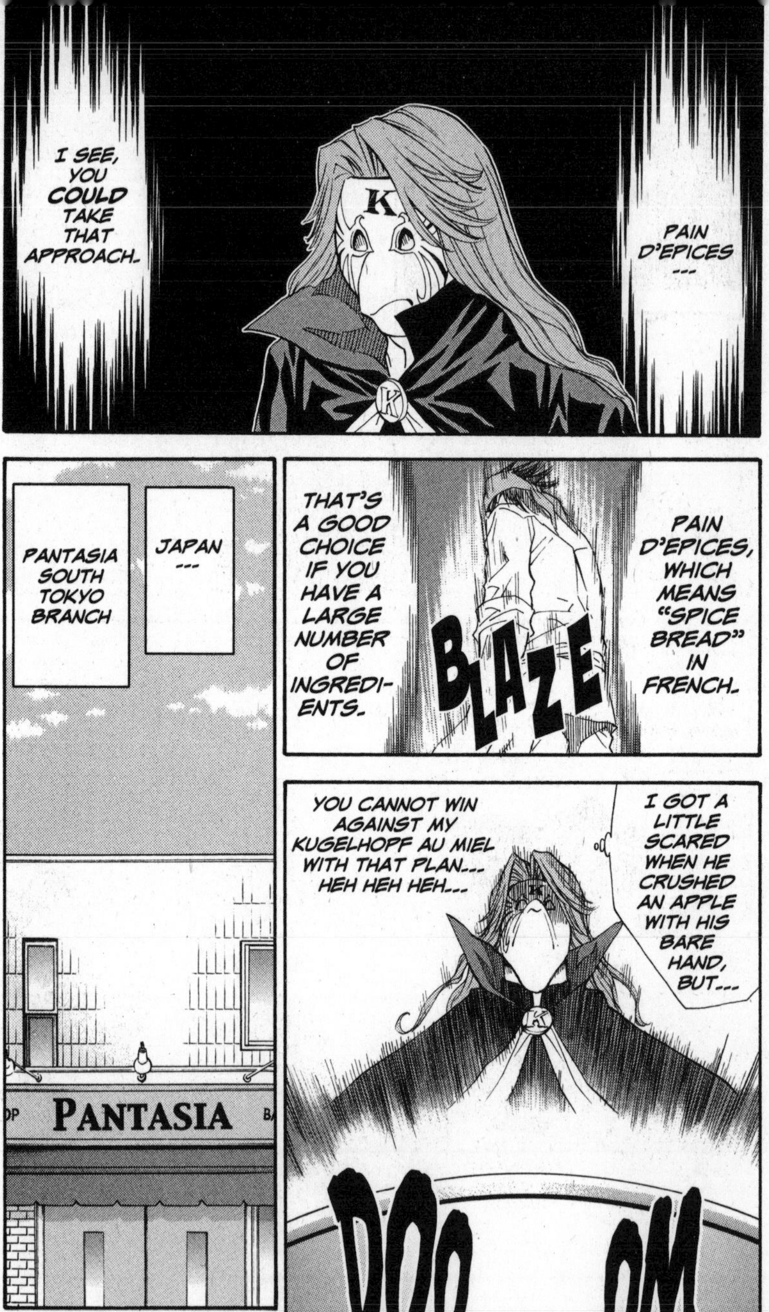
PAIN D'EPICES ---
I SEE, YOU COULD TAKE THAT APPROACH.
PAIN D'EPICES, WHICH MEANS "SPICE BREAD" IN FRENCH.
BLAZE
THAT'S A GOOD CHOICE IF YOU HAVE A LARGE NUMBER OF INGREDI-ENTS.
I GOT A LITTLE SCARED WHEN HE CRUSHED AN APPLE WITH HIS BARE HAND, BUT...
YOU CANNOT WIN AGAINST MY KUGELHOPF AU MIEL WITH THAT PLAN... HEH HEH HEH...
DOO OM
JAPAN ---
PANTASIA SOUTH TOKYO BRANCH
PANTASIA

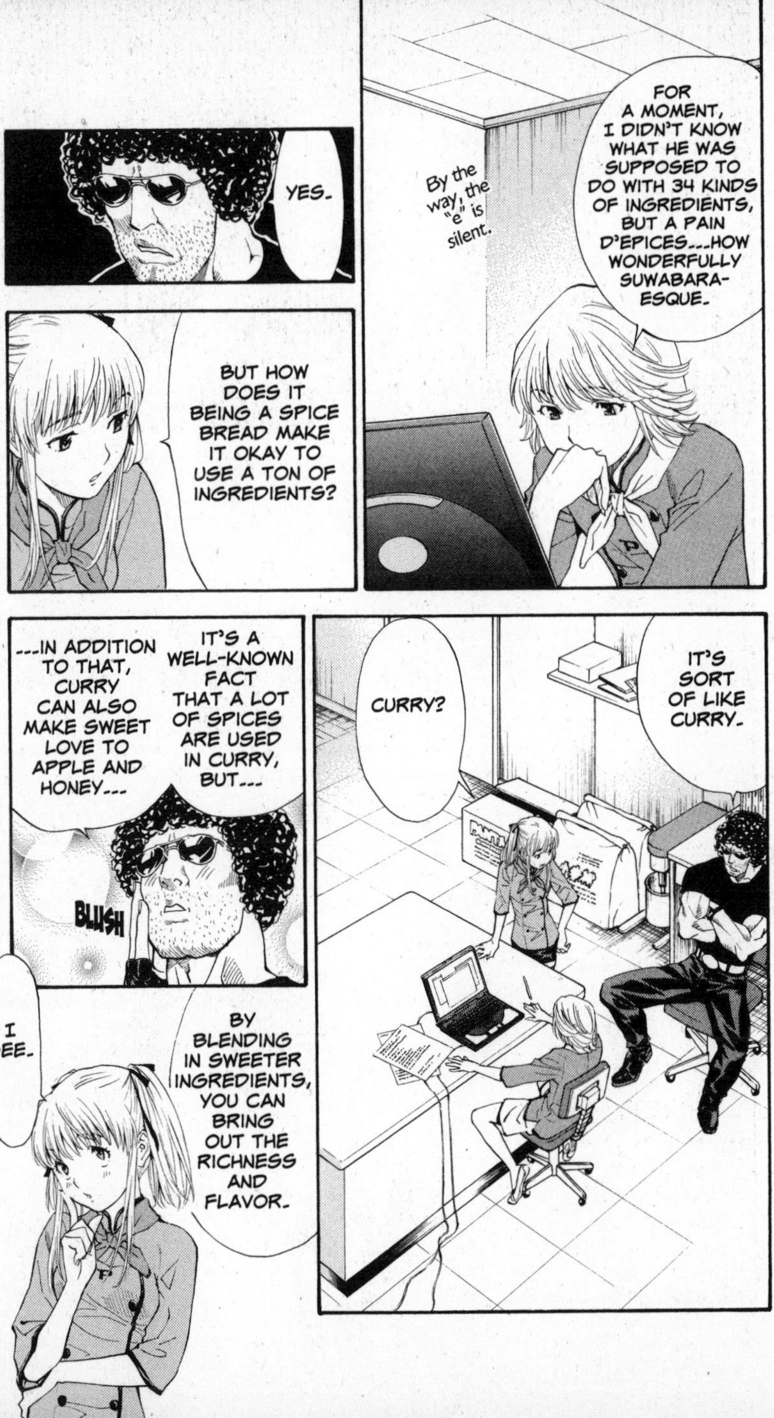
FOR A MOMENT, I DIDN'T KNOW WHAT HE WAS SUPPOSED TO DO WITH 34 KINDS OF INGREDIENTS, BUT A PAIN D'EPICES...HOW WONDERFULLY SUWABARA-ESQUE.
By the way, the "e" is silent.
YES.
BUT HOW DOES IT BEING A SPICE BREAD MAKE IT OKAY TO USE A TON OF INGREDIENTS?
IT'S SORT OF LIKE CURRY.
CURRY?
IT'S A WELL-KNOWN FACT THAT A LOT OF SPICES ARE USED IN CURRY, BUT...
...IN ADDITION TO THAT, CURRY CAN ALSO MAKE SWEET LOVE TO APPLE AND HONEY...
BLUSH
BY BLENDING IN SWEETER INGREDIENTS, YOU CAN BRING OUT THE RICHNESS AND FLAVOR.
I SEE.

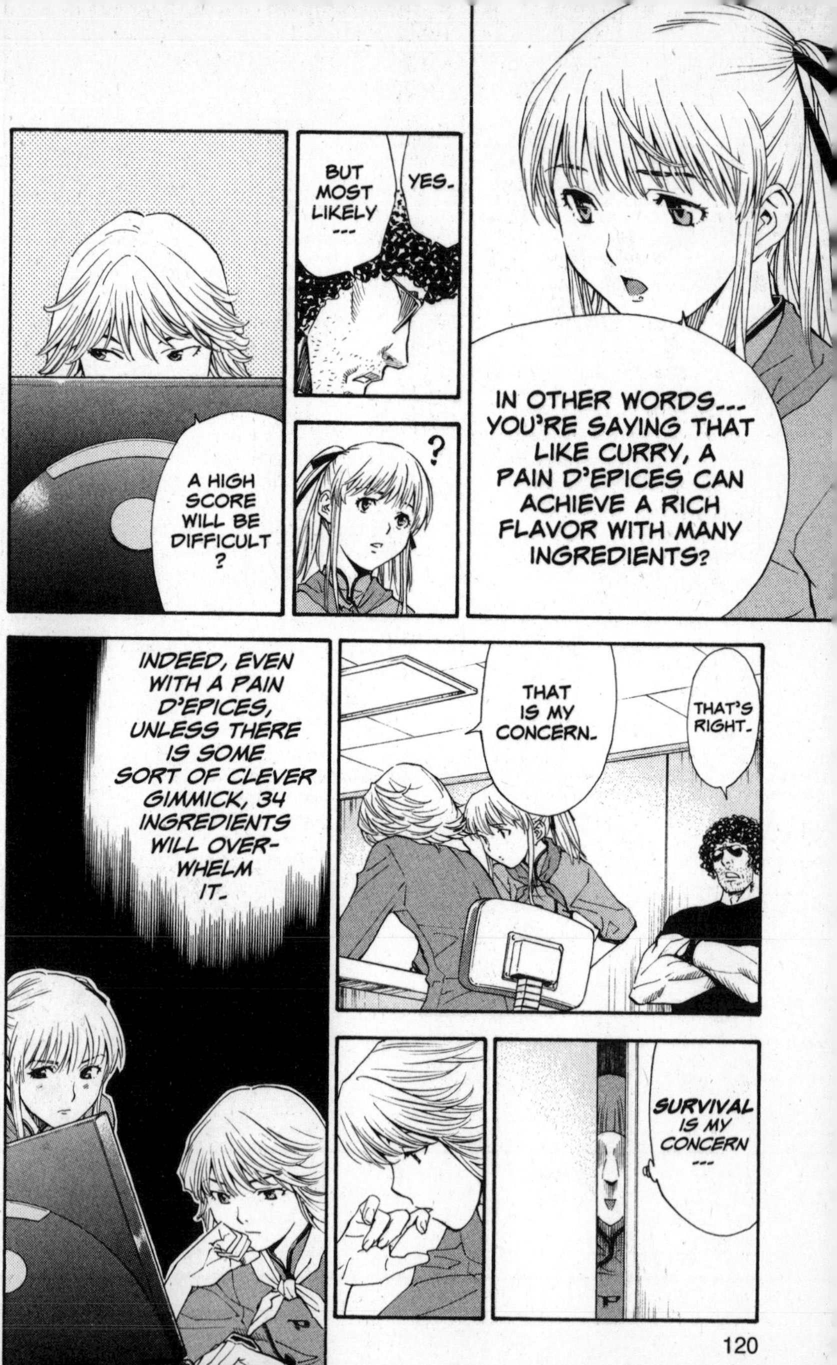
IN OTHER WORDS... YOU'RE SAYING THAT LIKE CURRY, A PAIN D'EPICES CAN ACHIEVE A RICH FLAVOR WITH MANY INGREDIENTS?
YES.
BUT MOST LIKELY...
?
A HIGH SCORE WILL BE DIFFICULT?
THAT'S RIGHT.
THAT IS MY CONCERN.
SURVIVAL IS MY CONCERN...
INDEED, EVEN WITH A PAIN D'EPICES, UNLESS THERE IS SOME SORT OF CLEVER GIMMICK, 34 INGREDIENTS WILL OVER-WHELM IT.

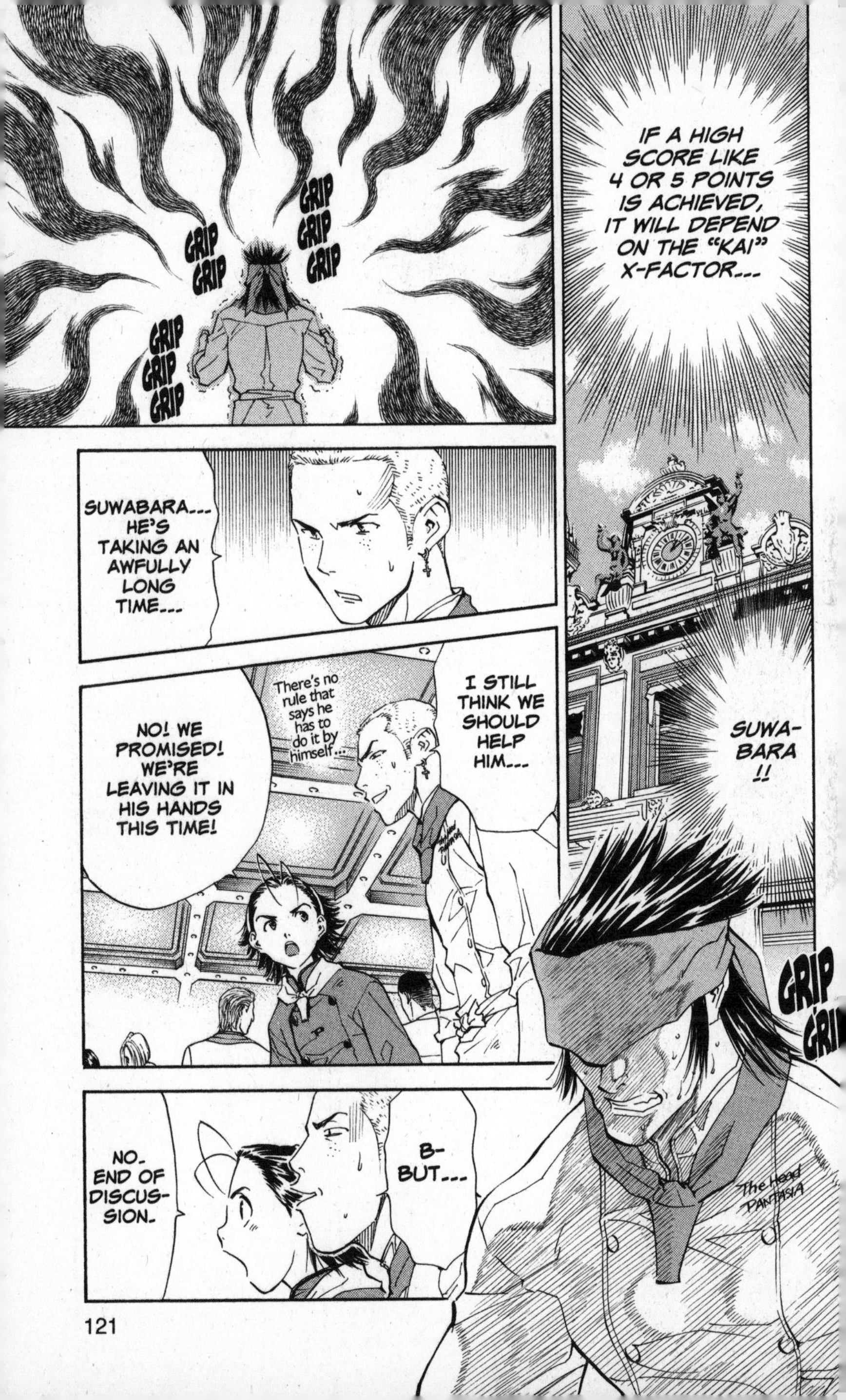
IF A HIGH SCORE LIKE 4 OR 5 POINTS IS ACHIEVED, IT WILL DEPEND ON THE "KAI" X-FACTOR...
SUWA-BARA !!
GRIP GRI
The Head PANTASIA
GRIP GRIP GRIP
GRIP GRIP
GRIP GRIP GRIP
SUWABARA... HE'S TAKING AN AWFULLY LONG TIME...
I STILL THINK WE SHOULD HELP HIM...
There's no rule that says he has to do it by himself...
NO! WE PROMISED! WE'RE LEAVING IT IN HIS HANDS THIS TIME!
B-BUT...
NO. END OF DISCUSSION.

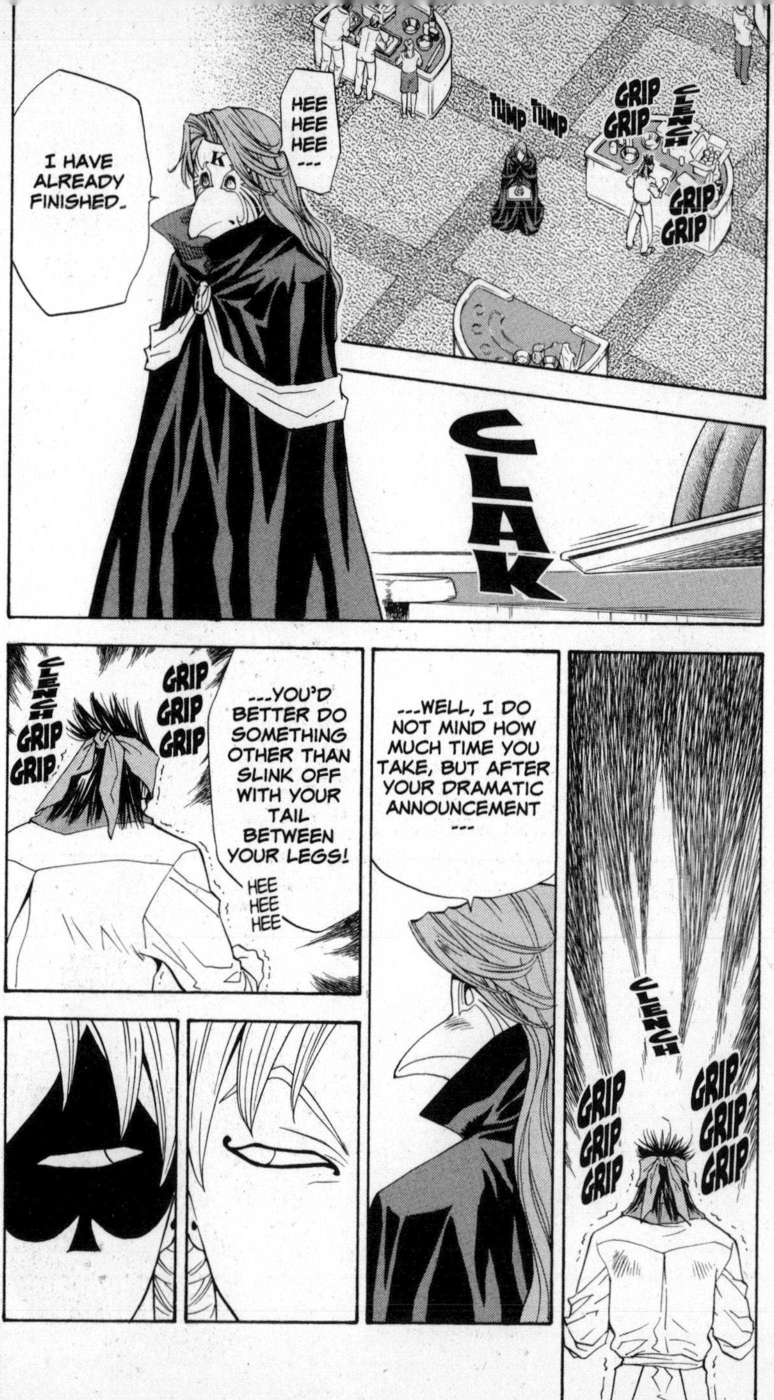
GRIP GRIP
CLENCH
GRIP GRIP
TUMP TUMP
HEE HEE HEE ---
I HAVE ALREADY FINISHED.
CLAK
CLENCH
GRIP GRIP GRIP
GRIP GRIP GRIP
---WELL, I DO NOT MIND HOW MUCH TIME YOU TAKE, BUT AFTER YOUR DRAMATIC ANNOUNCEMENT ---
GRIP GRIP GRIP
CLENCH
GRIP GRIP
---YOU'D BETTER DO SOMETHING OTHER THAN SLINK OFF WITH YOUR TAIL BETWEEN YOUR LEGS!
HEE HEE HEE

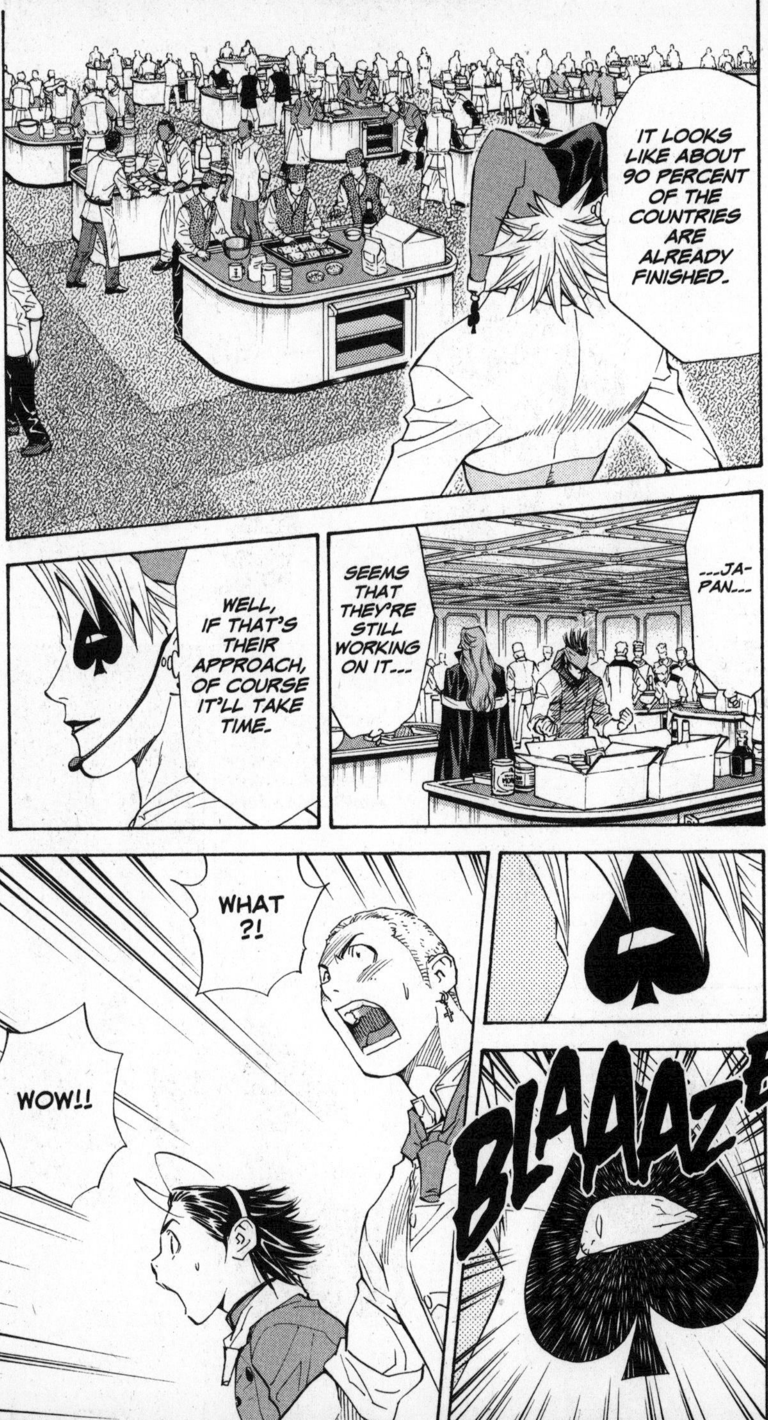
IT LOOKS LIKE ABOUT 90 PERCENT OF THE COUNTRIES ARE ALREADY FINISHED.
---JA-PAN---
SEEMS THAT THEY'RE STILL WORKING ON IT---
WELL, IF THAT'S THEIR APPROACH, OF COURSE IT'LL TAKE TIME.
BLAAAZE
WHAT ?!
WOW!!

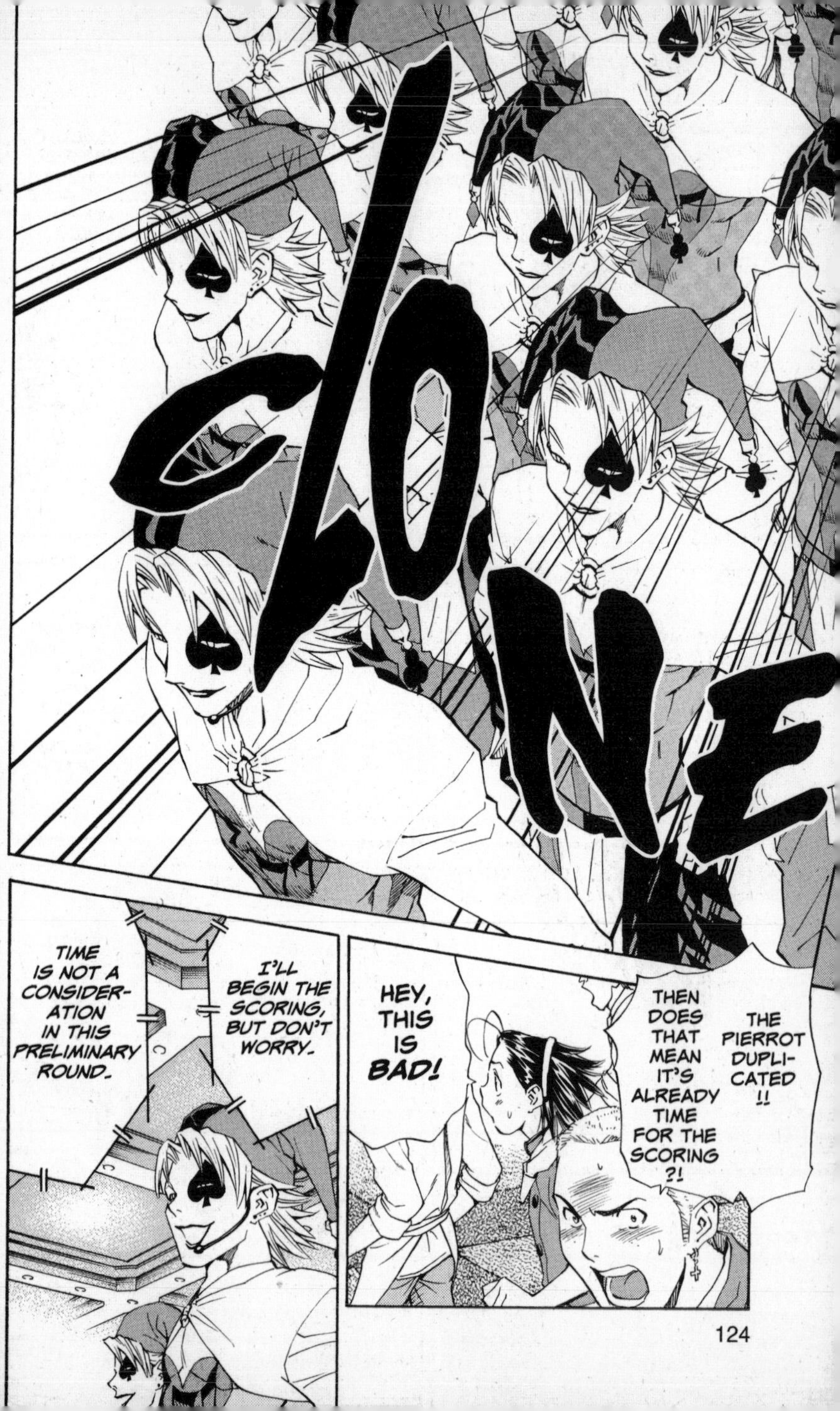
CLONE
THE PIERROT DUPLICATED!!
THEN DOES THAT MEAN IT'S ALREADY TIME FOR THE SCORING?!
HEY, THIS IS BAD!
I'LL BEGIN THE SCORING, BUT DON'T WORRY.
TIME IS NOT A CONSIDERATION IN THIS PRELIMINARY ROUND.

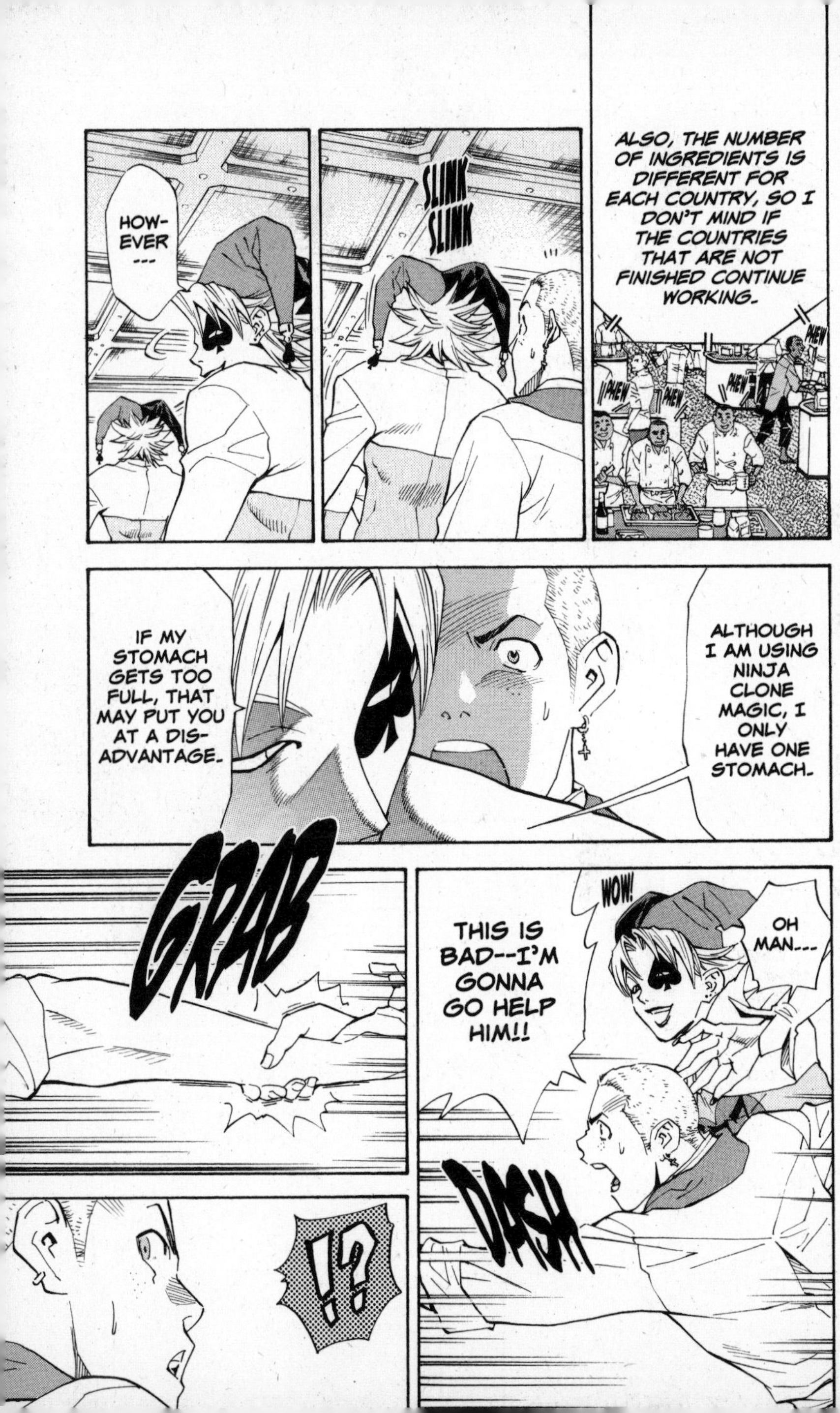

ALSO, THE NUMBER OF INGREDIENTS IS DIFFERENT FOR EACH COUNTRY, SO I DON'T MIND IF THE COUNTRIES THAT ARE NOT FINISHED CONTINUE WORKING.
PHEW
PHEW
PHEW
PHEW
SLINK SLINK
HOW-EVER...
ALTHOUGH I AM USING NINJA CLONE MAGIC, I ONLY HAVE ONE STOMACH.
IF MY STOMACH GETS TOO FULL, THAT MAY PUT YOU AT A DIS-ADVANTAGE.
OH MAN...
WOW!
THIS IS BAD--I'M GONNA GO HELP HIM!!
DASH
GRAB
!?

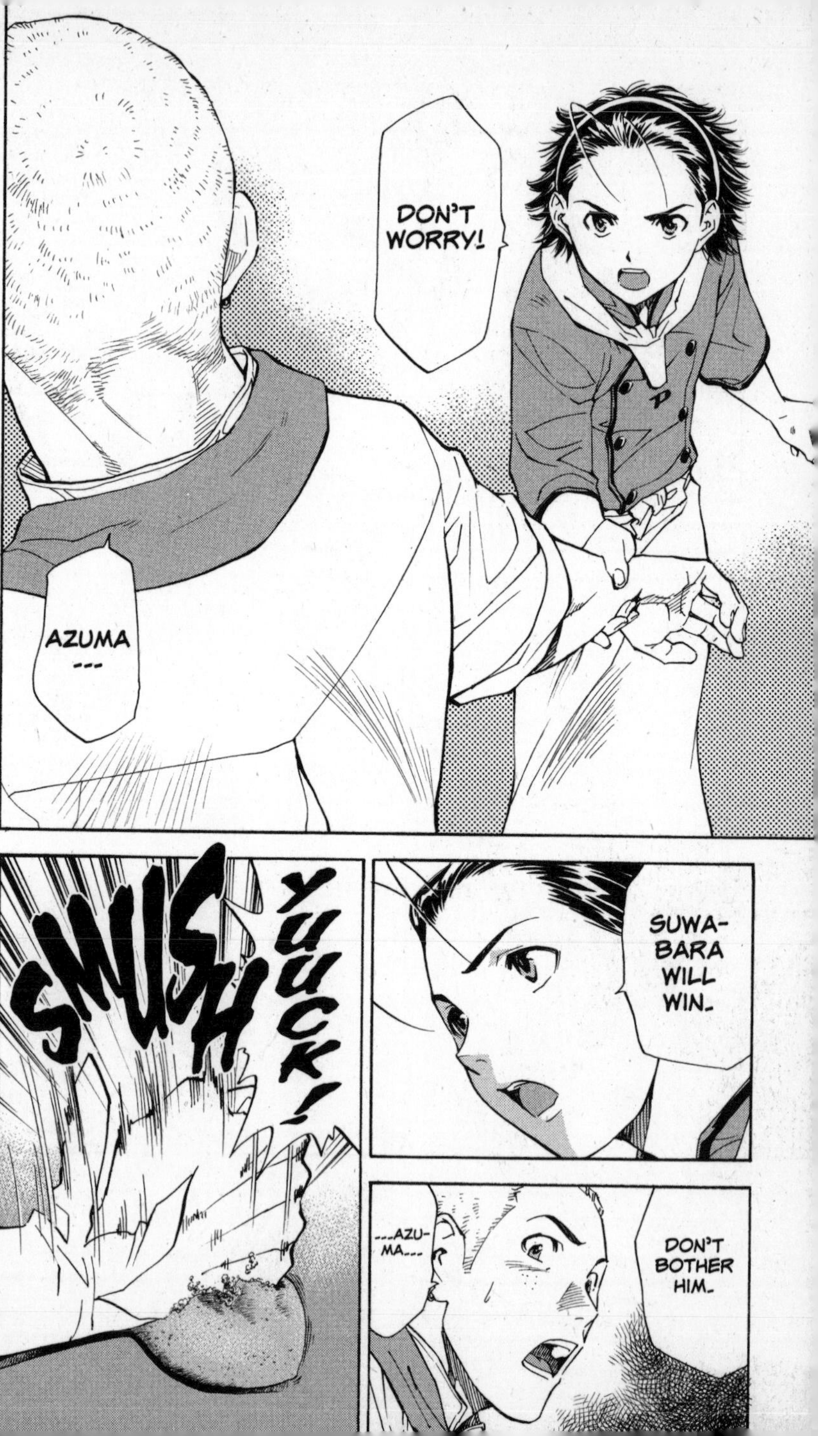
DON'T WORRY!
AZUMA...
SUWA-BARA WILL WIN.
DON'T BOTHER HIM.
...AZU-MA...
YUUCK!
SMUSH

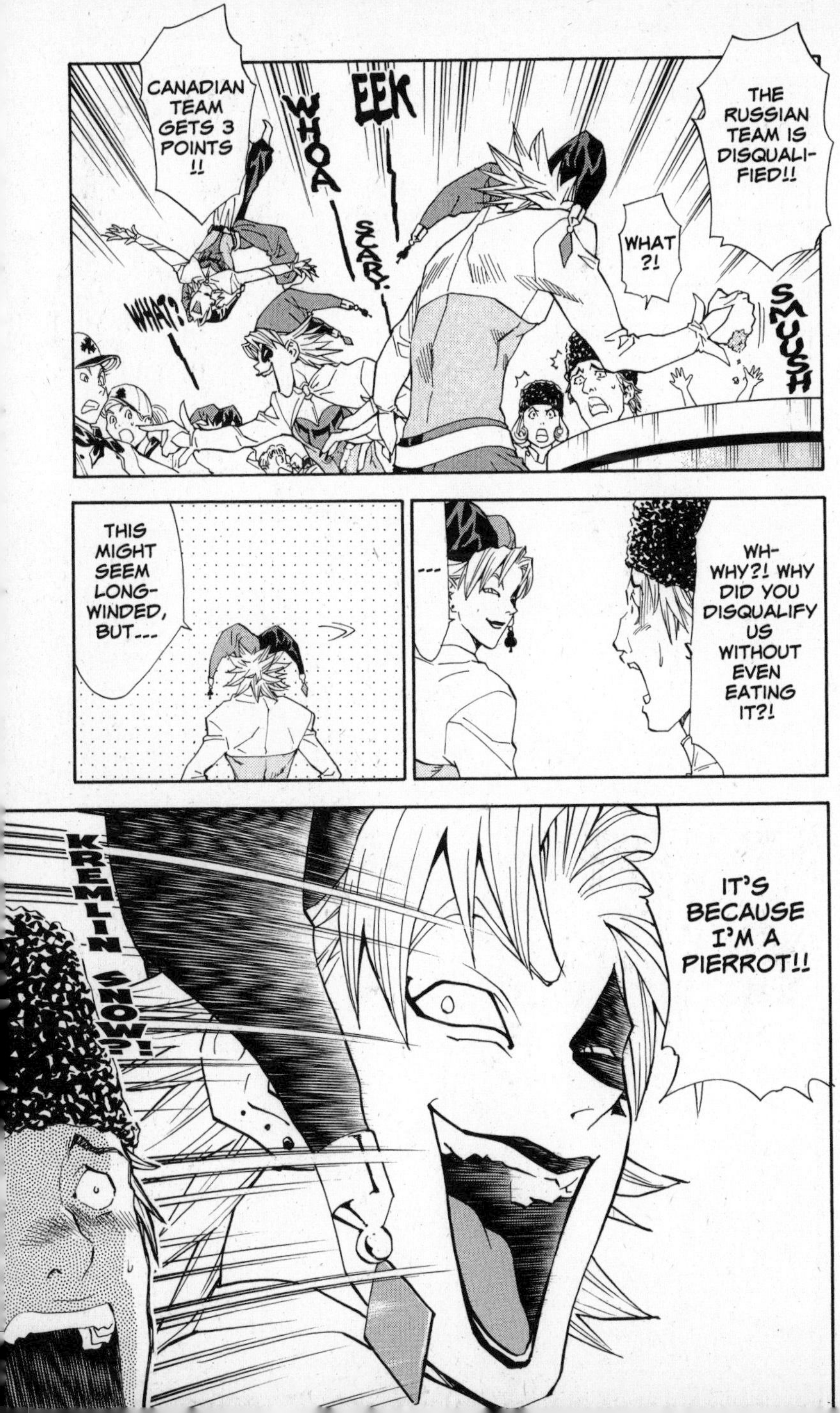
THE RUSSIAN TEAM IS DISQUALIFIED!!
EEK
CANADIAN TEAM GETS 3 POINTS!!
WHOA
SCARY
WHAT?!
SMUSH
WHAT?
WH- WHY?! WHY DID YOU DISQUALIFY US WITHOUT EVEN EATING IT?!
...
THIS MIGHT SEEM LONG-WINDED, BUT...
IT'S BECAUSE I'M A PIERROT!!
KREMLIN SNOW?!

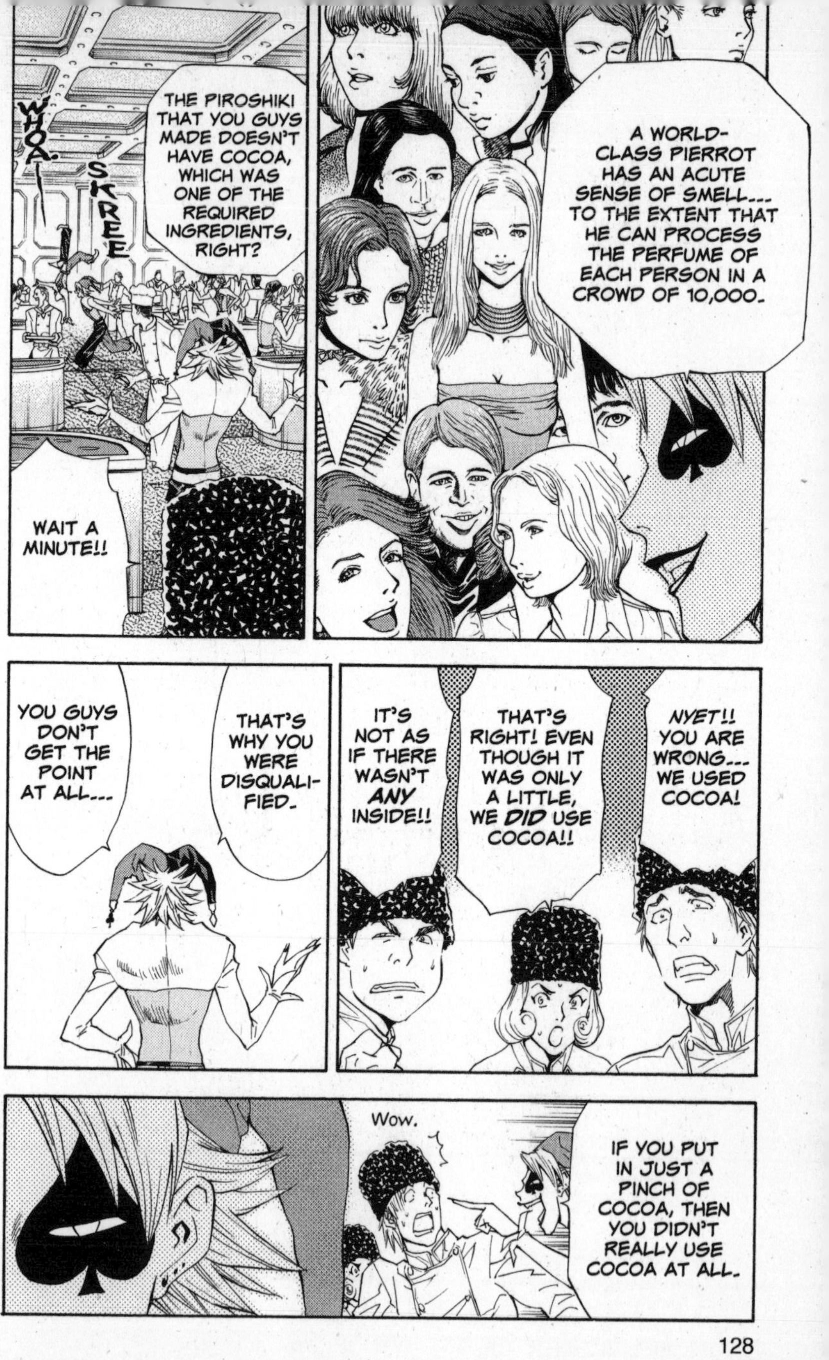
A WORLD-CLASS PIERROT HAS AN ACUTE SENSE OF SMELL... TO THE EXTENT THAT HE CAN PROCESS THE PERFUME OF EACH PERSON IN A CROWD OF 10,000.
THE PIROSHIKI THAT YOU GUYS MADE DOESN'T HAVE COCOA, WHICH WAS ONE OF THE REQUIRED INGREDIENTS, RIGHT?
SKREE
WHOA!
WAIT A MINUTE!!
NYET!! YOU ARE WRONG... WE USED COCOA!
THAT'S RIGHT! EVEN THOUGH IT WAS ONLY A LITTLE, WE *DID* USE COCOA!!
IT'S NOT AS IF THERE WASN'T *ANY* INSIDE!!
THAT'S WHY YOU WERE DISQUALIFIED.
YOU GUYS DON'T GET THE POINT AT ALL...
IF YOU PUT IN JUST A PINCH OF COCOA, THEN YOU DIDN'T REALLY USE COCOA AT ALL.
Wow.

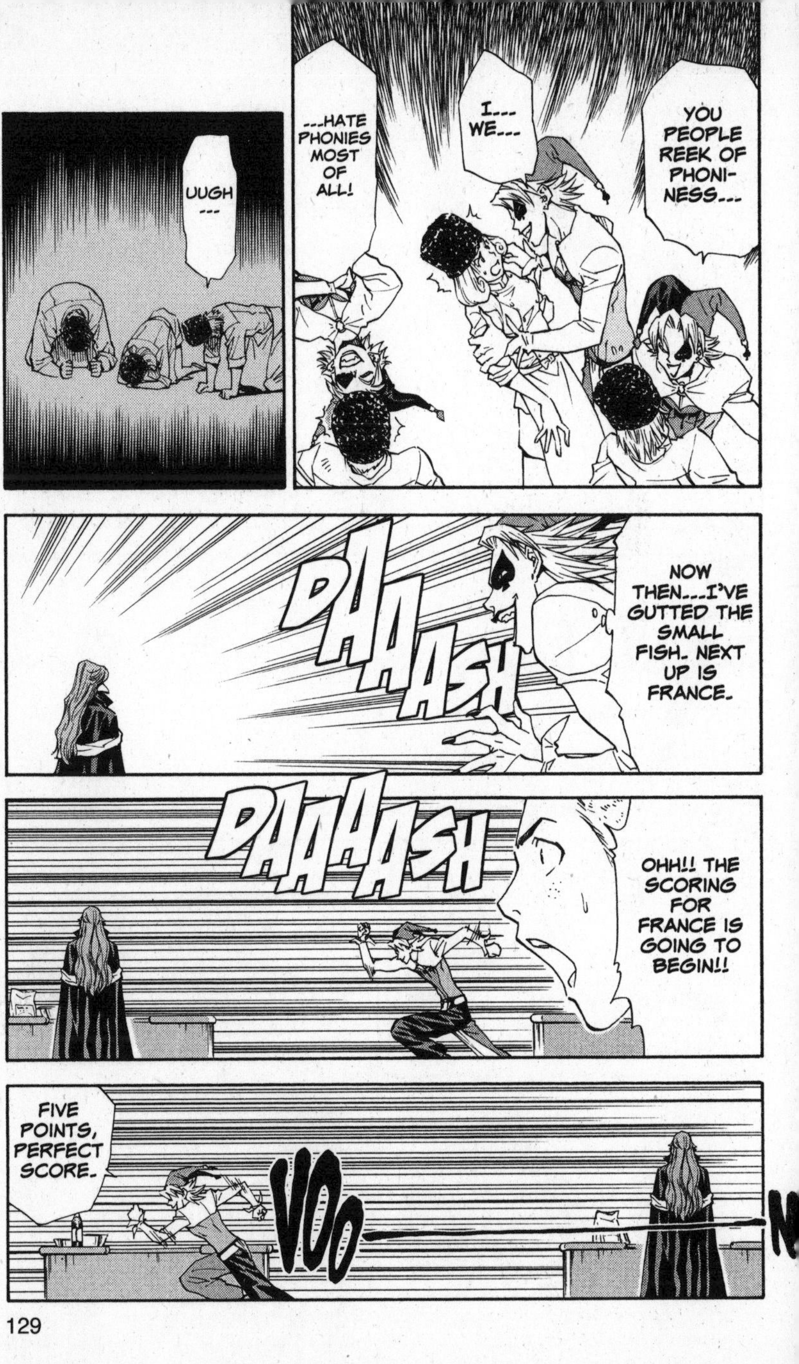
YOU PEOPLE REEK OF PHONINESS...
I... WE...
...HATE PHONIES MOST OF ALL!
UUGH ...
NOW THEN...I'VE GUTTED THE SMALL FISH. NEXT UP IS FRANCE.
DAAASH
OHH!! THE SCORING FOR FRANCE IS GOING TO BEGIN!!
DAAAAASH
VOON
FIVE POINTS, PERFECT SCORE.

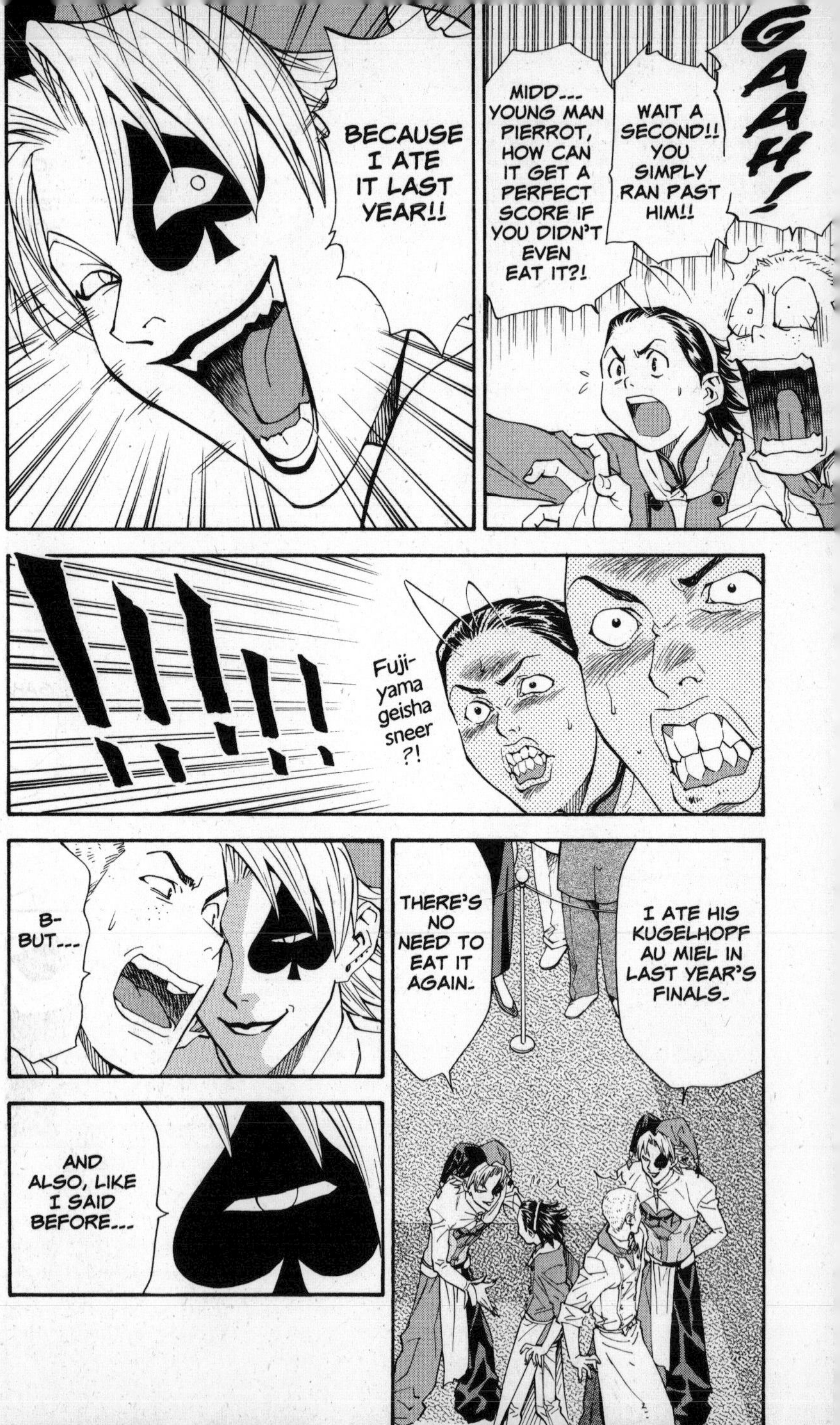
GAAAH!
WAIT A SECOND!! YOU SIMPLY RAN PAST HIM!!
MIDD... YOUNG MAN PIERROT, HOW CAN IT GET A PERFECT SCORE IF YOU DIDN'T EVEN EAT IT?!
BECAUSE I ATE IT LAST YEAR!!
Fuji-yama geisha sneer?!
!!!!!
I ATE HIS KUGELHOPF AU MIEL IN LAST YEAR'S FINALS.
THERE'S NO NEED TO EAT IT AGAIN.
B-BUT...
AND ALSO, LIKE I SAID BEFORE...

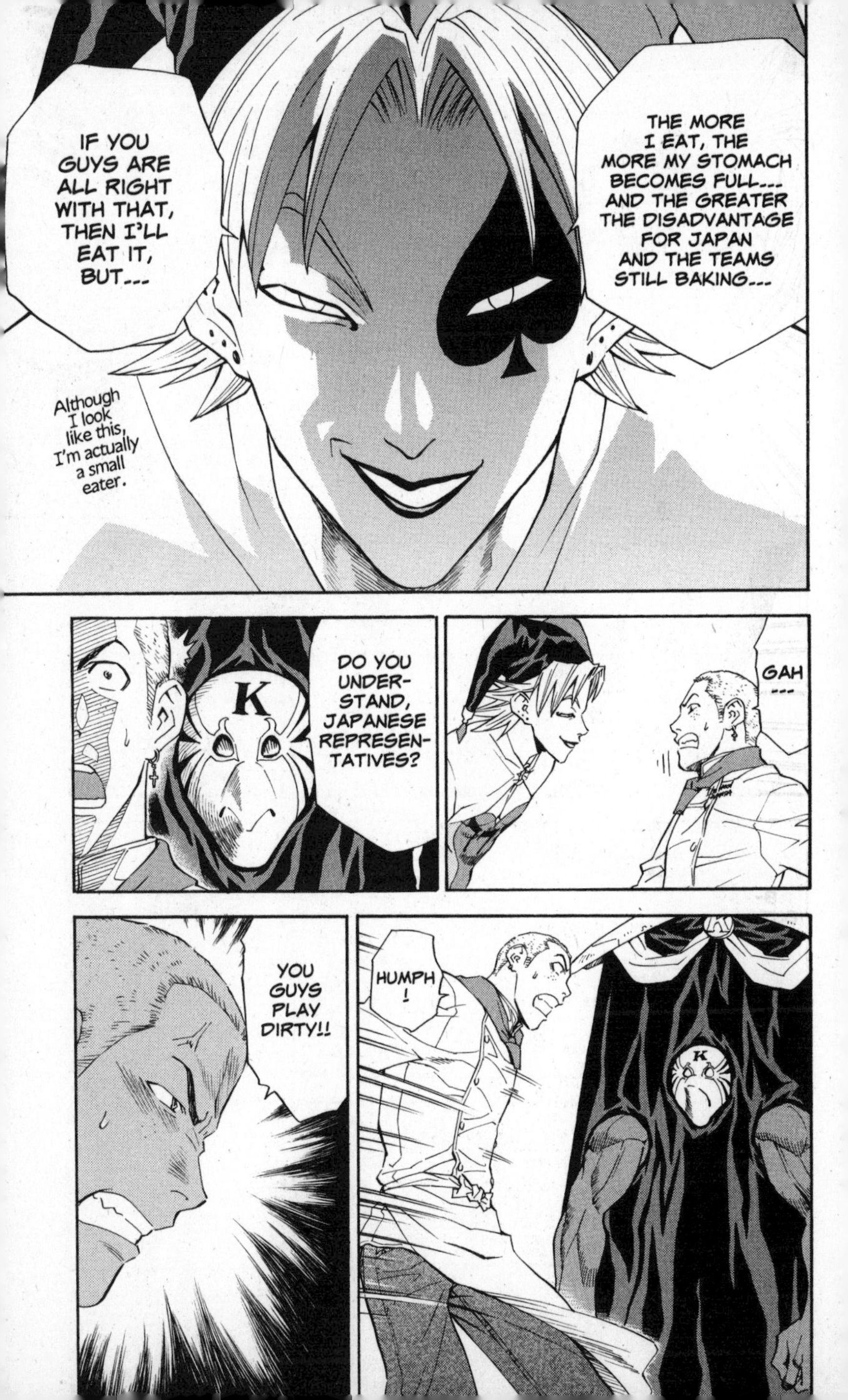
THE MORE I EAT, THE MORE MY STOMACH BECOMES FULL... AND THE GREATER THE DISADVANTAGE FOR JAPAN AND THE TEAMS STILL BAKING...
IF YOU GUYS ARE ALL RIGHT WITH THAT, THEN I'LL EAT IT, BUT...
Although I look like this, I'm actually a small eater.
GAH...
DO YOU UNDERSTAND, JAPANESE REPRESENTATIVES?
HUMPH!
YOU GUYS PLAY DIRTY!!

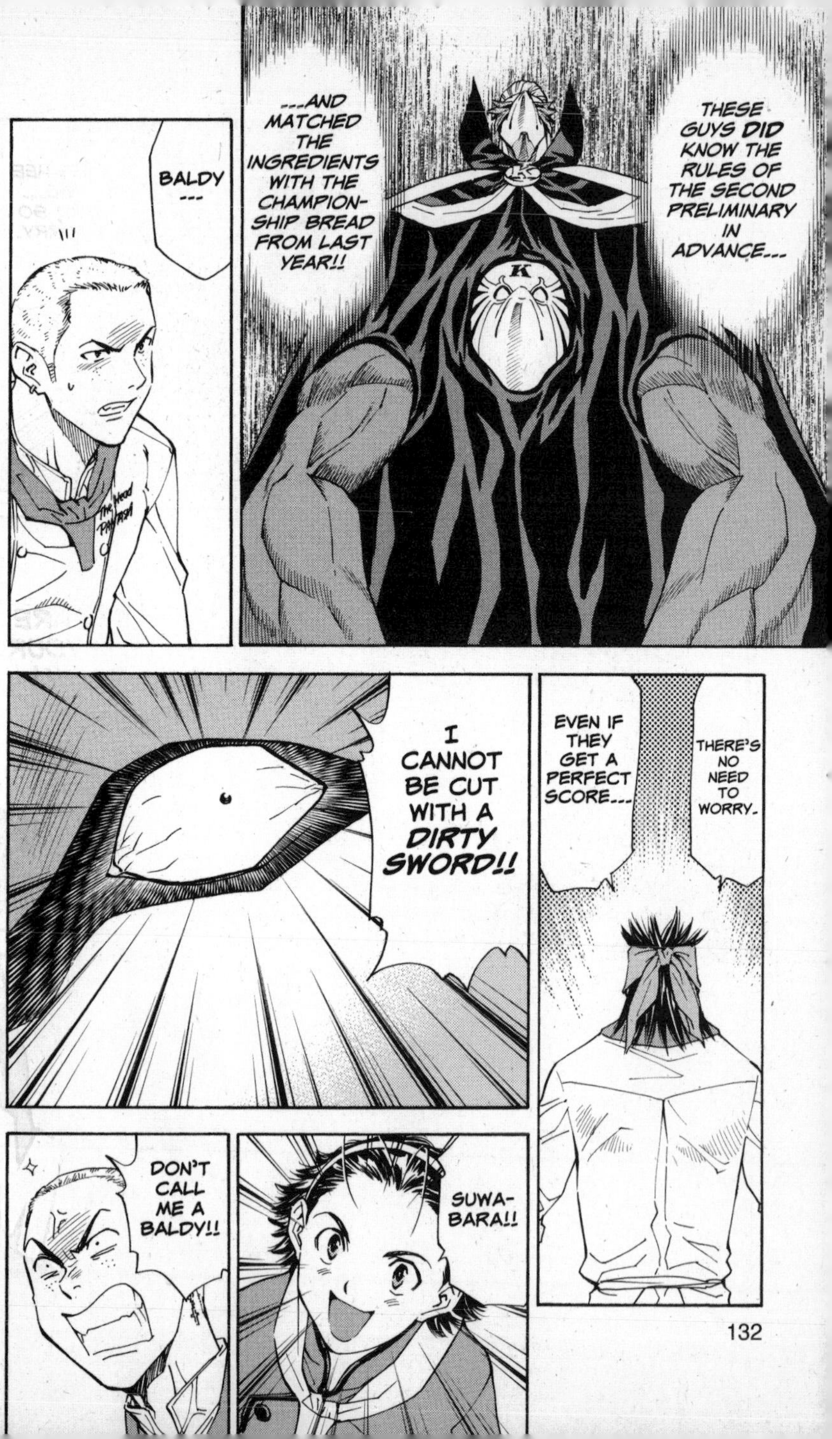
THESE GUYS DID KNOW THE RULES OF THE SECOND PRELIMINARY IN ADVANCE...
...AND MATCHED THE INGREDIENTS WITH THE CHAMPIONSHIP BREAD FROM LAST YEAR!!
BALDY ---
THERE'S NO NEED TO WORRY.
EVEN IF THEY GET A PERFECT SCORE...
I CANNOT BE CUT WITH A DIRTY SWORD!!
SUWA-BARA!!
DON'T CALL ME A BALDY!!

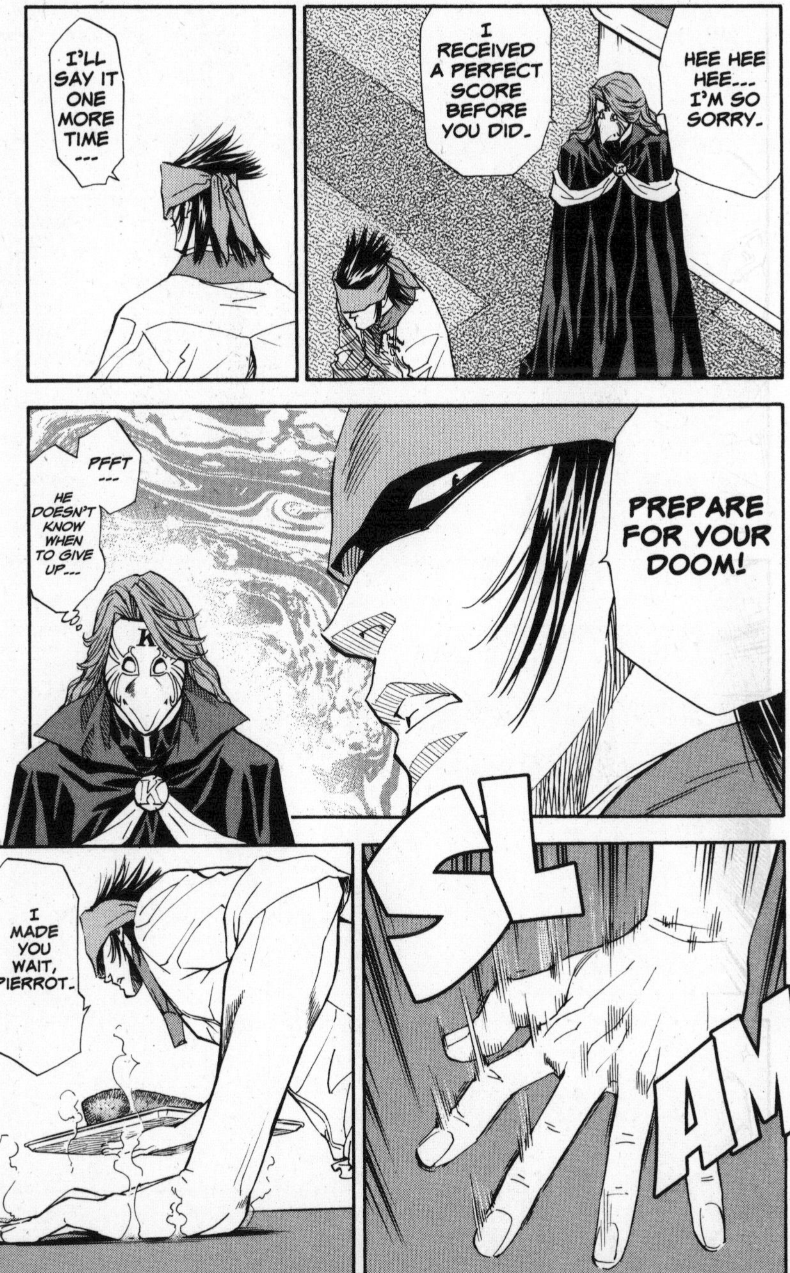
HEE HEE HEE... I'M SO SORRY.
I RECEIVED A PERFECT SCORE BEFORE YOU DID.
I'LL SAY IT ONE MORE TIME ...
PREPARE FOR YOUR DOOM!
PFFT ...
HE DOESN'T KNOW WHEN TO GIVE UP...
SL
AM
I MADE YOU WAIT, PIERROT.

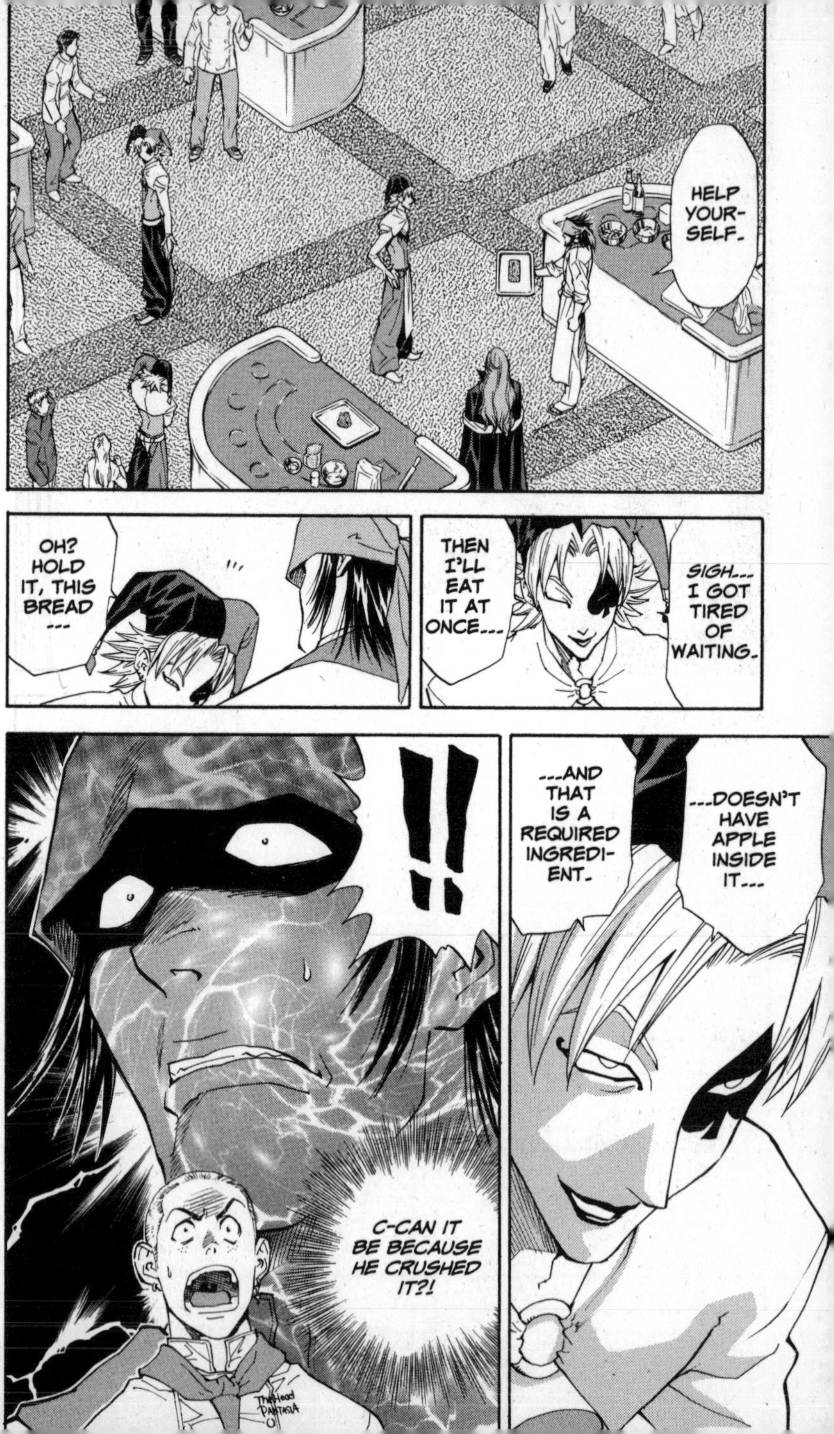
HELP YOURSELF.
SIGH... I GOT TIRED OF WAITING.
THEN I'LL EAT IT AT ONCE...
OH? HOLD IT, THIS BREAD ---
...DOESN'T HAVE APPLE INSIDE IT...
...AND THAT IS A REQUIRED INGREDIENT.
!!
C-CAN IT BE BECAUSE HE CRUSHED IT?!

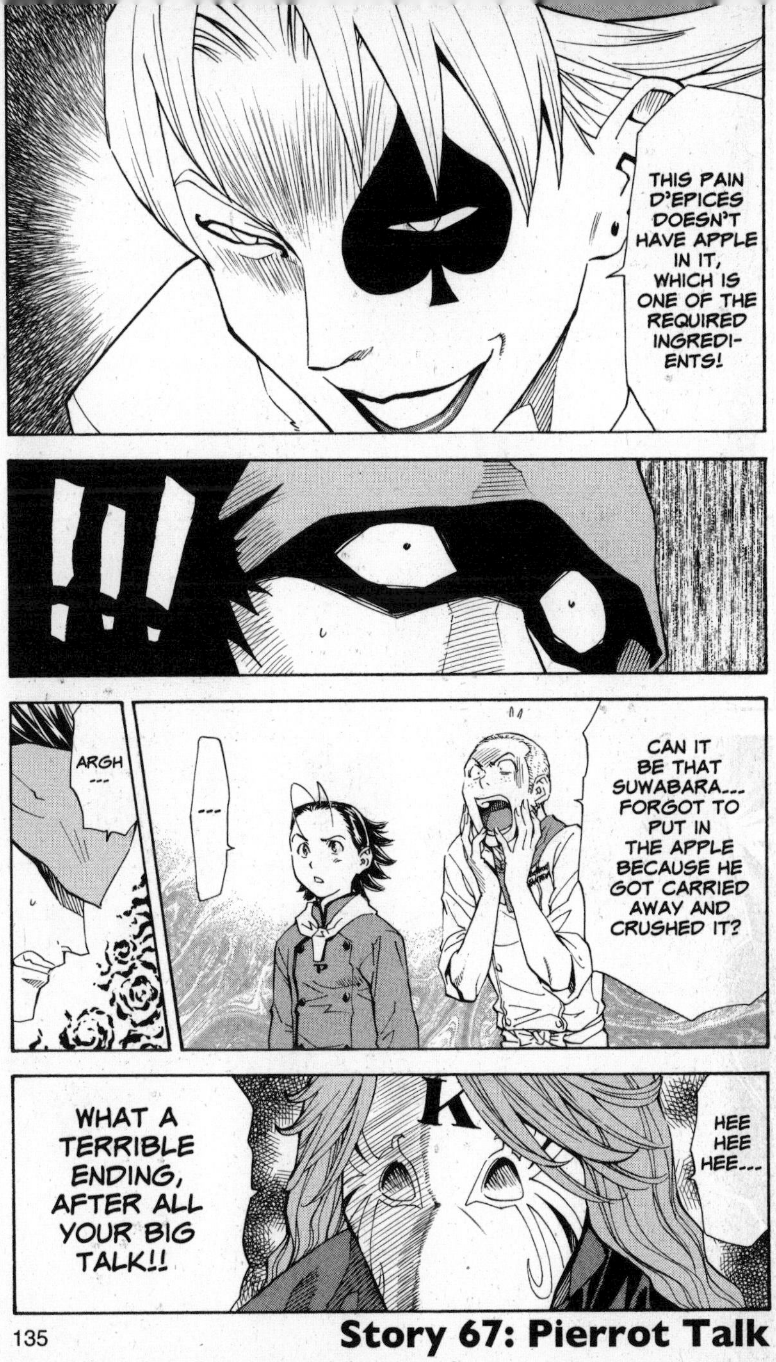
THIS PAIN D'EPICES DOESN'T HAVE APPLE IN IT, WHICH IS ONE OF THE REQUIRED INGREDI-ENTS!
!!!
CAN IT BE THAT SUWABARA... FORGOT TO PUT IN THE APPLE BECAUSE HE GOT CARRIED AWAY AND CRUSHED IT?
...
ARGH ...
HEE HEE HEE...
WHAT A TERRIBLE ENDING, AFTER ALL YOUR BIG TALK!!

Story 67: Pierrot Talk

Story 67: Pierrot Talk

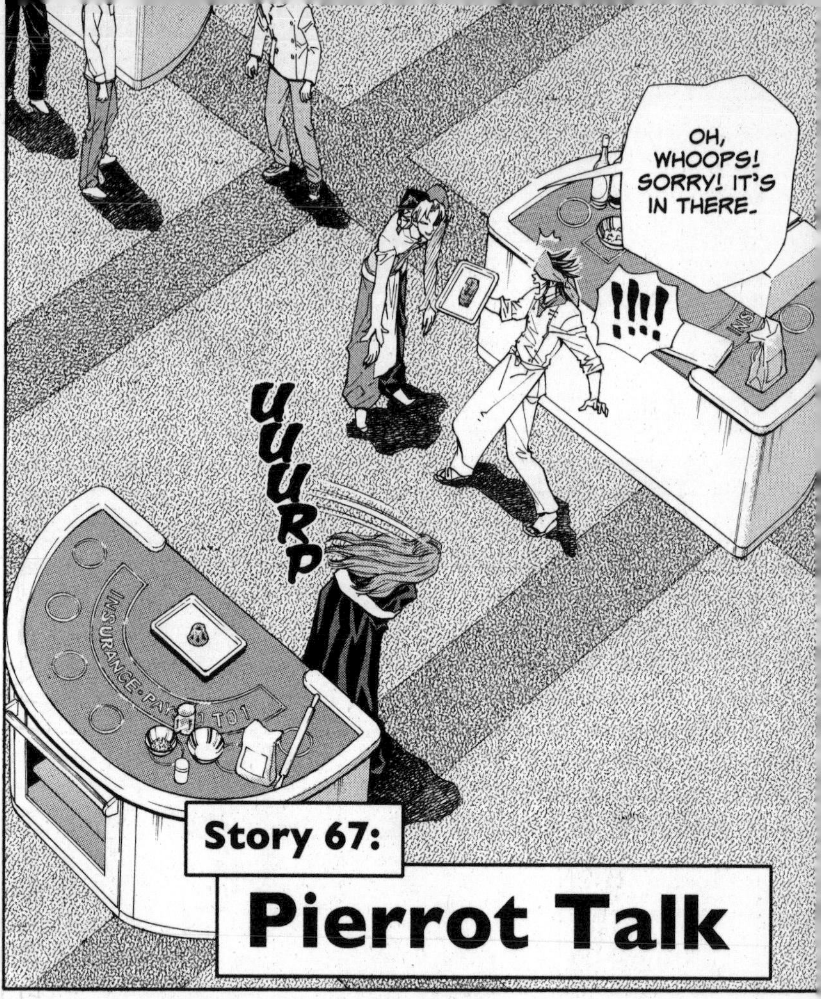
OH, WHOOPS! SORRY! IT'S IN THERE.
!!!!
UUURP

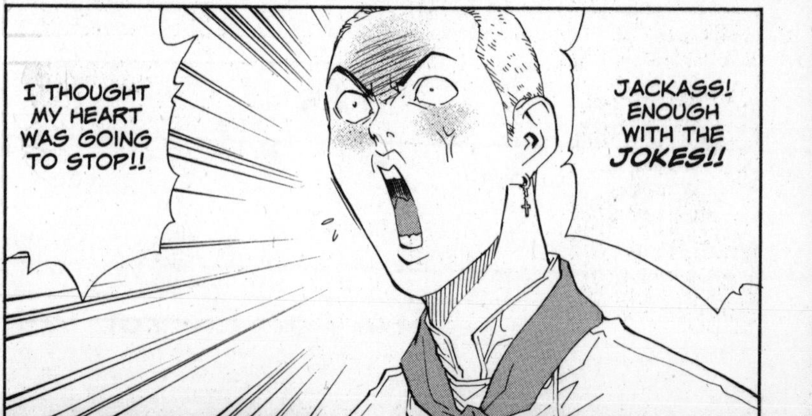
JACKASS! ENOUGH WITH THE JOKES!!
I THOUGHT MY HEART WAS GOING TO STOP!!

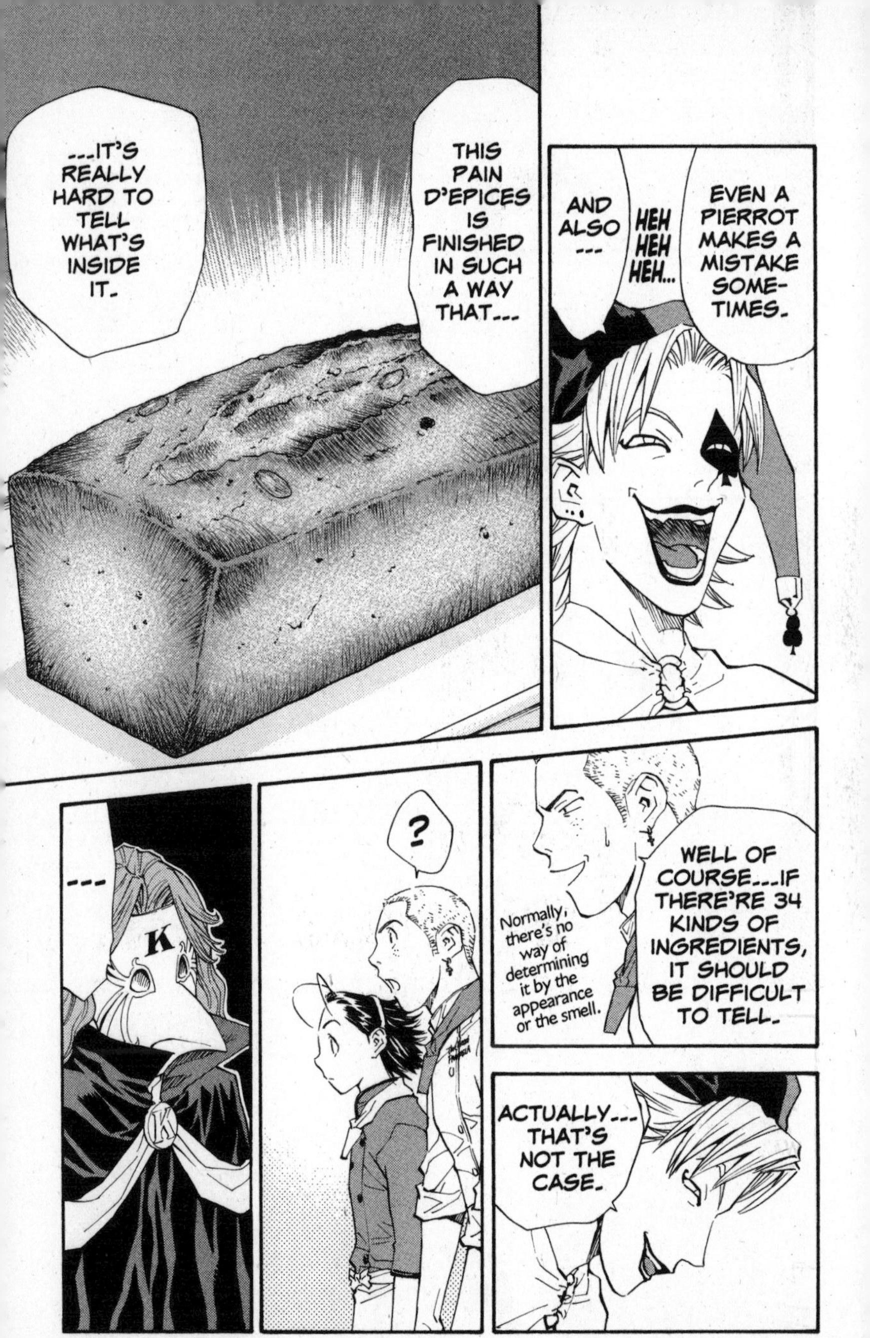
EVEN A PIERROT MAKES A MISTAKE SOMETIMES.
HEH HEH HEH...
AND ALSO ...
THIS PAIN D'EPICES IS FINISHED IN SUCH A WAY THAT...
...IT'S REALLY HARD TO TELL WHAT'S INSIDE IT.
WELL OF COURSE...IF THERE'RE 34 KINDS OF INGREDIENTS, IT SHOULD BE DIFFICULT TO TELL.
Normally, there's no way of determining it by the appearance or the smell.
ACTUALLY... THAT'S NOT THE CASE.
?
...

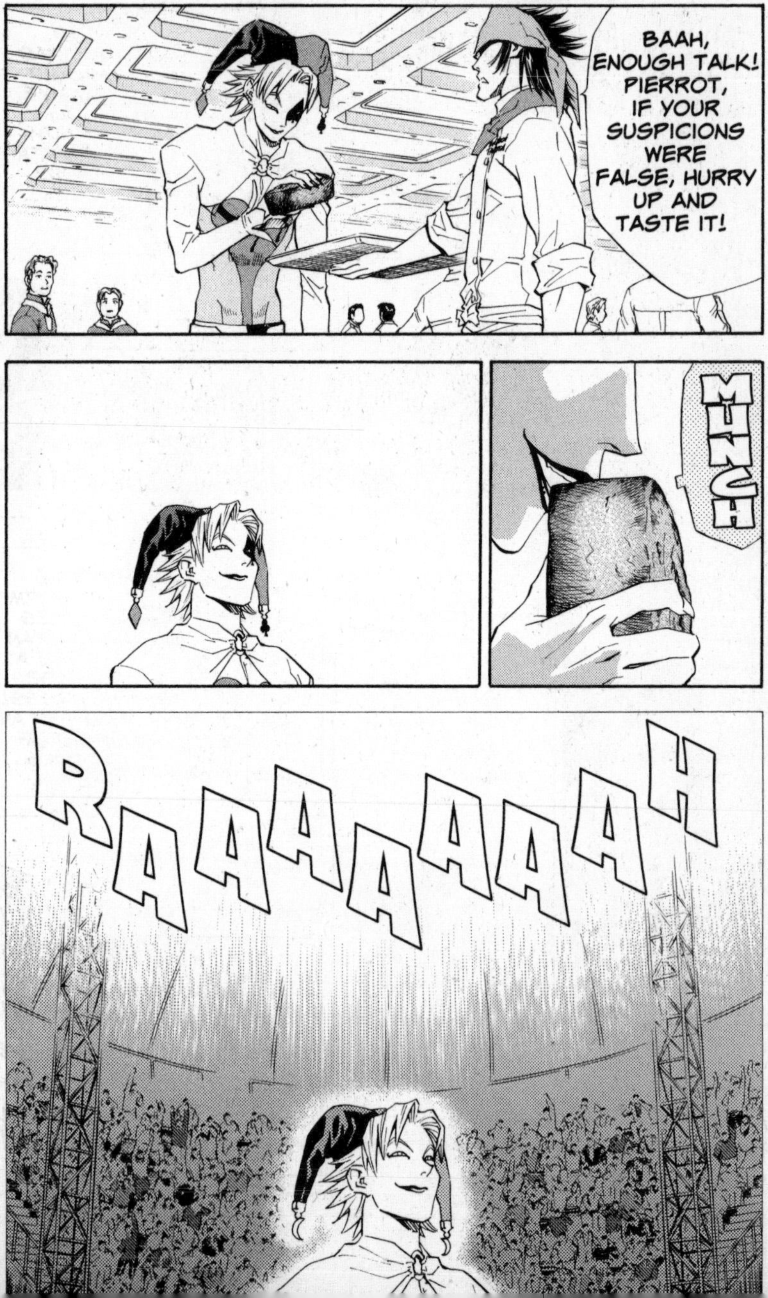
BAAH, ENOUGH TALK! PIERROT, IF YOUR SUSPICIONS WERE FALSE, HURRY UP AND TASTE IT!
MUNCH
RAAAAAAAH

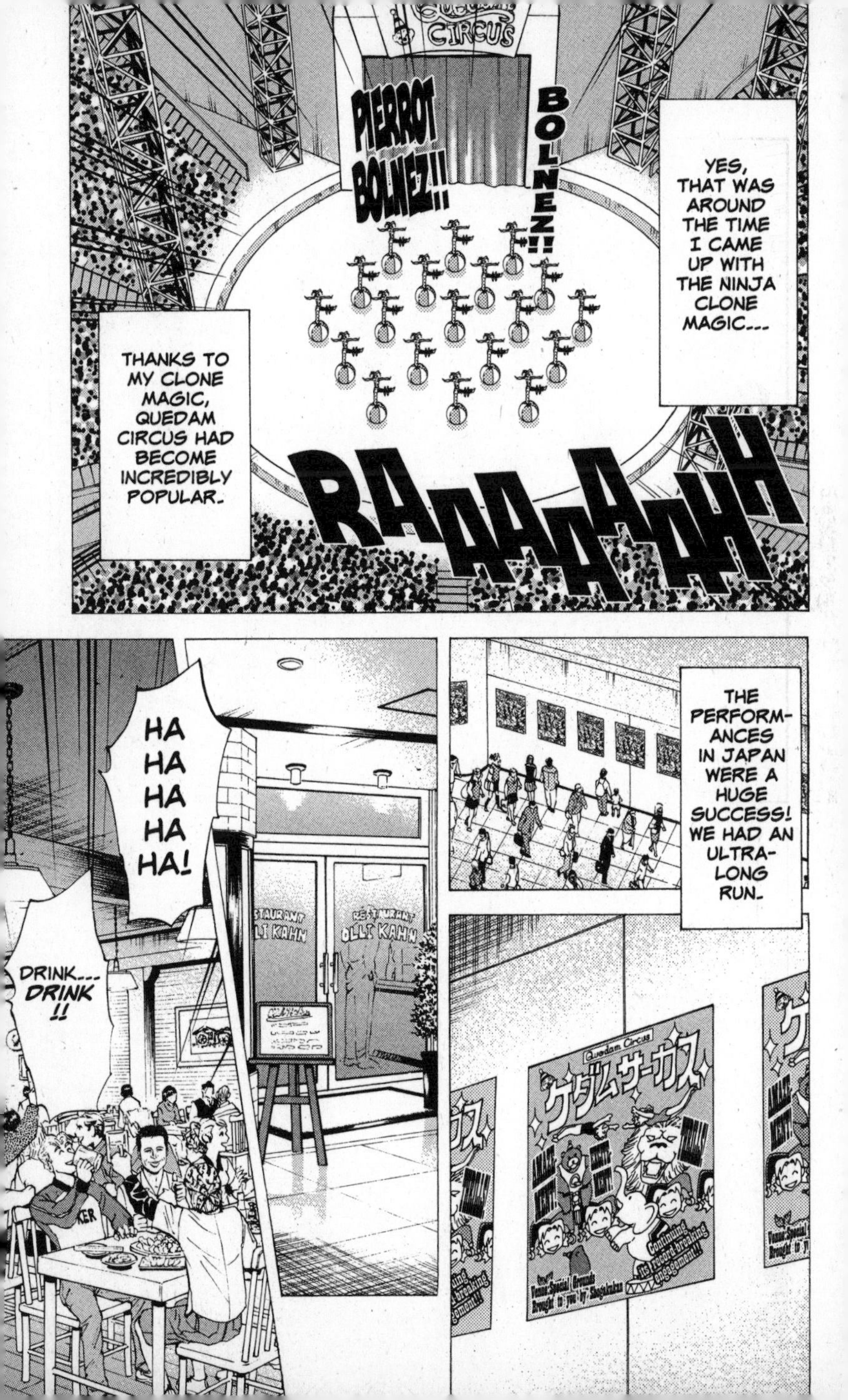
CIRCUS
YES, THAT WAS AROUND THE TIME I CAME UP WITH THE NINJA CLONE MAGIC...
PIERROT BOLNEZ!!
BOLNEZ!!
THANKS TO MY CLONE MAGIC, QUEDAM CIRCUS HAD BECOME INCREDIBLY POPULAR.
RAAAAAAAH
THE PERFORMANCES IN JAPAN WERE A HUGE SUCCESS! WE HAD AN ULTRA-LONG RUN.
Quedam Circus
ケダムサーカス
AMAZEMENT!
EXCITEMENT!
THRILL!
Continuing its record breaking engagement!!
Venue: Special Grounds
Brought to you by Shogakukan
HA HA HA HA HA HA!
DRINK... DRINK!!
RESTAURANT OLLI KAHN

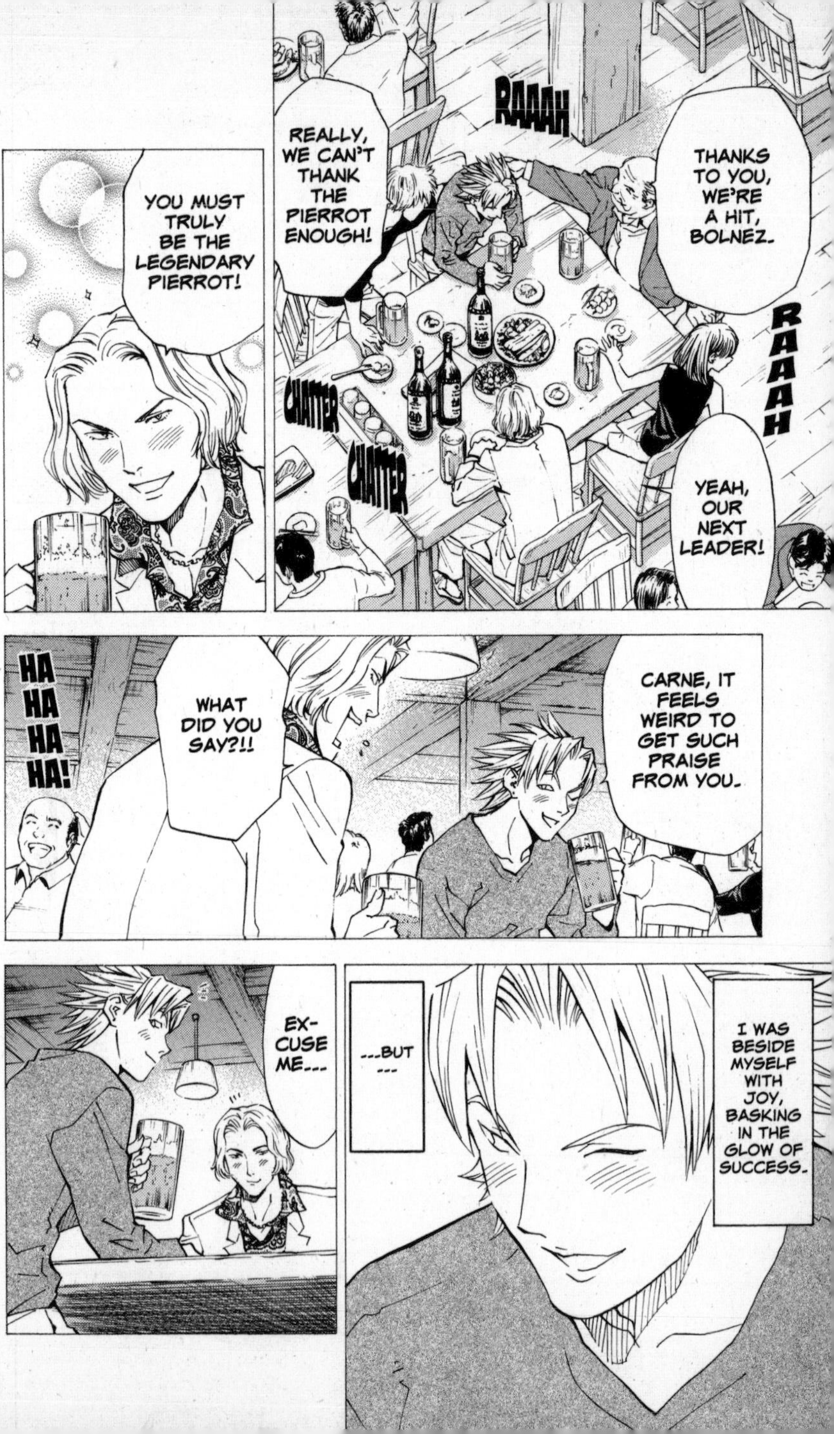
THANKS TO YOU, WE'RE A HIT, BOLNEZ.
RAAAH
REALLY, WE CAN'T THANK THE PIERROT ENOUGH!
RAAAH
YEAH, OUR NEXT LEADER!
CHATTER
CHATTER
YOU MUST TRULY BE THE LEGENDARY PIERROT!
CARNE, IT FEELS WEIRD TO GET SUCH PRAISE FROM YOU.
WHAT DID YOU SAY?!!
HA HA HA HA!
I WAS BESIDE MYSELF WITH JOY, BASKING IN THE GLOW OF SUCCESS.
...BUT ...
EX-CUSE ME...

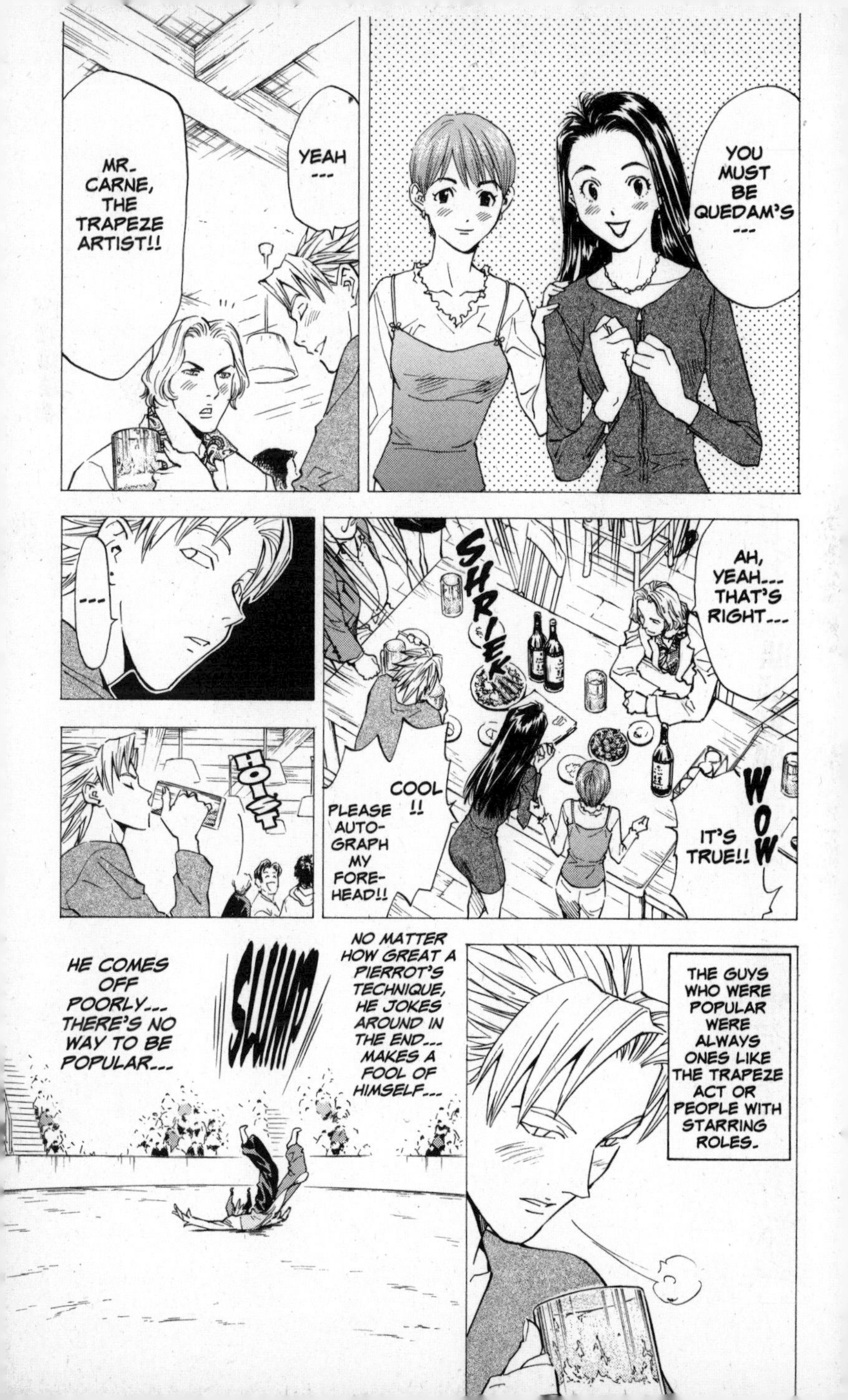
YOU MUST BE QUEDAM'S ---
YEAH ---
MR. CARNE, THE TRAPEZE ARTIST!!
SHRIEK
AH, YEAH... THAT'S RIGHT...
WOW
IT'S TRUE!!
COOL!!
PLEASE AUTOGRAPH MY FOREHEAD!!

HOIST
THE GUYS WHO WERE POPULAR WERE ALWAYS ONES LIKE THE TRAPEZE ACT OR PEOPLE WITH STARRING ROLES.
NO MATTER HOW GREAT A PIERROT'S TECHNIQUE, HE JOKES AROUND IN THE END... MAKES A FOOL OF HIMSELF...
SLUMP
HE COMES OFF POORLY... THERE'S NO WAY TO BE POPULAR...

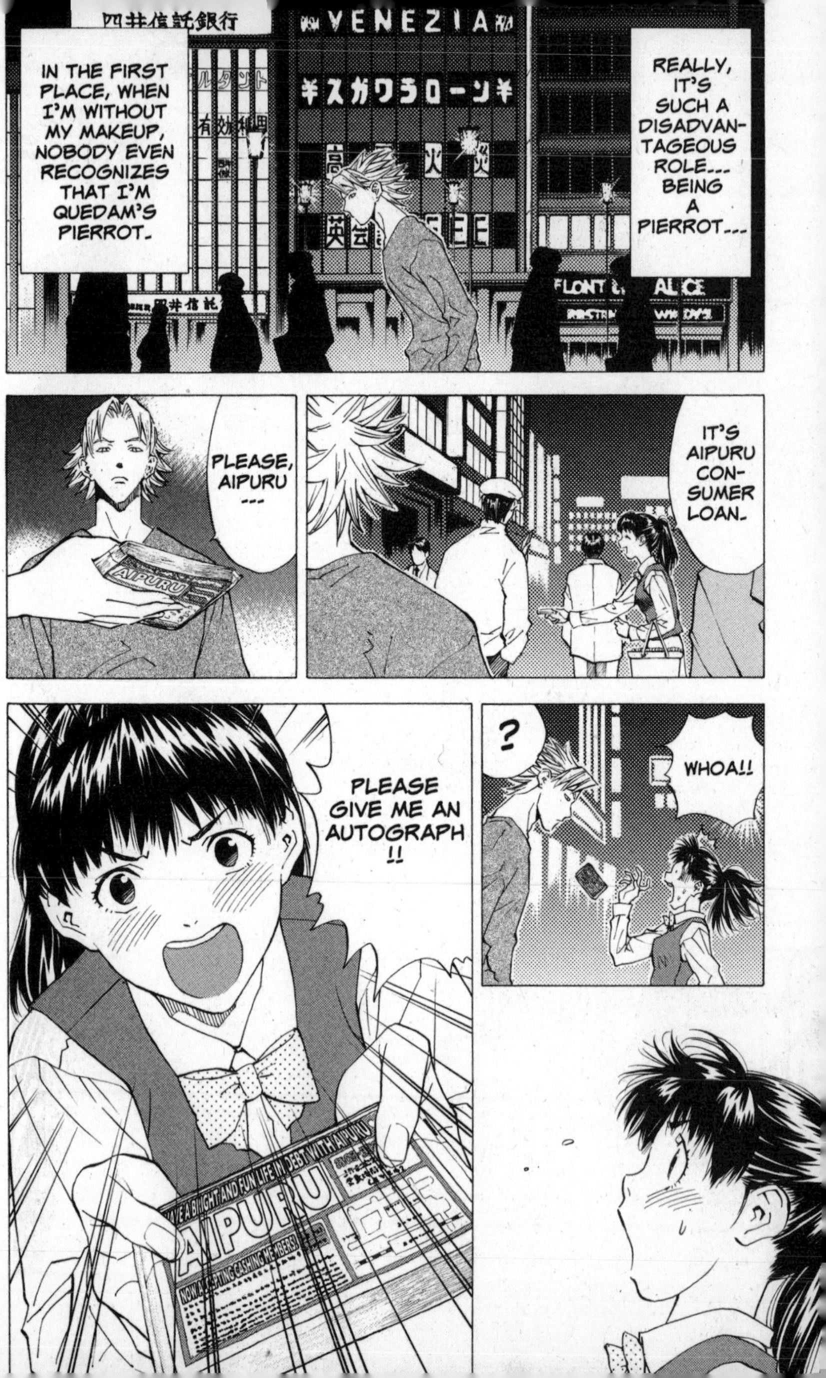
VENEZIA
REALLY, IT'S SUCH A DISADVANTAGEOUS ROLE... BEING A PIERROT...
IN THE FIRST PLACE, WHEN I'M WITHOUT MY MAKEUP, NOBODY EVEN RECOGNIZES THAT I'M QUEDAM'S PIERROT.
IT'S AIPURU CONSUMER LOAN.
PLEASE, AIPURU ...
AIPURU
WHOA!!
?
PLEASE GIVE ME AN AUTOGRAPH !!
AIPURU

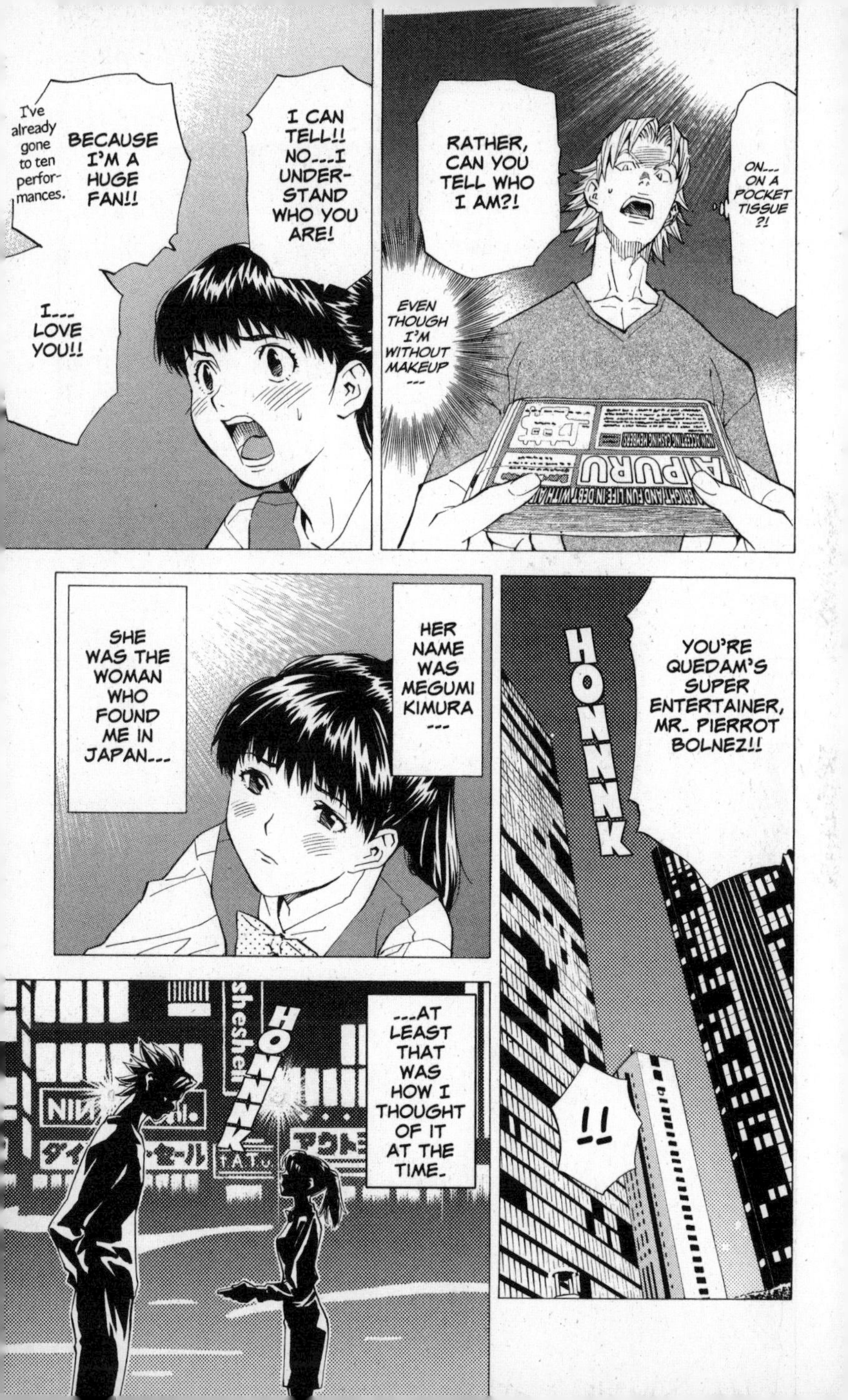
ON... ON A POCKET TISSUE ?!
RATHER, CAN YOU TELL WHO I AM?!
EVEN THOUGH I'M WITHOUT MAKEUP ---
AIPURU
NOW ACCEPTING CASHING MEMBERS
I CAN TELL!! NO...I UNDER-STAND WHO YOU ARE!
BECAUSE I'M A HUGE FAN!!
I've already gone to ten perfor-mances.
I... LOVE YOU!!
HONNNK
YOU'RE QUEDAM'S SUPER ENTERTAINER, MR. PIERROT BOLNEZ!!
!!
HER NAME WAS MEGUMI KIMURA ---
SHE WAS THE WOMAN WHO FOUND ME IN JAPAN...
...AT LEAST THAT WAS HOW I THOUGHT OF IT AT THE TIME.
HONNNK

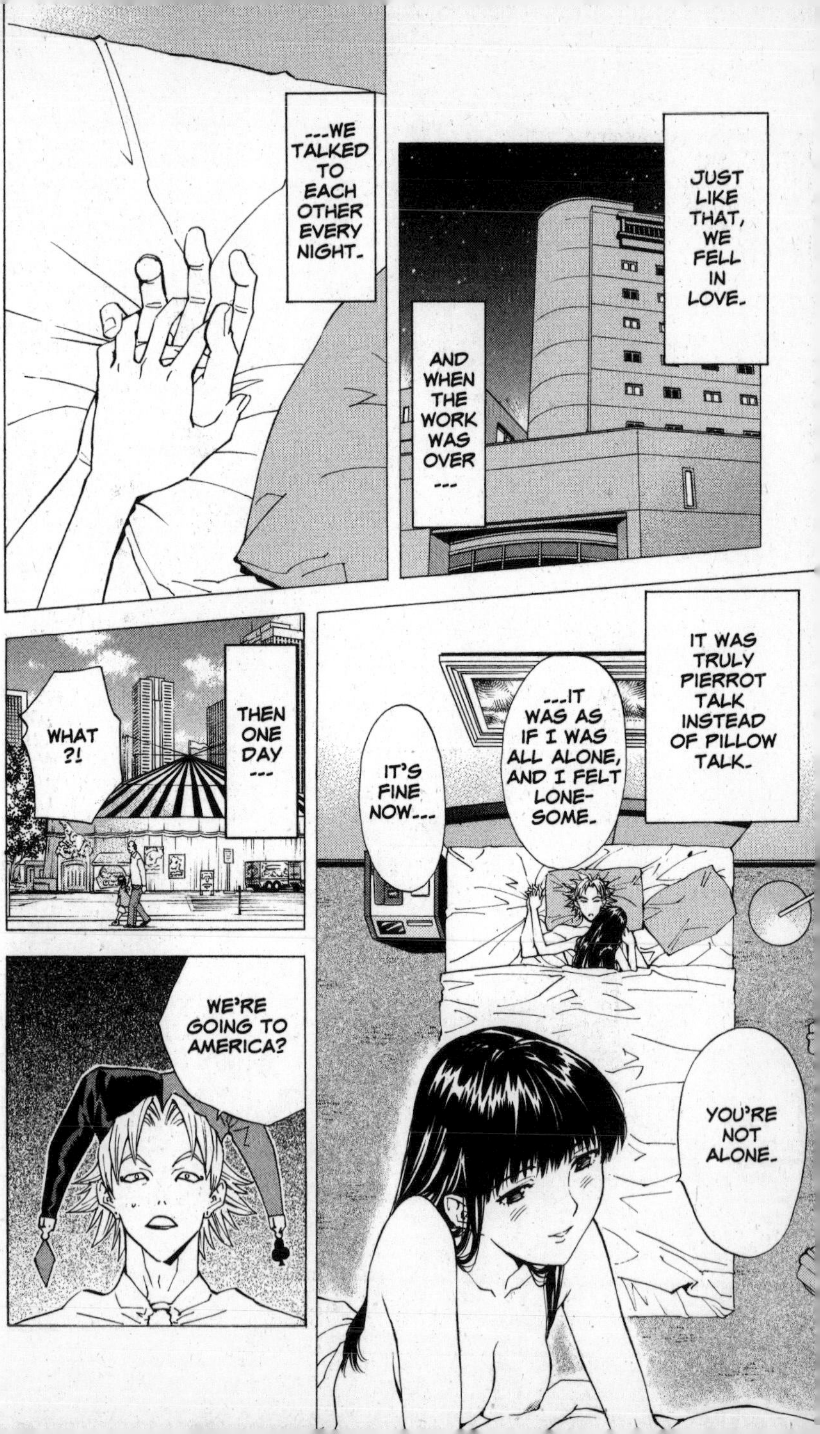
JUST LIKE THAT, WE FELL IN LOVE.
AND WHEN THE WORK WAS OVER---
---WE TALKED TO EACH OTHER EVERY NIGHT.
IT WAS TRULY PIERROT TALK INSTEAD OF PILLOW TALK.
---IT WAS AS IF I WAS ALL ALONE, AND I FELT LONE-SOME.
IT'S FINE NOW---
YOU'RE NOT ALONE.
THEN ONE DAY---
WHAT?!
WE'RE GOING TO AMERICA?

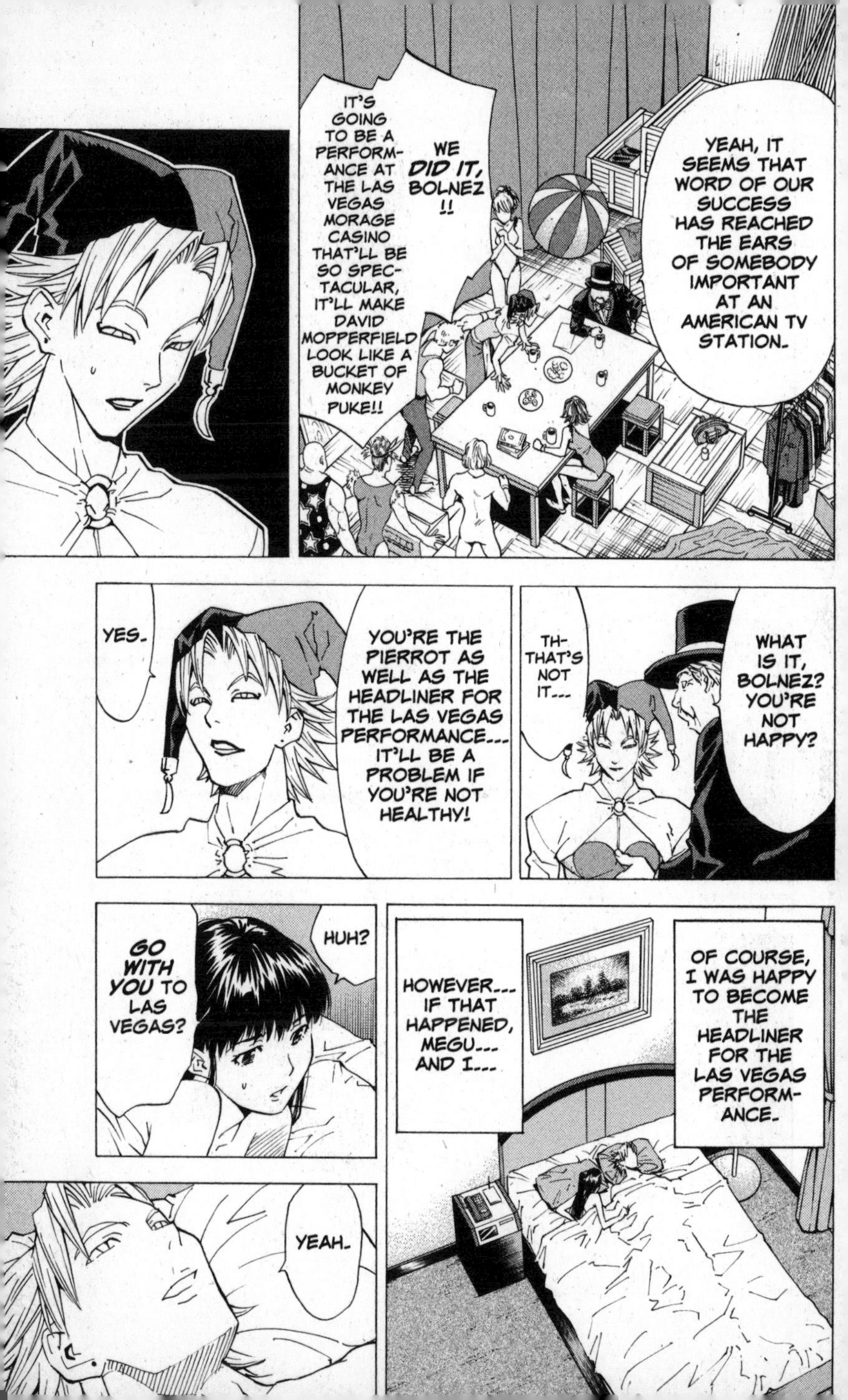
YEAH, IT SEEMS THAT WORD OF OUR SUCCESS HAS REACHED THE EARS OF SOMEBODY IMPORTANT AT AN AMERICAN TV STATION.
WE DID IT, BOLNEZ!!
IT'S GOING TO BE A PERFORMANCE AT THE LAS VEGAS MORAGE CASINO THAT'LL BE SO SPECTACULAR, IT'LL MAKE DAVID MOPPERFIELD LOOK LIKE A BUCKET OF MONKEY PUKE!!
WHAT IS IT, BOLNEZ? YOU'RE NOT HAPPY?
TH-THAT'S NOT IT...
YOU'RE THE PIERROT AS WELL AS THE HEADLINER FOR THE LAS VEGAS PERFORMANCE... IT'LL BE A PROBLEM IF YOU'RE NOT HEALTHY!
YES.
OF COURSE, I WAS HAPPY TO BECOME THE HEADLINER FOR THE LAS VEGAS PERFORMANCE.
HOWEVER... IF THAT HAPPENED, MEGU... AND I...
HUH?
GO WITH YOU TO LAS VEGAS?
YEAH.

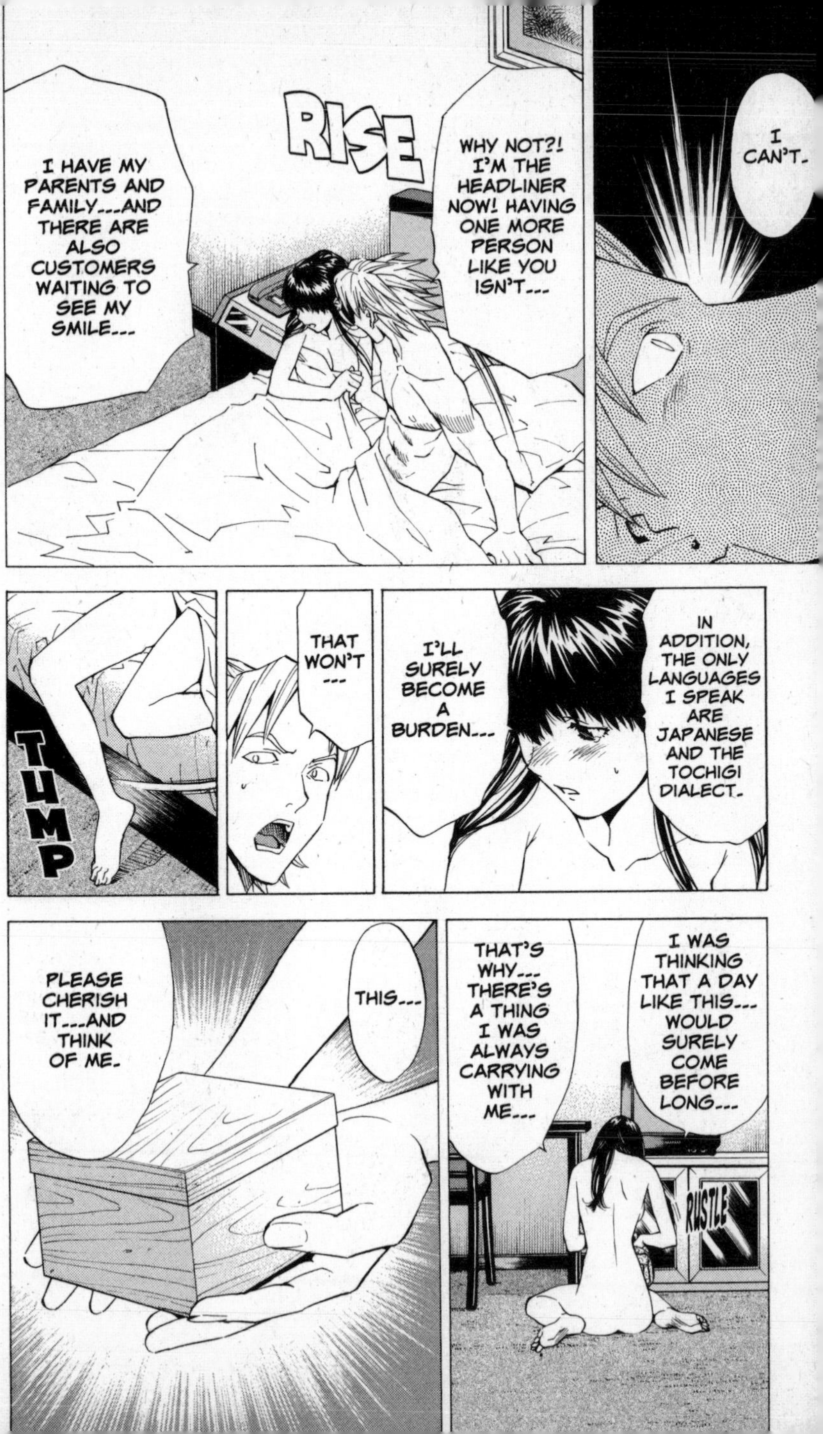
I CAN'T.
WHY NOT?! I'M THE HEADLINER NOW! HAVING ONE MORE PERSON LIKE YOU ISN'T...
RISE
I HAVE MY PARENTS AND FAMILY...AND THERE ARE ALSO CUSTOMERS WAITING TO SEE MY SMILE...
IN ADDITION, THE ONLY LANGUAGES I SPEAK ARE JAPANESE AND THE TOCHIGI DIALECT.
I'LL SURELY BECOME A BURDEN...
THAT WON'T ...
TUMP
I WAS THINKING THAT A DAY LIKE THIS... WOULD SURELY COME BEFORE LONG...
THAT'S WHY... THERE'S A THING I WAS ALWAYS CARRYING WITH ME...
RUSTLE
THIS...
PLEASE CHERISH IT...AND THINK OF ME.

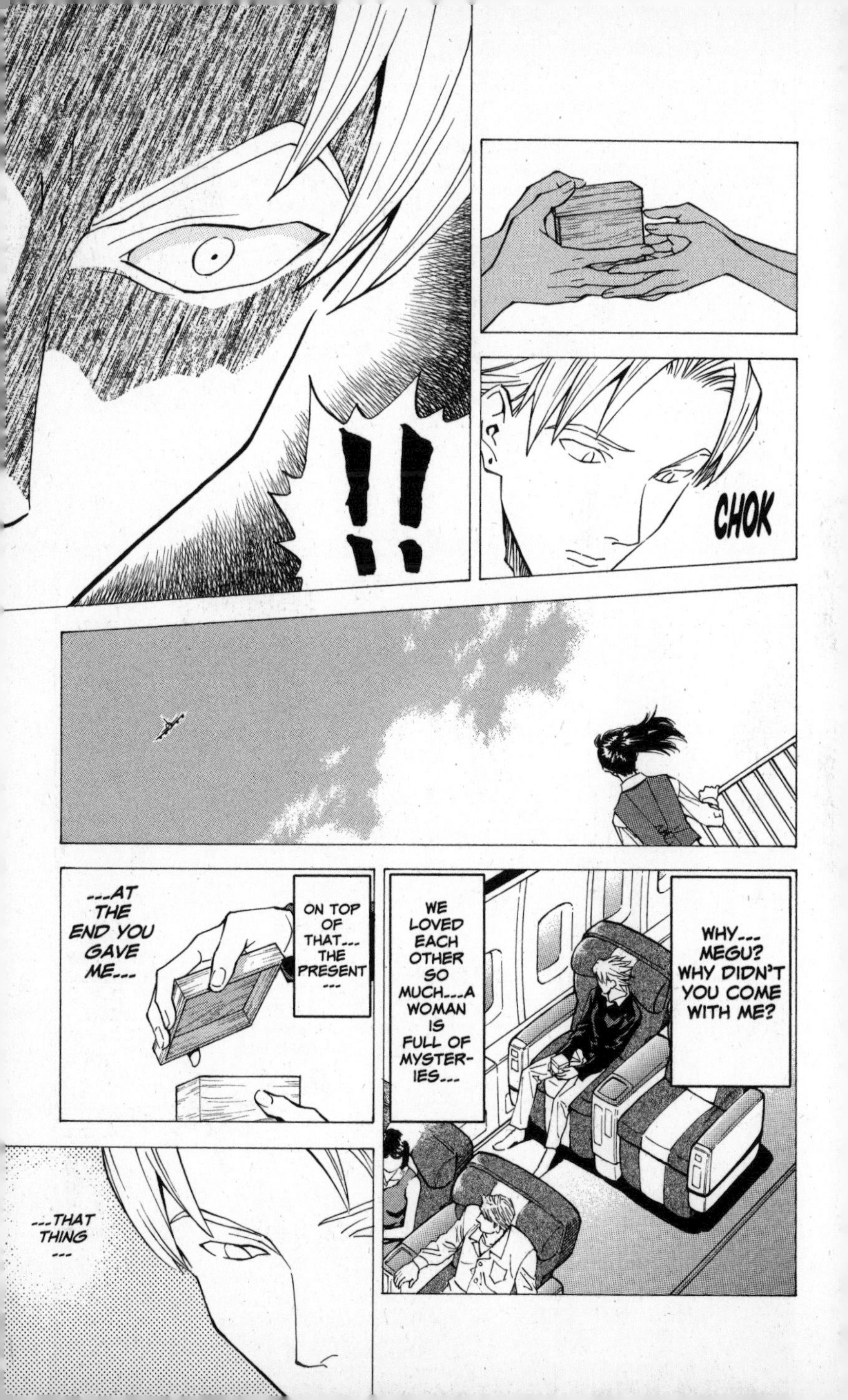
CHOK
!!
WHY... MEGU? WHY DIDN'T YOU COME WITH ME?
WE LOVED EACH OTHER SO MUCH...A WOMAN IS FULL OF MYSTER-IES...
ON TOP OF THAT... THE PRESENT ...
...AT THE END YOU GAVE ME...
...THAT THING ...

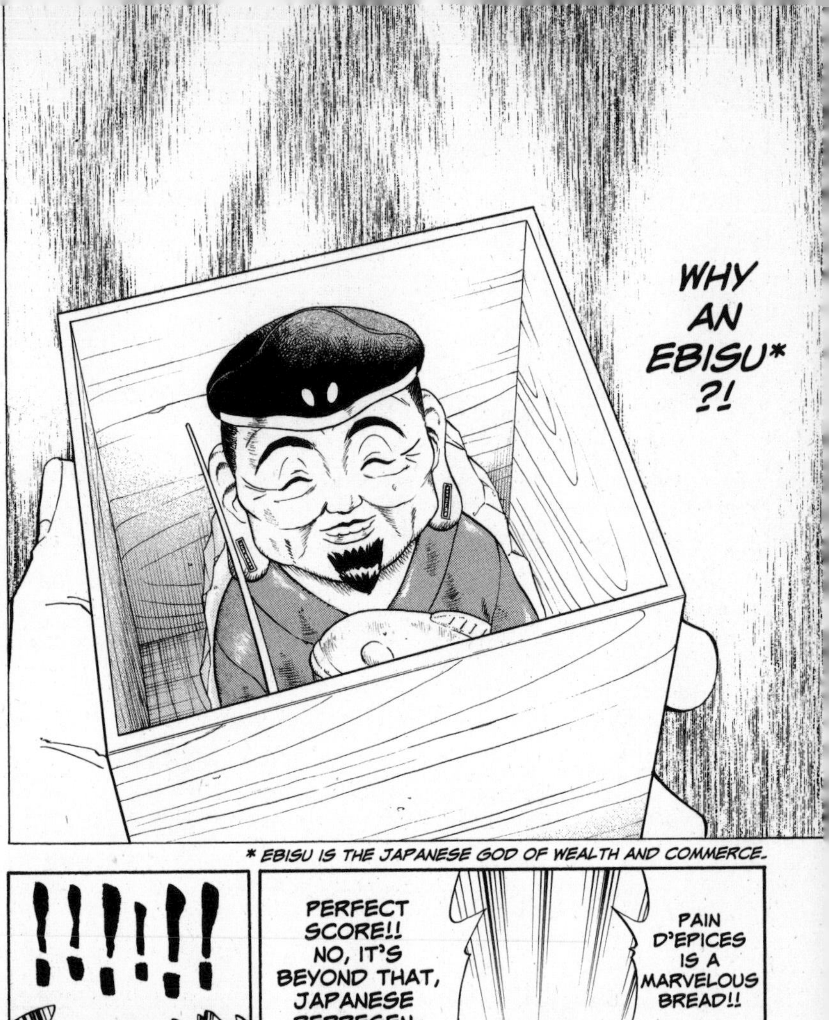
WHY AN EBISU* ?!

* EBISU IS THE JAPANESE GOD OF WEALTH AND COMMERCE.

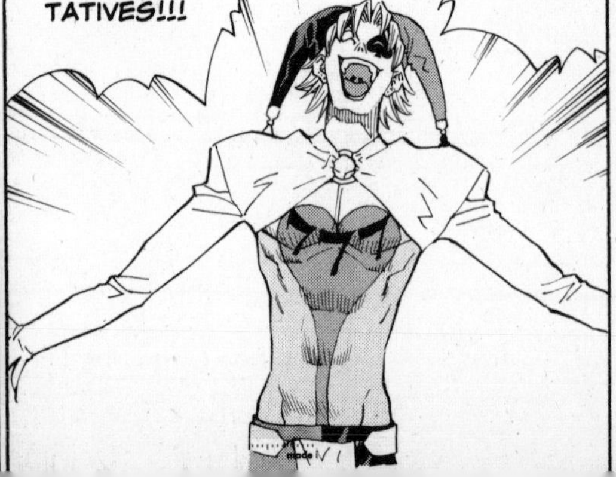
PAIN D'EPICES IS A MARVELOUS BREAD!!
PERFECT SCORE!! NO, IT'S BEYOND THAT, JAPANESE REPRESEN-TATIVES!!!

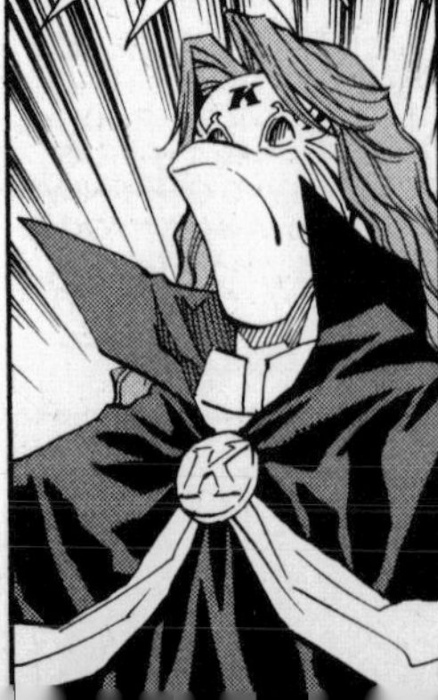
!!!!!!

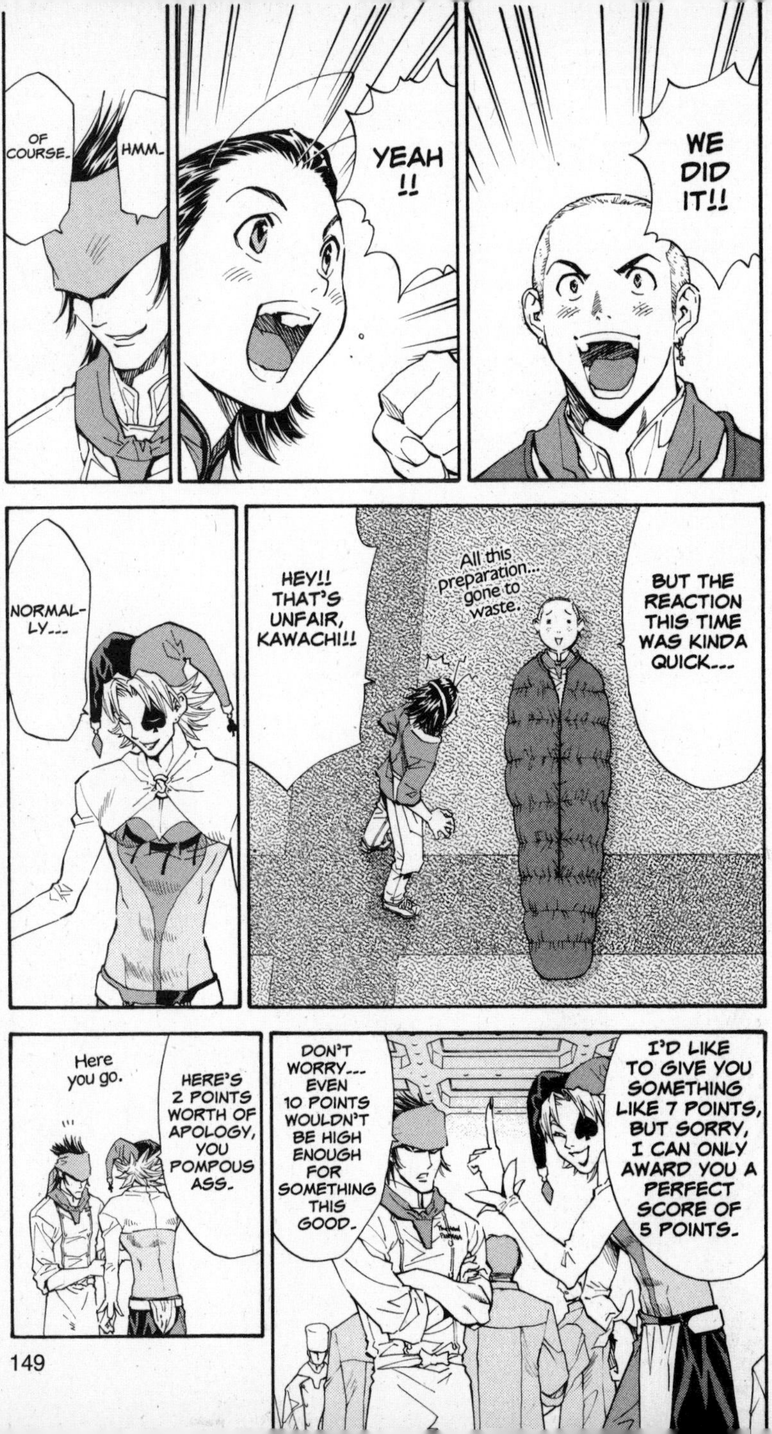
WE DID IT!!
YEAH!!
HMM...
OF COURSE...
BUT THE REACTION THIS TIME WAS KINDA QUICK...
All this preparation... gone to waste.
HEY!! THAT'S UNFAIR, KAWACHI!!
NORMAL-LY...
I'D LIKE TO GIVE YOU SOMETHING LIKE 7 POINTS, BUT SORRY, I CAN ONLY AWARD YOU A PERFECT SCORE OF 5 POINTS.
DON'T WORRY... EVEN 10 POINTS WOULDN'T BE HIGH ENOUGH FOR SOMETHING THIS GOOD.
HERE'S 2 POINTS WORTH OF APOLOGY, YOU POMPOUS ASS.
Here you go.

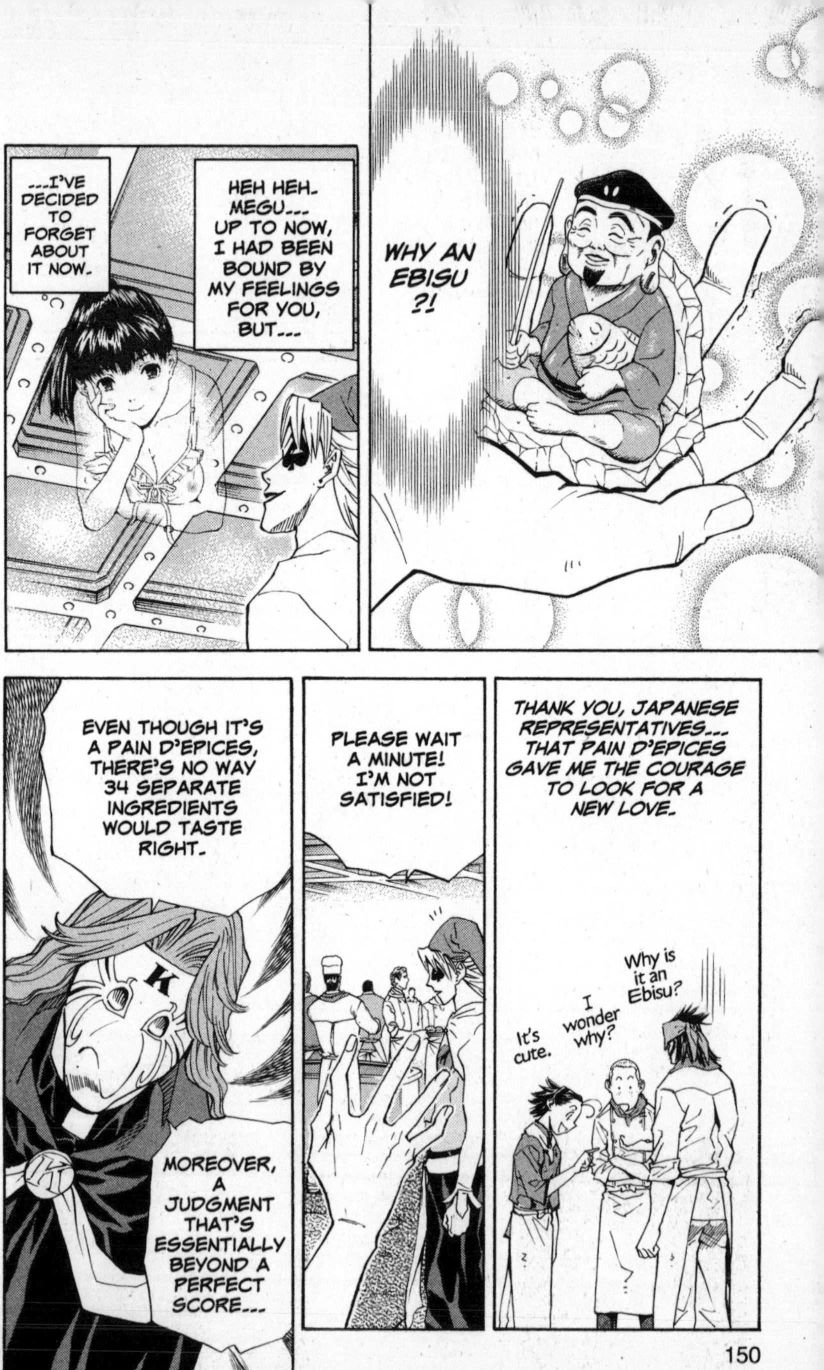
WHY AN EBISU ?!
HEH HEH. MEGU... UP TO NOW, I HAD BEEN BOUND BY MY FEELINGS FOR YOU, BUT...
...I'VE DECIDED TO FORGET ABOUT IT NOW.
THANK YOU, JAPANESE REPRESENTATIVES... THAT PAIN D'EPICES GAVE ME THE COURAGE TO LOOK FOR A NEW LOVE.
Why is it an Ebisu?
I wonder why?
It's cute.
PLEASE WAIT A MINUTE! I'M NOT SATISFIED!
EVEN THOUGH IT'S A PAIN D'EPICES, THERE'S NO WAY 34 SEPARATE INGREDIENTS WOULD TASTE RIGHT.
MOREOVER, A JUDGMENT THAT'S ESSENTIALLY BEYOND A PERFECT SCORE...

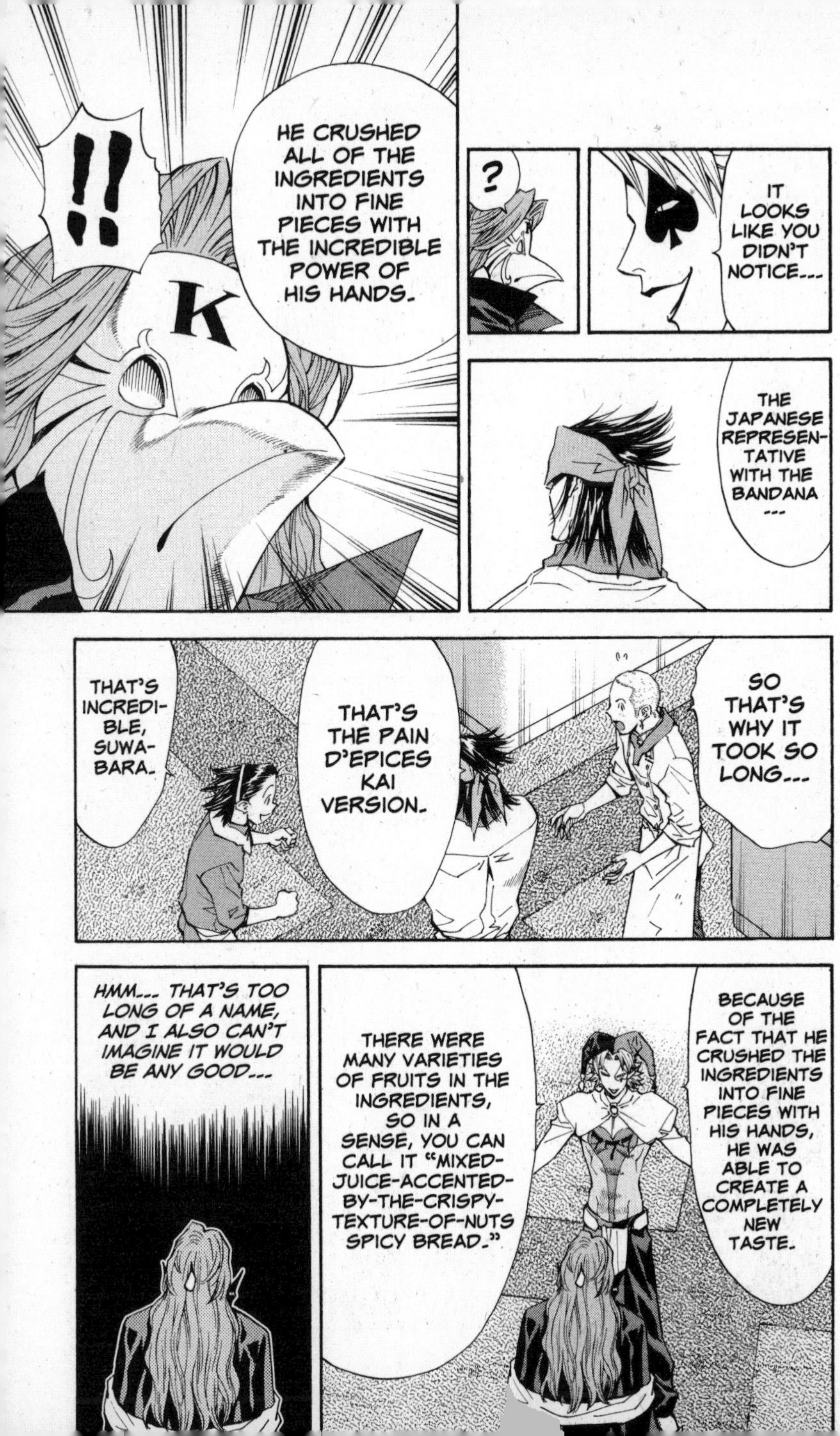
IT LOOKS LIKE YOU DIDN'T NOTICE...
?
THE JAPANESE REPRESENTATIVE WITH THE BANDANA...
!!
HE CRUSHED ALL OF THE INGREDIENTS INTO FINE PIECES WITH THE INCREDIBLE POWER OF HIS HANDS.
SO THAT'S WHY IT TOOK SO LONG...
THAT'S THE PAIN D'EPICES KAI VERSION.
THAT'S INCREDIBLE, SUWABARA.
BECAUSE OF THE FACT THAT HE CRUSHED THE INGREDIENTS INTO FINE PIECES WITH HIS HANDS, HE WAS ABLE TO CREATE A COMPLETELY NEW TASTE.
THERE WERE MANY VARIETIES OF FRUITS IN THE INGREDIENTS, SO IN A SENSE, YOU CAN CALL IT "MIXED-JUICE-ACCENTED-BY-THE-CRISPY-TEXTURE-OF-NUTS SPICY BREAD."
HMM... THAT'S TOO LONG OF A NAME, AND I ALSO CAN'T IMAGINE IT WOULD BE ANY GOOD...

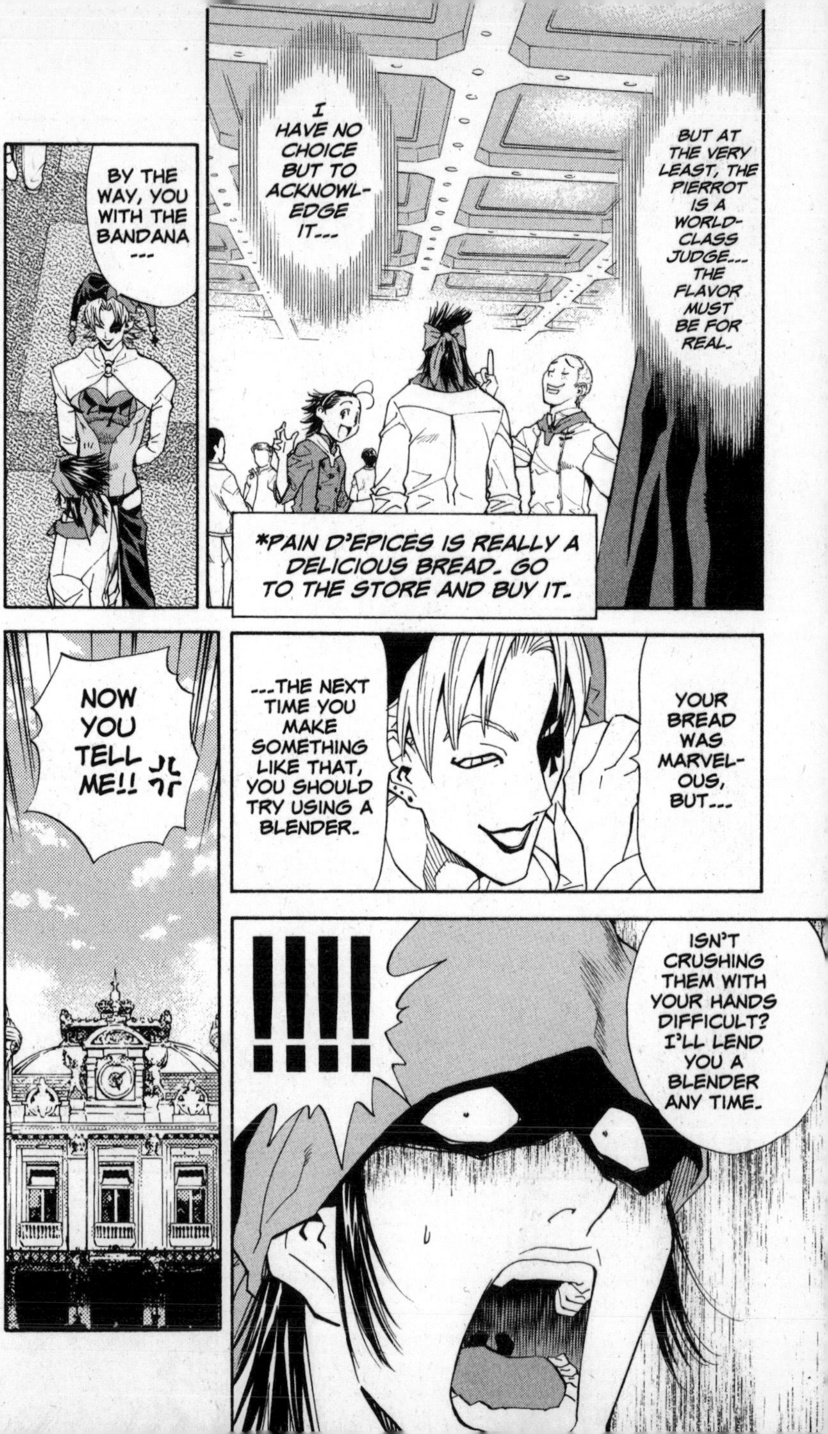
BUT AT THE VERY LEAST, THE PIERROT IS A WORLD-CLASS JUDGE... THE FLAVOR MUST BE FOR REAL.
I HAVE NO CHOICE BUT TO ACKNOWL-EDGE IT...
*PAIN D'EPICES IS REALLY A DELICIOUS BREAD. GO TO THE STORE AND BUY IT.
BY THE WAY, YOU WITH THE BANDANA ---
YOUR BREAD WAS MARVEL-OUS, BUT---
---THE NEXT TIME YOU MAKE SOMETHING LIKE THAT, YOU SHOULD TRY USING A BLENDER.
ISN'T CRUSHING THEM WITH YOUR HANDS DIFFICULT? I'LL LEND YOU A BLENDER ANY TIME.
!!!!
NOW YOU TELL ME!!

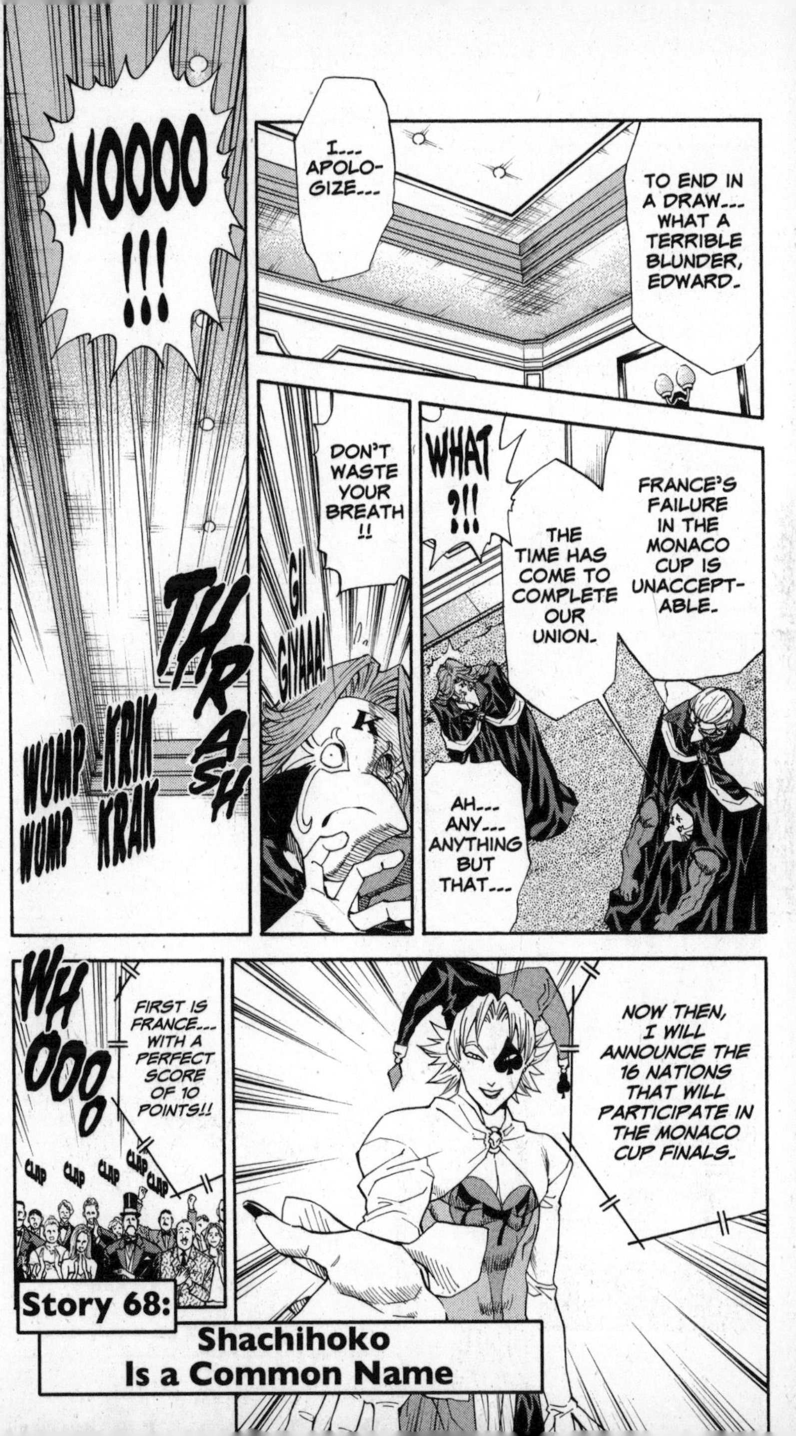

TO END IN A DRAW... WHAT A TERRIBLE BLUNDER, EDWARD.
I... APOLOGIZE...
FRANCE'S FAILURE IN THE MONACO CUP IS UNACCEPTABLE.
THE TIME HAS COME TO COMPLETE OUR UNION.
WHAT ?!!
AH... ANY... ANYTHING BUT THAT...
DON'T WASTE YOUR BREATH !!
GI GIYAAA!
NOOOO !!! !!!
THRASH
KRIK KRAK
WUMP WUMP
NOW THEN, I WILL ANNOUNCE THE 16 NATIONS THAT WILL PARTICIPATE IN THE MONACO CUP FINALS.
FIRST IS FRANCE... WITH A PERFECT SCORE OF 10 POINTS!!
WHOOOO
CLAP CLAP CLAP CLAP

Story 68: Shachihoko Is a Common Name

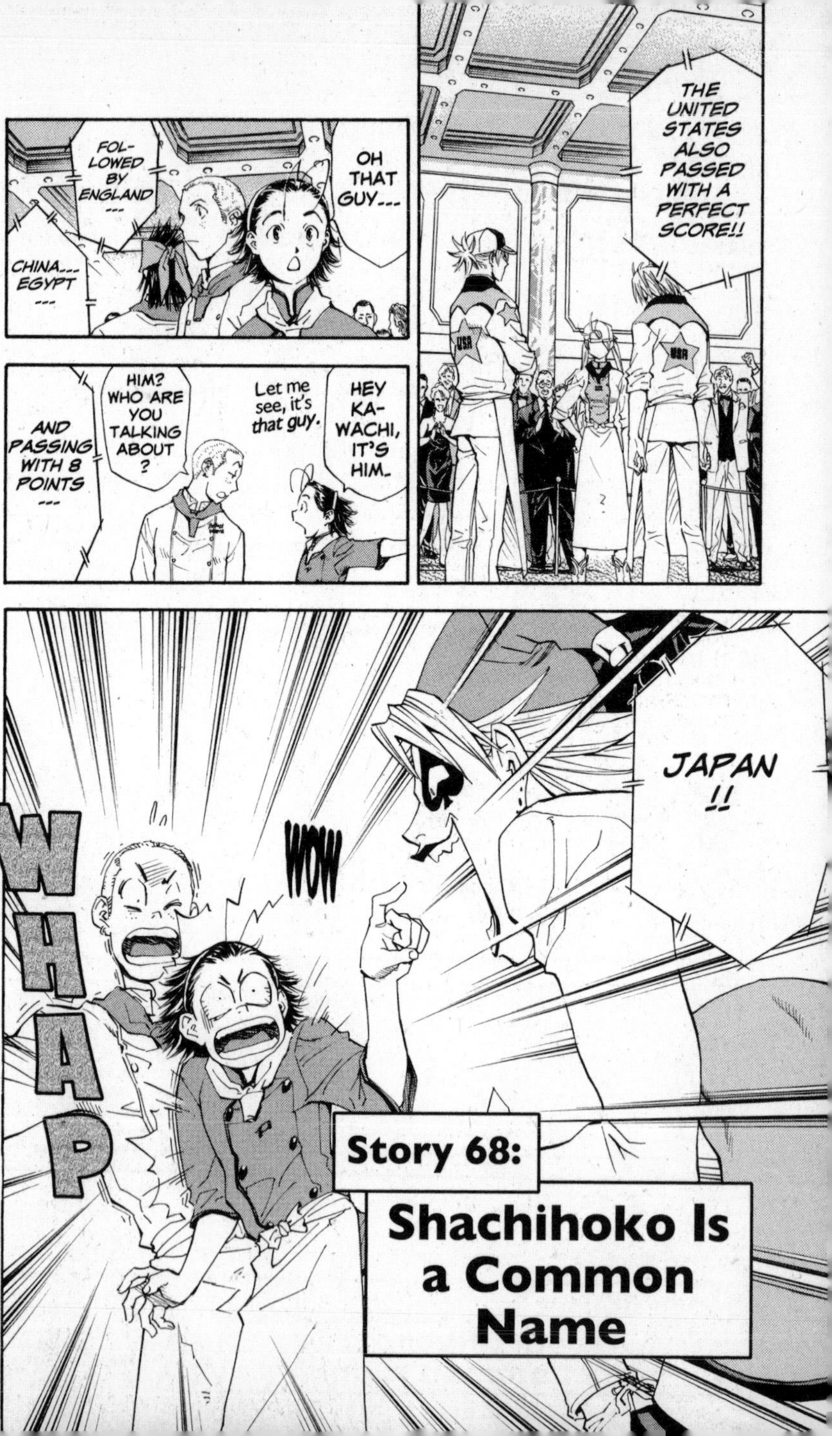
THE UNITED STATES ALSO PASSED WITH A PERFECT SCORE!!
OH THAT GUY...
FOL-LOWED BY ENGLAND...
CHINA... EGYPT...
HEY KA-WACHI, IT'S HIM.
Let me see, it's that guy.
HIM? WHO ARE YOU TALKING ABOUT?
AND PASSING WITH 8 POINTS...
JAPAN!!
WOW
WHAP
Story 68:
Shachihoko Is a Common Name

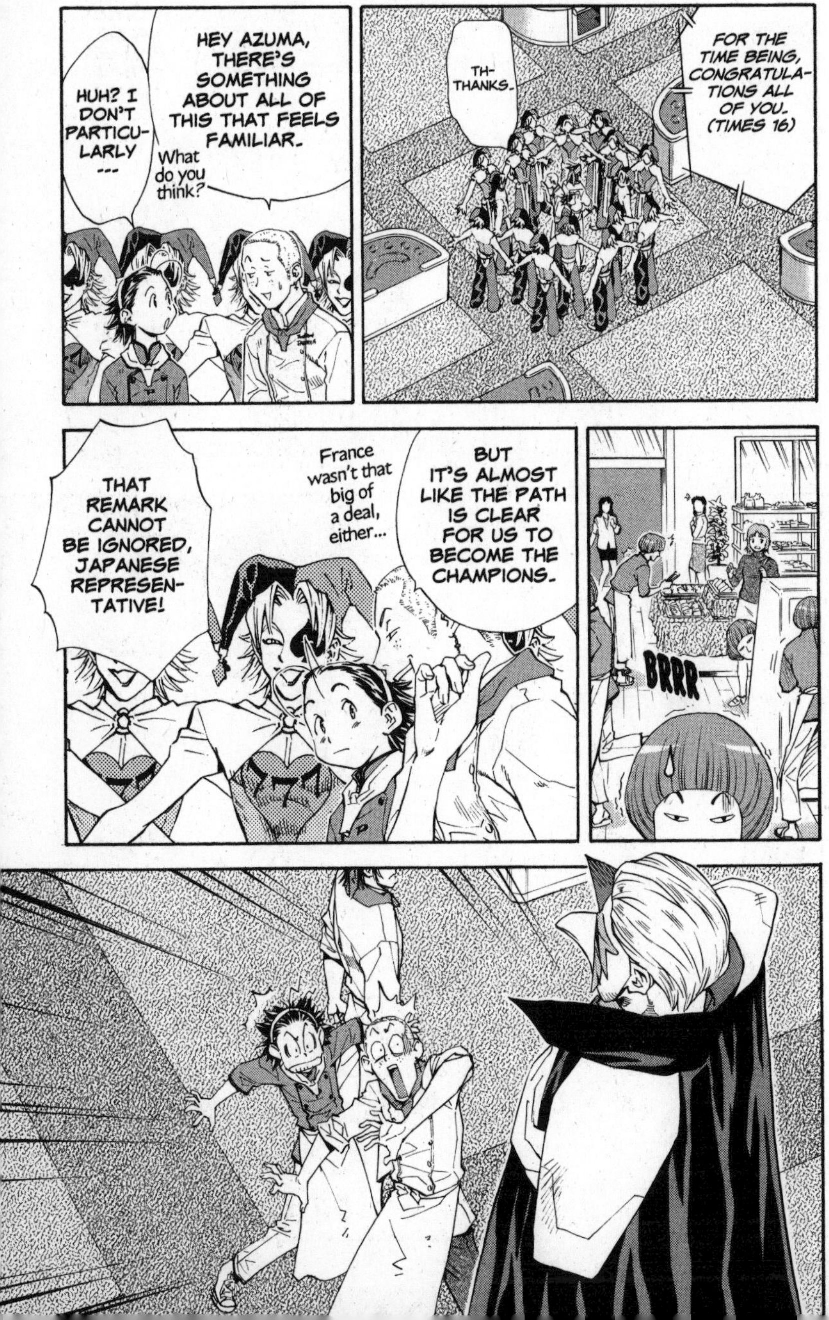
FOR THE TIME BEING, CONGRATULATIONS ALL OF YOU. (TIMES 16)
TH-THANKS.
HEY AZUMA, THERE'S SOMETHING ABOUT ALL OF THIS THAT FEELS FAMILIAR.
What do you think?
HUH? I DON'T PARTICULARLY ---
BRRR-
BUT IT'S ALMOST LIKE THE PATH IS CLEAR FOR US TO BECOME THE CHAMPIONS.
France wasn't that big of a deal, either...
THAT REMARK CANNOT BE IGNORED, JAPANESE REPRESENTATIVE!

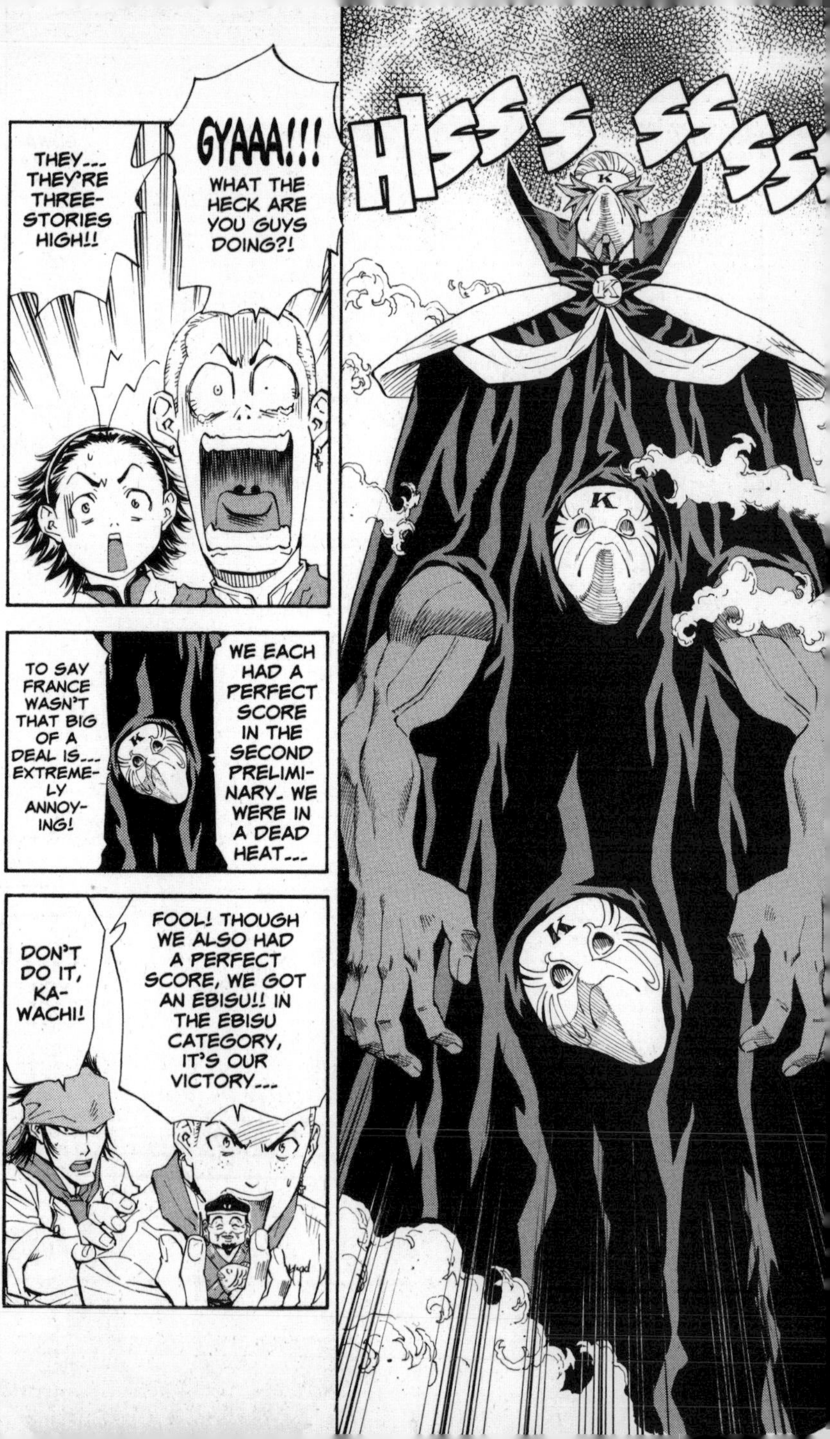
HISSS SSSS
GYAAA!!! WHAT THE HECK ARE YOU GUYS DOING?!
THEY... THEY'RE THREE-STORIES HIGH!!
WE EACH HAD A PERFECT SCORE IN THE SECOND PRELIMINARY. WE WERE IN A DEAD HEAT...
TO SAY FRANCE WASN'T THAT BIG OF A DEAL IS... EXTREMELY ANNOYING!
FOOL! THOUGH WE ALSO HAD A PERFECT SCORE, WE GOT AN EBISU!! IN THE EBISU CATEGORY, IT'S OUR VICTORY...
DON'T DO IT, KAWACHI!

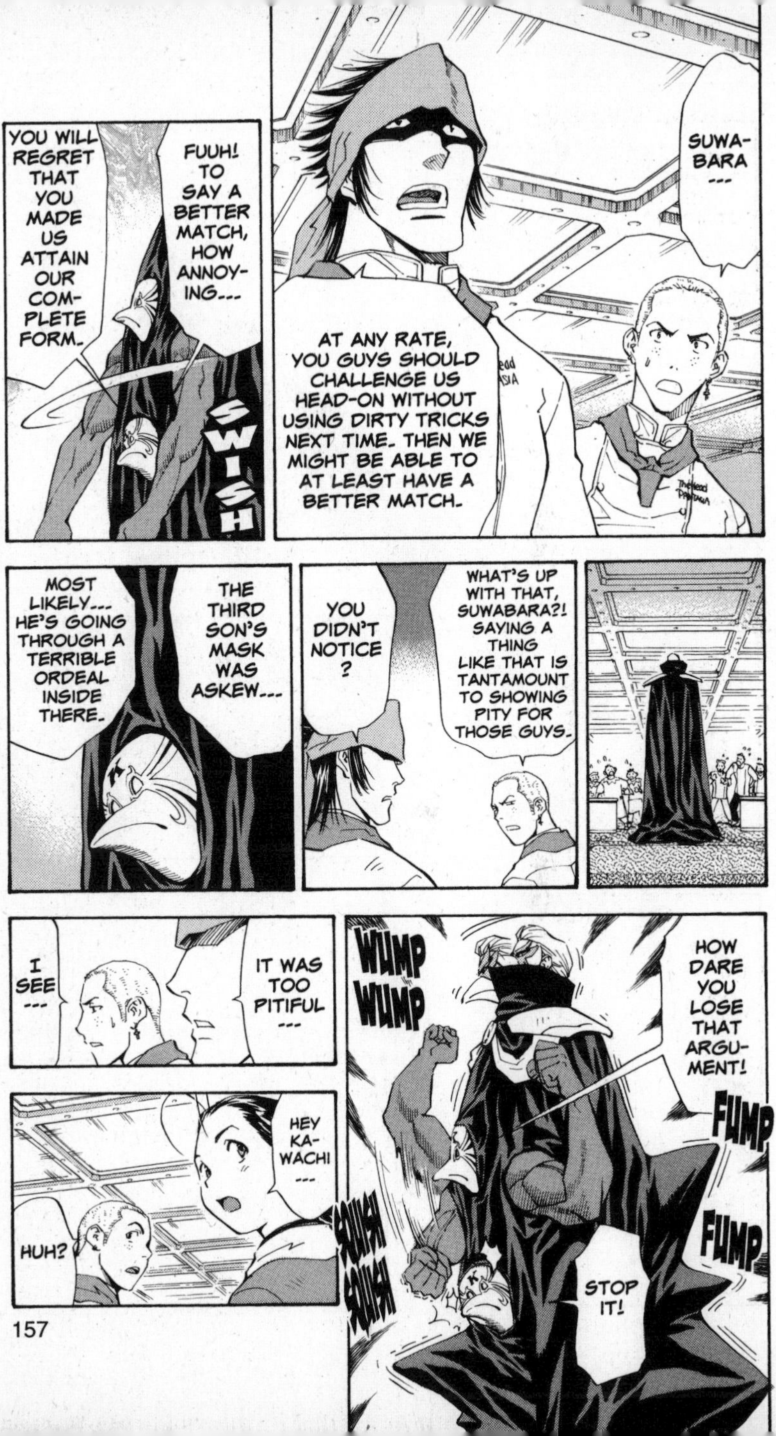
SUWA-BARA---
AT ANY RATE, YOU GUYS SHOULD CHALLENGE US HEAD-ON WITHOUT USING DIRTY TRICKS NEXT TIME. THEN WE MIGHT BE ABLE TO AT LEAST HAVE A BETTER MATCH.
FUUH! TO SAY A BETTER MATCH, HOW ANNOY-ING---
YOU WILL REGRET THAT YOU MADE US ATTAIN OUR COM-PLETE FORM.
SWISH
WHAT'S UP WITH THAT, SUWABARA?! SAYING A THING LIKE THAT IS TANTAMOUNT TO SHOWING PITY FOR THOSE GUYS.
YOU DIDN'T NOTICE?
THE THIRD SON'S MASK WAS ASKEW---
MOST LIKELY--- HE'S GOING THROUGH A TERRIBLE ORDEAL INSIDE THERE.
HOW DARE YOU LOSE THAT ARGU-MENT!
WUMP WUMP
FUMP
FUMP
SQUISH SQUISH
STOP IT!
IT WAS TOO PITIFUL ---
I SEE ---
HEY KA-WACHI ---
HUH?

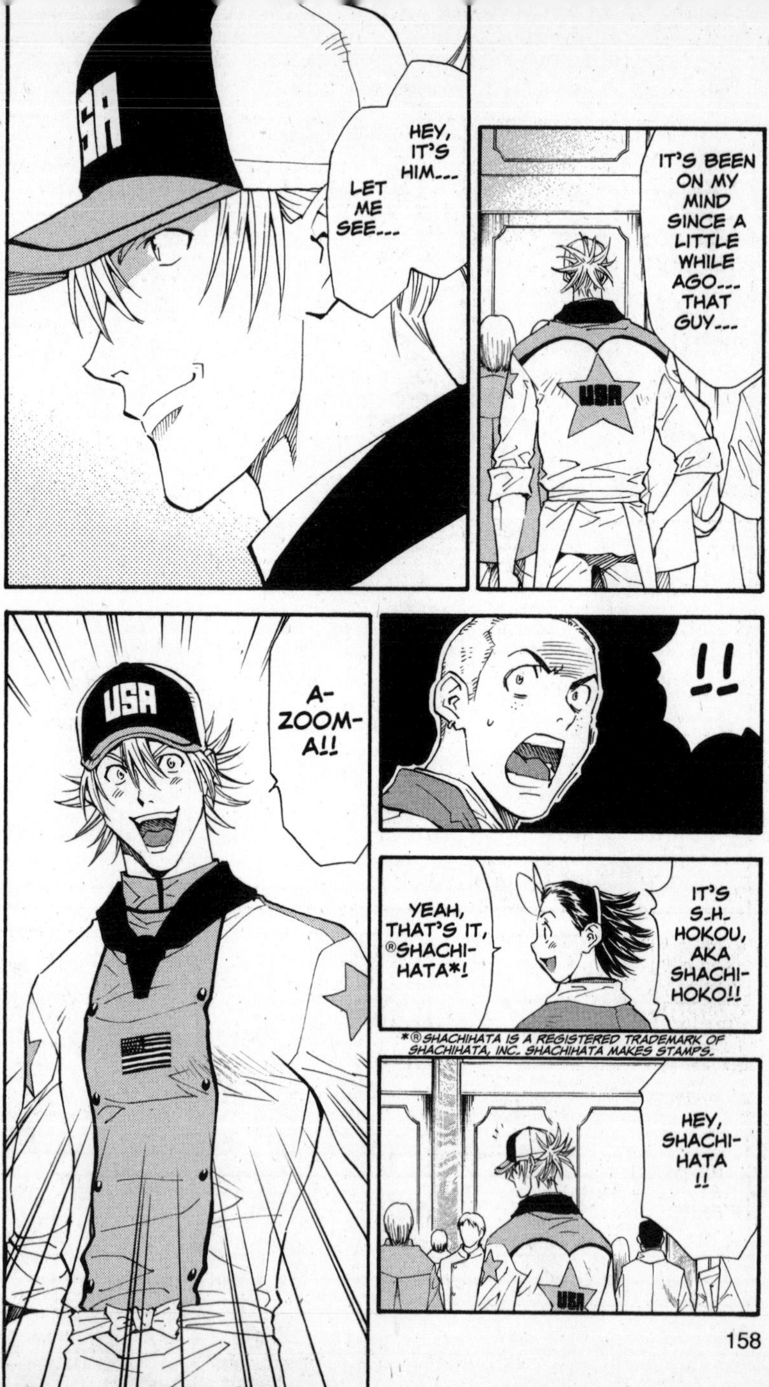
IT'S BEEN ON MY MIND SINCE A LITTLE WHILE AGO... THAT GUY...
HEY, IT'S HIM...
LET ME SEE...
USA
!!
IT'S S-H-HOKOU, AKA SHACHI-HOKO!!
YEAH, THAT'S IT, ®SHACHI-HATA*!
*® SHACHIHATA IS A REGISTERED TRADEMARK OF SHACHIHATA, INC. SHACHIHATA MAKES STAMPS.
HEY, SHACHI-HATA!!
USA
USA
A-ZOOM-A!!

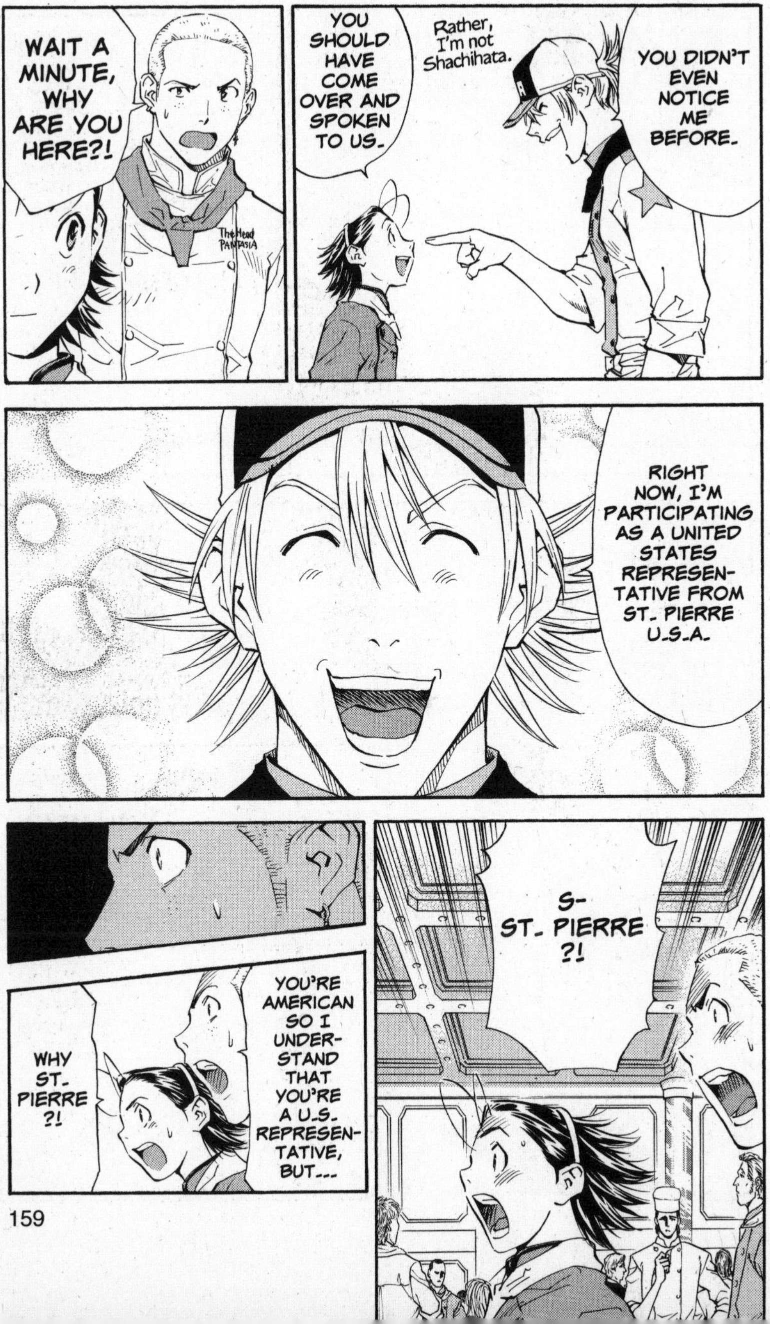
YOU DIDN'T EVEN NOTICE ME BEFORE.
Rather, I'm not Shachihata.
YOU SHOULD HAVE COME OVER AND SPOKEN TO US.
WAIT A MINUTE, WHY ARE YOU HERE?!
The Head PANTASIA
RIGHT NOW, I'M PARTICIPATING AS A UNITED STATES REPRESEN-TATIVE FROM ST. PIERRE U.S.A.
S- ST. PIERRE ?!
YOU'RE AMERICAN SO I UNDER-STAND THAT YOU'RE A U.S. REPRESEN-TATIVE, BUT...
WHY ST. PIERRE ?!

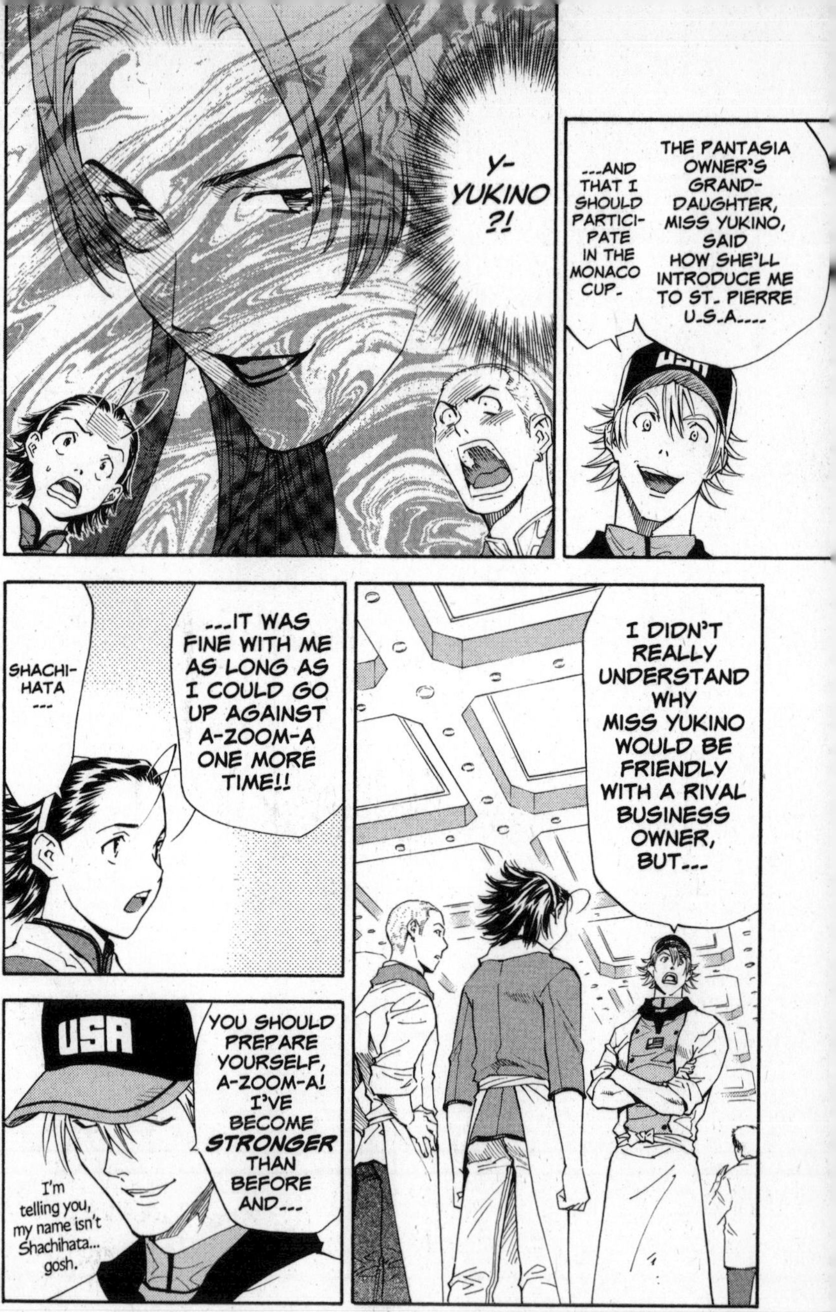
THE PANTASIA OWNER'S GRAND-DAUGHTER, MISS YUKINO, SAID HOW SHE'LL INTRODUCE ME TO ST. PIERRE U.S.A....
...AND THAT I SHOULD PARTICIPATE IN THE MONACO CUP.
Y-YUKINO?!
I DIDN'T REALLY UNDERSTAND WHY MISS YUKINO WOULD BE FRIENDLY WITH A RIVAL BUSINESS OWNER, BUT...
...IT WAS FINE WITH ME AS LONG AS I COULD GO UP AGAINST A-ZOOM-A ONE MORE TIME!!
SHACHIHATA...
YOU SHOULD PREPARE YOURSELF, A-ZOOM-A! I'VE BECOME *STRONGER* THAN BEFORE AND...
I'm telling you, my name isn't Shachihata... gosh.

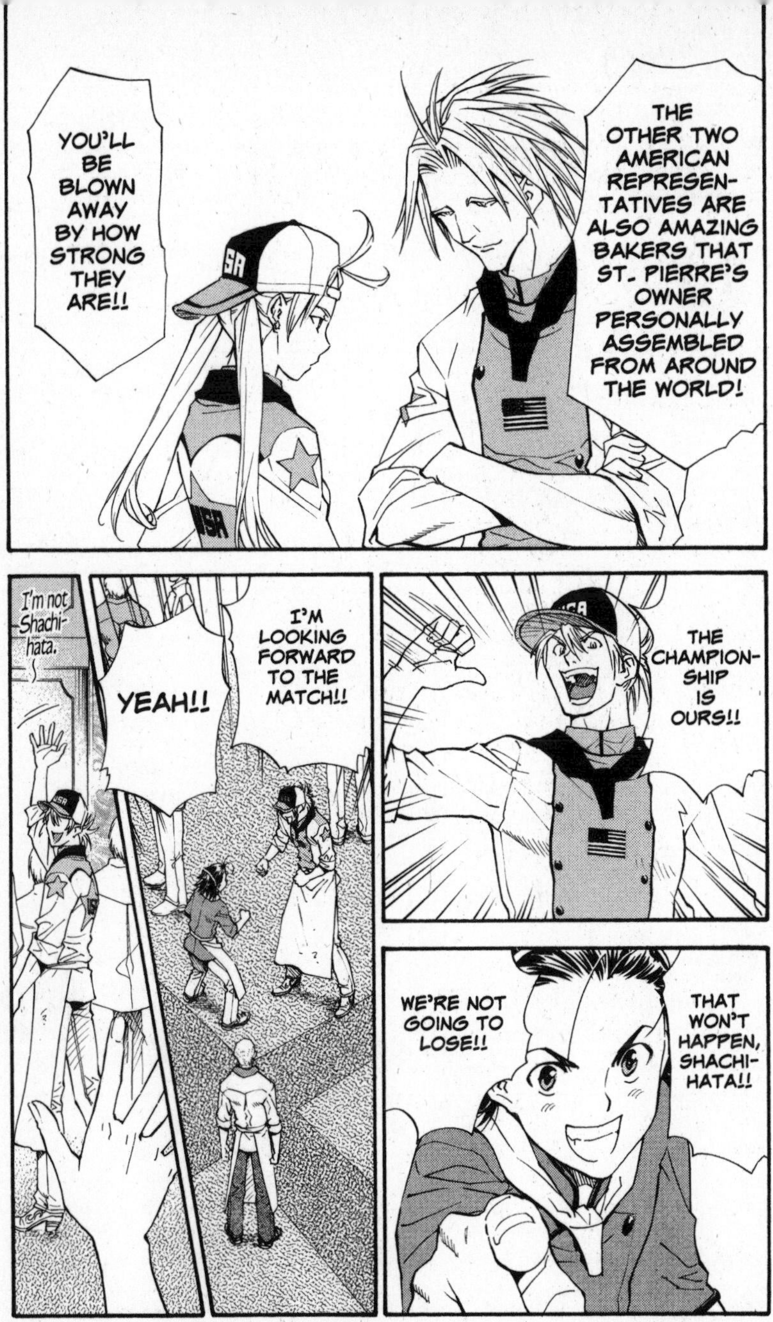
THE OTHER TWO AMERICAN REPRESEN-TATIVES ARE ALSO AMAZING BAKERS THAT ST. PIERRE'S OWNER PERSONALLY ASSEMBLED FROM AROUND THE WORLD!
YOU'LL BE BLOWN AWAY BY HOW STRONG THEY ARE!!
THE CHAMPION-SHIP IS OURS!!
THAT WON'T HAPPEN, SHACHI-HATA!!
WE'RE NOT GOING TO LOSE!!
I'M LOOKING FORWARD TO THE MATCH!!
YEAH!!
I'm not Shachi-hata.

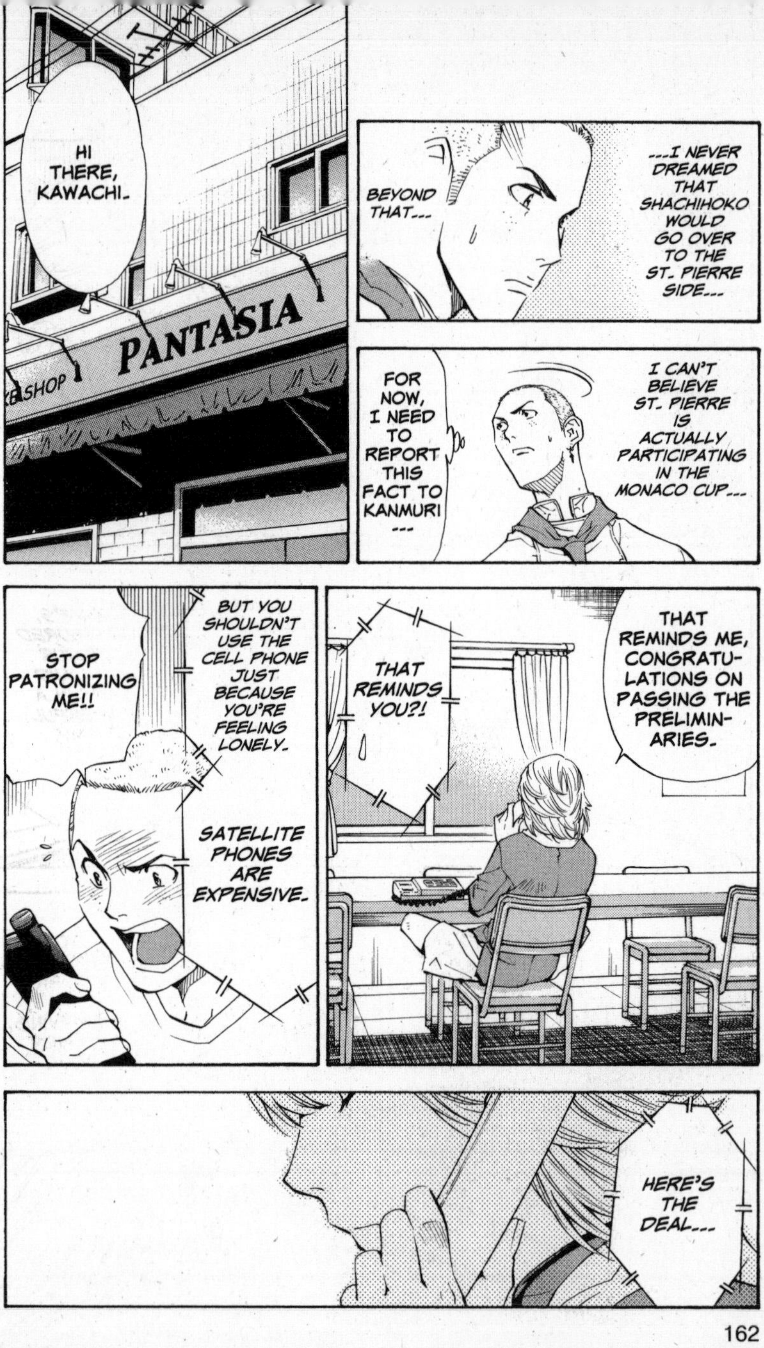
...I NEVER DREAMED THAT SHACHIHOKO WOULD GO OVER TO THE ST. PIERRE SIDE...
BEYOND THAT...
I CAN'T BELIEVE ST. PIERRE IS ACTUALLY PARTICIPATING IN THE MONACO CUP...
FOR NOW, I NEED TO REPORT THIS FACT TO KANMURI ...
KESHOP
PANTASIA
HI THERE, KAWACHI.
THAT REMINDS ME, CONGRATULATIONS ON PASSING THE PRELIMINARIES.
THAT REMINDS YOU?!
BUT YOU SHOULDN'T USE THE CELL PHONE JUST BECAUSE YOU'RE FEELING LONELY.
STOP PATRONIZING ME!!
SATELLITE PHONES ARE EXPENSIVE.
HERE'S THE DEAL...

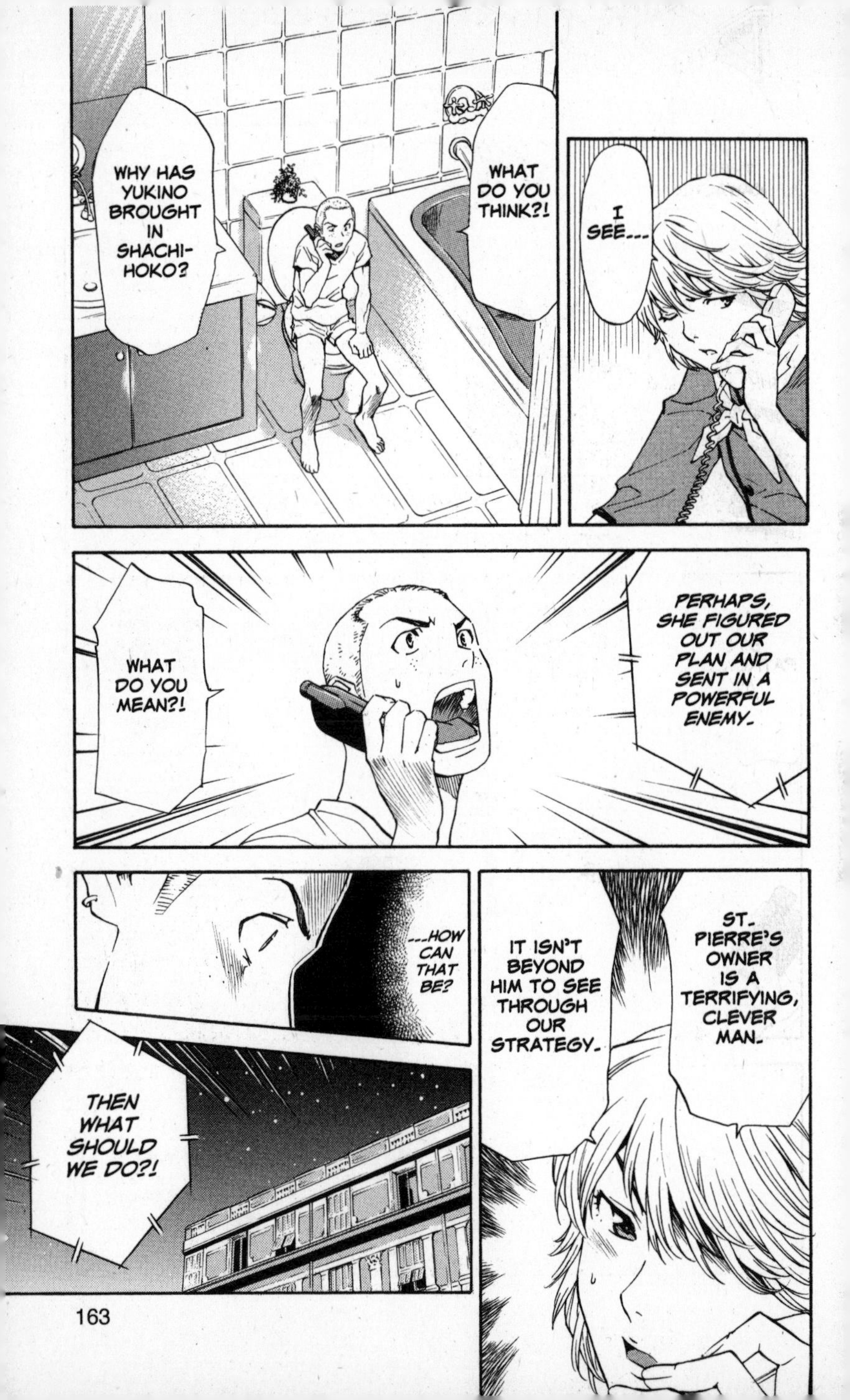
I SEE...
WHAT DO YOU THINK?!
WHY HAS YUKINO BROUGHT IN SHACHI-HOKO?
PERHAPS, SHE FIGURED OUT OUR PLAN AND SENT IN A POWERFUL ENEMY.
WHAT DO YOU MEAN?!
ST. PIERRE'S OWNER IS A TERRIFYING, CLEVER MAN.
IT ISN'T BEYOND HIM TO SEE THROUGH OUR STRATEGY.
...HOW CAN THAT BE?
THEN WHAT SHOULD WE DO?!

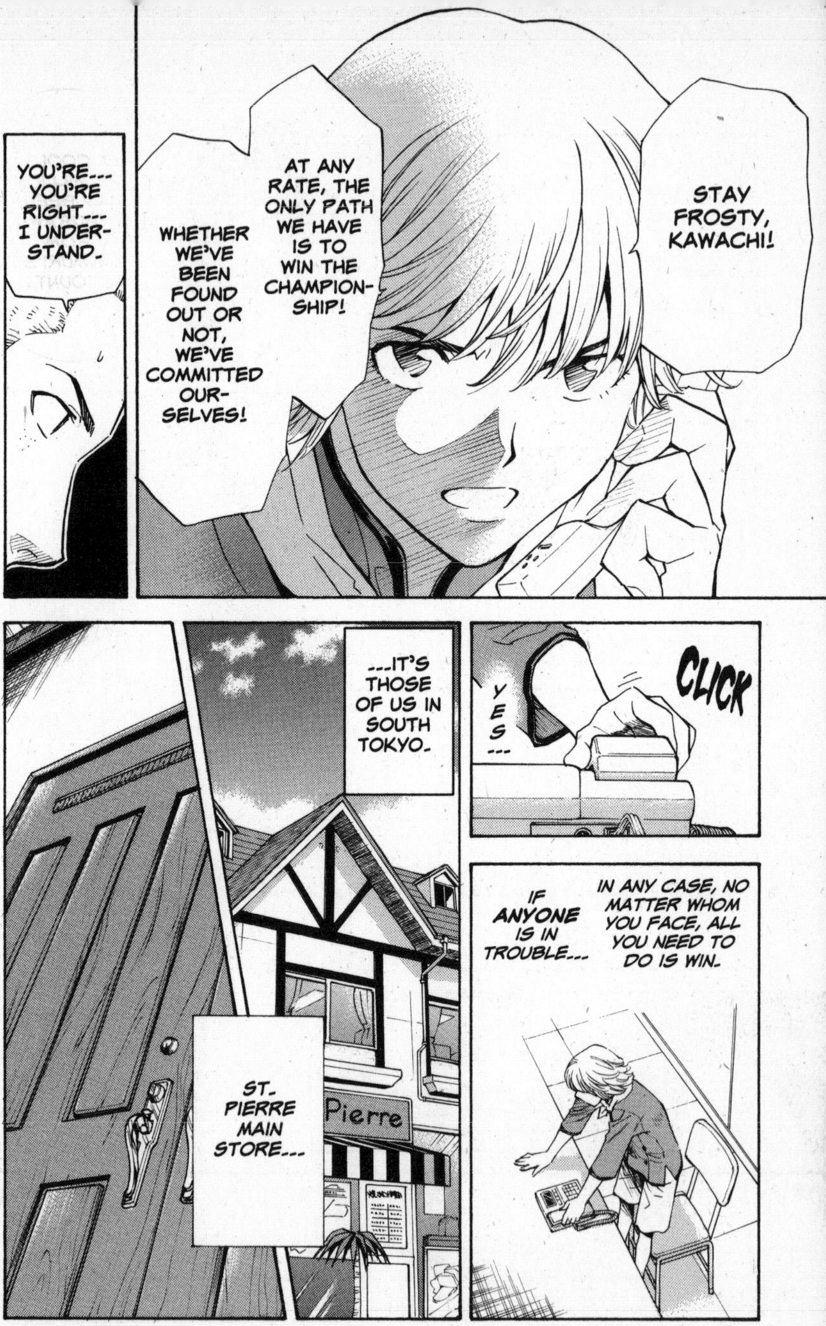
STAY FROSTY, KAWACHI!
AT ANY RATE, THE ONLY PATH WE HAVE IS TO WIN THE CHAMPIONSHIP!
WHETHER WE'VE BEEN FOUND OUT OR NOT, WE'VE COMMITTED OURSELVES!
YOU'RE... YOU'RE RIGHT... I UNDERSTAND.
CLICK
YES...
IN ANY CASE, NO MATTER WHOM YOU FACE, ALL YOU NEED TO DO IS WIN.
IF ANYONE IS IN TROUBLE...
...IT'S THOSE OF US IN SOUTH TOKYO.
ST. PIERRE MAIN STORE...
Pierre

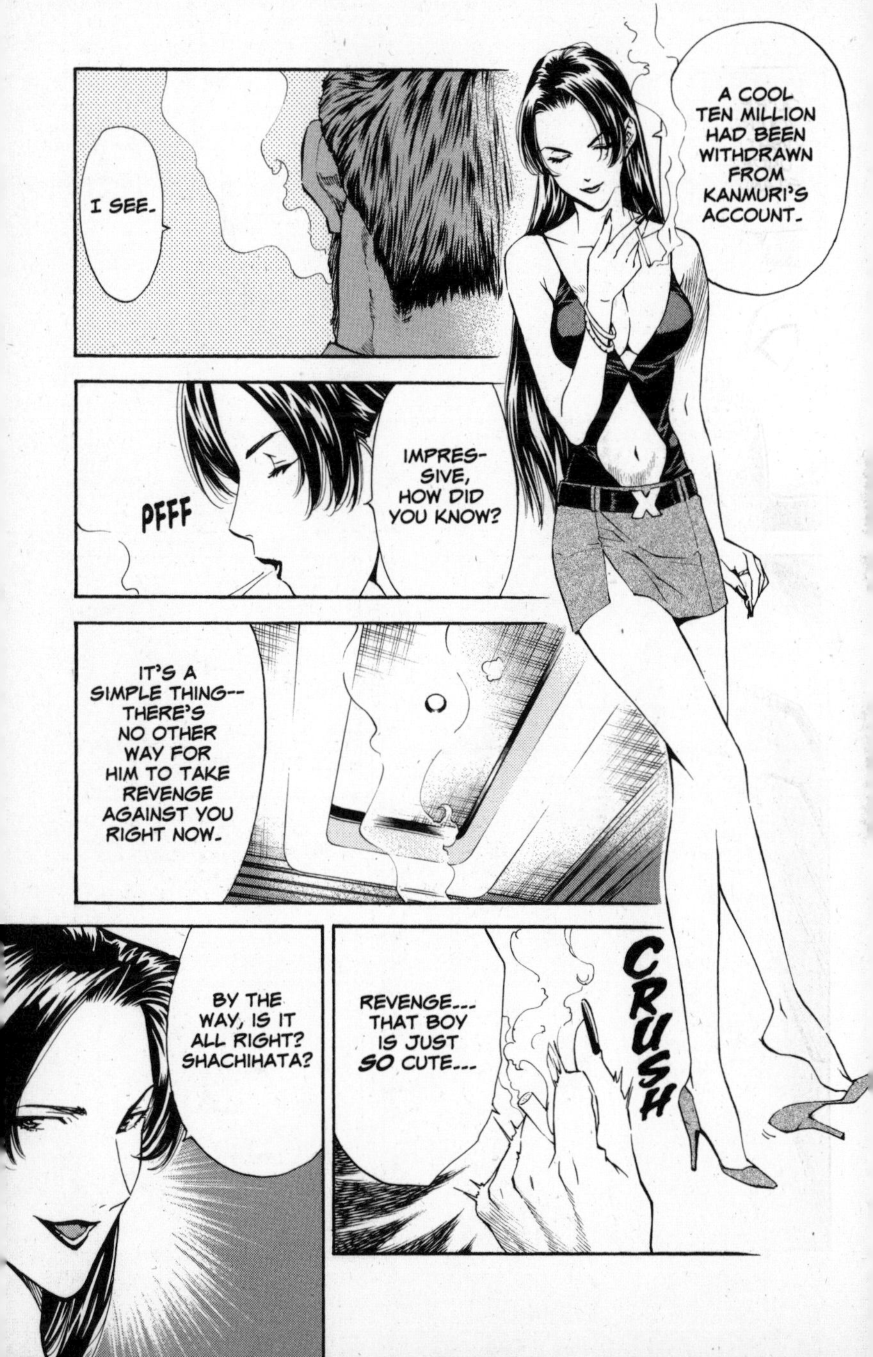
A COOL TEN MILLION HAD BEEN WITHDRAWN FROM KANMURI'S ACCOUNT.
I SEE.
IMPRES-SIVE, HOW DID YOU KNOW?
PFFF
IT'S A SIMPLE THING-- THERE'S NO OTHER WAY FOR HIM TO TAKE REVENGE AGAINST YOU RIGHT NOW.
REVENGE... THAT BOY IS JUST *SO* CUTE...
CRUSH
BY THE WAY, IS IT ALL RIGHT? SHACHIHATA?

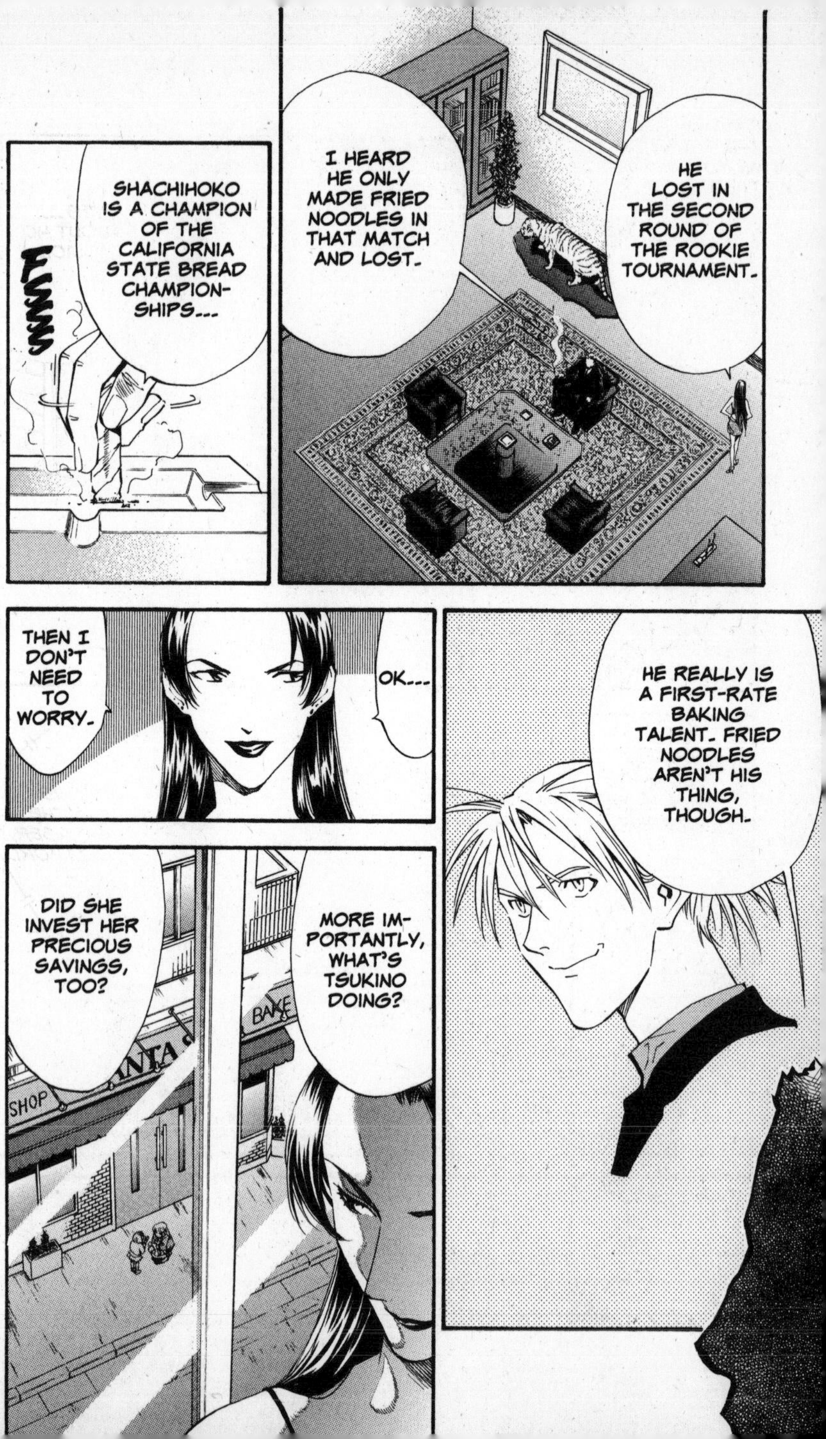
HE LOST IN THE SECOND ROUND OF THE ROOKIE TOURNAMENT.
I HEARD HE ONLY MADE FRIED NOODLES IN THAT MATCH AND LOST.
SHACHIHOKO IS A CHAMPION OF THE CALIFORNIA STATE BREAD CHAMPION-SHIPS...
FSSSS
HE REALLY IS A FIRST-RATE BAKING TALENT. FRIED NOODLES AREN'T HIS THING, THOUGH.
OK...
THEN I DON'T NEED TO WORRY.
MORE IM-PORTANTLY, WHAT'S TSUKINO DOING?
DID SHE INVEST HER PRECIOUS SAVINGS, TOO?
BAKE
SHOP

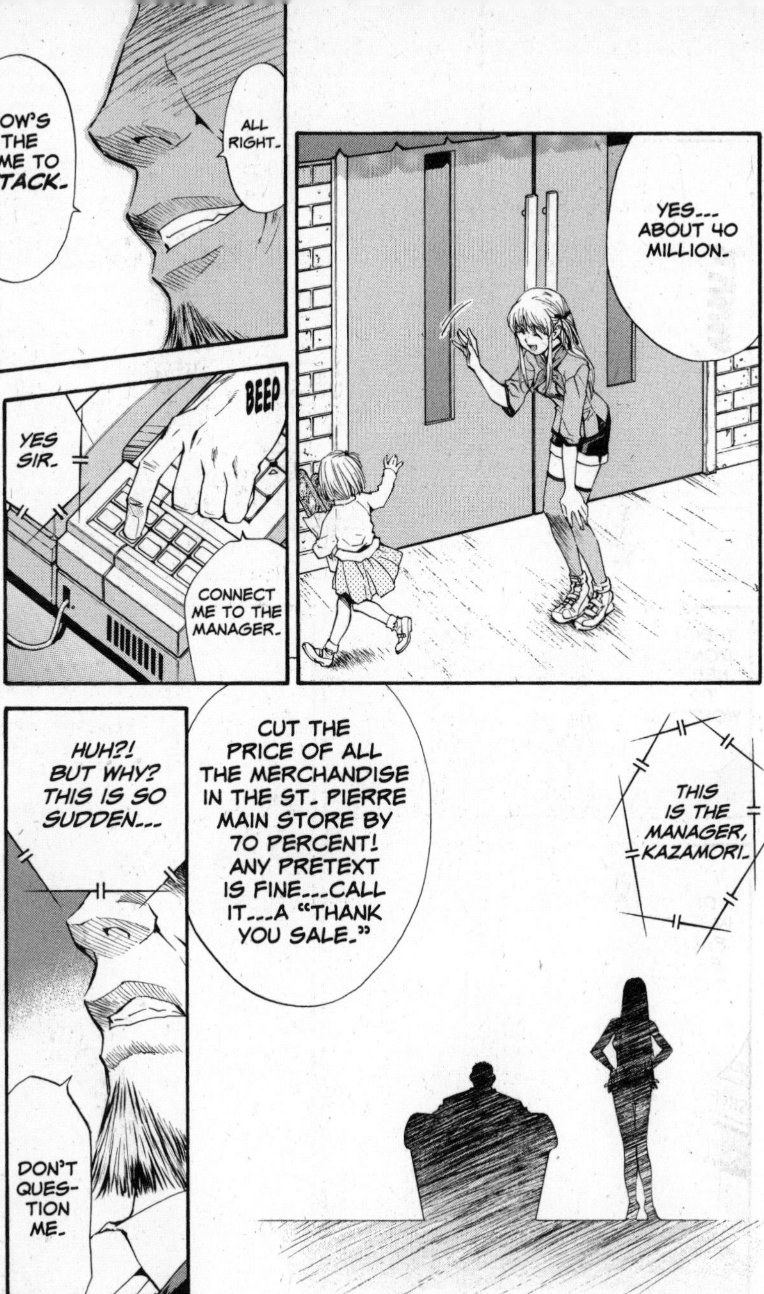
YES... ABOUT 40 MILLION.
ALL RIGHT.
NOW'S THE TIME TO ATTACK.
BEEP
CONNECT ME TO THE MANAGER.
YES SIR.
THIS IS THE MANAGER, KAZAMORI.
CUT THE PRICE OF ALL THE MERCHANDISE IN THE ST. PIERRE MAIN STORE BY 70 PERCENT! ANY PRETEXT IS FINE...CALL IT...A "THANK YOU SALE."
HUH?! BUT WHY? THIS IS SO SUDDEN...
DON'T QUES- TION ME.

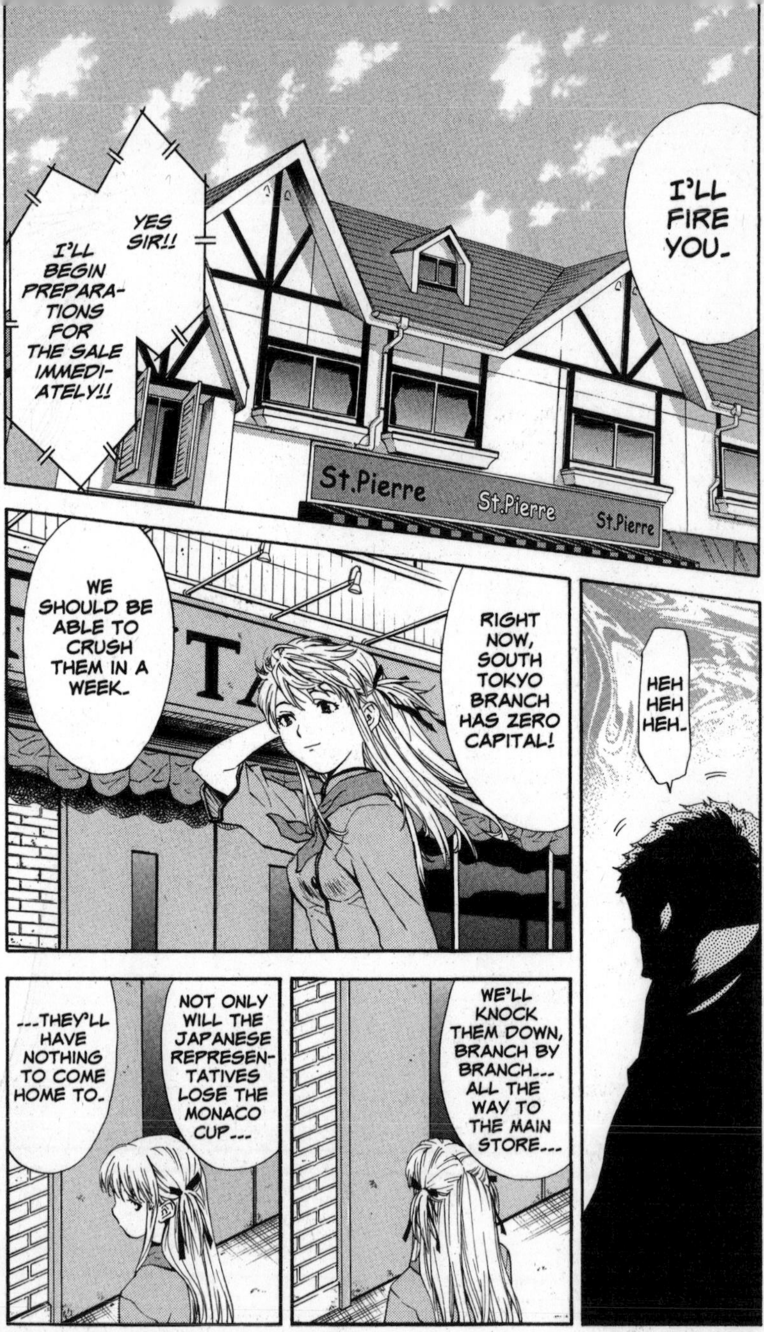
I'LL FIRE YOU...
YES SIR!!
I'LL BEGIN PREPARATIONS FOR THE SALE IMMEDIATELY!!
St.Pierre
St.Pierre
St.Pierre
HEH HEH HEH...
RIGHT NOW, SOUTH TOKYO BRANCH HAS ZERO CAPITAL!
WE SHOULD BE ABLE TO CRUSH THEM IN A WEEK...
WE'LL KNOCK THEM DOWN, BRANCH BY BRANCH... ALL THE WAY TO THE MAIN STORE...
NOT ONLY WILL THE JAPANESE REPRESENTATIVES LOSE THE MONACO CUP...
...THEY'LL HAVE NOTHING TO COME HOME TO...

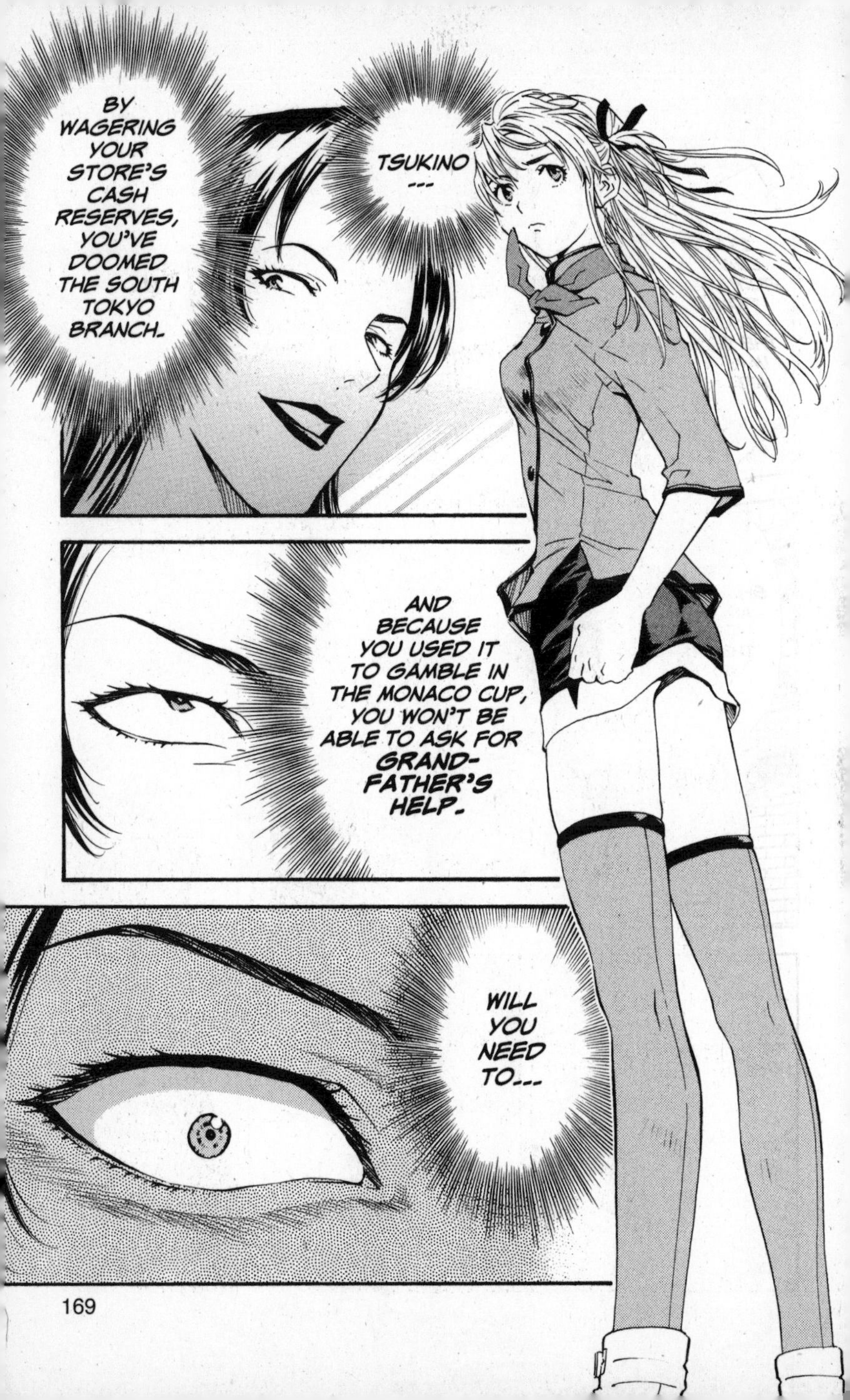

TSUKINO---
BY WAGERING YOUR STORE'S CASH RESERVES, YOU'VE DOOMED THE SOUTH TOKYO BRANCH.
AND BECAUSE YOU USED IT TO GAMBLE IN THE MONACO CUP, YOU WON'T BE ABLE TO ASK FOR **GRANDFATHER'S** HELP.
WILL YOU NEED TO...

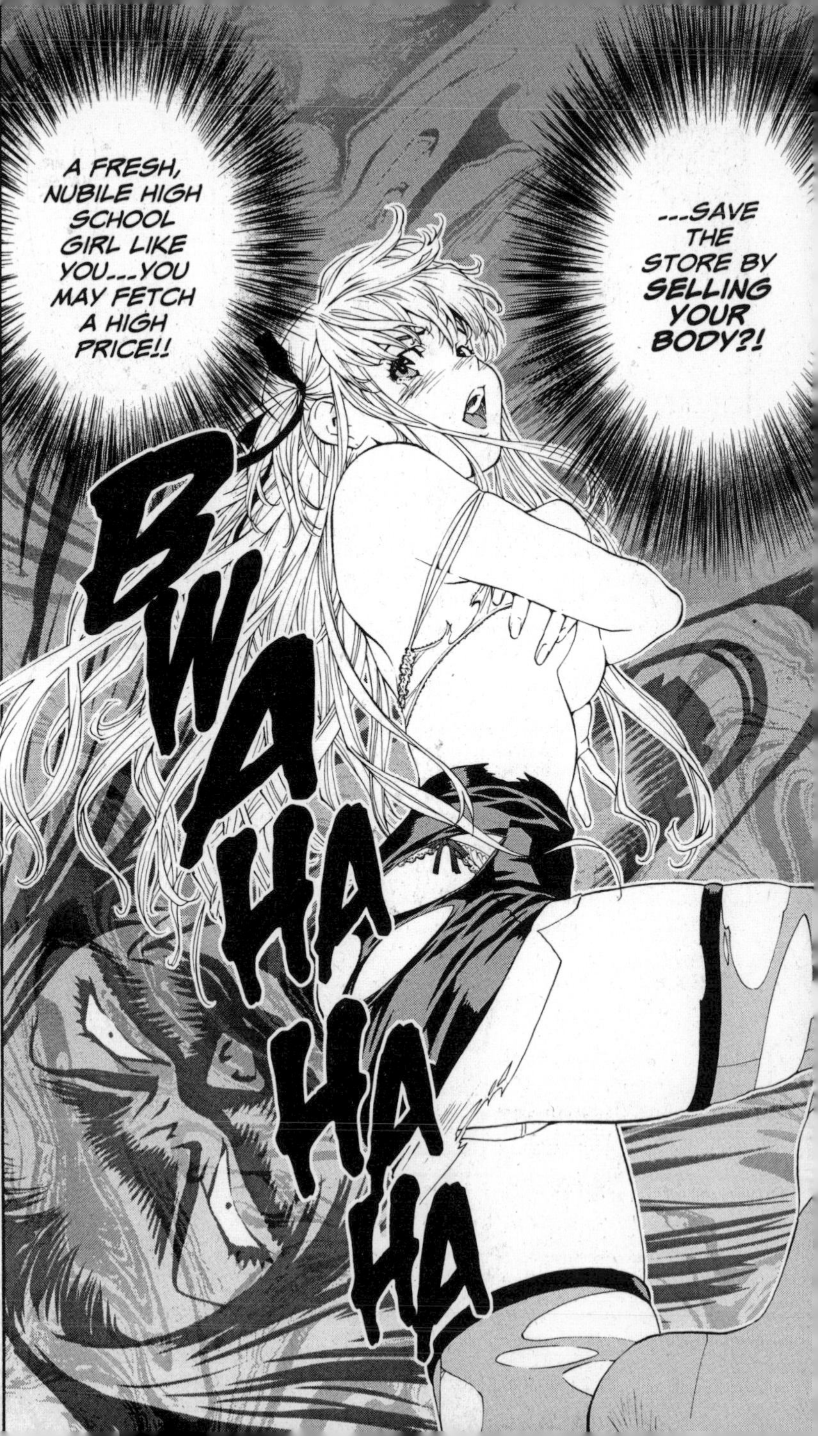
---SAVE THE STORE BY SELLING YOUR BODY?!
A FRESH, NUBILE HIGH SCHOOL GIRL LIKE YOU---YOU MAY FETCH A HIGH PRICE!!
BWAHAHAHAHA

Story 69: Kinoshita and the Circus

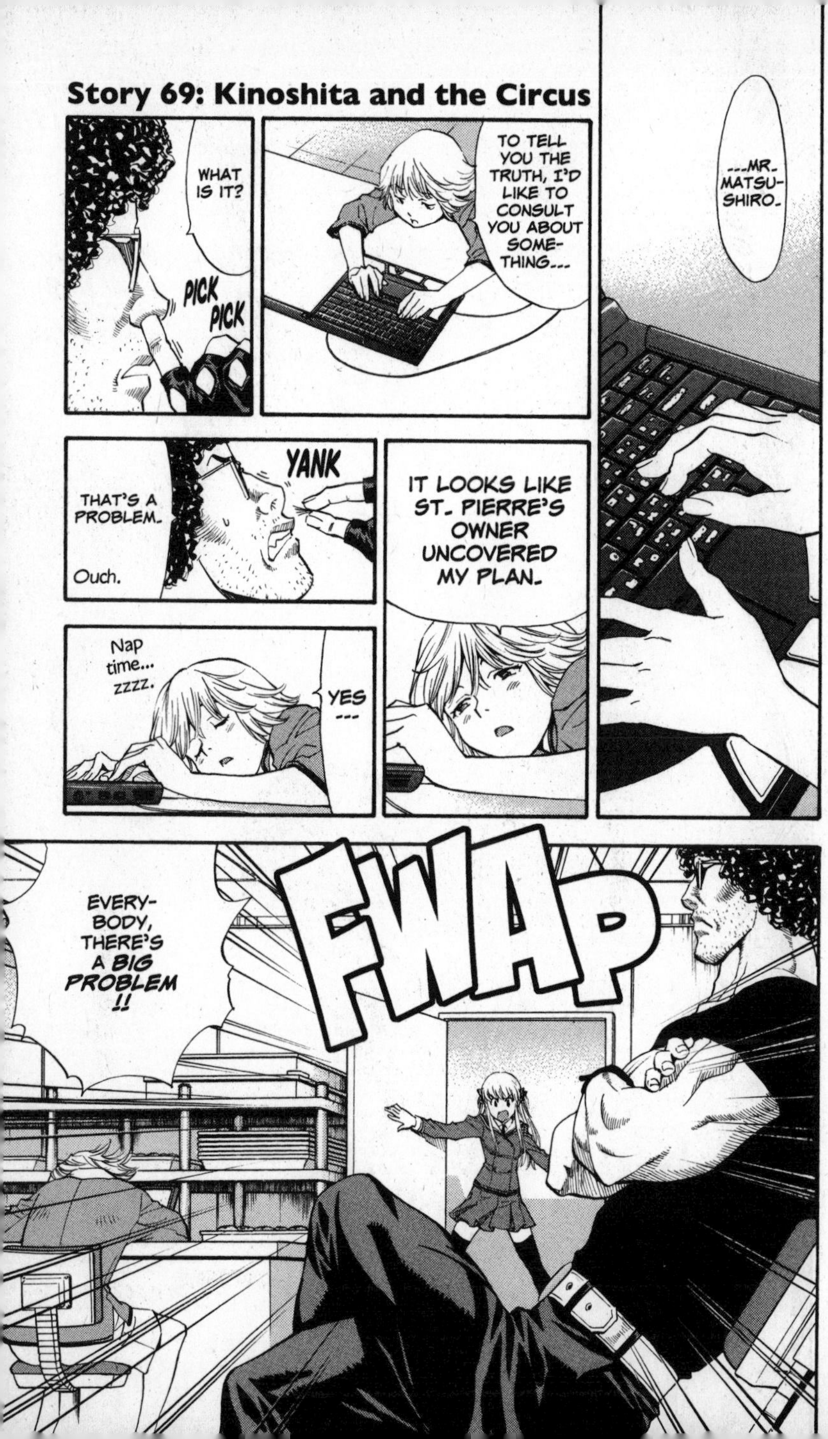
---MR. MATSUSHIRO.
TO TELL YOU THE TRUTH, I'D LIKE TO CONSULT YOU ABOUT SOMETHING...
WHAT IS IT?
PICK PICK
IT LOOKS LIKE ST. PIERRE'S OWNER UNCOVERED MY PLAN.
YANK
THAT'S A PROBLEM.
Ouch.
YES ---
Nap time... zzzz.
FWAP
EVERYBODY, THERE'S A *BIG PROBLEM* !!

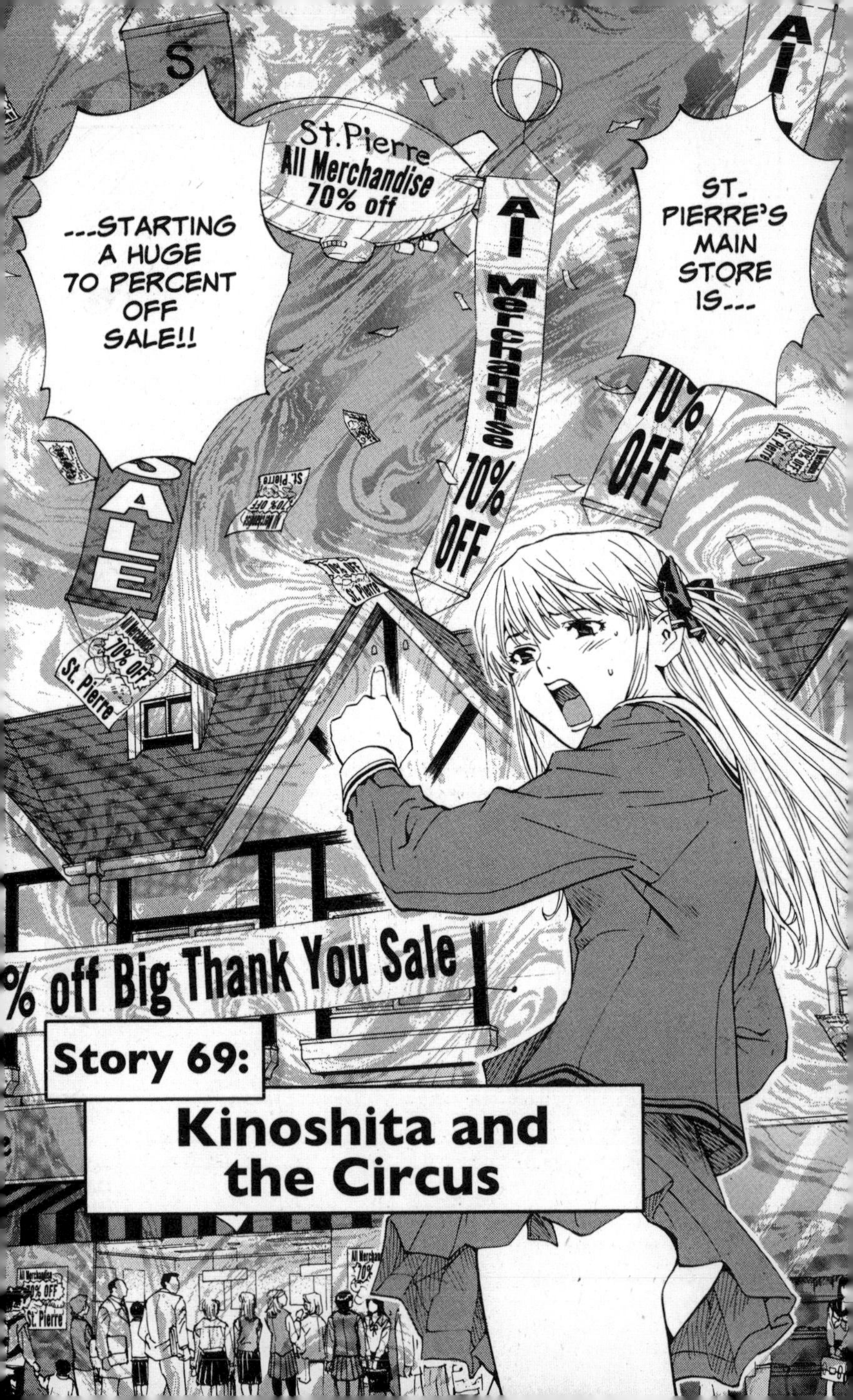
ST. PIERRE'S MAIN STORE IS...
...STARTING A HUGE 70 PERCENT OFF SALE!!
St. Pierre All Merchandise 70% off
All Merchandise 70% OFF
70% OFF
SALE
% off Big Thank You Sale
Story 69:
Kinoshita and the Circus

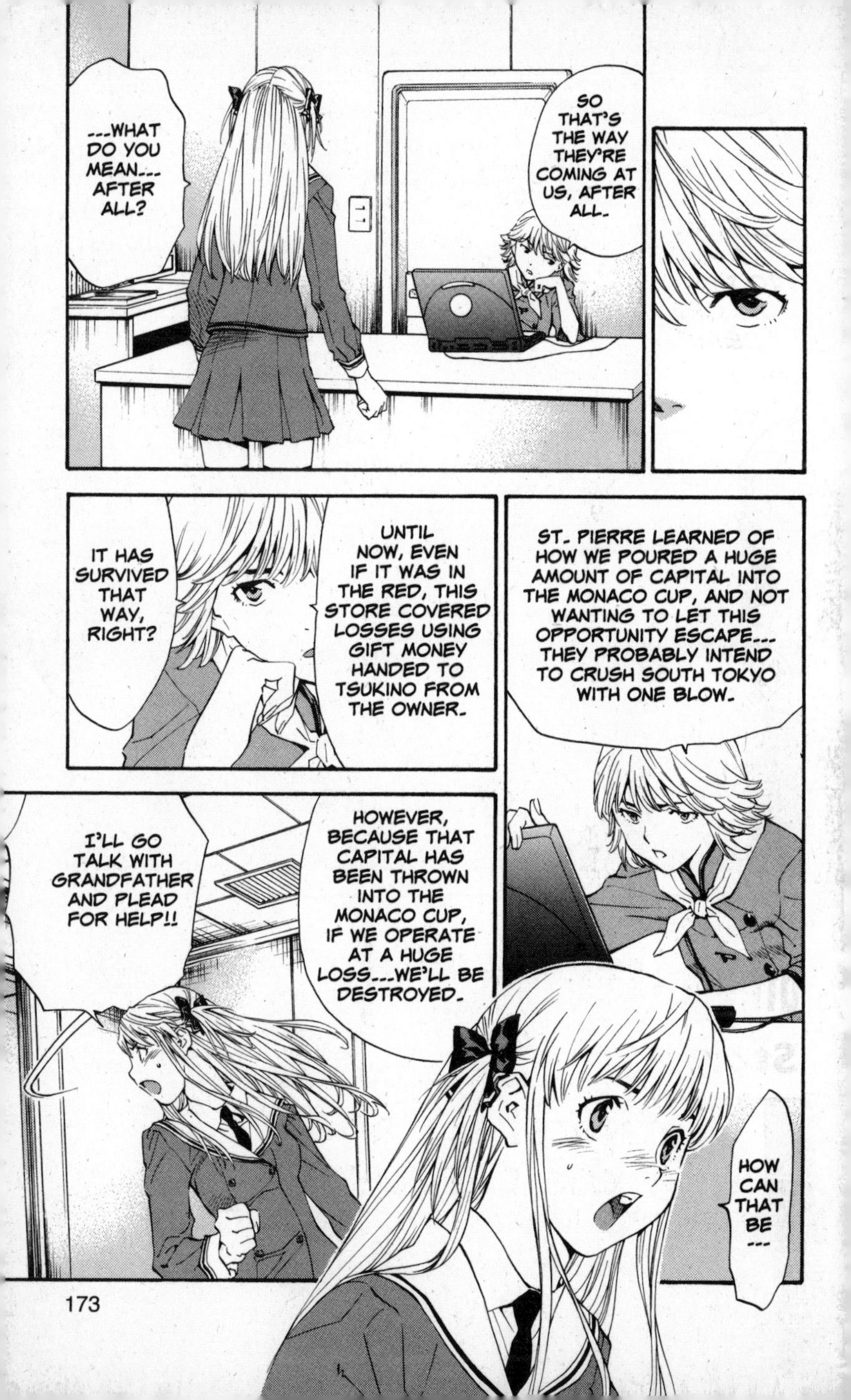
SO THAT'S THE WAY THEY'RE COMING AT US, AFTER ALL.
...WHAT DO YOU MEAN... AFTER ALL?
ST. PIERRE LEARNED OF HOW WE POURED A HUGE AMOUNT OF CAPITAL INTO THE MONACO CUP, AND NOT WANTING TO LET THIS OPPORTUNITY ESCAPE... THEY PROBABLY INTEND TO CRUSH SOUTH TOKYO WITH ONE BLOW.
UNTIL NOW, EVEN IF IT WAS IN THE RED, THIS STORE COVERED LOSSES USING GIFT MONEY HANDED TO TSUKINO FROM THE OWNER.
IT HAS SURVIVED THAT WAY, RIGHT?
HOWEVER, BECAUSE THAT CAPITAL HAS BEEN THROWN INTO THE MONACO CUP, IF WE OPERATE AT A HUGE LOSS...WE'LL BE DESTROYED.
HOW CAN THAT BE ---
I'LL GO TALK WITH GRANDFATHER AND PLEAD FOR HELP!!

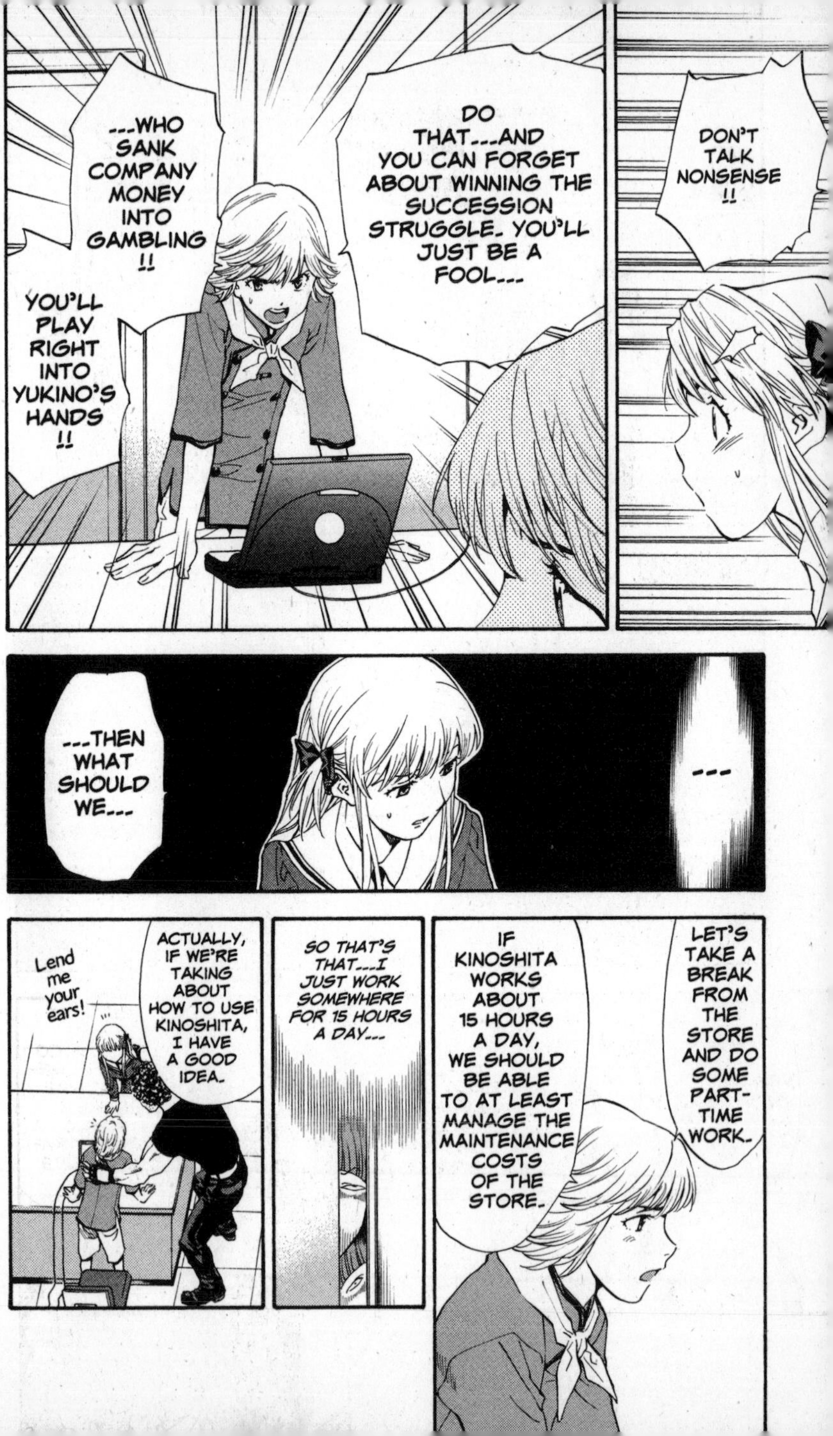
DON'T TALK NONSENSE!!
DO THAT...AND YOU CAN FORGET ABOUT WINNING THE SUCCESSION STRUGGLE. YOU'LL JUST BE A FOOL...
...WHO SANK COMPANY MONEY INTO GAMBLING!!
YOU'LL PLAY RIGHT INTO YUKINO'S HANDS!!
...
...THEN WHAT SHOULD WE...
LET'S TAKE A BREAK FROM THE STORE AND DO SOME PART-TIME WORK.
IF KINOSHITA WORKS ABOUT 15 HOURS A DAY, WE SHOULD BE ABLE TO AT LEAST MANAGE THE MAINTENANCE COSTS OF THE STORE.
SO THAT'S THAT...I JUST WORK SOMEWHERE FOR 15 HOURS A DAY...
ACTUALLY, IF WE'RE TAKING ABOUT HOW TO USE KINOSHITA, I HAVE A GOOD IDEA.
Lend me your ears!

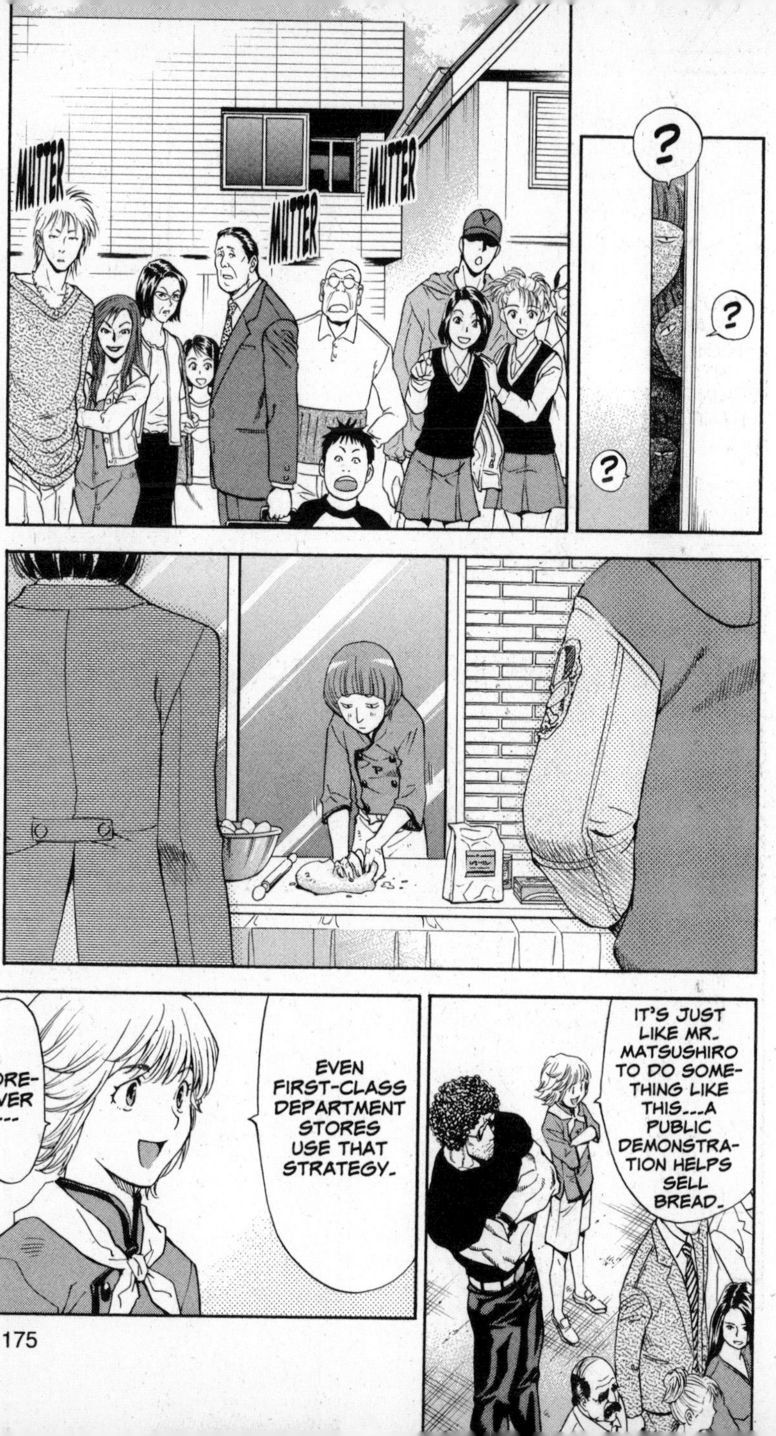
?
?
?
MUTTER
MUTTER
MUTTER
IT'S JUST LIKE MR. MATSUSHIRO TO DO SOME-THING LIKE THIS...A PUBLIC DEMONSTRA-TION HELPS SELL BREAD.
EVEN FIRST-CLASS DEPARTMENT STORES USE THAT STRATEGY.
MORE-OVER ...

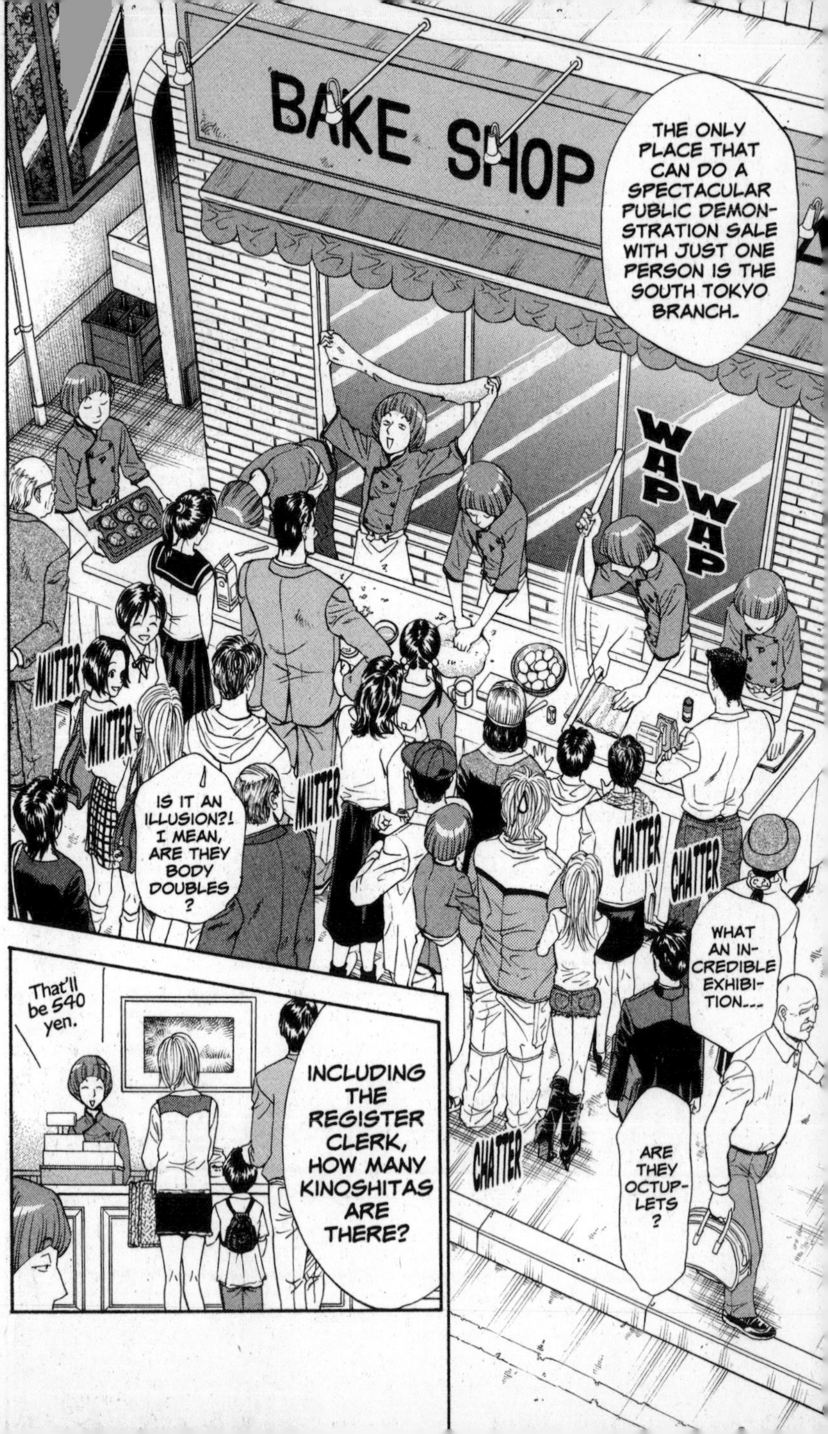
BAKE SHOP
THE ONLY PLACE THAT CAN DO A SPECTACULAR PUBLIC DEMONSTRATION SALE WITH JUST ONE PERSON IS THE SOUTH TOKYO BRANCH.
WAP WAP
CHATTER
CHATTER
WHAT AN INCREDIBLE EXHIBITION...
MUTTER
MUTTER
MUTTER
IS IT AN ILLUSION?! I MEAN, ARE THEY BODY DOUBLES?
ARE THEY OCTUPLETS?
CHATTER
INCLUDING THE REGISTER CLERK, HOW MANY KINOSHITAS ARE THERE?
That'll be 540 yen.

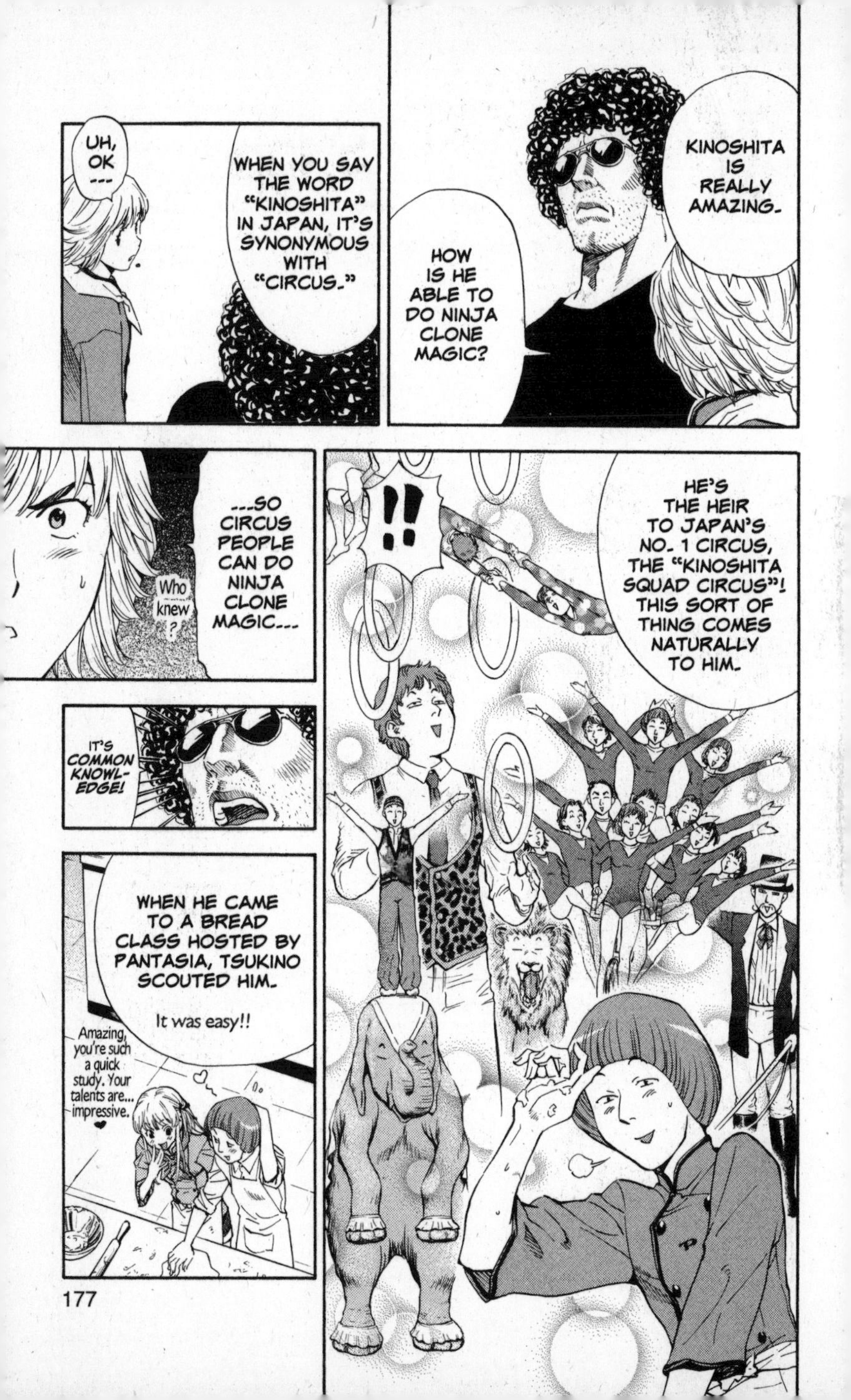

KINOSHITA IS REALLY AMAZING.
HOW IS HE ABLE TO DO NINJA CLONE MAGIC?
WHEN YOU SAY THE WORD "KINOSHITA" IN JAPAN, IT'S SYNONYMOUS WITH "CIRCUS."
UH, OK ...
HE'S THE HEIR TO JAPAN'S NO. 1 CIRCUS, THE "KINOSHITA SQUAD CIRCUS"! THIS SORT OF THING COMES NATURALLY TO HIM.
!!
...SO CIRCUS PEOPLE CAN DO NINJA CLONE MAGIC...
Who knew?
IT'S COMMON KNOWL-EDGE!
WHEN HE CAME TO A BREAD CLASS HOSTED BY PANTASIA, TSUKINO SCOUTED HIM.
It was easy!!
Amazing, you're such a quick study. Your talents are... impressive.

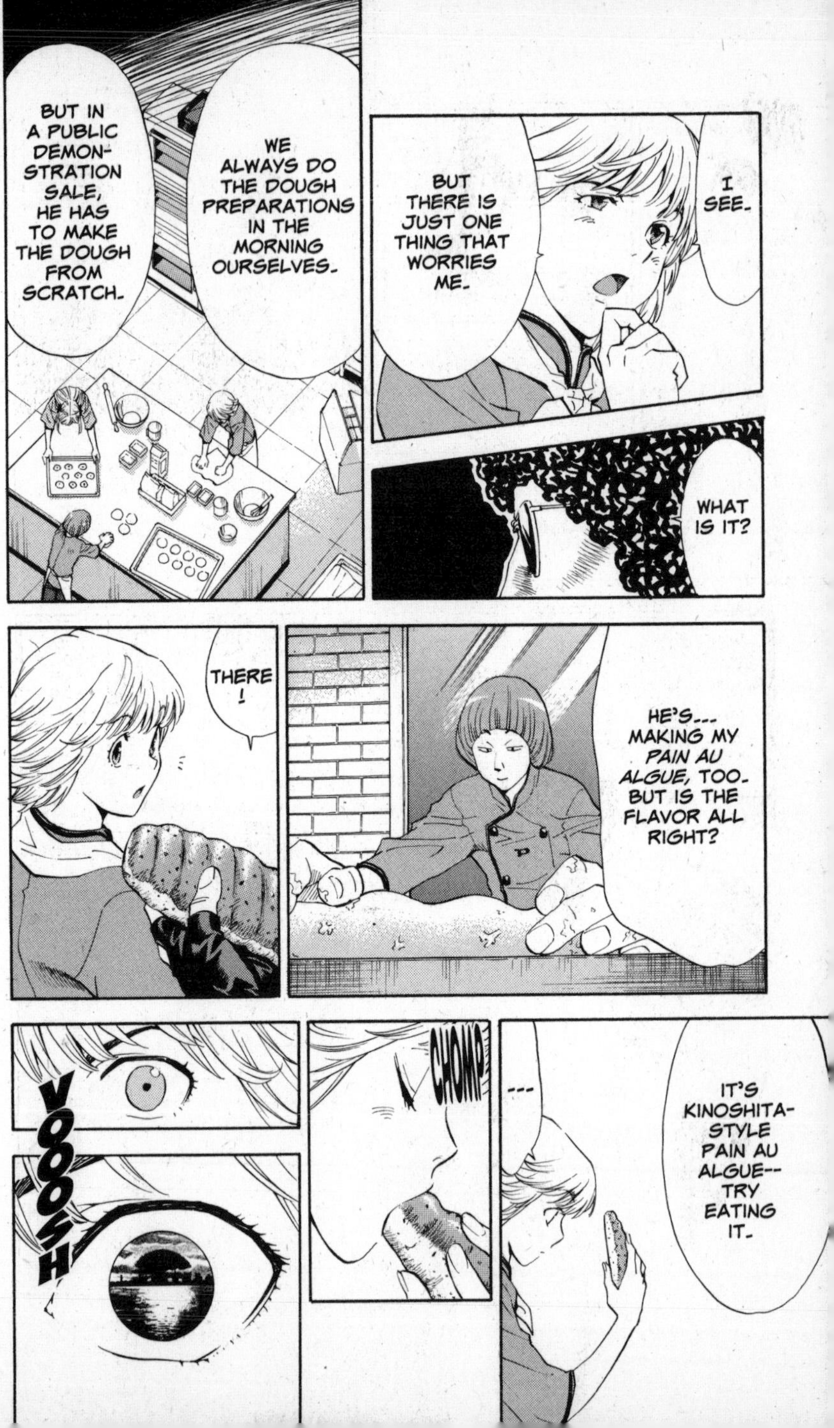
I SEE.
BUT THERE IS JUST ONE THING THAT WORRIES ME.
WHAT IS IT?
WE ALWAYS DO THE DOUGH PREPARATIONS IN THE MORNING OURSELVES.
BUT IN A PUBLIC DEMON-STRATION SALE, HE HAS TO MAKE THE DOUGH FROM SCRATCH.
HE'S... MAKING MY PAIN AU ALGUE, TOO. BUT IS THE FLAVOR ALL RIGHT?
THERE!
IT'S KINOSHITA-STYLE PAIN AU ALGUE--TRY EATING IT.
CHOMP
...
VOOOSH!

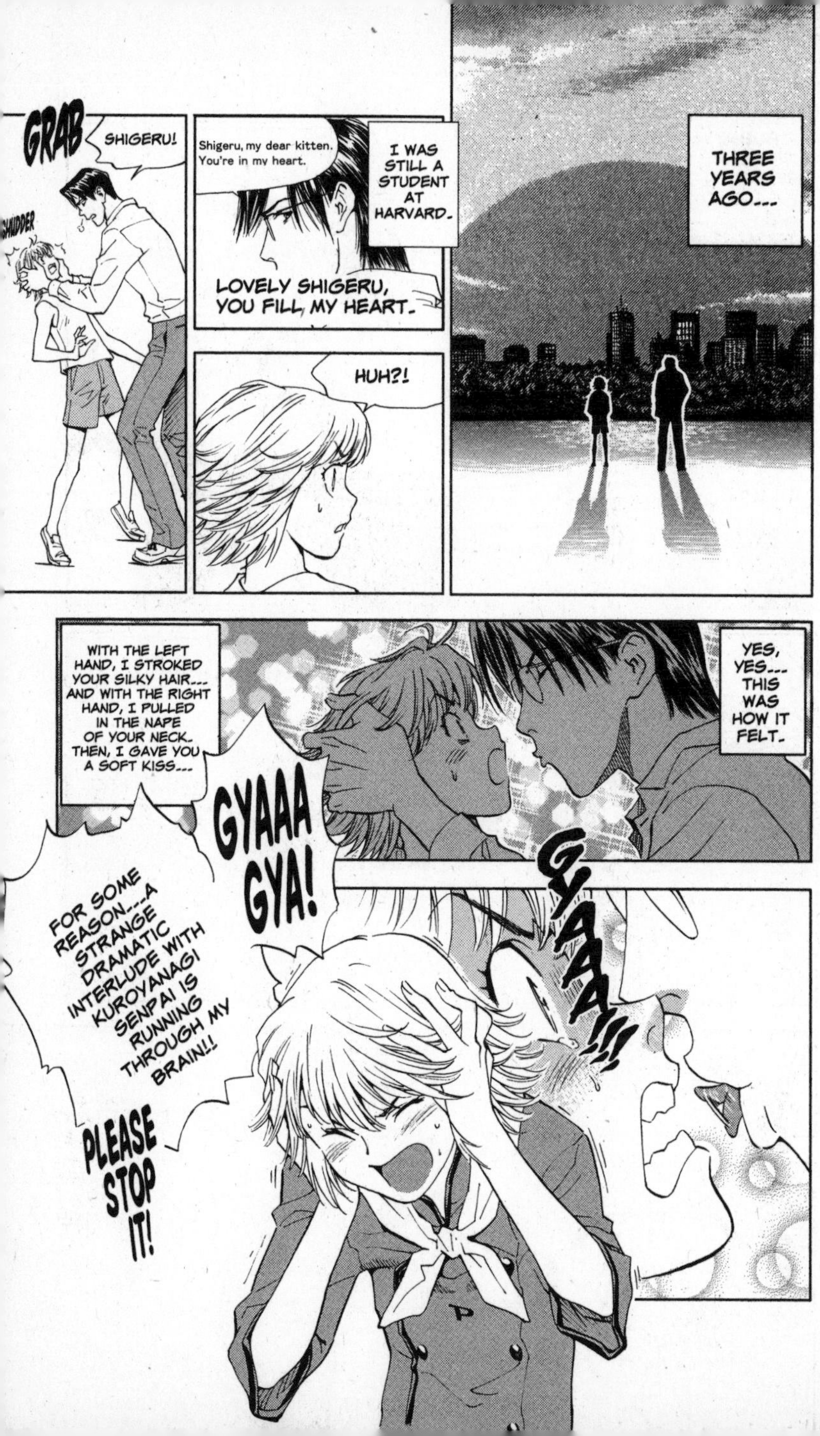
THREE YEARS AGO...
I WAS STILL A STUDENT AT HARVARD.
Shigeru, my dear kitten. You're in my heart.
LOVELY SHIGERU, YOU FILL MY HEART.
HUH?!
GRAB
SHIGERU!
SHUDDER
YES, YES... THIS WAS HOW IT FELT.
WITH THE LEFT HAND, I STROKED YOUR SILKY HAIR... AND WITH THE RIGHT HAND, I PULLED IN THE NAPE OF YOUR NECK. THEN, I GAVE YOU A SOFT KISS...
GYAAA!!!
GYAAA GYA!
FOR SOME REASON...A STRANGE DRAMATIC INTERLUDE WITH KUROYANAGI SENPAI IS RUNNING THROUGH MY BRAIN!!
PLEASE STOP IT!

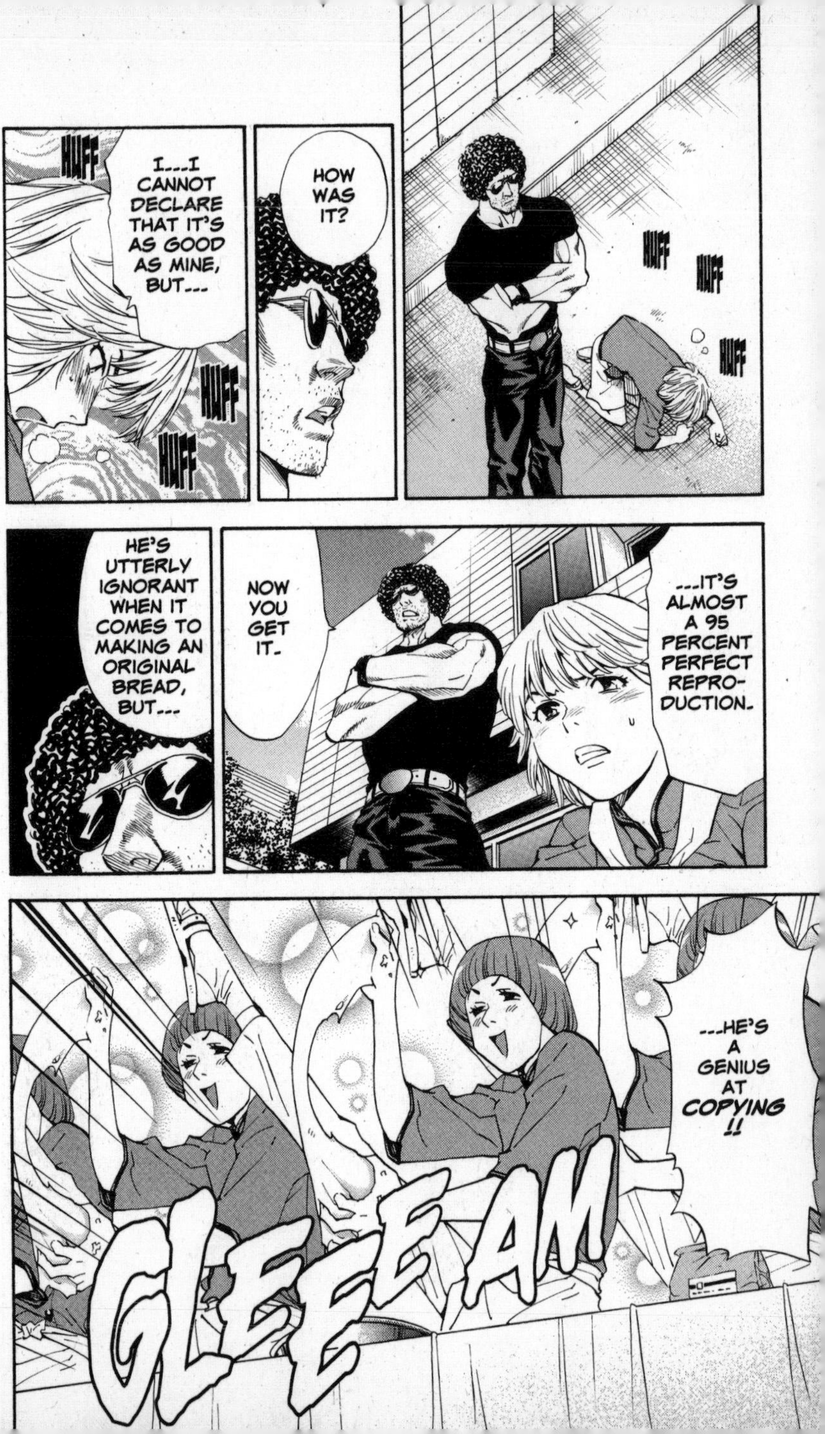
HUFF
HUFF
HUFF
HOW WAS IT?
HUFF
I...I CANNOT DECLARE THAT IT'S AS GOOD AS MINE, BUT...
HUFF
HUFF
...IT'S ALMOST A 95 PERCENT PERFECT REPRODUCTION.
NOW YOU GET IT.
HE'S UTTERLY IGNORANT WHEN IT COMES TO MAKING AN ORIGINAL BREAD, BUT...
...HE'S A GENIUS AT COPYING!!
GLEEEAM

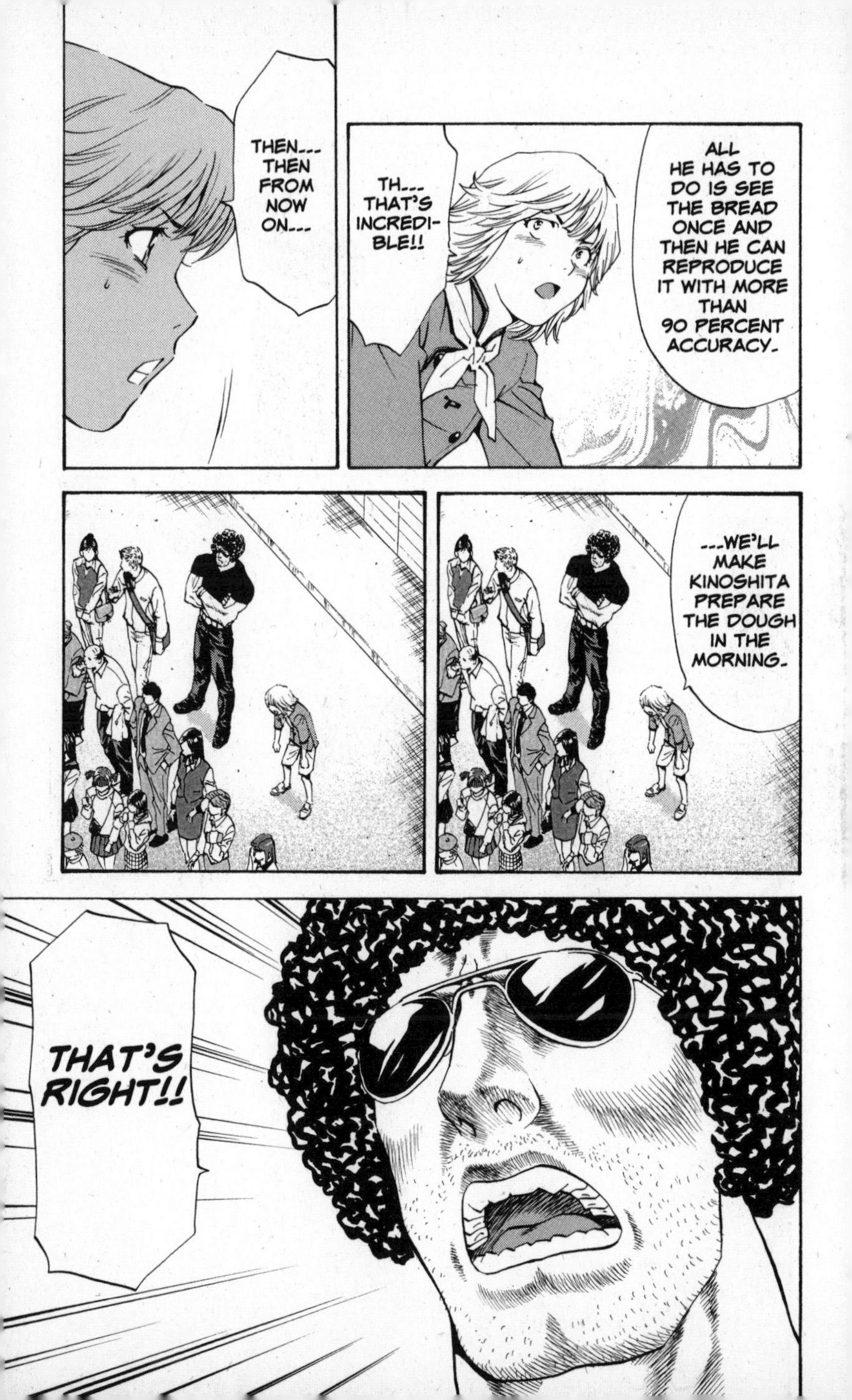
ALL HE HAS TO DO IS SEE THE BREAD ONCE AND THEN HE CAN REPRODUCE IT WITH MORE THAN 90 PERCENT ACCURACY.
TH... THAT'S INCREDIBLE!!
THEN... THEN FROM NOW ON...
...WE'LL MAKE KINOSHITA PREPARE THE DOUGH IN THE MORNING.
THAT'S RIGHT!!

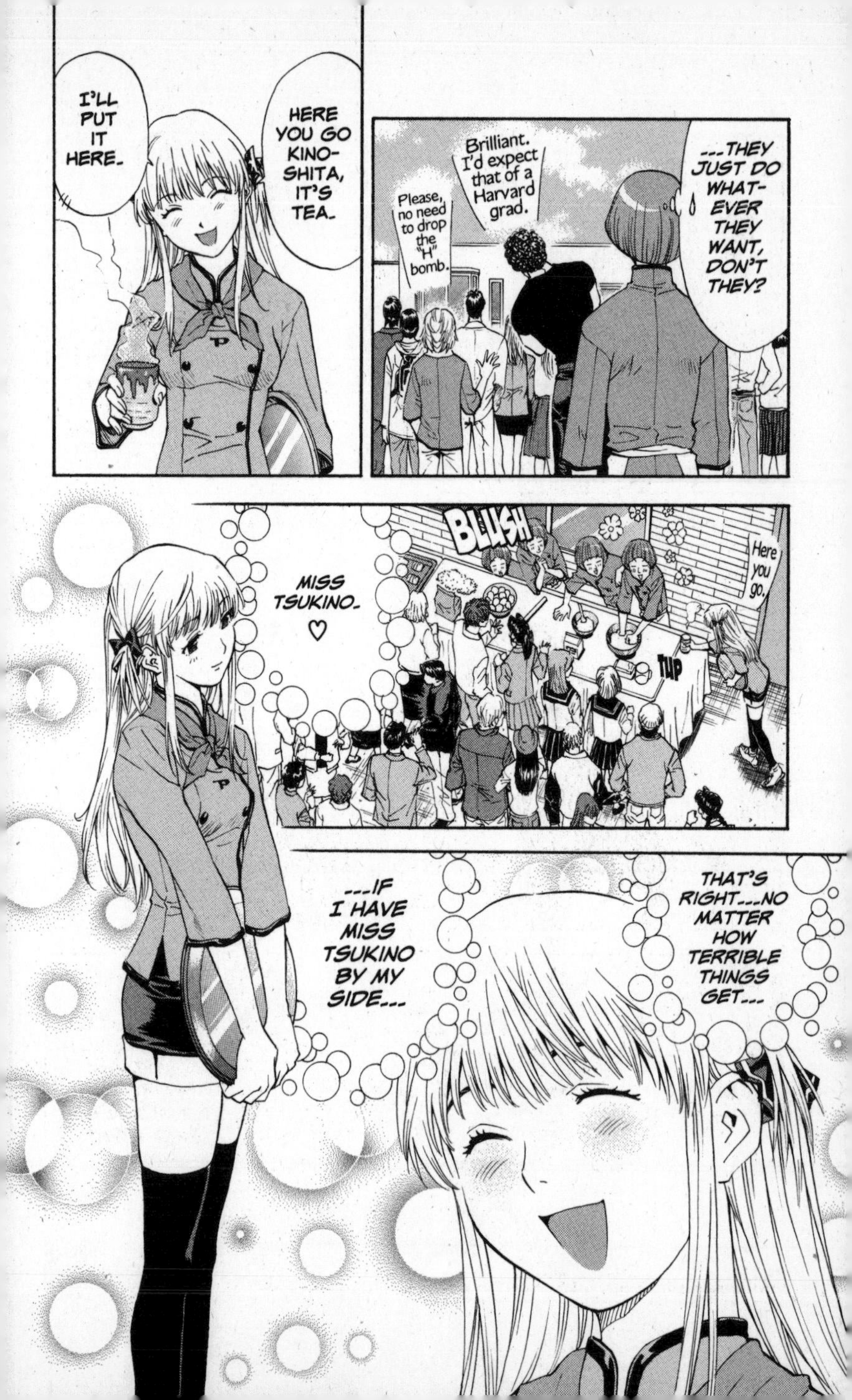
...THEY JUST DO WHATEVER THEY WANT, DON'T THEY?
Brilliant. I'd expect that of a Harvard grad.
Please, no need to drop the "H" bomb.
HERE YOU GO KINOSHITA, IT'S TEA...
I'LL PUT IT HERE...
Here you go.
BLUSH
TUP
MISS TSUKINO... ♡
THAT'S RIGHT...NO MATTER HOW TERRIBLE THINGS GET...
...IF I HAVE MISS TSUKINO BY MY SIDE...

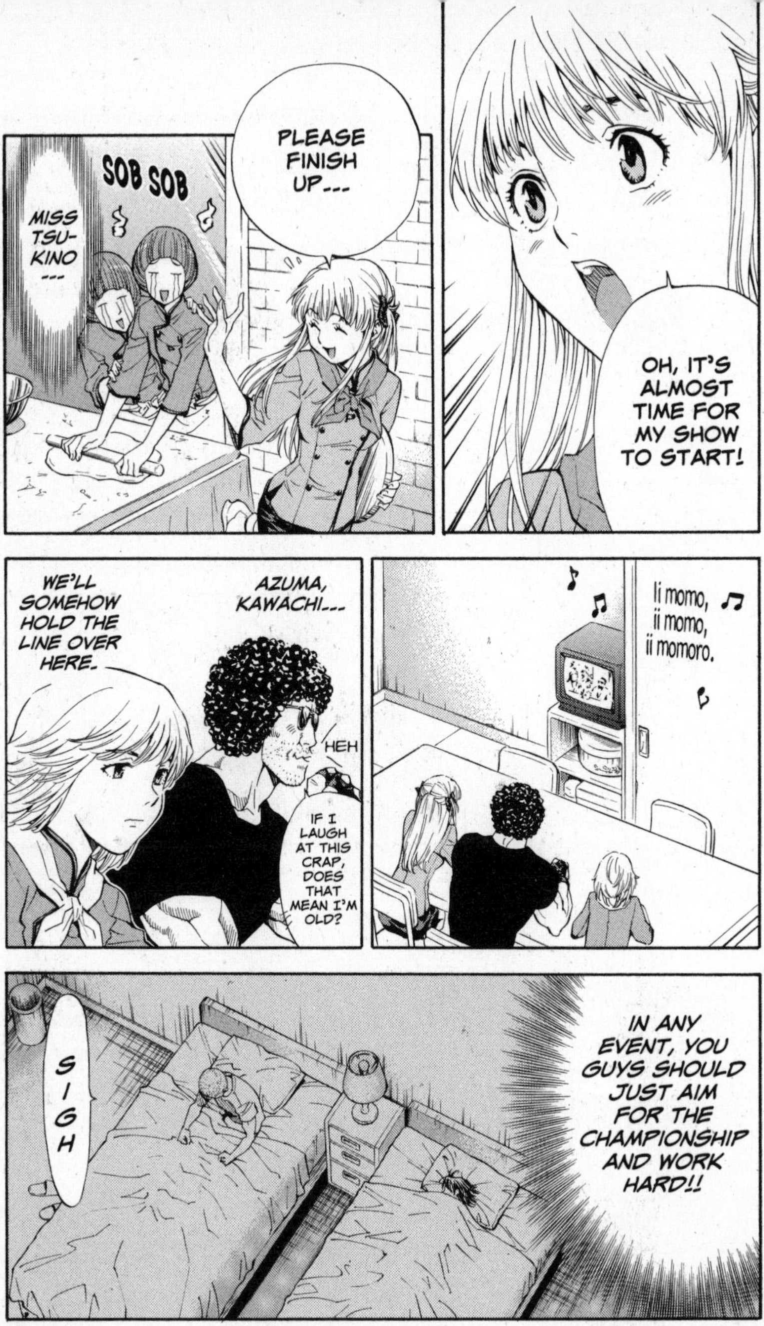
OH, IT'S ALMOST TIME FOR MY SHOW TO START!
PLEASE FINISH UP...
SOB SOB
MISS TSU-KINO...
Ii momo, ii momo, ii momoro.
AZUMA, KAWACHI...
WE'LL SOMEHOW HOLD THE LINE OVER HERE.
HEH
IF I LAUGH AT THIS CRAP, DOES THAT MEAN I'M OLD?
IN ANY EVENT, YOU GUYS SHOULD JUST AIM FOR THE CHAMPIONSHIP AND WORK HARD!!
SIGH

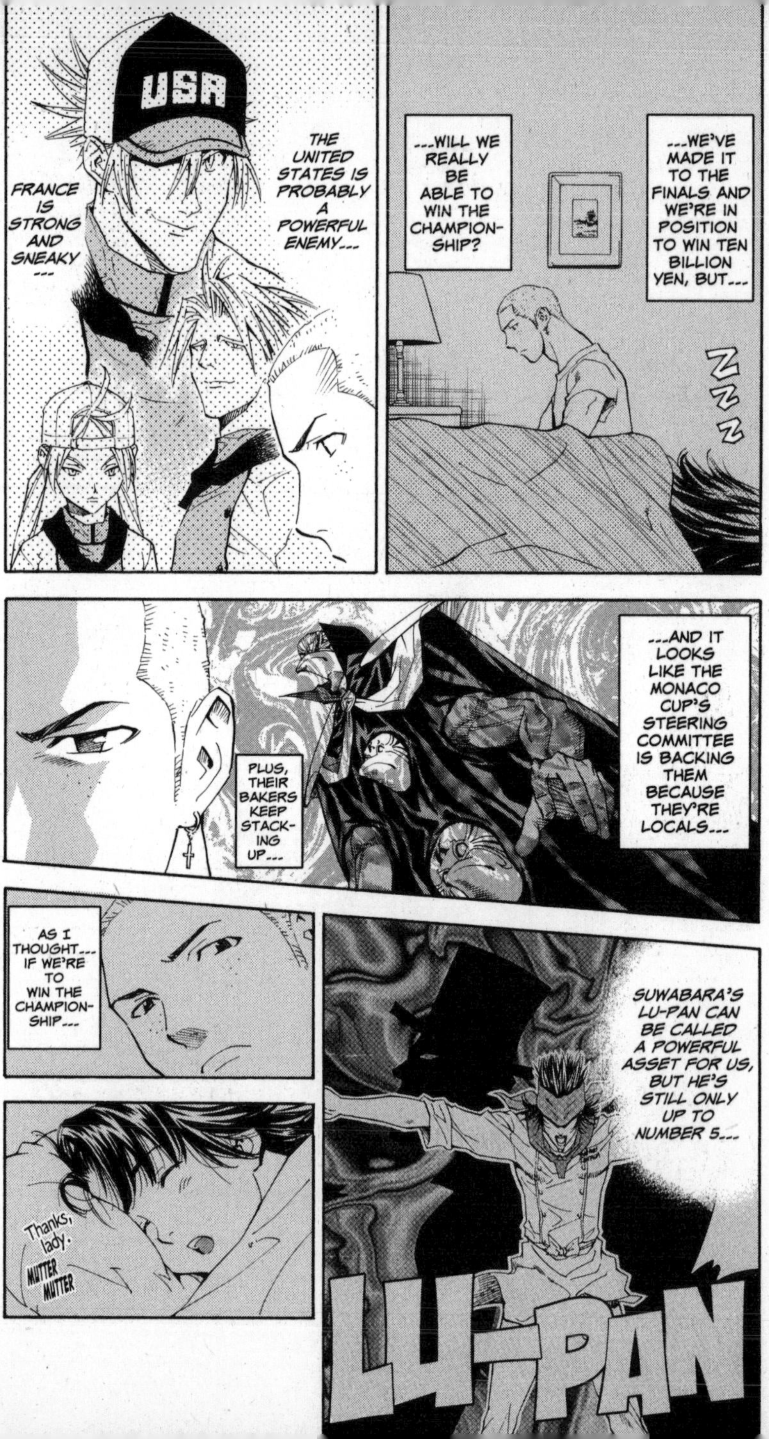
---WE'VE MADE IT TO THE FINALS AND WE'RE IN POSITION TO WIN TEN BILLION YEN, BUT---
---WILL WE REALLY BE ABLE TO WIN THE CHAMPION-SHIP?
ZZZ
THE UNITED STATES IS PROBABLY A POWERFUL ENEMY---
USA
FRANCE IS STRONG AND SNEAKY---
---AND IT LOOKS LIKE THE MONACO CUP'S STEERING COMMITTEE IS BACKING THEM BECAUSE THEY'RE LOCALS---
PLUS, THEIR BAKERS KEEP STACK-ING UP---
SUWABARA'S LU-PAN CAN BE CALLED A POWERFUL ASSET FOR US, BUT HE'S STILL ONLY UP TO NUMBER 5---
LU-PAN
AS I THOUGHT--- IF WE'RE TO WIN THE CHAMPION-SHIP---
Thanks, lady.
MUTTER MUTTER

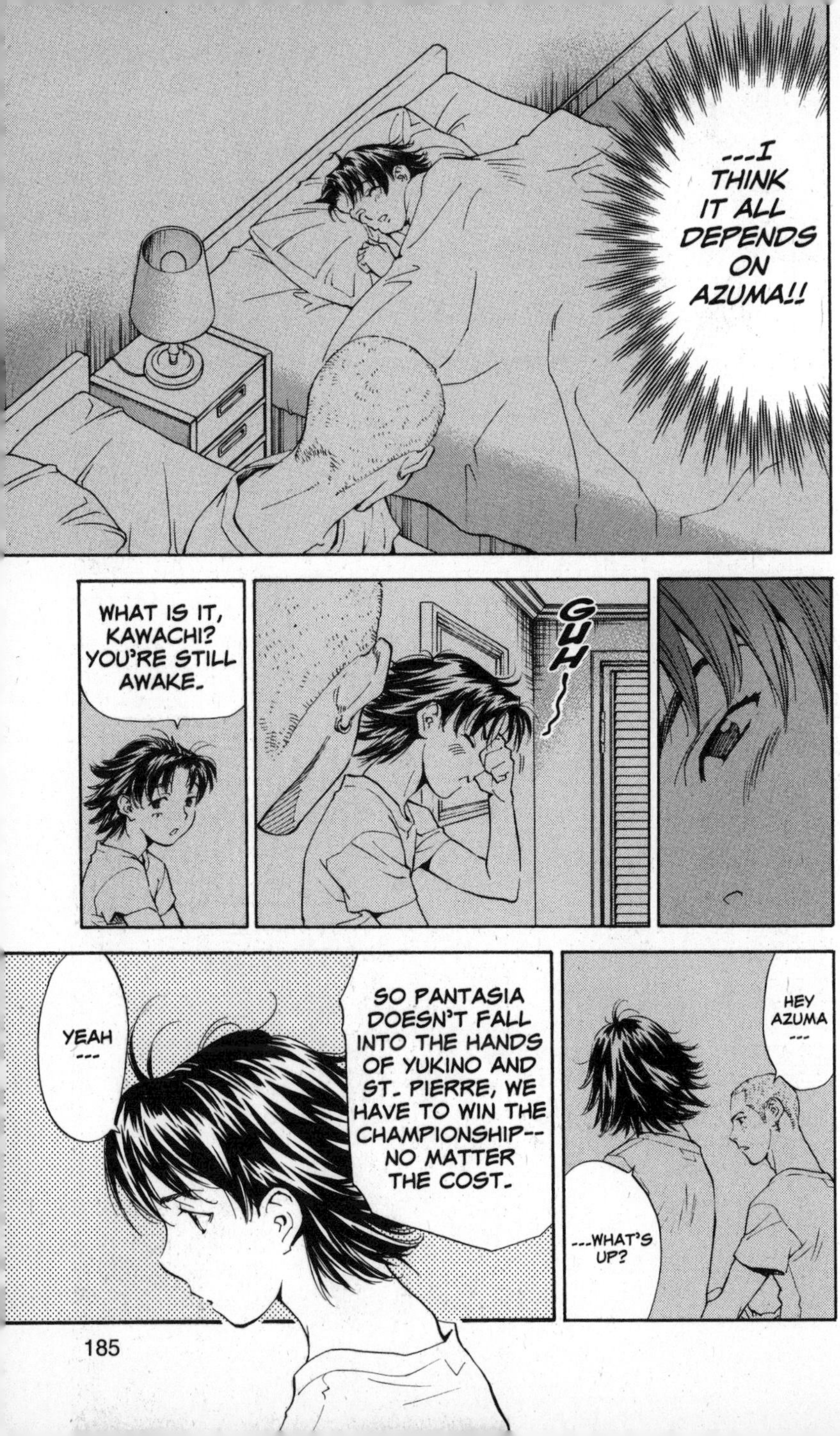
---I THINK IT ALL DEPENDS ON AZUMA!!
GUH!!
WHAT IS IT, KAWACHI? YOU'RE STILL AWAKE.
HEY AZUMA ---
---WHAT'S UP?
SO PANTASIA DOESN'T FALL INTO THE HANDS OF YUKINO AND ST. PIERRE, WE HAVE TO WIN THE CHAMPIONSHIP-- NO MATTER THE COST.
YEAH ---

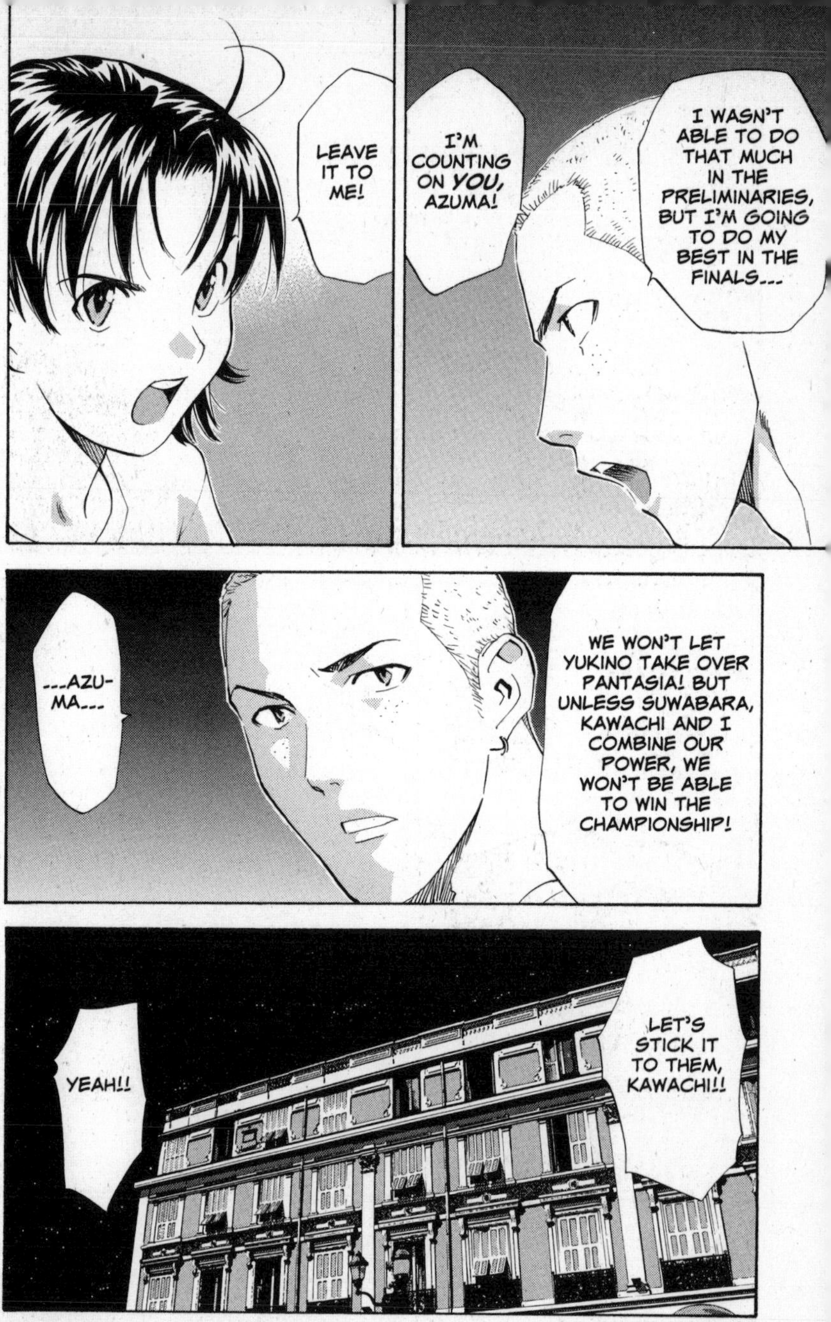
I WASN'T ABLE TO DO THAT MUCH IN THE PRELIMINARIES, BUT I'M GOING TO DO MY BEST IN THE FINALS...
I'M COUNTING ON *YOU*, AZUMA!
LEAVE IT TO ME!
WE WON'T LET YUKINO TAKE OVER PANTASIA! BUT UNLESS SUWABARA, KAWACHI AND I COMBINE OUR POWER, WE WON'T BE ABLE TO WIN THE CHAMPIONSHIP!
...AZU-MA...
LET'S STICK IT TO THEM, KAWACHI!!
YEAH!!

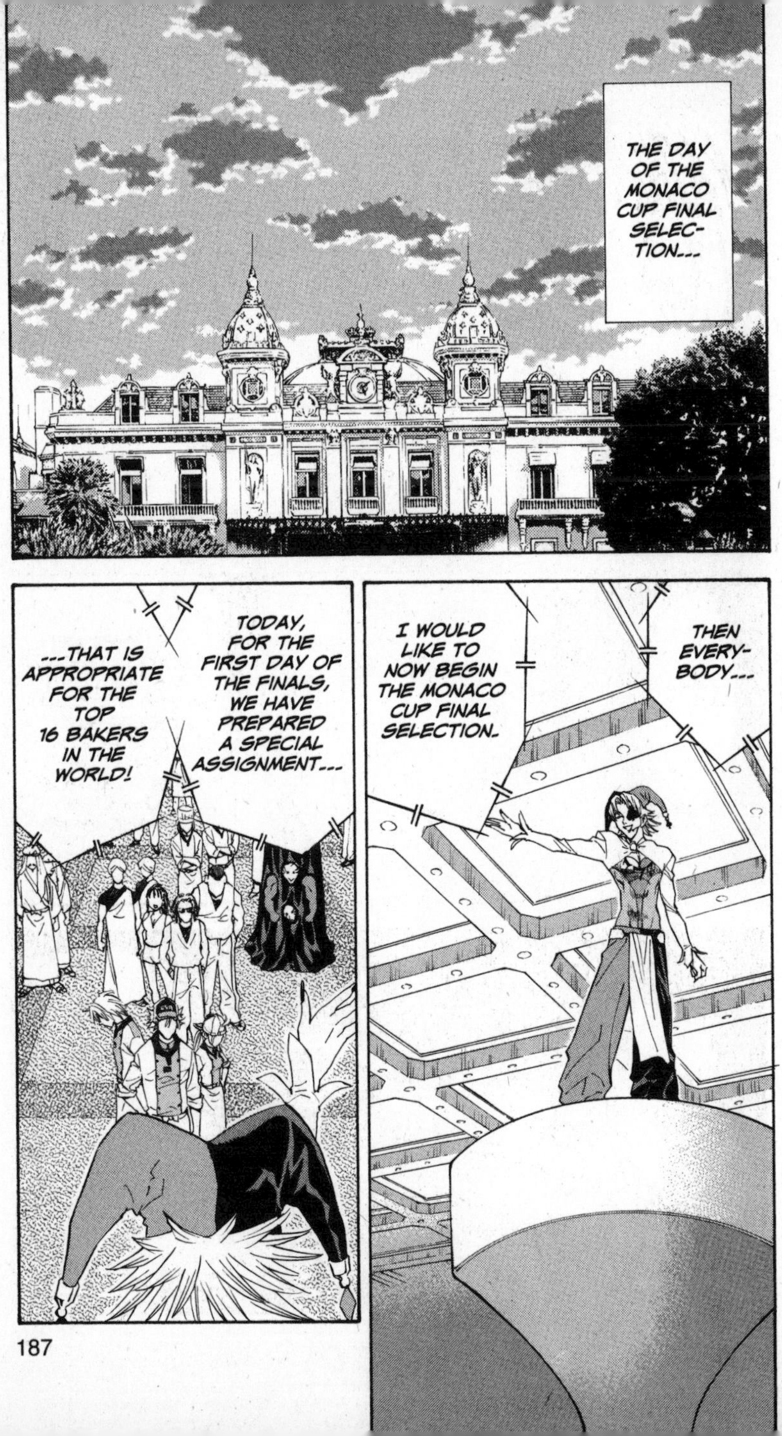
THE DAY OF THE MONACO CUP FINAL SELECTION...
THEN EVERYBODY...
I WOULD LIKE TO NOW BEGIN THE MONACO CUP FINAL SELECTION.
TODAY, FOR THE FIRST DAY OF THE FINALS, WE HAVE PREPARED A SPECIAL ASSIGNMENT...
...THAT IS APPROPRIATE FOR THE TOP 16 BAKERS IN THE WORLD!

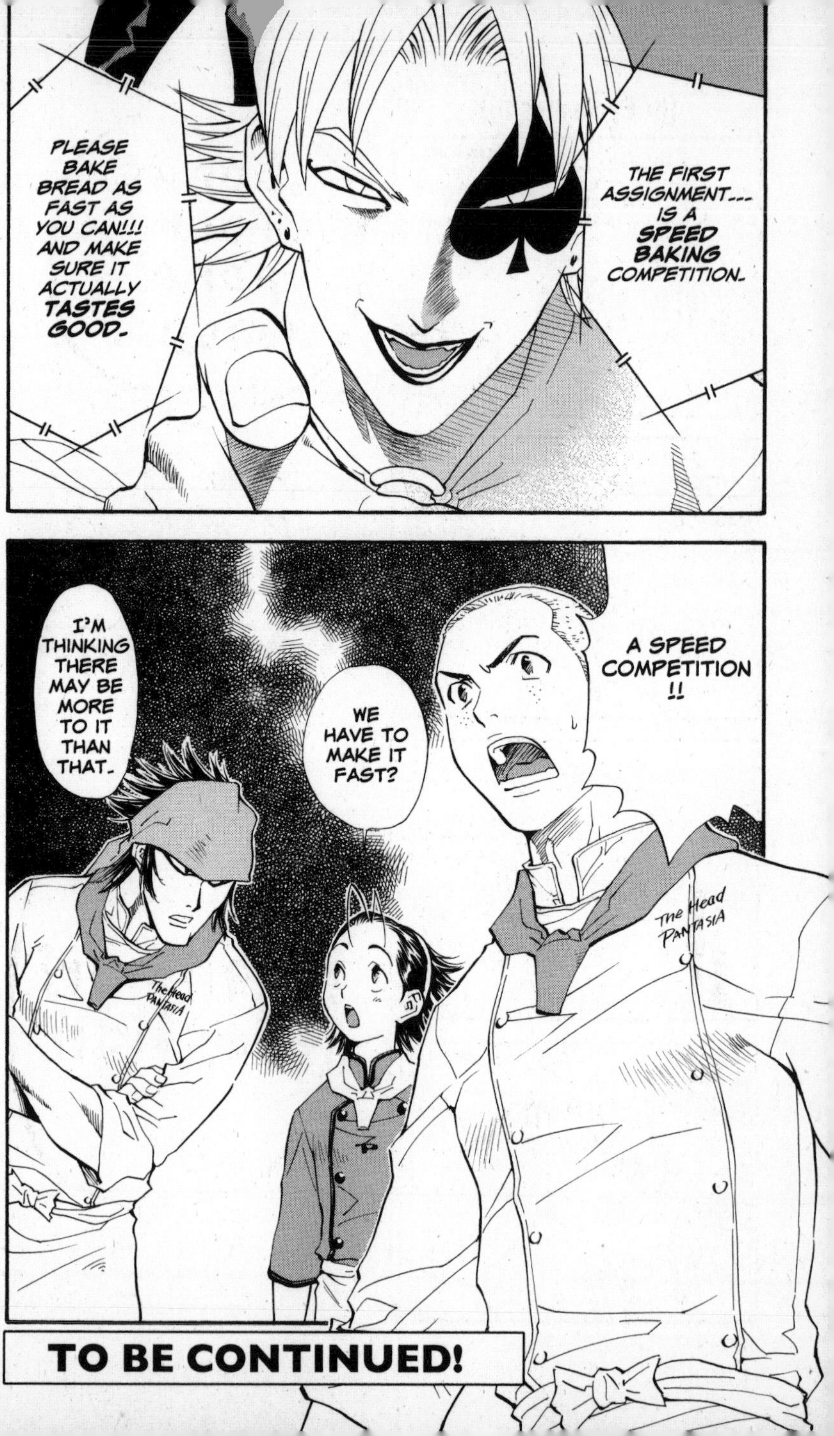
THE FIRST ASSIGNMENT... IS A SPEED BAKING COMPETITION.
PLEASE BAKE BREAD AS FAST AS YOU CAN!!! AND MAKE SURE IT ACTUALLY TASTES GOOD.
A SPEED COMPETITION!!
The Head PANTASIA
WE HAVE TO MAKE IT FAST?
I'M THINKING THERE MAY BE MORE TO IT THAN THAT.
The Head PANTASIA
TO BE CONTINUED!

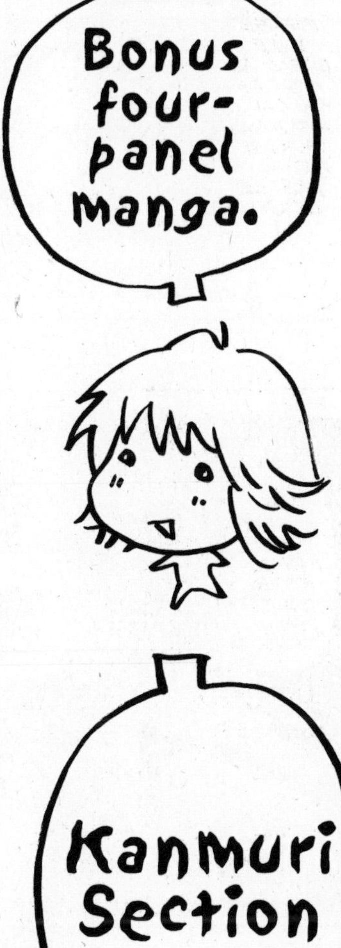
Bonus four-panel manga.
Kanmuri Section

((((•Eyelashes•))))

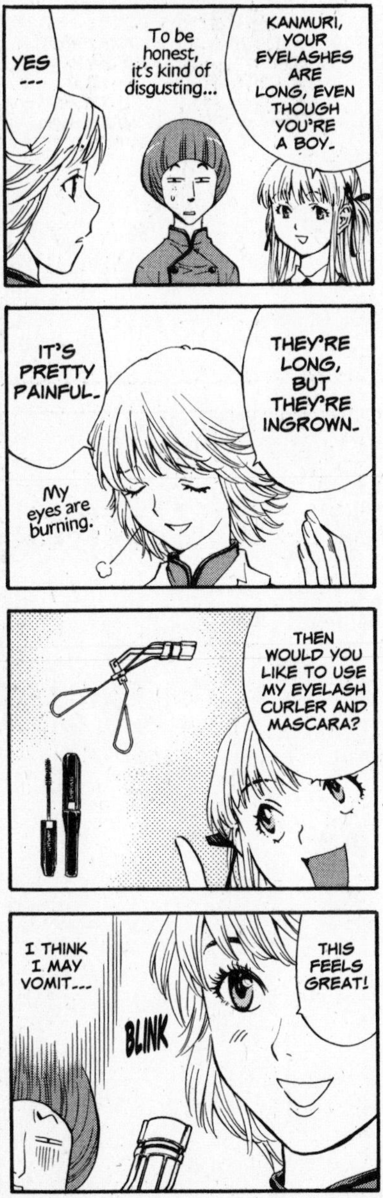
KANMURI, YOUR EYELASHES ARE LONG, EVEN THOUGH YOU'RE A BOY.
To be honest, it's kind of disgusting...
YES---
THEY'RE LONG, BUT THEY'RE INGROWN.
IT'S PRETTY PAINFUL.
My eyes are burning.
THEN WOULD YOU LIKE TO USE MY EYELASH CURLER AND MASCARA?
THIS FEELS GREAT!
I THINK I MAY VOMIT---
BLINK

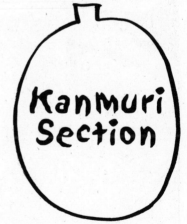

Masochism

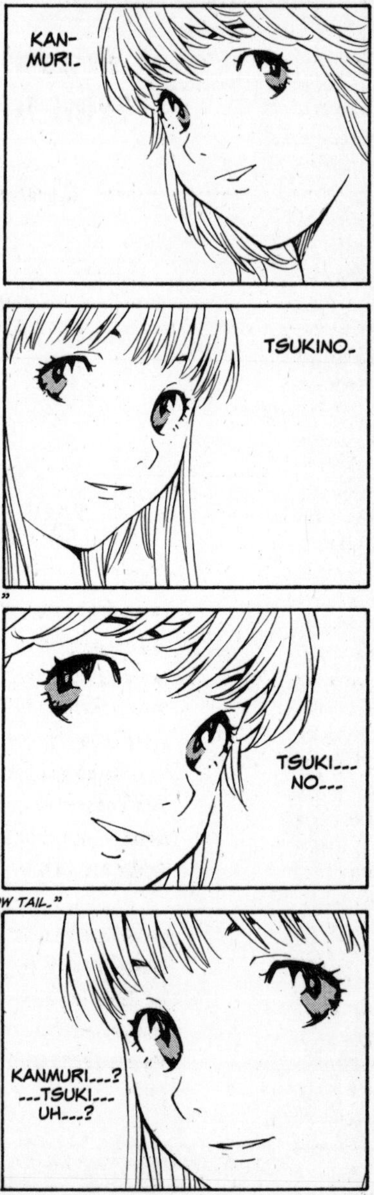
KAN-
MURI.
TSUKINO.
TSUKI...
NO...
KANMURI...?
...TSUKI...
UH...?

Kanmuri

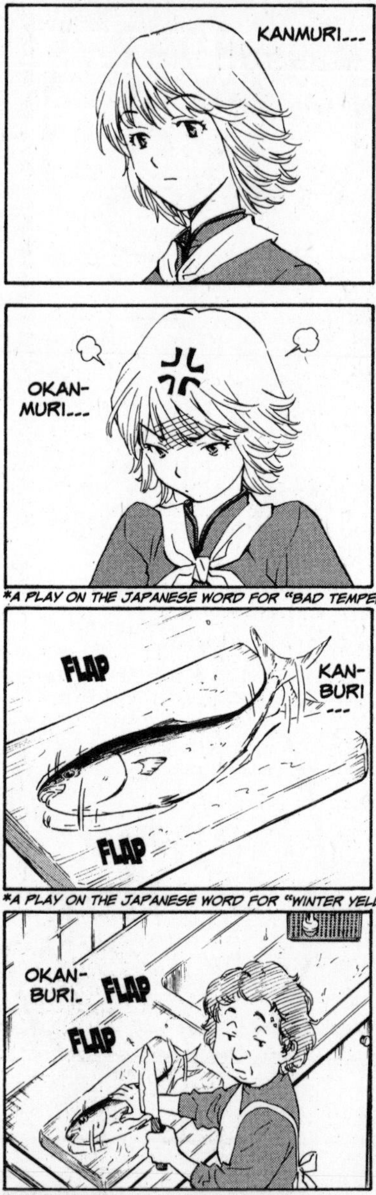
KANMURI...
OKAN-
MURI...
KAN-
BURI
...
FLAP
FLAP
OKAN-
BURI.
FLAP
FLAP

*A PLAY ON THE JAPANESE WORD FOR "BAD TEMPER."

*A PLAY ON THE JAPANESE WORD FOR "WINTER YELLOW TAIL."

*UM, JAPANESE FOR "WHAT LOOKS LIKE A TYPICAL MOTHER." PLEASE LAUGH.

Freshly Baked!! Mini Information

Castella Ja-pan

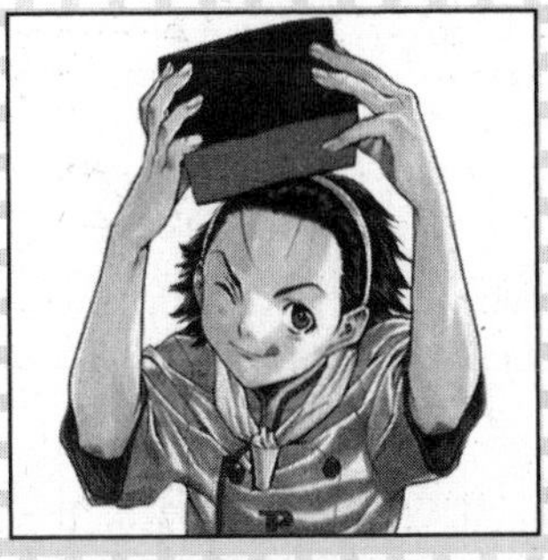

The number one difference between castella and castella bread is whether or not you let it ferment. Whipping the eggs produces the soft feel of castella, but if you're going to make it bread-style, fermenting it produces the soft feel. Which one tastes better? It depends on your preference, but regular castella is more moist while the bread-like version has a slightly lighter feel to it.

For people who have the time to spare, please try making it by putting yeast into the castella dough. You should come to understand that castella made bread-style is pretty good, too.

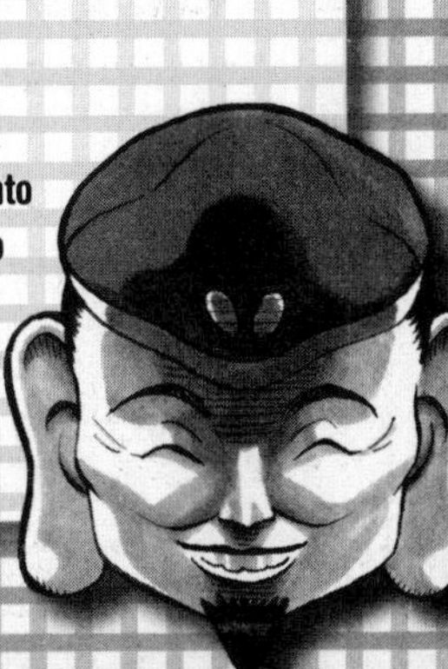

YAKITATE!! JAPAN
VOL. 8

STORY AND ART BY
TAKASHI HASHIGUCHI

English Adaptation/Drew Williams
Translation/Noritaka Minami
Touch-up Art & Lettering/Steve Dutro
Cover Design/Yukiko Whitley
Editor/Kit Fox

Editor in Chief, Books/Alvin Lu
Editor in Chief, Magazines/Marc Weidenbaum
VP of Publishing Licensing/Rika Inouye
VP of Sales/Gonzalo Ferreyra
Sr. VP of Marketing/Liza Coppola
Publisher/Hyoe Narita

Published by VIZ Media, LLC
P.O. Box 77010
San Francisco, CA 94107

10 9 8 7 6 5 4 3 2 1
First printing, November 2007

www.viz.com

store.viz.com